EAST CRETAN WHITE-ON-DARK WARE

Studies on a Handmade Pottery
of the Early to Middle Minoan Periods

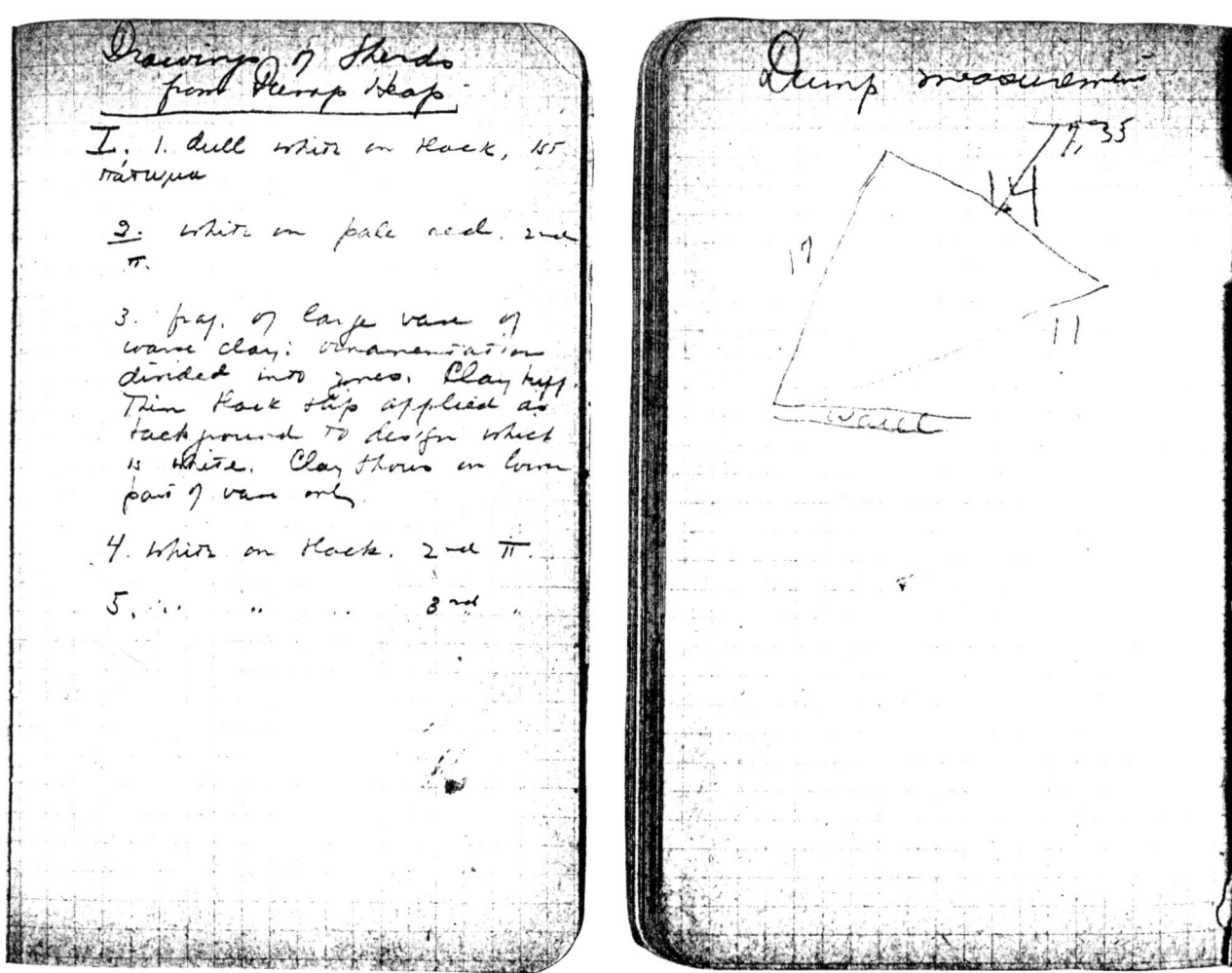

Two pages from the notebook of Edith Hall Dohan describing the North Trench at Gournia where White-on-dark Ware was first found in quantity.

University Museum Monograph 51

EAST CRETAN WHITE-ON-DARK WARE

Studies on a Handmade Pottery of the Early to Middle Minoan Periods

Philip P. Betancourt

With contributions from

Thomas Bakas	John A. Gifford	George Rapp, Jr.
Philip P. Betancourt	Gail Gosser	Susan Sapareto
Harriet Blitzer	Nicholas Hartmann	Charles P. Swann
Albert D. Frost	Yannis Maniatis	Maria Voyatzoglou
Thomas K. Gaisser	Frederick R. Matson	Robert G. White
N.-H. J. Gangas	George H. Myer	

Published by
THE UNIVERSITY MUSEUM
University of Pennsylvania
1984

Design, editing, production
Publications Division, The University Museum

Typesetting and Printing
The Sheridan Press
Hanover, Pennsylvania

Library of Congress Cataloging in Publication Data
Main entry under title:

East Cretan White-on-dark Ware.

   (University Museum monography; 51)
   Bibliography: p.
   1. Crete—Antiquities—Addresses, essays, lectures.
2. Pottery, Minoan—Dating—Addresses, essays, lectures.
3. Pottery, Minoan—Expertising—Addresses, essays,
lectures. 4. Pottery—Greece—Crete—Dating—Addresses,
essays, lectures. 5. Pottery—Greece—Crete—Expertising—
Addresses, essays, lectures. 6. Slipware—Greece—Crete—
Addresses, essays, lectures. 7. Greece—Antiquities—
Addresses, essays, lectures. I. Betancourt, Philip P., 1936– .
II. Series.
DF221.C8E27 1983   939'.18   84-2237
ISBN 0-934718-57-1

Copyright © 1984
THE UNIVERSITY MUSEUM
University of Pennsylvania
Philadelphia
All rights reserved
Printed in the United States of America

Dedicated to Edith Hall Dohan
who first recognized the
importance of White-on-dark Ware.

Table of Contents

LIST OF FIGURES ix
LIST OF PLATES xiii
LIST OF TABLES xiv
ADDRESSES OF CONTRIBUTING AUTHORS xvi
ABBREVIATIONS xvii
CREDITS FOR PHOTOGRAPHS AND FIGURES xviii
PREFACE xix

PART I. INTRODUCTION
    1. Introduction to the Studies, *by Philip P. Betancourt* 1

PART II. THE CHRONOLOGY AND STYLE OF EAST CRETAN WHITE-ON-DARK WARE
    2. Deposits and Chronology, *by Philip P. Betancourt* 6
    3. The Decorative Motifs, *by Philip P. Betancourt* 21
    4. Analysis of the Shapes, *by Philip P. Betancourt* 35

PART III. CHARACTERIZATION STUDIES
    5. Physical Characteristics of the Fabric, Slip and Paint, *by Frederick R. Matson* 52
    6. Ceramic Petrography, *by George H. Myer* 60
    7. Mössbauer Investigation of the Fabric, *by N.-H. J. Gangas and Th. Bakas* 67
    8. Studies on the Gournian White Slip, *by Philip P. Betancourt, Thomas K. Gaisser, Frederick R. Matson, George H. Myer, and Robert G. White* 71
    9. Firing Conditions of White-on-Dark Ware from Eastern Crete, *by Yannis Maniatis* 75
    10. Porosity Studies, *by Nicholas Hartmann* 78
    11. Proton Microprobe Analysis of White-on-dark Ware, *by Thomas K. Gaisser and Charles P. Swann* 83
    12. Neutron Activation and Cluster Analysis, *by George Rapp, Jr. and John A. Gifford* 91
    13. Photoacoustic Examination of White-on-dark Ware from Gournia, *by Albert D. Frost* 105
    14. Xeroradiography Analysis, *by Robert H. Johnston and Philip P. Betancourt* 114

3-2.	Chevrons and Triangles.	23
3-3.	Triangles (cont.) and Parallel Vertical Lines.	24
3-4.	Diamonds, Dot Bands, and Wavy Lines.	25
3-5.	Quirks and J-Spirals.	26
3-6.	Semicircles and Crescents.	27
3-7.	Circles.	28
3-8.	Triglyphs and Metopes and Zigzags.	29
3-9.	Zigzags (cont.).	30
3-10.	Pictorials and Miscellaneous.	31
4-1.	Shapes 1 and 2. Open conical shapes.	40
4-2.	Shapes 3, 4, and 5. Open conical, semiglobular, and cylindrical shapes.	42
4-3.	Shapes 6, 7, and 8. Open rounded and carinated shapes and jugs.	44
4-4.	Shape 9. Bridge spouted jars.	46
4-5.	Shapes 10, 11, and 12. Teapots, jars, and pyxides.	48
4-6.	Shape 13 and misc. shapes.	49
7-1.	Mössbauer spectra of the as received samples at 4.2 K (left column) and 74 K (right column).	68
7-2.	Relative areas of spectral components plotted versus measuring temperature of the samples.	69
7-3.	Mössbauer spectra of the as received samples (left column) and the samples refired at 1100% C (right column). The spectra were obtained at 293 K.	70
10-1.	Apparent porosity (P_a) values, displaying as a histogram.	80
10-2.	Apparent porosity (P_a) plotted as a function of Si content (determined as SiO_2).	80
10-3.	Apparent porosity (P_a) plotted as a function of Ca content (determined as CaO).	81
11-1.	A comparison between Ca and Y from EM III and MM I-III Gournia.	87
11-2.	A comparison between Ni and Sr from EM III and MM I-III Gournia.	89
12-1.	Sherd samples, K-means clustering.	98
12-2.	Clay samples plus all sherds, K-means clustering.	98
12-3.	Clay samples plus sherds from Gournia and Vasilike, K-means cluster analysis.	99
13-1.	Block diagram of experimental equipment used for photoacoustical measurements.	106
13-2.	Schematic diagram of the distribution of illumination flux and temperature at and below the sample surface for a thermally homogenous material.	107

FIGURES

13-3.	Schematic diagram of the distribution of illumination flux and temperature at and below the surface of a sample.	107
13-4.	Variation in the photoacoustic signal strength as a function of chopping rate for several illumination spots on the design side surface of sherd MS 4615-2.	108
13-5.	Variation in relative photoacoustic response (fixed chopping rate of 12 Hz) as the illumination spot is moved linearly across the sample surface.	108
13-6.	Linear scan plot of PA response made on the design side surface of MS 4615-2.	109
13-7.	Linear scan plot of PA response made on the interior surface of MS 4615-2; right side as shown.	109
13-8.	Linear scan plot of PA response made on the interior surface of MS 4615-2.	109
13-9.	Map of equal photoacoustic signal strength contours for the interior surface of MS 4615-2.	109
13-10.	(a) Linear scan plot of relative PA signal on the inside surface of MS 4615.28.	110
	(b) Linear scan plot of relative PA signal on the inside surface of MS 4615-45.	110
13-11.	(a) Linear scan plot of relative PA signal on the inside surface of MS 4615-20.	111
	(b) Linear scan plot of relative PA signal on the inside surface of MS 4615-21.	111
13-12.	Linear scan plot of the relative PA signal on the inside of MS 4615-36.	111
13-13.	Linear scan plot of relative PA signal on the design side surface of MS 4615-10.	112
13-14.	(a) Map of equal PA signal strength contours for the design side surface of MS 4615-10.	112
	(b) Drawing of the xeroradiography image of MS 4615-10 showing air bubbles included within the body of the clay.	112
14-1.	Reconstructions of shapes of White-on dark Ware.	115
15-1.	Geological sketch map of the Isthmus of Ierapetra (greatly simplified from Fortuin's 1977 map), with the 17 sample locations of the present study.	120
17-1.	The turntable, elevation.	134
17-2.	The turntable, plan.	135
17-3.	The "Dressing" operation.	136
17-4.	The "Milking" operation.	136
17-5.	The "String" operation.	136
17-6.	The "Pulling" operation.	137
17-7.	Levelling the clay between the fingers.	137
17-8.	The "Knuckling" operation.	137

17-9.	The "Rib" operation.	137
17-10.	Applying the "Belt."	137
17-11.	Elevation of the kiln.	140
17-12.	Plan of the kiln.	140
18-1.	Map of Crete showing locations mentioned in the text.	144
18-2.	Detail of the Eparchy of Ierapetra, showing Kentri and the land and sea routes by which Kentri pottery was distributed in Crete.	144
18-3.	Plan of a Τσικαλαριό, or potter's workshop, in the village of Kentri.	146
18-4.	A less frequently used potter's workshop. Plan.	147
18-5.	Types of vessels formerly and presently produced in Kentri.	150
18-6.	Types of vessels formerly and presently produced in Kentri (cont).	151
19-1.	A painting from Tomb 2 at Beni Hasan, from the early Middle Kingdom, showing potters at work in a workshop.	160

Plates

Frontispiece.	Two pages from the notebook of Edith Hall Dohan describing the North Trench at Gournia.
1.	White-on-dark Ware from Mokhlos (A-F) and Palaikastro (G).
2.	Vases from Mokhlos (A), the Gulf of Mirabello area (B-E), Pseira (F), and Palaikastro (G).
3.	Vases from the gulf of Mirabello area (A) and Knossos (B).
4.	Cross sections of sherds from Gournia.
5.	SEM photomicrographs.
6.	SEM photomicrographs.
7.	SEM Photomicrographs.
8.	Thin section (A-B) and SEM photomicrographs (C-F).
9.	Photographically enhanced xeroradiographs.
10.	Photographically enhanced xeroradiographs.
11.	Localities for clay samples.
12.	Cross sections (A-C) and the exterior (D) of sherds from Gournia.
13.	Steps in the manufacture of a rounded cup.
14.	A potter's workshop at Thrapsano (A-D) and scenes near Kentri (E-F).
15.	A potter's workshop at Kentri.
16.	Kilns at Kentri.
17.	Kilns and vessels at Kentri.
18.	Analyzed sherds listed in the Appendix: nos. 1–24.
19.	Analyzed sherds listed in the Appendix: nos. 25–45.
20.	Analyzed sherds and vases listed in the Appendix: nos. 46–60.
21.	Analyzed sherds and vases listed in the Appendix: nos. 61–70.
22.	Analyzed sherds and vases listed in the Appendix: nos. 71–75.

Tables

2-I.	Principal contexts containing East Cretan White-on-dark Ware.	7
4-I.	The most characteristic shapes of East Cretan White-on-dark Ware.	36
4-II.	Shapes from the North Trench at Gournia.	37
4-III.	Shapes from Ossuary III in the Ellenika Cemetery, Palaikastro.	38
5-I.	Chemical compositions of Gournian EM III and MM sherds.	55
6-I.	Inclusions larger than 10 micrometers in sherds from EM III Gournia.	61
6-II.	Inclusions in MM I-III sherds from Gournia.	62
6-III.	Inclusions in EM III sherds from Mokhlos.	63
6-IV.	Inclusions in EM III sherds from Vasilike.	64
6-V.	Inclusions in sherds from Priniatikos Pyrgos, East Crete, and Knossos.	64
8-I.	Elemental percentages (by weight) for the white slip on sherds from Gournia.	72
8-II.	Elemental percentages (by weight) for MS 4615-13.	73
9-I.	Firing conditions of East Cretan White-on-dark Ware.	76
10-I.	Values for saturated weight in air, dry weight in air, saturated weight in water, and apparent porosity for EM III sherds.	79
10-II.	Average apparent porosities for 26 EM III sherds grouped according to vessel shape.	82
11-I.	Composition of the standard.	84
11-II.	Average concentrations of elements.	85
11-III.	Concentrations relative to the Gournian EM III group.	88
12-I.	Concentrations for 21 elements.	92
12-II.	Corrected concentrations for eight elements.	96

12-III.	Clay samples, K-means clustering based on eight elements.	100
12-IV.	Sherds, K-means clustering.	101
12-V.	Clay samples plus all sherds, K-means clustering.	102
12-VI.	Clay samples plus sherds from Gournia and Vasilike, K-means clustering.	103
15-I.	Clay samples presented as a stratigraphic column.	121
15-II.	Munsell colors and calcium carbonate percentages of marl samples.	122
15-III.	Descriptive grain-size statistics of four marl samples.	122
15-IV.	Composition of clay samples.	124
17-I.	Operations in the making of one strip.	138
17-II.	Time table for one jar.	139
19-I.	Variables in the sherds from EM III Gournia.	161

Addresses of Contributing Authors

Dr. Thomas Bakas
University of Ioannina
First Institute of Physics
Ioannina, Greece

Prof. Philip P. Betancourt
Department of Art History
Temple University
Philadelphia, Pennsylvania 19122
U.S.A.

Dr. Harriet Blitzer
62 Fairfield St.
Buffalo, New York 14214
U.S.A.

Prof. Albert D. Frost
Department of Electrical
 and Computer Engineering
University of New Hampshire
Durham, New Hampshire 03824
U.S.A.

Prof. Thomas K. Gaisser
Bartol Research Foundation
 of the Franklin Institute
University of Delaware
Newark, Delaware 19711
U.S.A.

Prof. N.-H. J. Gangas
K. Palama St., 3
452 21 Ioannina
Greece

Prof. John A. Gifford
Department of Anthropology
University of Miami
P.O. Box 248106
Coral Gables, Florida 33124
U.S.A.

Ms. Gail Gosser
23 North Richardson
Lansdale, Pennsylvania 19146
U.S.A.

Dr. Nicholas Hartmann
MASCA
University Museum
The University of Pennsylvania
Philadelphia, Pennsylvania 19104
U.S.A.

Prof. Robert Johnston
Dean, College of Fine
 and Applied Arts
Rochester Institute of Technology
1 Lomb Memorial Drive
Rochester, New York 14623
U.S.A.

Dr. Y. Maniatis
Nuclear Research Center
 "Demokritos"
Aghia Paraskevi
Attiki, Greece

Prof. Frederick R. Matson
Department of Anthropology
409 Carpenter Bld.
Pennsylvania State University
University Park,
 Pennsylvania 16802
U.S.A.

Prof. George H. Myer
Department of Geology
Temple University
Philadelphia, Pennsylvania 19122
U.S.A.

Prof. George Rapp, Jr.
Dean, College of Letters
 and Sciences
108 Mathematics-Geology
 Building
University of Minnesota
Duluth, Minnesota 55812
U.S.A.

Ms. Susan Sapareto
118 W. 69th St. 5A
New York, N.Y. 10023
U.S.A.

Prof. Charles P. Swann
Bartol Research Foundation
 of the Franklin Institute
University of Delaware
Newark, Delaware 19711
U.S.A.

Ms. Maria Voyatzoglou
85 Hesperidon
Callithea
Athens, Greece

Dr. Robert G. White
Laboratory for Research
 in the Structure of Matter
University of Pennsylvania
Philadelphia, Pennsylvania 19104
U.S.A.

Abbreviations

Abbreviations of journals follow the conventions suggested by the *American Journal of Archaeology*, vol. 82, no. 1, 1978.

Abbreviations of Museums

AK	Akademisches Kunstmuseum, Bonn
AM	Ashmolean Museum, Oxford
AN	Museum, Aghios Nikolaos
BM	British Museum, London
ERM	Ella Riegel Museum, Bryn Mawr College, Bryn Mawr
FM	Fitzwilliam Museum, Cambridge
HM	Archaeological Museum, Herakleion
KSM	Stratigraphical Museum, Knossos
MHC	Art Museum, Mount Holyoke College, South Hadley, Mass.
MFA	Museum of Fine Arts, Boston
MMA	Metropolitan Museum of Art, New York
NMC	National Museum, Copenhagen
Penn	University Museum, University of Pennsylvania, Philadelphia

Credits for Photographs and Figures

Kristin Anderson, by courtesy of the Museum of Fine Arts, Boston, Cornelius C. Vermeule, curator of Greek and Roman art
 Pls. 1B–C, 1E–F, 21, nos. 61–67.

Ashmolean Museum, Oxford
 Pls. 1G, 3B, 20, nos. 55–60.

Philip P. Betancourt
 Pls. 13, 14A–D, 19, nos. 36–45, 20, nos. 46–54; Figs. 1–1C–D, 1–1G, 1–2 nos. 1, 4–5, 7, 10, 12–14, and 16, 2–3, 3–1, 4–1 to 4–6, 19–1.

Harriet Blitzer
 Pls. 14E–F, 15, 16, 17; Figs. 18–1 to 18–6.

Mrs. E. Dohan
 Frontispiece

Trustees of the British Museum, London
 Pls. 2B–E, 3A.

Stacey Frost
 Figs. 13–1 to 13–14.

Thomas K. Gaisser and Charles P. Swann
 Figs. 11–1 to 11–2.

N.-H. J. Gangas
 Figs. 7–1 to 7–3.

John A. Gifford
 Pl. 11, Fig. 15–1.

John A. Gifford and George Rapp, Jr.
 Figs. 12–1 to 12–3.

Lori Grove
 Figs. 1–1A, 1–1F, 1–1H.

Debi Harlan
 Fig. 14–1.

Nicholas Hartmann
 Pls. 4, 12, 18, 19, nos. 25–35, 21, nos. 68–70, 22, nos. 72 and 74–75; Figs. 10–1 to 10–3.

Barbara Hayden
 Figs. 1–1B, 1–1E, 1–2 nos. 2–3, 6, 8–9, 11, and 15, 2–1.

Hirmer Fotoarchiv, Munich
 Pl. 1A.

Robert H. Johnston (xeroradiographs), photographically enhanced by Robert Kushner
 Pls. 9A, 9C, 9E, 10A, 10C, 10E, 10G.

Yannis Maniatis
 Pl. 8C–F.

Frederick R. Matson
 Pls. 5–7.

Metropolitan Museum of Art, New York
 Pl. 2F.

George H. Myer
 Pl. 8A–B.

By courtesy of Wolf-Dietrich Niemeier
 Fig. 2–2.

By courtesy of the University Museum, University of Pennsylvania
 Figs. 2–5 to 2–14.

R. K. Vincent, Jr., by courtesy of the Archaeological Museum, Herakleion, John Sakellarakis, director
 Pls. 1D, 2A, 2G.

Preface

Much has been made in our generation about "New Archaeology" versus "Old Archaeology," about the value of modern methods as opposed to traditional techniques. In this study the distinctions do not exist. All archaeology is a study of the past, and the present endeavor brings together a range of methodology and expertise: traditional; recently developed; innovative; and on the cutting edge of science. In some ways, the East Cretan White-on-dark Ware Project represents a new way of looking at archaeological pottery. Its contribution is not so much in the quality of the parts as in the concept of the whole, a commitment to a coordinated examination of archaeological artifacts from many different points of view, both traditional and new. It suggests that only the sum of many facets can help the historian gain perspectives on the way objects were made and used, what they say about their society, and what they meant to those who used them.

The subject chosen for investigation is particularly well suited to this type of study. East Cretan White-on-dark Ware was made at a crucial turning point in history, just before the first palatial society of ancient Europe incorporated the Cretan landscape into a new artistic and economic (and presumably also political) structure. It thus offers information on a formative period for complex urban society in Europe, a subject that is very little known.

Thanks are extended to many organizations and individuals for assistance with the project, but particularly to those who made the pottery under their jurisdiction available for study and/or analysis:

D. M. Bailey, British Museum, London.
Dietrich von Bothmer, Metropolitan Museum of Art, New York.
Gerald Cadogan, Pyrgos Excavations, Pyrgos, Crete.
B. F. Cook, British Museum, London.
Costis Davaras, the Museum, Aghios Nikolaos, Crete.
G. Roger Edwards, University Museum, University of Pennsylvania.
Spyros Iakovidis, University Museum, University of Pennsylvania.
Doro Levi, Phaistos Excavations, Phaistos, Crete.
Machteld Mellink, Ella Riegel Museum, Bryn Mawr College, Bryn Mawr, Pennsylvania.
Jean-Claude Poursat, Malia Excavations, Malia, Crete.
John Sakellarakis, Archaeological Museum, Herakleion, Crete.
Joseph W. Shaw, Kommos Excavations, Pitsidia, Crete.
Iannis Tzedakis, Archaeological Museum, Khania, Crete.
Cornelius C. Vermeule and Emily Vermeule, Museum of Fine Arts, Boston.
Michael Vickers, Ashmolean Museum, Oxford.
Peter Warren, Knossos Excavations, Knossos, Crete.
Wendy M. Watson, Art Museum, Mount Holyoke College, South Hadley, Massachusetts.

Assistance in working in Greece was given by the American School of Classical Studies in Athens, the British School of Archaeology in Athens, and the Greek Archaeological Service. Other individuals offered many kinds of help. Our thanks go particularly to Sinclair Hood, Robert Koehl, Deng Jeng Lee, Jennifer Moody, Wolf-Dietrich Niemeier, Robert M. Winokur, David Pease, Malcolm Wiener, and Florence Wolsky.

Portions of the research and publication of the entire project were assisted by grants from the National Endowment for the Humanities, Grant no. RO-158-79-1363, Temple University, and The University Museum, University of Pennsylvania. The stylistic analysis was assisted by a grant from Temple University to Philip P. Betancourt. A grant from the Xerox Corporation to Robert H. Johnston, Dean and Professor at the Rochester Institute of Technology, in Rochester, New York, made possible the application of xeroradiography to this study. The energy dispersive spectroscopy of Robert G. White was done at the Electron Microscope Facility, Laboratory for Research in the Structure of Matter, University of Pennsylvania, supported by the National Science Foundation, grant no. DMR-7923647. Thanks are extended to The Pennsylvania State University for the ceramic technology studies conducted by Frederick R. Matson. The replication studies of Susan Sapareto and Gail Gosser are indebted to the use of the Ceramics Area, Tyler School of Art, Temple University. The porosity studies of Nicholas Hartmann were done at the Museum Applied Science Center for Archaeology, University of Pennsylvania. The neutron activation analyses of George Rapp, Jr. and John A. Gifford were done as part of the Reactor Sharing Program under DOE contract E-(11-1)-2144 to the University of Wisconsin Reactor Facility, Richard Cashwell, Director. The photoacoustic spectroscopy analysis of Albert D. Frost is indebted to the Research Laboratory of Archaeometry and the History of Art, Oxford University, and to the Department of Electrical and Computer Engineering, University of New Hampshire, Durham, N.H. The ethnological studies of Maria Voyatzoglou were supported in part by the Polytechnical School, Thessaloniki University.

Additional acknowledgements are listed under the individual chapters.

Philip P. Betancourt
1982

Part I

1

Introduction to the Studies

Philip P. Betancourt

At the close of the Early Bronze Age, a handmade pottery decorated with white linear ornament became very popular in eastern Crete. It used a light colored fabric with part or all of the exterior surface covered by a slip that would fire red to brown to black, and a slightly creamy off-white decoration was painted over the dark slip. The ornament was nearly always linear, employing a variety of simple geometric motifs, used singly or combined in repeating or alternating patterns.

This pottery, called White-on-dark Ware, is important to Cretan archaeology for several reasons. As the principal fine ware of Early Minoan III in eastern Crete (overlapping with Middle Minoan IA in the central part of the island), it defines a chronological phase, so that its presence can be used to date other artifacts. Historically, it marks the beginning of a long Middle Bronze Age tradition of white-painted and polychrome pottery. During this period, Middle Minoan IB–III, the fine Kamares Ware of the Minoan palaces became a major art form, and it greatly influenced the monumental wall paintings and the other arts of the Late Bronze Age in Crete. Since the technology used to produce the dark slip of White-on-dark Ware is ancestral to the "black glaze" of Classical Greek pottery, and since Minoan artistic styles were transmitted to the Mycenaeans and from them to the Classical Greeks and Romans, this early pottery stands at the beginning of a long and important tradition.

Found in both houses and tombs, White-on-dark Ware must have served as the main fine ware of its time. It was made in many shapes (Fig. 1–1 and pl. 1): cups and bowls for serving and drinking; jugs, spouted jars, and teapots for pouring; larger jars for storage; shallow bowls for general use; and specialized shapes for many different purposes. Even a few anthropomorphic figures are known, like the strange woman with pierced breasts shown in pl. 1A. Because many of the same shapes are found in both settlements and tombs, a given type might have had more than one function. Although coarse and undecorated pots were made in large numbers, only a few other decorated fine wares were used in eastern Crete at this time; at the height of its popularity White-on-dark Ware shared its position with only a few other fine vases (mostly painted with simple dark designs).

Following the ceramic nomenclature system suggested by Rice (1976), the ware is defined chiefly by its surface treatment. The ornament, mostly lines, consists of spirals, quirks, triangles, chevrons, arcs, and other abstract motifs. They often form horizontal bands of ornament that are interesting and attractive. Their background, the dark-firing slip, sets off the white and creates a pleasing contrast.

Only hand techniques were used. Shapes were serviceable and utilitarian, with profiles that flowed smoothly with no sharp carinations (see the profile drawings in Fig. 1–2). Nonfunctional ceramic additions such as ornamental knobs or extra handles were not used. The walls were usually worked to a uniform thickness except where a lip might be thickened as in Fig. 1–2, nos. 8–15. Handles were round or flattened coils, and spouts and bases were made separately and joined on. The style was simple and straightforward, with the aesthetic qualities carried by the ornament and the overall shape of the vessel.

White-on-dark Ware itself does not represent a break with earlier ceramic tradition; it cannot be the result of a sudden influx of new ideas. Most of the shapes and many aspects of the technology are inherited from earlier periods, and its ornamental system develops only gradually. We are dealing with

Fig. 1–1. East Cretan White-on-dark Ware. All from EM III. Scale 1:3. A. Rounded cup from Vasilike (HM 5294). B. Spouted, conical bowl from Vasilike (Penn MS 4238). C. Teapot from Vasilike (HM 5249). D. Jug from Mokhlos (HM 5449). E. Bowl from Vasilike (Penn MS 4237). F. Conical cup from Malia (HM 8656). G. Conical cup with pronounced base from Vasilike (Penn MS 4234). H. Conical bowl with frying pan handle from Vasilike (HM unnumbered).

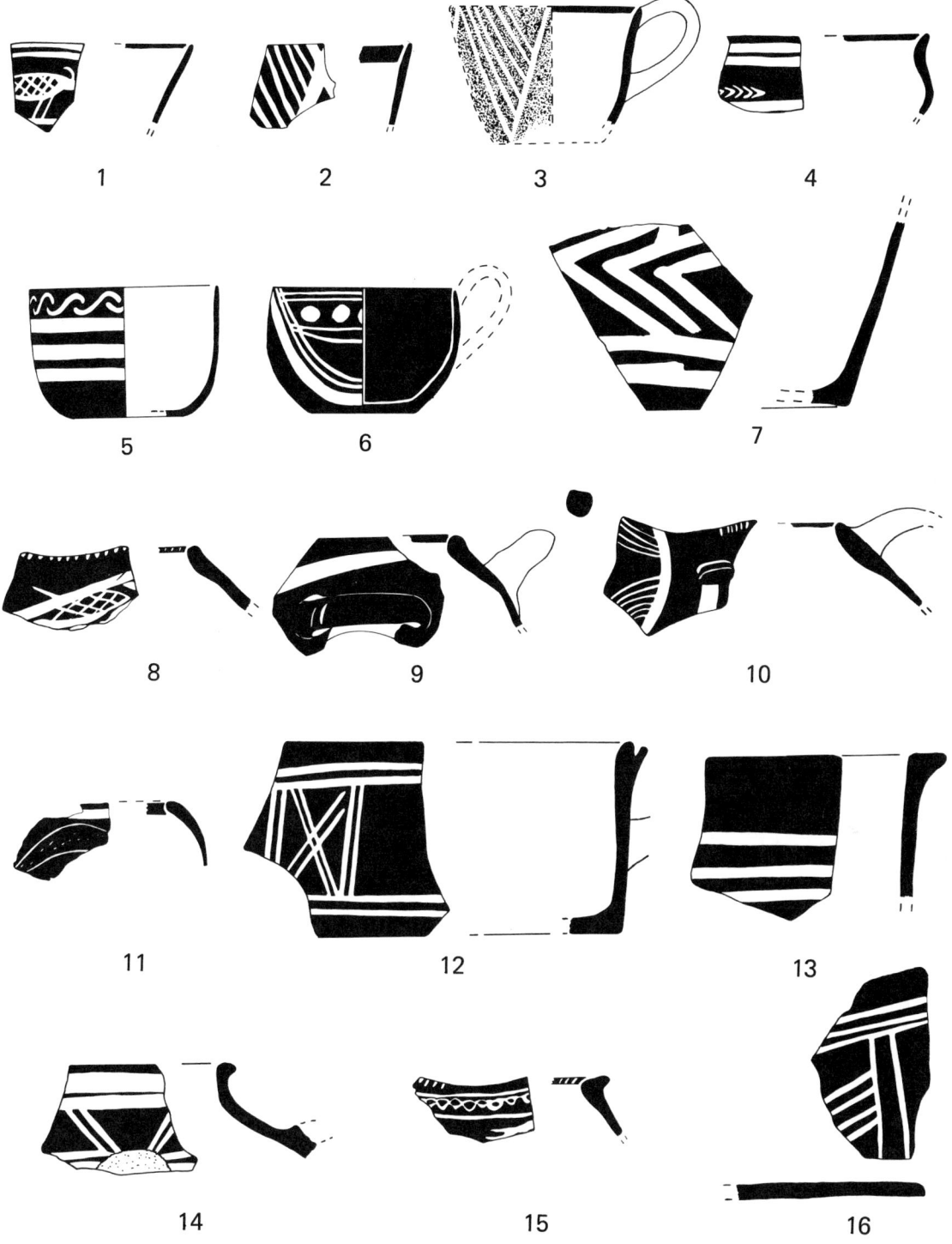

Fig. 1–2. Profiles of East Cretan White-on-dark Ware. Scale 1:3. 1. Cup from Gournia (MMA 07.232.197). 2. Cup from Gournia (Penn MS 4615–29). 3. Cup from Gournia (Penn MS 4615–1). 4. Cup or bowl from Gournia (MMA 07.232.18). 5. Rounded cup from Vasilike (MHC BAI 14–B). 6. Cup from Pseira (Penn MS 4233). 7. Conical jar from Vasilike (MHC BAI 14–A). 8. Bridge spouted jar from Gournia (Penn MS 4615–27). 9. Bridge spouted jar from Gournia (Penn MS 4615–26). 10. Bridge spouted jar with three handles from Gournia (MMA 07.232.162). 11. Bridge spouted jar from Gournia (Penn MS 4615–22). 12. Pyxis from Gournia (MMA 07.232.71). 13. Jar from Gournia (ERM P–531). 14. Teapot from eastern Crete (ERM P–519). 15. Teapot from Gournia (Penn MS 4615–43). 16. Lid from eastern Crete (ERM P–518).

a local Cretan development that was well grounded in the pottery of the Early Bronze Age.

The *floruit* of the ware came at a turning point in Minoan history. In the period immediately following, Middle Minoan IB, important palaces were constructed at Knossos, Phaistos, and other Cretan centers. The polychrome Kamares Ware which developed out of White-on-dark Ware was essentially a palatial style, and its principal development was at these centers. But what was the situation in EM III–MM IA? Was White-on-dark Ware the product of household industries, was it made in a series of village workshops, or were there already regional pottery producers? Answers to these questions are fundamental to any interpretation of the palatial economy which grew out of the earlier situation. Kamares Ware used both the technology and the style of White-on-dark Ware, and its production must have been a major factor in the nature and direction of the palace economy.

The East Cretan White-on-dark Ware Project

In order to better understand the White-on-dark Ware of eastern Crete, a research team composed of specialists from several disciplines collaborated to examine many aspects of the pottery. The investigations were carried out both in the United States and in Greece, using a variety of analytical methods. The results were coordinated and compared during the progress of the research, so that the results obtained by one investigator might complement and enhance the conclusions of others. The research was conducted over a period of four years, from 1978 to 1982, and a preliminary report of the findings appeared in 1982 (Betancourt 1982).

The principal investigators include:

Thomas Bakas received a first degree in Physics from the University of Ioannina, Ioannina, Greece, in February 1976. Since then he has been working with Professor N-H. Gangas in Mössbauer spectroscopy and is now completing the requirements for his Ph.D thesis.

Philip P. Betancourt, Professor of Art History at Temple University and Consulting Scholar and Visiting Lecturer, University Museum, University of Pennsylvania, is an archaeologist with a specialization in Minoan pottery. He contributed the stylistic analyses and several other sections, and he also acted as director of the project.

Harriet Blitzer is an archaeologist who specializes in the history of technology. Her section is on the ethnology of Kentri.

Albert D. Frost is a physicist and Professor of Electrical Engineering at the University of New Hampshire. He wrote on photoacoustic examination of surfaces, a nondestructive technique he has developed for use with archaeological materials.

Thomas K. Gaisser is a physicist at the Bartol Research Foundation of the Franklin Institute at the University of Delaware. Professor Gaisser collaborated on the analyses by Proton Induced X-ray Emission (PIXE).

N.-H. J. Gangas is Professor of Physics at the University of Ioannina. Among his specializations is the application of Mössbauer spectroscopy to ancient pottery studies, which he contributed to this volume.

John A. Gifford was a geologist at the Archaeometry Laboratory, University of Minnesota, Duluth, when he conducted the research presented in this volume. He specialized in the application of geological studies to the archaeology of the Eastern Mediterranean and contributed sections on geology and neutron activation analysis.

Gail Gosser is a professional potter with experience in hand techniques and kiln construction. She collaborated on the replication of ancient techniques when she was a candidate for the MFA degree at the Tyler School of Art of Temple University.

Nicholas Hartmann is an archaeologist affiliated with the Museum Applied Science Center for Archaeology, University Museum, University of Pennsylvania. His work on porosity measurement is included in the volume.

Robert H. Johnston, Dean of the College of Fine and Applied Arts, Rochester Institute of Technology, is an anthropologist, potter, and ethnographer. He contributed the section on xeroradiography, an archaeological analysis technique he helped to develop.

Yannis Maniatis is a physicist at the Nuclear Research Center "Demokritos," Aghia Paraskeve, Attiki, Greece. A specialist in the early history of pyrotechnology in Greece, he contributed the section on firing temperature analysis.

Frederick R. Matson, a ceramic engineer and archaeologist, is Professor Emeritus at Pennsylvania State University, State College. He has extensive experience with the archaeological pottery of the Mediterranean and Near Eastern cultures and contributed the section on physical characterization by SEM and other methods.

George H. Myer, a geologist at Temple University, Philadelphia, specializes in mineralogy and ceramic petrography. Professor Myer offered sections on geology and pottery characterization.

George Rapp, Jr., Dean of the College of Letters and Science, University of Minnesota, Duluth, is an archaeological geologist and geochemist with extensive experience in the Eastern Mediterranean. He presented the neutron activation analysis.

Susan Sapareto is a professional potter who works with hand methods. She is an experienced kiln builder and collaborated on the replication studies at the time she was a candidate for the MFA degree at the Tyler School of Art, Temple University.

Charles P. Swann, Professor of Physics at the Bartol Research Foundation of the Franklin Institute, University of Delaware, collaborated on the studies by proton microprobe (PIXE).

Maria Voyatzoglou is a professional potter, living in Athens. She has done extensive work on the ethnology of folk potters in Crete, and she contributed a section on the potters of Thrapsano.

Robert G. White is Supervisor, Electron Microscopy Center, Laboratory for Research in the structure of Matter and Instructor in the School of Materials Science and Engineering, University of Pennsylvania. He contributed the study of X-ray spectroscopy.

The major results of the team's investigations show East Cretan White-on-dark Ware to be a vigorous and dynamic regional tradition, a ware made at many stylistically interrelated centers. The potters were well aware of the characteristics of their materials, making good use of the resources available to them. Their products were attractive and serviceable, and they added an aesthetically pleasing note to the life of the time.

References

Betancourt, P. P. et al. 1982. Preliminary Results from the East Cretan White-on-dark Ware Project. In *Archaeological Ceramics,* ed. J. S. Olin and A. D. Franklin, Washington, D.C.

Rice, P. M. 1976. Rethinking the Ware Concept. *American Antiquity* 41:538–43.

Part II

2

Deposits and Chronology

Philip P. Betancourt

East Cretan White-on-dark Ware is by no means the earliest white-painted ceramics of Crete. Wares decorated with white pigment are known from Knossos from as early as Early Neolithic I (Furness 1953: 115), and at the beginning of the Early Bronze Age a pottery with white designs called Lebena Ware is found in the Mesara and adjacent areas (for discussion see Branigan 1970: 27). Other isolated examples of the technology also exist. East Cretan White-on-dark Ware differs from these other styles both in its repertoire of shapes and in its style of ornamentation, though a relation could conceivably exist in the technology or in the use of white lines on a contrasting background.

Several writers have discussed the stylistic development of Minoan pottery in the period from Early Minoan III to Middle Minoan I (see especially Warren 1965; Zois 1968: chap. 6; 1968B; 1969; Betancourt 1977; Andreou 1978). Their researches have clarified the position of White-on-dark Ware with respect to the other wares of this period, and its general stratigraphic position is fairly well understood: the earliest sherds come from the end of Early Minoan IIB; many pieces date to EM III and MM IA; and the style gradually merges into later traditions in MM IB, with some motifs surviving later.

Eastern Crete is an archaeological (and perhaps cultural) region at the end of the third millennium B.C., and the local pottery has its own characteristics. Its chronology and style can be related to the rest of the island, but some periods (like the very long East Cretan EM III) do not seem to match exactly. The relevant stylistic periods in eastern Crete are currently defined by Minoan archaeologists in the following way:

EM IIB is characterized by large quantities of mottled red to black to brown Vasilike Ware, Red Burnished Ware, and Brown Burnished Ware. It is principally defined by the pottery from Period II at Myrtos (Warren 1972).

EM III, when White-on-dark Ware largely replaces Vasilike Ware and other heavily burnished pottery, is stratified above EM IIB at several sites in eastern Crete (for Vasilike see Seager 1904–1905: 218–20; 1906–1907: 114, 118–9; for Palaikastro see Dawkins 1903–1904: 199–200; 1904–1905: 273; Bosanquet and Dawkins 1923: 8; for Pseira see Seager 1910: 17; for Mokhlos see Seager 1909: 278–79). Comparisons with contexts from central Crete suggest that the latter part of east Cretan EM III overlaps with central Cretan MM IA (see Warren 1965: 25–27; Betancourt 1977).

MM IA begins with the introduction of red paint for decoration on some vases (Hood 1971: 39). White-on-dark Ware continues, but with the addition of some new shapes and motifs.

MM IB begins with the first extensive use of vases made on the potter's wheel. The new technique is rare at first, and most shapes continue to be manufactured by hand.

The chronology of these periods may be best understood by examining the pottery from several well stratified sites in eastern Crete (fig. 2–1). From these contexts, White-on-dark Ware may be divided into three successive phases (Table 2–I). In the Early Phase, dated to EM IIB and known chiefly from Period II at Myrtos, the ware represents only a small percentage of the decorated pottery. Motifs are simple, with chevrons and hatched triangles predominating. The Middle Phase, defined from contexts dated to east Cretan EM III (Knossian EM III to early MM IA), has a richer vocabulary of shapes and decorations. This is the mature phase of the ware, and its

Fig. 2–1. Map of eastern Crete showing the main sites with East Cretan White-on-dark Ware.

TABLE 2-I
Principal contexts containing East Cretan White-on-dark Ware

Early Phase
1. Period II, Myrtos
Middle Phase
1. North Trench, Gournia
2. Well Deposit, Vasilike
3. Deposit in Block A, Mokhlos
4. Deposit in Block C, Mokhlos
5. Deposit in Delta 32, Palaikastro
6. Deposit in a Field West of Block Delta, Palaikastro
7. Ossuary III at Ellenika, Palaikastro
8. Floor Deposits on Kastri, Palaikastro
Late Phase
1. Period IIa-b, Pyrgos, Myrtou
2. Deposit Beneath House D, Mokhlos
3. South Houses, Malia
4. House B. Vasilike

style is fully formed. The North Trench at Gournia is the principal deposit, and Gournia may be regarded as the type-site. Other good contexts include a well deposit at Vasilike, deposits in Blocks A and C at Mokhlos, and several deposits from Palaikastro. The Late Phase spans the time from MM IA to MM IB. While many of the features of the Middle Phase persist into this period, new changes and motifs appear as well. Polychrome vessels, which define the beginning of MM IA, and wheelmade shapes, which begin in MM IB, are contemporary with the handmade ware with white decoration. Deposits include Period IIa–b at Pyrgos Myrtou, a deposit beneath House D at Mokhlos, the South Houses at Malia, House B at Vasilike, and several other contexts. By the end of the phase White-on-dark Ware has evolved into later traditions.

The White-on-dark Ware of central and western Crete is less well studied than the east Cretan variety. Only small amounts have been published, and there are few good deposits. Strata from Knossos, however, prove that a post-Vasilike Ware phase with white linear decoration but with no added red paint does exist in the central part of the island (Hood 1961–1962: 93; 1966). This period must coincide with at least part of east Cretan EM III. The pottery decorated with white paint continues into central Cretan MM IA, and it is likely that a phase with simple white decoration predates the Kamares Ware period throughout the island.

Central Cretan and West Cretan White-on-dark Ware is very different from the eastern pottery. The vessel shapes are distinct and the ornament less complex. Neither spirals nor circle motifs are usual. Plain horizontal bands are particularly common, while diagonal lines, hatching, dots, and other simple designs also occur. A teapot from Knossos decorated with rising arcs (pl. 3B) is typical of the best pottery from the phase in north central Crete (for other Knossian examples see Zois 1968B: pl. 30; Branigan 1970: 32). Sherds from Stavromenos, near Rethymnon, illustrate the style from western Crete (fig. 2–2). Some of the motifs here, like the dot band flanked by lines,

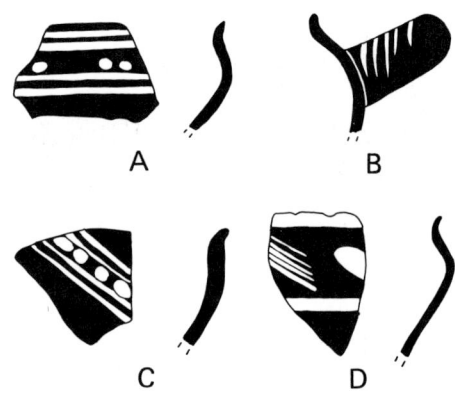

Fig. 2–2. A selection of sherds of White-on-dark Ware from Stavromenos, near Rethymnon in western Crete. Scale 1:3. A. Two sherds from a bridge spouted jar. B.–D. Sherds from cups.

may be closely compared with east Cretan designs, but the more complex eastern ornaments are not found (for the site see Schiering 1982). In the Mesara plain in southern Crete handmade shapes with white designs also occur before the period of elaborate polychrome decoration. Like the other white decorated wares, they gradually give way in favor of a more complex decorative repertoire. The clearest stratigraphy in this region comes from Kommos where bridge spouted jars and other shapes with white linear motifs persist into MM IB, after the introduction of wheelmade pottery (see the examples in fig. 2–3).

Only one sherd which may be East Cretan White-on-dark Ware has been found outside of Crete. It comes from a jar with circle motifs connected by multiple connecting lines from a Middle Bronze I level at Lerna on the Greek mainland.[1] It is clearly an import at the site, but its place of origin (probably near the Gulf of Mirabello) is not known.

Only in eastern Crete can the style be divided into three clear phases. These phases are both stylistic and chronological periods in this part of the island, and several generalizations may be made about each one. They are here presented in terms of specific deposits.

Early Phase

PERIOD II AT MYRTOS

The EM II settlement at Myrtos has two architectural periods. The later phase, destroyed at the end of EM IIB, uses large quantities of Vasilike Ware in addition to several other kinds of pottery (Warren 1972). Fine Gray Ware, typical of the earlier period at the site, is not found in this level, and dark linear decoration, another early EM II feature, is uncommon. Eleven catalogued pieces from Myrtos have white-on-dark decoration. All come from Period II (Fig. 2–4).

Several variations may be noted in the technique. In seven instances the white paint is on a dark ground,

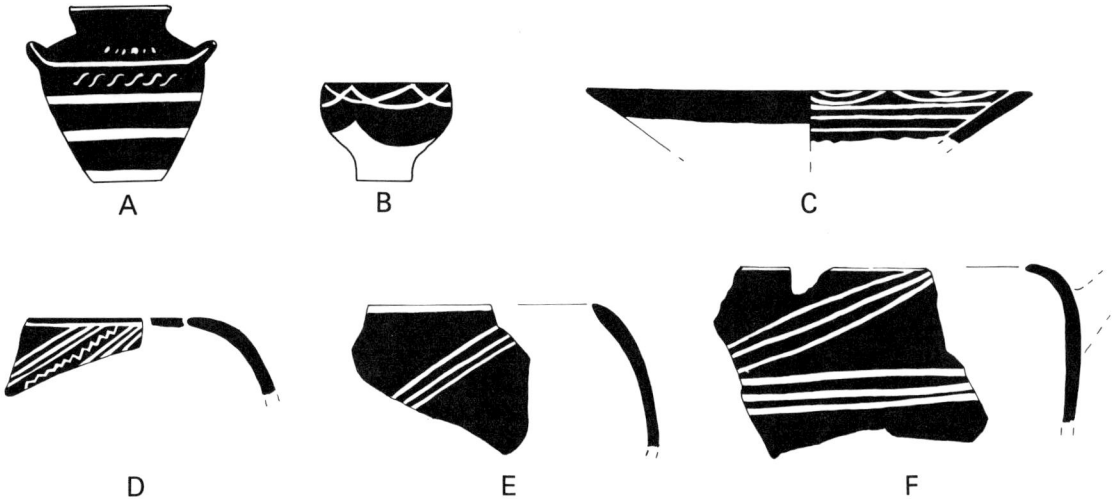

Fig. 2–3. South Cretan White-on-dark Ware. A. Jar from Platanos, MM I–IIA, HM no. 6860. B. Conical cup from Aghia Triada, MM I, HM no. 4090. C. Bowl from Kommos, MM IB, excav. no. C 5941. D.–F. Bridge spouted jars from Kommos, MM IB, excav. nos. C 5940, C 5953, and C 5072. Scale 1:3.

in three it is on a burnished red ground, and in one case it is on an unburnished red surface. This lack of standardization, perhaps to be expected in a new style, contrasts with the more uniform character of the white-painted pottery in later deposits.

The early motifs seem simple and stiff in comparison with the richness of the decorative vocabulary in the later phases of the style. Elements include chevrons (fig. 2–4, C–G), vertical lines (A), and simple zigzags. No curvilinear motifs are known. Shapes include the conical cup or bowl (D–E), the shallow, open bowl (C), the cup (F–G), and the wide mouthed jug (Warren 1972: fig. 87), all of which continue into the next phase.

OTHER DEPOSITS FROM THE EARLY PHASE

Only a few other early contexts with White-on-dark Ware are known. Seager found several examples of white-painted decoration on sherds from his Period III at Vasilike even though, as at Myrtos, the stratum contained mostly mottled Vasilike Ware and other EM II pottery (Seager 1904–1905: 217; 1906–1907: 116). The white lines were painted on top of the same burnished red to black slip typical of Vasilike Ware. A burial from Aghia Photia included a spouted, conical bowl with white linear decoration on a similarly mottled surface (Boyd 1904–1905: pl. 25 no. 3; Hawes et al. 1908: color pl. A4), and other vases in this style come from Pseira (Seager 1910: 17).

Middle Phase

THE NORTH TRENCH AT GOURNIA

White-on-dark Ware was found at several places at Gournia (Boyd 1904–1905: 185–86; Hall 1908), especially in a large hollow northeast of Quarter A, usually called the North Trench (Hall 1904–1905; 1908; see Frontispiece). The deposit was apparently a large dump. It contained a great mass of broken pottery, and two hundred baskets of sherds were recovered, almost all undecorated coarse wares. Most of the decorated pieces had white-painted ornament, though a few used a dark-on-light technique (see the examples in figs. 2–10 and 2–12). Only a sherd or two of EM I–II was present.

The North Trench provides a large selection of White-on-dark Ware (figs. 2–5 to 12). Among the shapes, discussed more fully in chap. 4, cups (figs. 2–5 to 6) and bridge spouted jars (figs. 2–8 to 9) are the most popular pieces. Other forms include teapots (fig. 2–12, no. 2), lids (fig. 2–11, no. 1), jugs (fig. 2–11 nos. 2, 4, and 8), and other shapes. The decorations are very advanced over those of Period II at Myrtos. Spirals, circle motifs, quirks, and other curvilinear designs have now joined the rectilinear ornament pre-

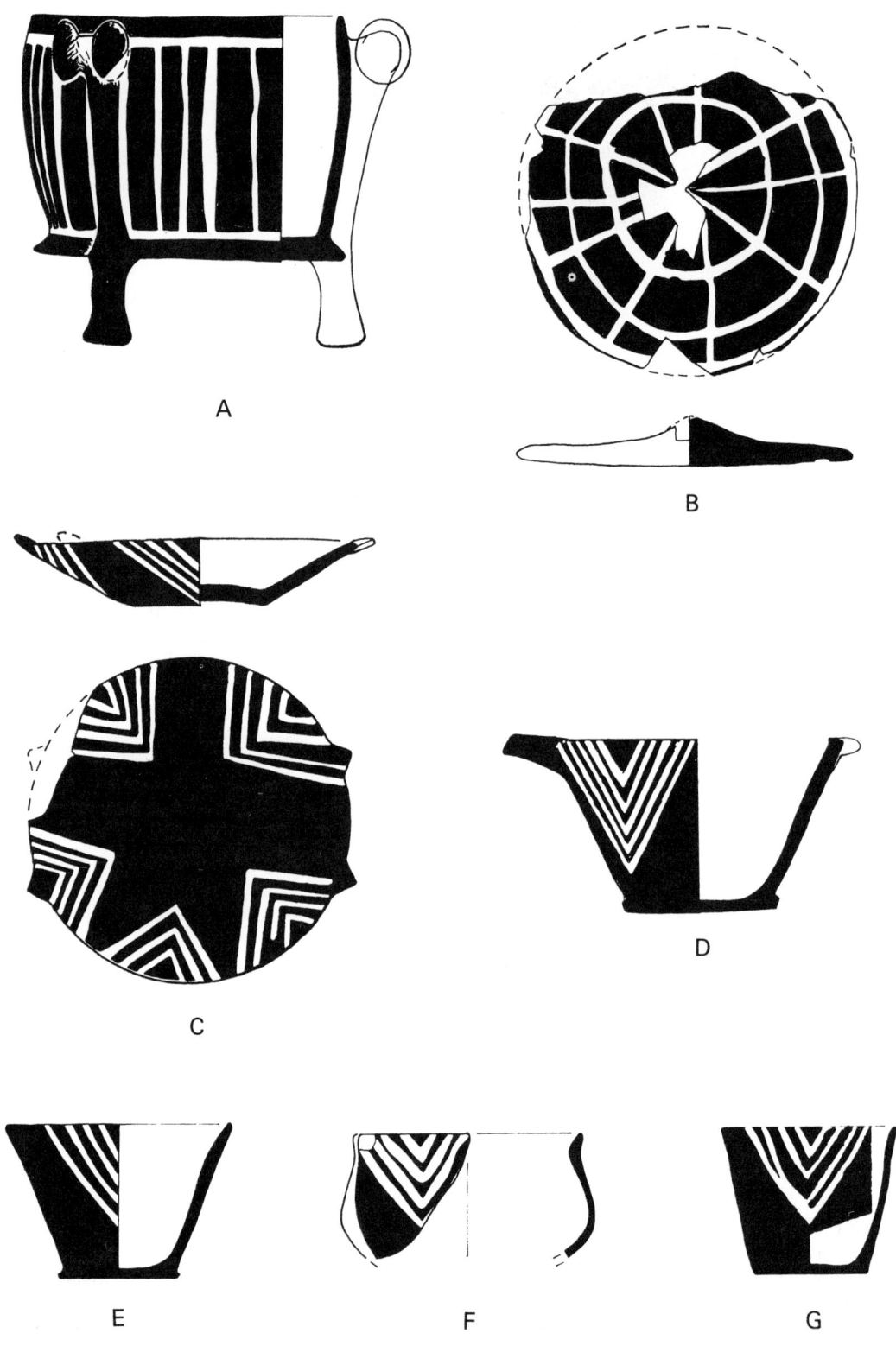

Fig. 2–4. Ceramic vases decorated with white linear decoration from Period II at Myrtos (White-on-dark Ware, Early Phase).

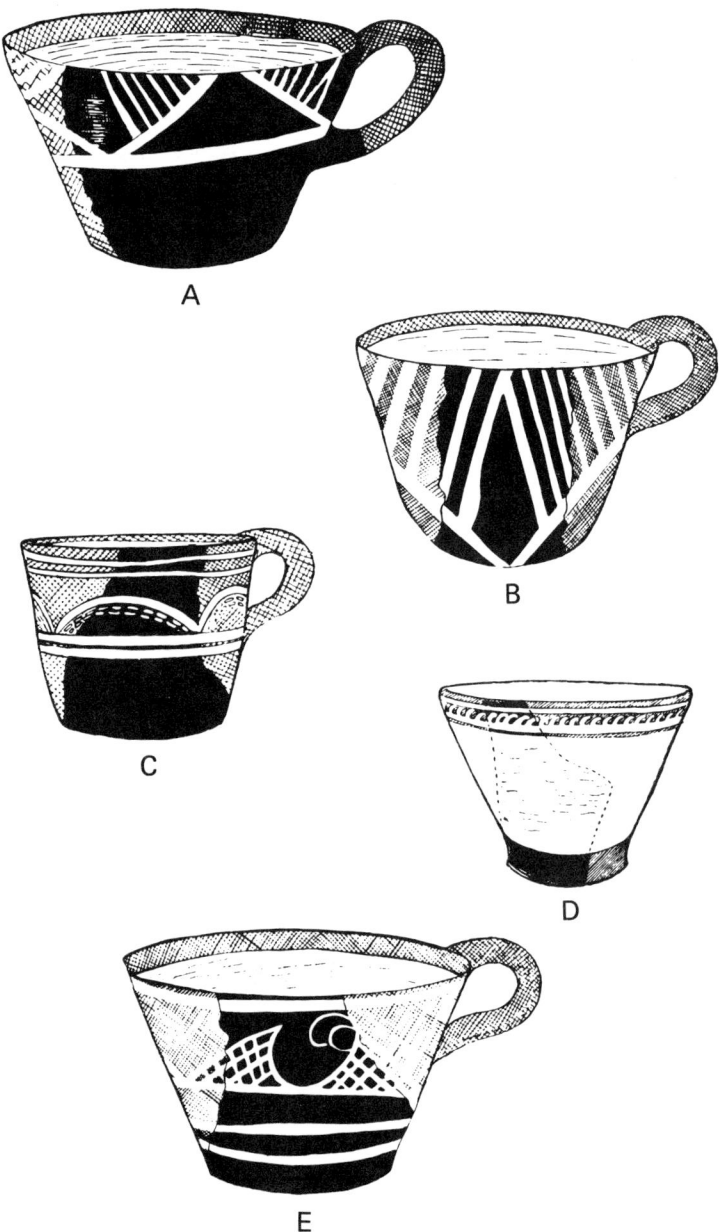

Fig. 2–5. Restored cups from the North Trench at Gournia. After Hall 1904–1905: pl. 26.

ferred in the Early Phase (see the fuller discussion in chap. 3). A few designs are zoomorphic (fig. 2–7, no. 28 and 2–9, nos. 11, 13). No red paint is found on any of the published sherds. Because of the homogeneous character of this large deposit, Gournia may be regarded as the type-site for the main phase of East Cretan White-on-dark Ware, and its material defines EM III in eastern Crete.

WELL DEPOSIT AT VASILIKE

In 1906 Richard Seager excavated a well with a large deposit of White-on-dark Ware at Vasilike (1906–1907: 118–23). Vasilike Ware, the type-ware for EM IIB, was found in some quantity only in the lowest meter of the fill, perhaps establishing the date at which the well was dug. Almost all of the decorated

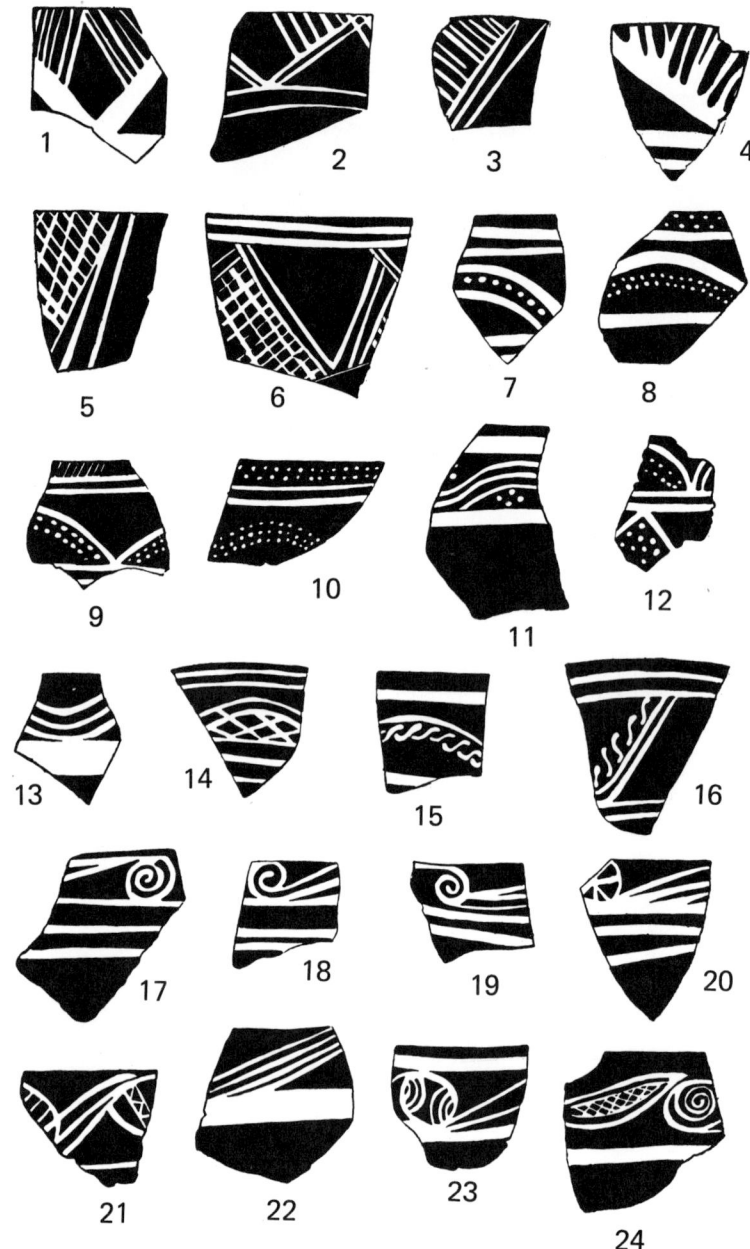

Fig. 2–6. Cup fragments from the North Trench at Gournia. Scale 2:5. After Hall 1904–1905: pl. 27.

pottery from the rest of the deposit was in the light-on-dark technique (published pieces from this deposit include Seager 1906–1907: figs. 3a–c, 4, 5, 6, 13, and pl. 30a).

Since most of the pottery was never published, we must depend on Seager's descriptions for much of our knowledge about the deposit as a whole. The shapes and decorations seem similar to those of the North Trench group, but the correspondence is not exact, and Seager thought that the deposit at Vasilike might be a little later in date. Crosshatched circles and lozenges, common at Gournia, are reportedly absent from the group found in the well. A cup with a convex profile and small horizontal handles set low on the body is found there but not in the North Trench material. The published pottery from Vasilike, how-

Fig. 2–7. Cup fragments from the North Trench at Gournia. Scale 2:5. After Hall 1904–1905: pl. 28.

ever, has many affinities with the sherds from Gournia. Hatched and crosshatched triangles, chevrons, quirks, and dotted arcs are all found in both contexts. Conical bowls and cups, teapots, bridge spouted jars, and other similar shapes connect the two deposits as well. Since no red paint seems to have been used in either group, they are probably not very far apart in date.

DEPOSIT IN BLOCK A AT MOKHLOS

Information on the White-on-dark Ware from Mokhlos is provided by a deposit from Block A, from a level stratified above an EM II phase within rooms built during EM II (Seager 1909: 278 and fig. 6). Evidently there was no architectural break between the two periods at this spot. Conical and rounded

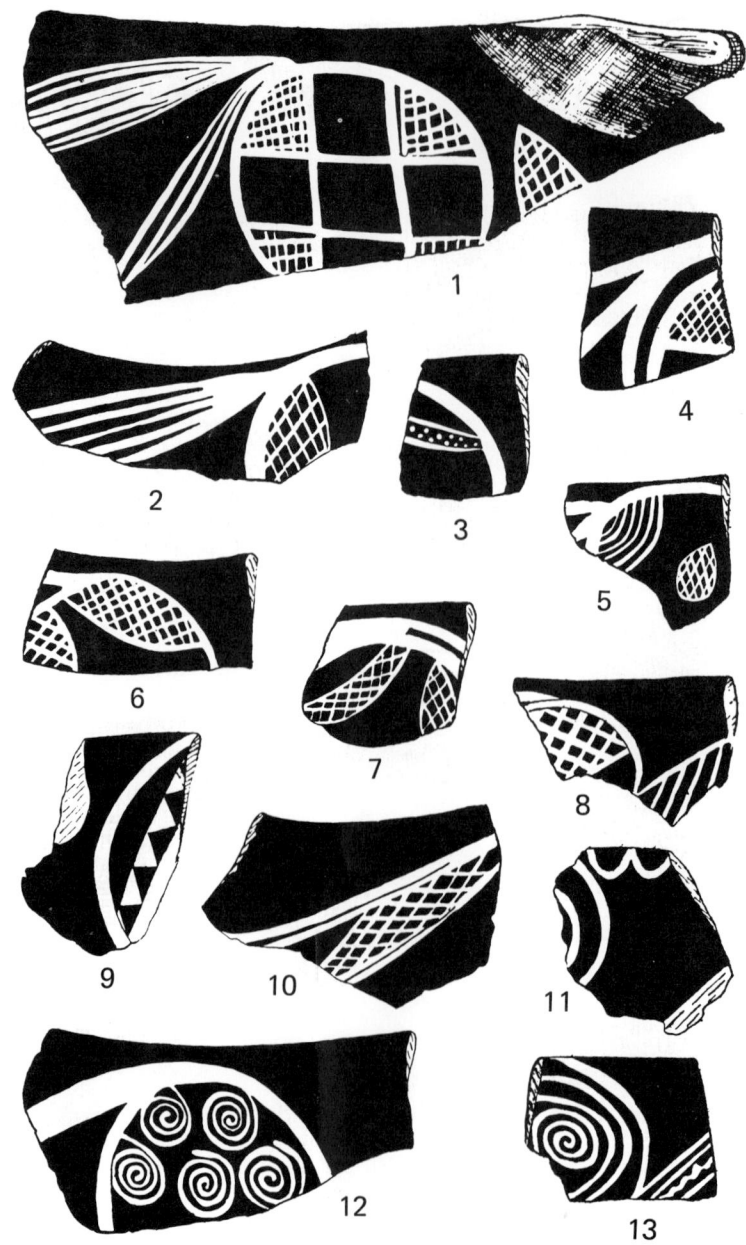

Fig. 2–8. Bridge spouted jar fragments from the North Trench at Gournia. Scale 2:5. After Hall 1904–1905: pl. 29.

cups and other typical EM III shapes associate the level with the material from the North Trench, but a few MM I sherds are present as well.

DEPOSIT IN BLOCK C AT MOKHLOS

Twenty EM III vases and an unspecified number of sherds come from a deposit in Block C at Mokhlos (Seager 1909: 283–84, figs. 7, 8, and 13 center row, nos. 2–4 and bottom row). All the White-on-dark Ware may be compared very closely with the Well Deposit at Vasilike and the North Trench at Gournia. Although the sherds and several of the vases were never published, it seems likely the deposit is mostly (or all?) from EM III rather than later.

DEPOSIT IN DELTA 32 AT PALAIKASTRO

An EM III deposit was found beneath an early MM level in Delta 32 at Palaikastro (Dawkins 1903–1904: 198 and fig. 2a, g, and j–k). The style of the few

Fig. 2–9. Bridge spouted jar fragments from the North Trench at Gournia. Scale 2:5. After Hall 1904–1905: pl. 30.

published sherds agrees exactly with those from the North Trench at Gournia.

DEPOSIT IN A FIELD WEST OF BLOCK DELTA AT PALAIKASTRO

Several EM III sherds come from a deep trial trench in a field west of Block Delta at Palaikastro (Dawkins 1903–1904: 198–99 and fig. 2b–f, h, i, and l). Their style is similar to that of the sherds from the deposit in Delta 32. The most common shapes, cups and bridge spouted jars, are the same ones found in the North Trench.

OSSUARY III IN THE ELLENIKA CEMETERY, NEAR PALAIKASTRO

Forty-one complete vases were found in one of the rectangular built house tombs at Palaikastro (Dawkins 1904–1905: 269–72 and fig. 5a–b). All were in the same style, suggesting a brief period of use for the communal burial place. While only two drawings were

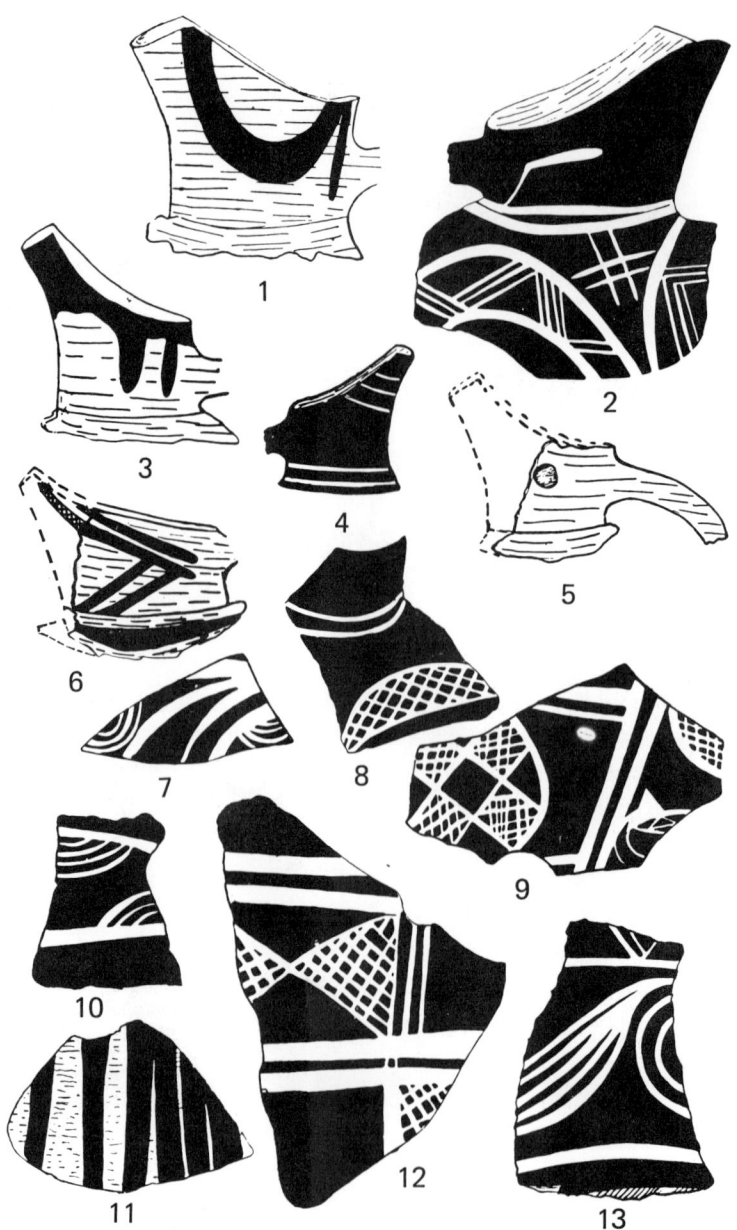

Fig. 2–10. Jug fragments and other shapes from the North Trench at Gournia. Scale 2:5. After Hall 1904–1905: pl. 31.

published, all the vessels were described, leaving no doubts as to their style. The shapes, mostly cups, are discussed more fully in chap. 3. The ornaments are typical of White-on-dark Ware in eastern Crete in the period preceding the introduction of red paint.

FLOOR DEPOSITS ON KASTRI, NEAR PALAIKASTRO

Several examples of White-on-dark Ware come from a large building on the hill of Kastri, near Palaikastro (Sackett, Popham and Warren 1965: 250, 269–72, 277–78, and pl. 72b–c). The building was apparently destroyed by an earthquake near the end of EM III. Since finds of similar style come from nearby (ibid., KA Trench 3), a sizeable community is perhaps indicated. The pottery is in the usual styles for this period, but it includes some unusual pieces, such as a jug with diagonal black lines across the body, each with two thin lines of added white paint (ibid., pl. 72c). No red paint occurs, suggesting a date before the beginning of east Cretan MM IA.

Fig. 2–11. Miscellaneous fragments from the North Trench at Gournia. Scale 2:5. After Hall 1904–1905: pl. 32.

OTHER DEPOSITS FROM THE MIDDLE PHASE

White-on-dark Ware comes from enough other contexts in eastern Crete to suggest a fairly good sized number of settlements at this time. Period IV at Vasilike, unfortunately disturbed by later building operations, has many pieces in this style (Seager 1904–1905: 211, 218–20; 1906–1907: 118–23). At Pseira a White-on-dark Ware stratum was also mixed with later pottery (Seager 1910: 17–18). A few other deposits come from the town at Mokhlos (Seager 1909: 288 and 291–93, mixed with MM I) and from the Mokhlos cemetery (Seager 1912: especially Tombs IV and V). Sphoungaras, with very poor stratigraphy, adds a few other examples (Hall 1912: 50–51 and fig. 23). Palaikastro has some additional deposits, for example from Block Khi (Dawkins 1904–1905: 269, 273, and fig 5c).

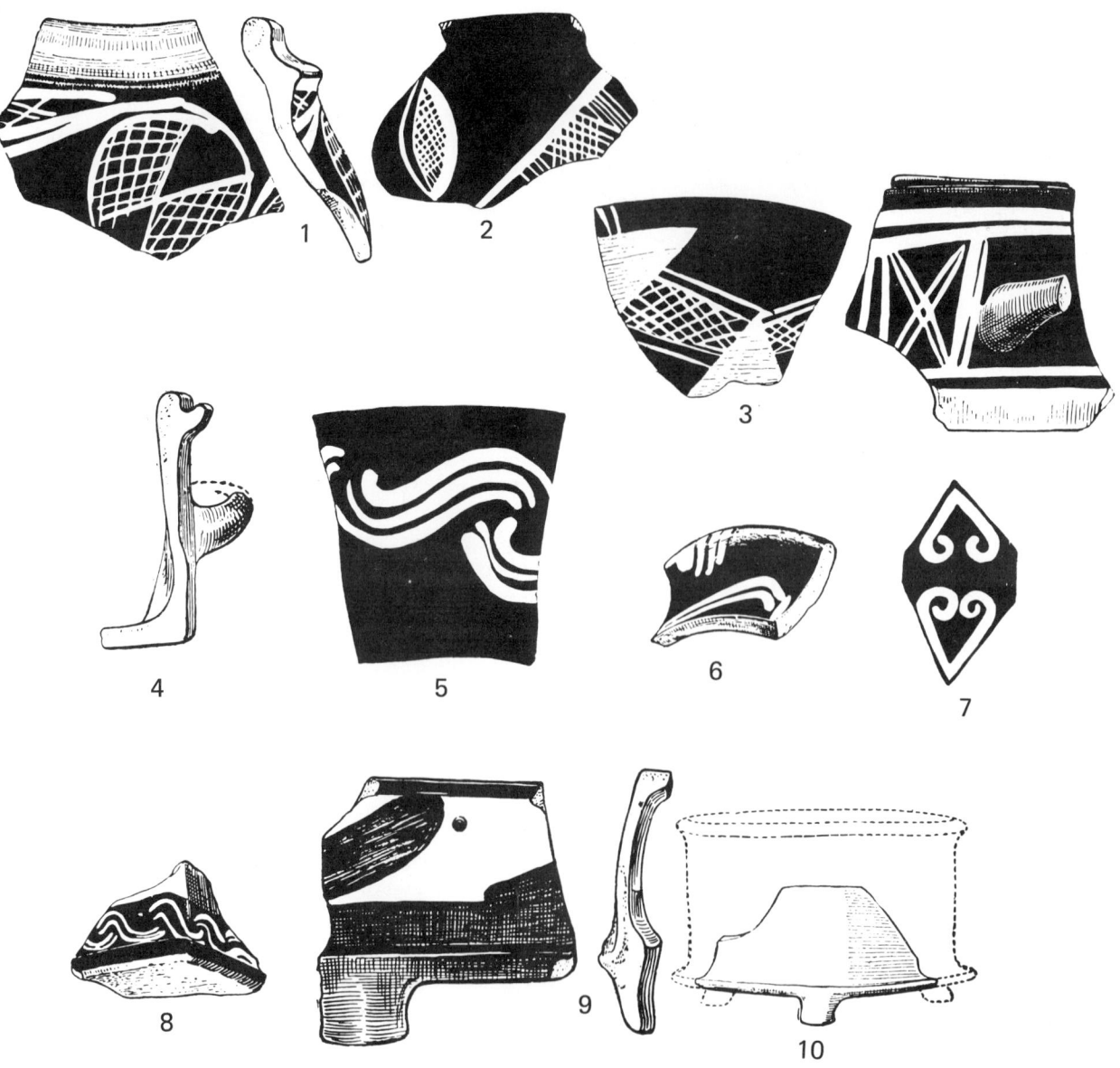

Fig. 2–12. Miscellaneous fragments from the North Trench at Gournia. Scale 2:5. After Hall 1904–1905: pl. 33.

Late Phase

PERIOD IIA–B AT PYRGOS, MYRTOU

Ceramic deposits with handmade pottery in the light-on-dark style and with a sparing use of red on some pieces come from the site of Pyrgos. They are found beneath strata with a few wheelmade vases, mostly cups (Cadogan 1974; 1978: 71–73; Andreou 1978: 82–92 and passim). This phase may be designated MM IA. Shapes include open bowls, conical cups, goblets, bridge spouted jars, and jugs. The cylindrical cup, the bridge spouted jar with an elongated lower body, and the jug with a cutaway spout represent advances over the earlier period. Many decorations continue the traditions of EM III: hatched triangles; hatched and crosshatched zones; festoons; arcs; and chevrons. Besides the use of red, which

Fig. 2–13. Six rounded cups from Vasilike. The shape, with small lugs or handles set low on the body, does not occur at Gournia. After Seager 1906–1907: fig. 4.

marks the beginning of the new phase rather easily, there are also new and more complex motifs like the whirl design (Cadogan 1974: pl. 17a; compare the vase with added red from Malia published by Chapouthier and Demargne 1962: pls. 7 and 37, no. 9220). More subtle is the beginning of the disintegration of the mature White-on-dark Ware compositional schemes. In EM III the style is especially rich in designs in which several individual elements are combined in creative and well organized syntactical arrangements. Simpler compositions now exist alongside the older schemes, and the tone of the style as a whole is diluted by the increased percentage of simple designs like multiple banding. The deposit is very similar to the earliest MM IB, distinguished chiefly by the addition of wheelmade cups to the existing ceramic inventory.

DEPOSIT BENEATH HOUSE D AT MOKHLOS

While only four vessels have been published from a deposit beneath a MM III floor at Mokhlos, the deposit as a whole has been described in some detail (Seager 1909: 290–93 and fig. 13 upper row). Eighteen whole vases and many fragments make up the unit. The latest pieces are carinated cups, and one, with two handles, has been illustrated (ibid., fig. 13 upper row no. 4). Carinated cups are a hallmark of MM IB. Other vases include cups with red bands, undecorated vessels, and several examples of White-on-dark Ware. Among these are late shapes like the cylindrical cup (ibid., upper row no. 2) as well as late decorations like the paneled motifs on the two-handled carinated cup.

THE SOUTH HOUSES AT MALIA

The remains of several houses are found beneath the level of the South Court and the southern edge of the palace at Malia (Chapouthier, Demargne, and

Fig. 2–14. Jug from House B at Vasilike. After Seager 1906–1907: fig. 7.

Dessene 1962: 13ff.). Their destruction may be dated to MM IB by the presence of a few wheelmade cups, but most of the pottery is handmade. Much of it is decorated in a conservative light-on-dark technique. Dark-on-light ornament is used as well, with the decoration laid directly onto the body of the vase. Red is also used on some pieces. The types—conical cups and bowls, goblets, bridge spouted jars, and other shapes—associate the style with the settlements in eastern Crete as much as with the central part of the island. Some of the light-on-dark motifs are like those of the North Trench at Gournia. Others, including an agrimilike design (fig. 3–10, no. 4) do not occur in the earlier stages of the White-on-dark Ware tradition.

HOUSE B AT VASILIKE

Two MM houses are known from Seager's excavations at Vasilike. From the earlier building, House B, come many complete vases, found in a deposit buried when the house was destroyed (Seager 1906–1907: 126–29; Betancourt 1977: 345–46 and ill. 1). Although only a small selection of the pottery has been published, enough pieces are known to establish the style. Most of the pottery is handmade. Pendant hatched triangles, chevrons, diagonal lines, and pendant concentric semicircles occur as dark-on-light decoration. A few polychrome pieces, including a wheelmade carinated cup with an undulating rim, put the date in MM IB or IIA. One jug with crosshatched semicircles on the shoulder is in the White-on-dark Ware tradition. While it has sometimes been regarded as an heirloom, Antonios Zois has shown that its shape, with a piriform body and a short spout, is perfectly at home in MM I (Zois 1968: 137 and 382–83, no. 37).

OTHER DEPOSITS FROM THE LATE PHASE

Many complete vases come from the cemetery at Malia, especially from a communal burial place called the *Premier Charnier* used from the latter part of the Early Bronze Age and the beginning of the Middle Bronze Age (Demargne 1945: 1–12). Deposit A at Sphoungaras and Seager's Period IV at Vasilike, both mentioned above, also seem to last into this period. Some of the burials at Pakheia Ammos are this early, or possibly even earlier (Seager 1916: nos. Ib, XIc). The MM I houses at Pseira may also be from this phase (Seager 1910: 17–20). A good MM IA deposit comes from Palaikastro, from Block Khi at Roussolakos (Sackett, Popham and Warren 1965: 251). Period IIc–d at Pyrgos, Myrtou, has the first wheelmade cups found at the site, and (as in House B at Vasilike) White-on-dark Ware is much less common than in Period IIa–b (Cadogan 1978; Andreou 1978: 77). The gradual decrease in the quantity of the ware in this period is fully understandable; it simply develops into the later Middle Bronze Age traditions.

Notes

1. Information on original hand written notes of E. Hall. Thanks are extended to Mrs. E. Dohan, daughter-in-law of Edith Hall Dohan, for lending the original manuscript to the author.

2. Thanks are extended to Carol Zerner for information on this important sherd.

References

Andreou, S. 1978. Pottery Groups of the Old Palace Period in Crete. Ph.D. Diss., University of Cincinnati.

Betancourt, P. P. 1977. Some Chronological Problems in the Middle Minoan Dark-on-Light Pottery of Eastern Crete. *AJA* 81: 341–53.

Bosanquet, R. C., and R. M. Dawkins. 1923. *The Unpublished Objects from the Palaikastro Excavations 1902–1906.* London.

Boyd, H. A. 1904–1905. Gournia. Report of the American Exploration Society's Excavations at Gournia, Crete, 1904. *Transactions of the Department of Archaeology, Free Museum of Science and Art* 1: 177–88.

Branigan, K. 1970. *The Foundations of Palatial Crete.* New York and Washington.

Cadogan, G. 1974. Myrtos: Pyrghos. *Archaeological Reports for 1973–74:* 37–39.

Cadogan, G. 1978. Pyrgos, Crete, 1970–7. *Archaeological Reports for 1977–78:* 70–84.

Chapouthier, F., and P. Demargne 1942. *Fouilles exécutées a Mallia, troisième rapport . . . Études crétoises* 6. Paris.

Chapouthier, F., P. Demargne, and A. Dessene 1962. *Fouilles exécutées a Mallia, quatrième rapport: Exploration du palais, (1929–1935 et 1946–1960), Études crétoises* 12. Paris.

Dawkins, R. M. 1903–1904. Excavations at Palaikastro III. *BSA* 10: 192–226.

Dawkins, R. M. 1904–1905. Excavations at Palaikastro IV. *BSA* 11: 258–92.

Demargne, P. 1945. *Fouilles exécutées a Mallia: Exploration des nécropoles (1921–1933), Études crétoises* 7. Paris.

Furness, A. 1953. The Neolithic Pottery of Knossos. *BSA* 48: 94–134.

Hall, E. H. 1904–1905. Early Painted Pottery from Gournia, Crete. *Transactions of the Department of Archaeology, Free Museum of Science and Art.* 1:191–205.

Hall, E. H. 1908. Early Minoan III Ware from the North Trench. In Hawes et al. 1908. Appendix E: 57.

Hall, E. H. 1912. *Excavations in Eastern Crete, Sphoungaras.* Philadelphia.

Hawes, H. B., B. E. Williams, R. B. Seager, and E. H. Hall. 1908. *Gournia, Vasiliki and other Prehistoric Sites on the Isthmus of Hierapetra, Crete.* Philadelphia.

Hood, M. S. F. 1961–1962. Stratigraphic Excavations at Knossos 1957–61. *KhChron* 15–16: pt. 1, 92–98.

Hood, M. S. F. 1966. The Early and Middle Minoan Periods at Knossos. *BICS* 13: 110–111.

Hood, M. S. F. 1971. *The Minoans.* New York and Washington.

Sackett, L. H., M. R. Popham, and P. M. Warren. 1965. Excavations at Palaikastro, VI. *BSA* 60: 248–314.

Schiering, W., and W. Müller and W.-D. Niemeier. 1982. Landbegehungen in Rethymnon und Umgebung. *AA:* 15–54.

Seager, R. B. 1904–1905. Excavations at Vasiliki, 1904. *Transactions of the Department of Archaeology, Free Museum of Science and Art* 1: 207–21.

Seager, R. B. 1906–1907, Report of Excavations at Vasiliki, Crete, in 1906. *Transactions of the Department of Archaeology, Free Museum of Science and Art* 2: 111–32.

Seager, R. B. 1909. Excavations on the Island of Mochlos, Crete, in 1908. *AJA* 13: 273–303.

Seager, R. B. 1910. *Excavations on the Island of Pseira, Crete.* Philadelphia.

Seager, R. B. 1912. *Explorations in the Island of Mochlos.* Boston and New York.

Seager, R. B. 1916. *The Cemetery of Pachyammos, Crete.* Philadelphia.

Warren, P. 1965. The first Minoan stone vases and Early Minoan chronology. *KrChron* 19: 7–43.

Warren, P. 1972. *Myrtos. An Early Bronze Age Settlement in Crete.* London.

Zois, A. A. 1968. Der Kamares-Stil. Werden und Wesen. Ph.D Diss. Eberhard-Karls-Universität, Tübingen.

Zois, A. A. 1968B. Ὑπάρχει ΠΜ III 'εποχή; Πεπραγμένα του Β' Διεθνοῦς κρητολογικοῦ Συνεδρίου: 141–56.

Zois, A. A. 1969. Προβλήματα χρονολογίας τῆς μινωϊκῆς κεραμεικῆς. Γοῦρνες. Τύλισος. Μάλια. Athens.

3

The Decorative Motifs

Philip P. Betancourt

The groundwork for the stylistic analysis of White-on-dark Ware has been laid down by Antonios Zois. In an important and useful article (1968B), he has demonstrated the essential unity of the style, isolating its major motifs and examining them in detail. His work is basic to all later stylistic studies of the ware, and the present analysis is a refinement that builds on his conclusions. Differences between this study and that of Zois include a more local focus (Zois discussed all of Crete while this study is limited to the eastern sites), a division of the style into three chronological phases, and a specialization that excludes the contemporary dark-on-light motifs.

Most of the style's vocabulary is linear and extremely simple.[1] Straight lines are normally either vertical, horizontal, or placed at a forty-five degree angle. Curved lines—spirals, waves, circles, arcs, and quirks—are used as well. Dots are arranged in lines or areas. Except for an occasional painted rectangle or other figure, solid or white areas are extremely rare.

The individual elements are combined together or used in series to make bands and other organizations that employ two types of syntax. The first, tectonic decoration, is based on the structure of the vessel. It emphasizes its component parts: spout; rim; neck; handle-zone; etc. An example, shown in the jug in fig. 1–1D, has the neck set off clearly from the handle-zone by placing a different decoration on each part. Unity decoration, an overall arrangement that stresses the total form, also occurs. The bowls with triangles or chevrons that expand toward the widest part of the vessel (fig. 1–1B, E–F, and H) are good examples of the type, and one may also note the teapots in which the decoration continues from the body onto the spout, creating a sweep of ornament at the vessel's greatest dimension (fig. 1–1C). The two classes of syntax are not as developed as in the Middle Minoan period (for which see Walberg 1976: 83–95; 1978), and a number of vases are intermediate between the two poles.

Within this syntax, the motifs are carefully arranged in circumcurrent or facial designs. In circumcurrent arrangements the motifs are repeated or alternated around the vase, usually in one or more bands. In facial compositions particular sides are selected for emphasis. Many of the facial designs use diagonal zones of ornament that curve around the body, creating a torsional movement that calls attention to the vessel's three-dimensional volume.

Several changes may be recognized during the style's chronological development, following the three phases discussed above. In the Early Phase (EM IIB) the designs are all extremely simple. Rectangular forms predominate, with chevrons and triangles being especially common. New designs—notably spirals, circles, and quirks—appear in the Middle Phase (EM III–MM IA). More of the ornament is curvilinear, and complicated arrangements (like the Triglyph and Metope designs or the Pictorial designs) are more common. The integrity of the style begins to break down in the Late Phase (MM IA–IB). Old elements continue, but they are joined by new details that have little in common with the traditional style. There is no precise line separating White-on-dark Ware from its successors. Elements with a new spirit, like the semicircle with tiny included concentric arcs or the circle with a whirling motif, are already outside the boundaries set down in the Middle Phase. They herald the end of the style, as White-on-dark Ware develops into the more elaborate decorative systems of Middle Minoan ceramics.

Fig. 3–1. Circles, used singly and with single, double, and complex connecting lines.

Individual Decorative Motifs

1. CHEVRONS

Chevrons may be horizontal or vertical. They begin in the Early Phase and persist during the entire style. Examples also occur in the dark-on-light pottery of MM I (Seager 1906–1907: figs. 9b and 10c).

2. TRIANGLES

Triangles, rising or pendant, are common. Variations are hatched or crosshatched, hatched at the corners, or filled with dots. The motif is particularly common on conical cups and bowls. It is used during the entire style.

3. PARALLEL VERTICAL LINES

This is a common motif in the Kamares Ware that follows immediately after White-on-dark Ware (Walberg 1976: fig. 50 Motif 33). It occurs during the entire period of White-on-dark Ware, both alone and as an alternation with other elements (see the Triglyph and Metope designs).

4. DIAMONDS

Horizontal bands composed of crosshatched diamonds occur occasionally in the ware. They are not known before the Middle Phase.

5. DOTTED BANDS

Bands and lines of dots are a regular feature of the Middle and Late Phases but are not known from the Early Phase. They sometimes form semicircles or triangles or follow the outlines of solid figures (see the Semicircles and Crescents). Large dots may be used as subsidiary decoration. The motif continues into Kamares Ware as the Repeated-Circle band (Walberg 1976: Motif 20).

6. WAVY LINES

Wavy lines begin in the Middle Phase. They occur in the North Trench and elsewhere, but they are not particularly common. Their popularity increases in the Kamares Ware of the Middle Minoan period (Walberg 1976: fig. 44 Motif 16).

7. QUIRKS

S-shaped figures, called quirks, are often used in series in the Middle and Late Phases. They are usually found in conjunction with solid lines, placed horizontally, diagonally, or in semicircles. In the Early and Classical Kamares periods they are more often used independently (Walberg 1976: figs. 38–39 Motif 8).

THE DECORATIVE MOTIFS

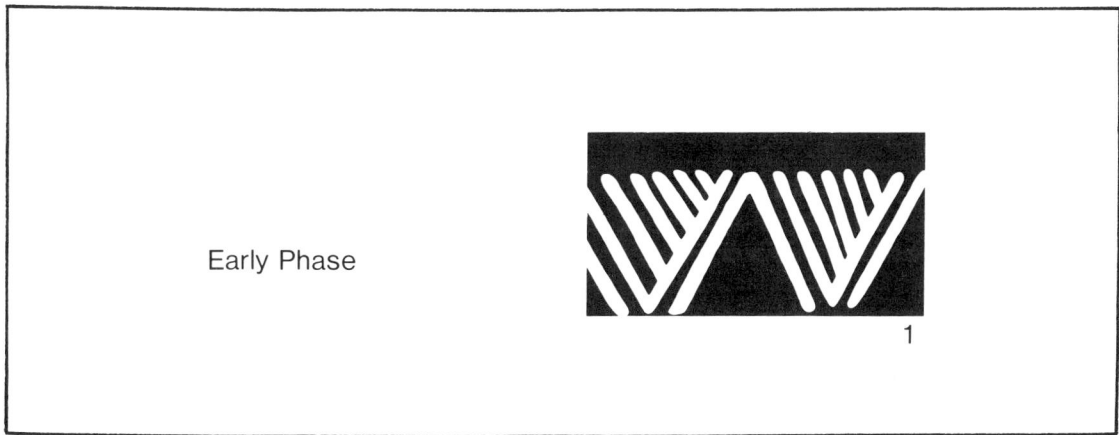

Fig. 3–2. Chevrons and Triangles.

2. Triangles (cont.)

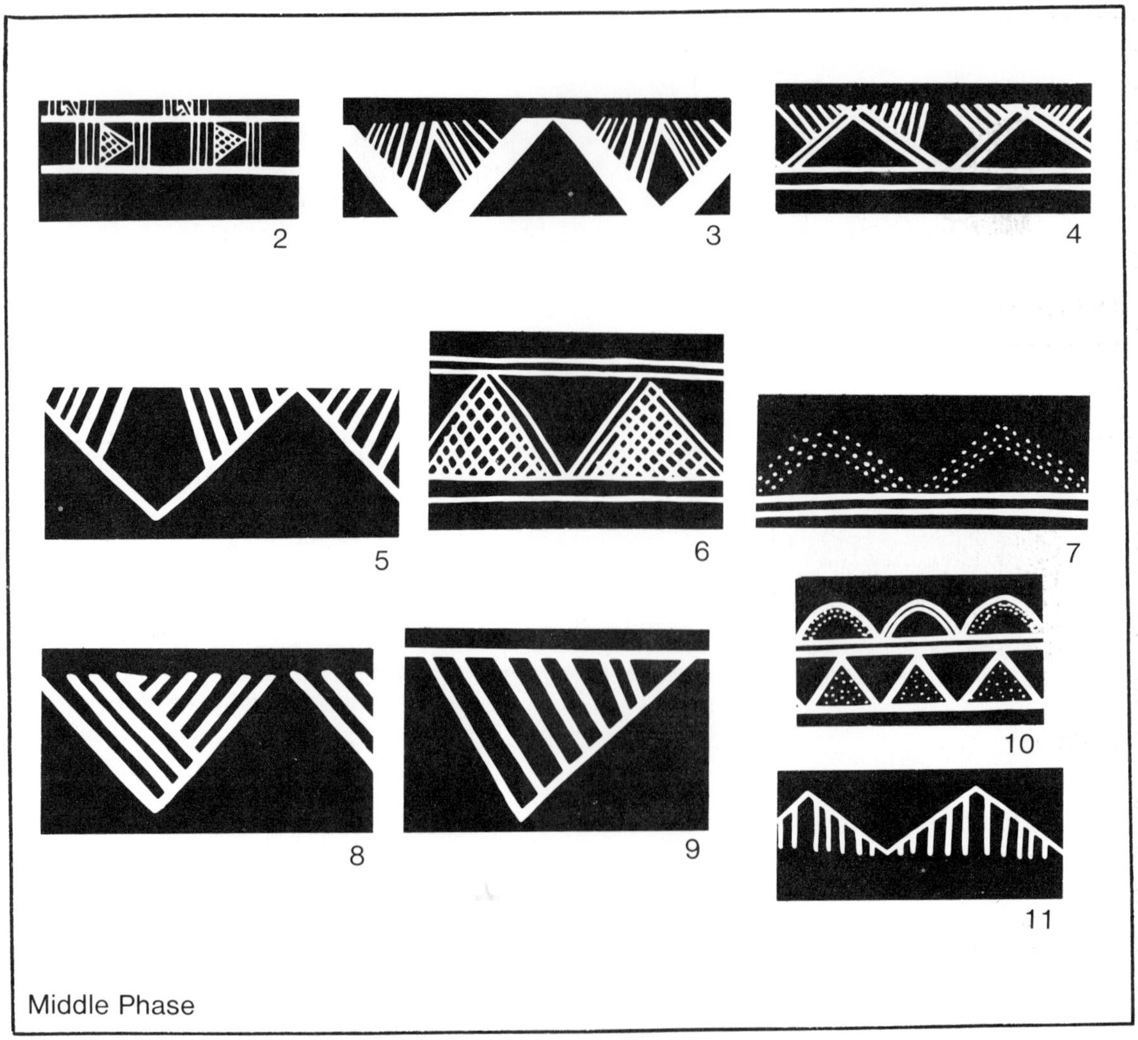

3. Parallel Vertical Lines

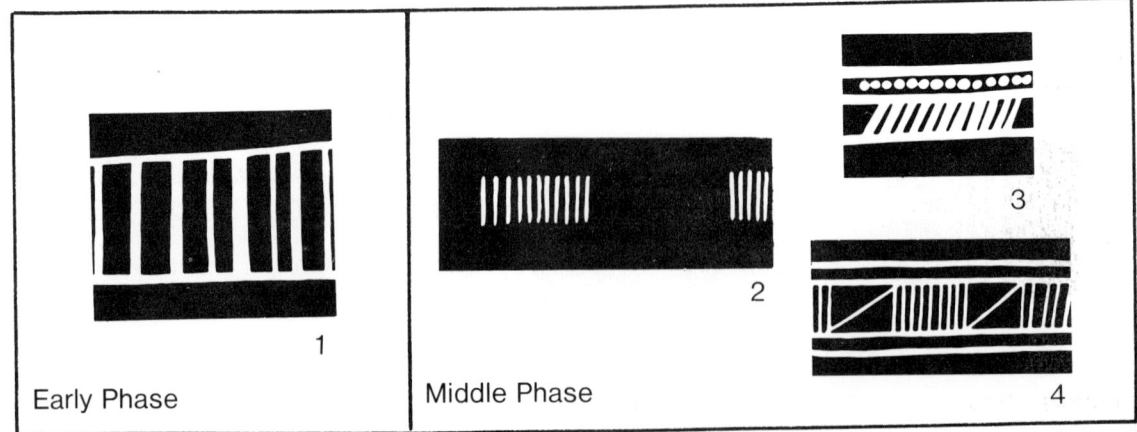

Fig. 3–3. Triangles (cont.) and Parallel Vertical Lines.

4. Diamonds

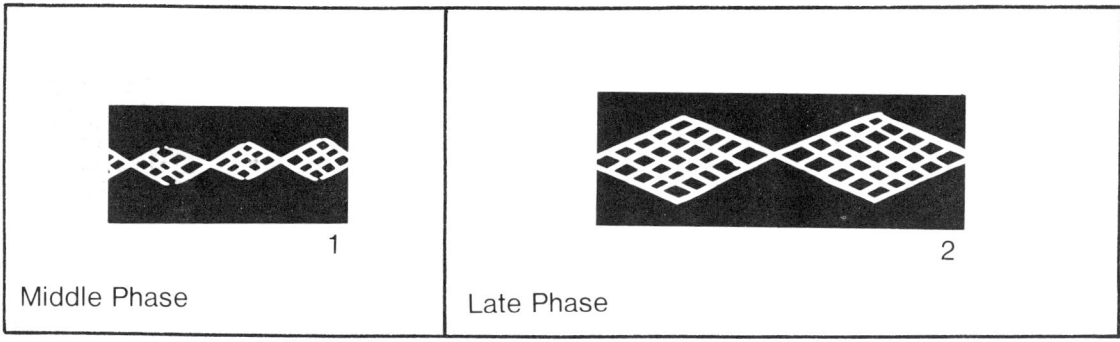

5. Dot Bands

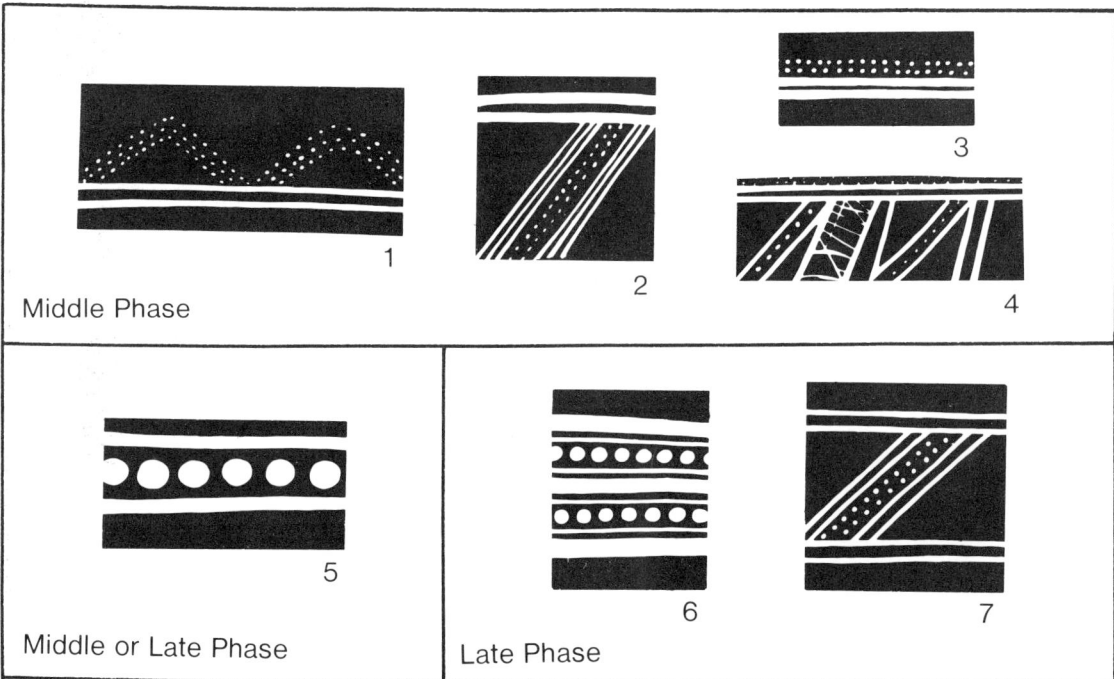

6. Wavy Lines

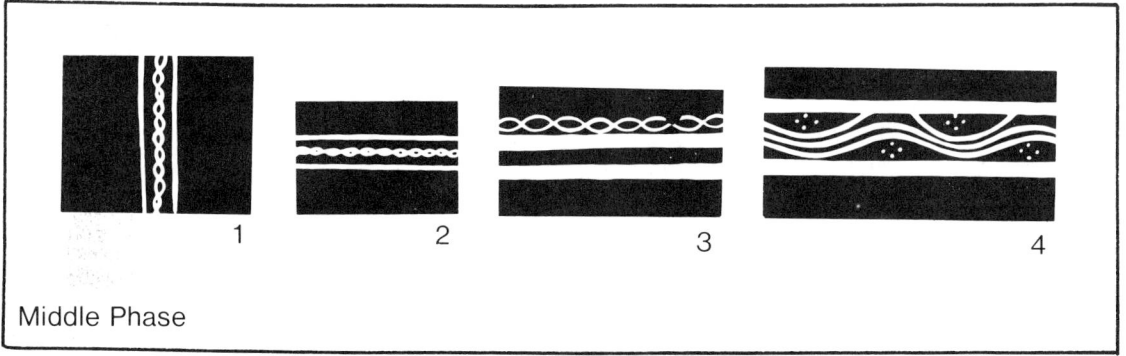

Fig. 3–4. Diamonds, Dot Bands, and Wavy Lines.

7. Quirks

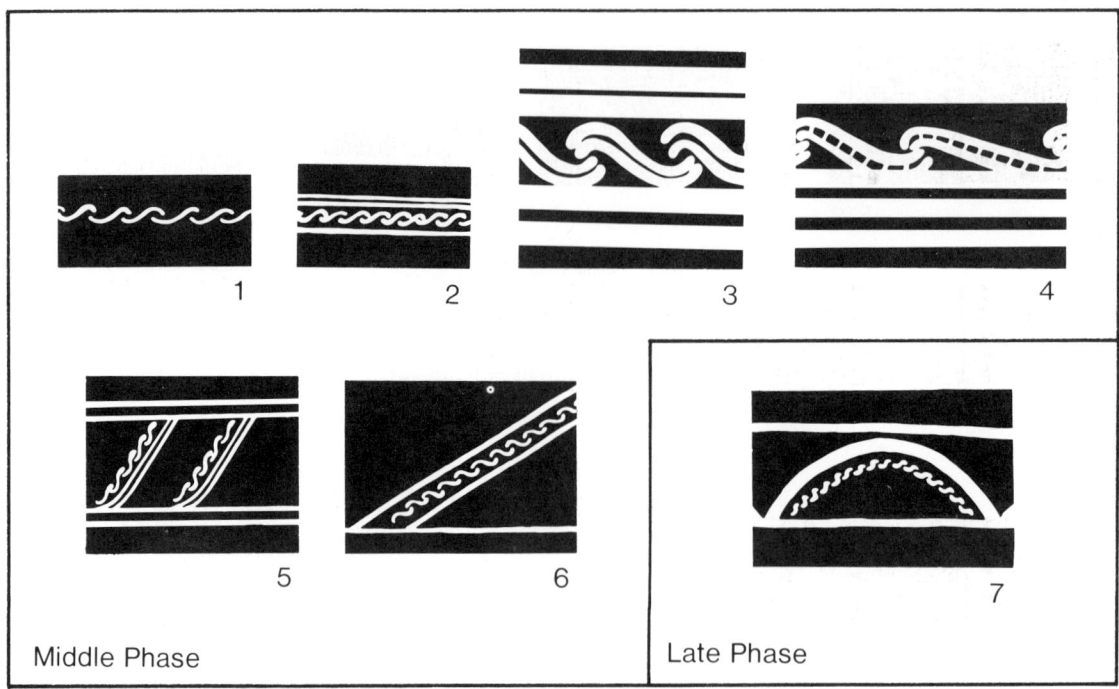

8. J-Spirals

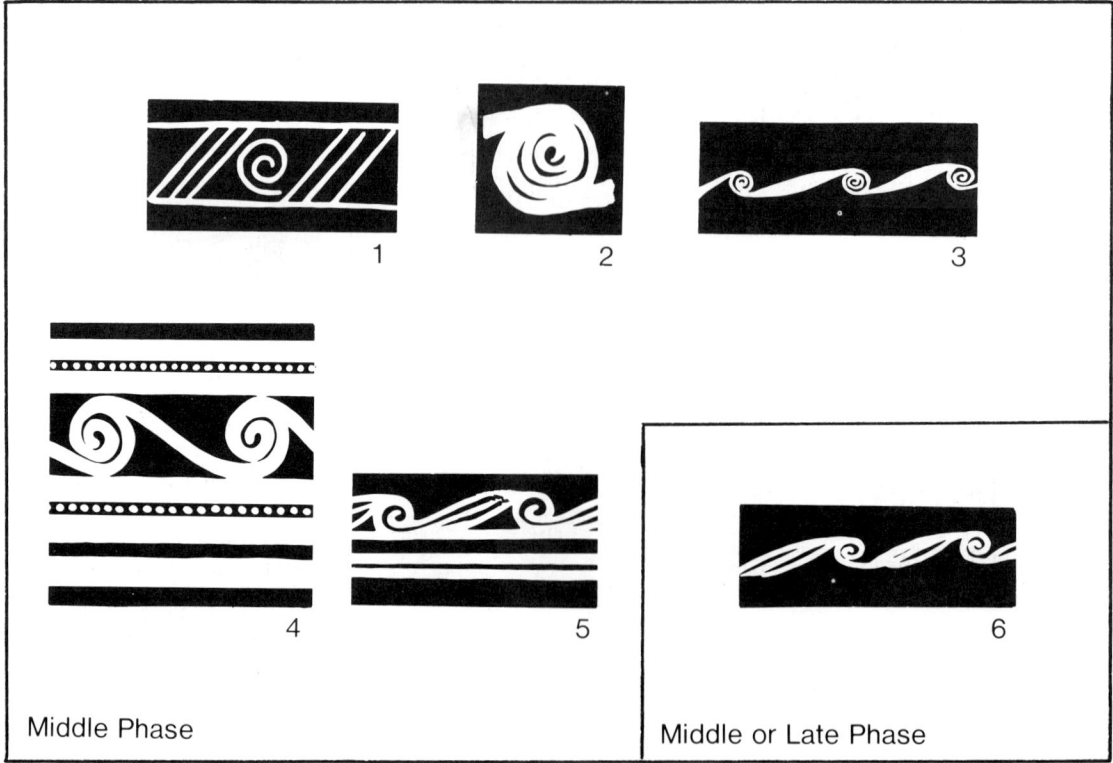

Fig. 3–5. Quirks and J-Spirals.

THE DECORATIVE MOTIFS

9. Semicircles and Crescents

Fig. 3–6. Semicircles and Crescents.

10. Circles

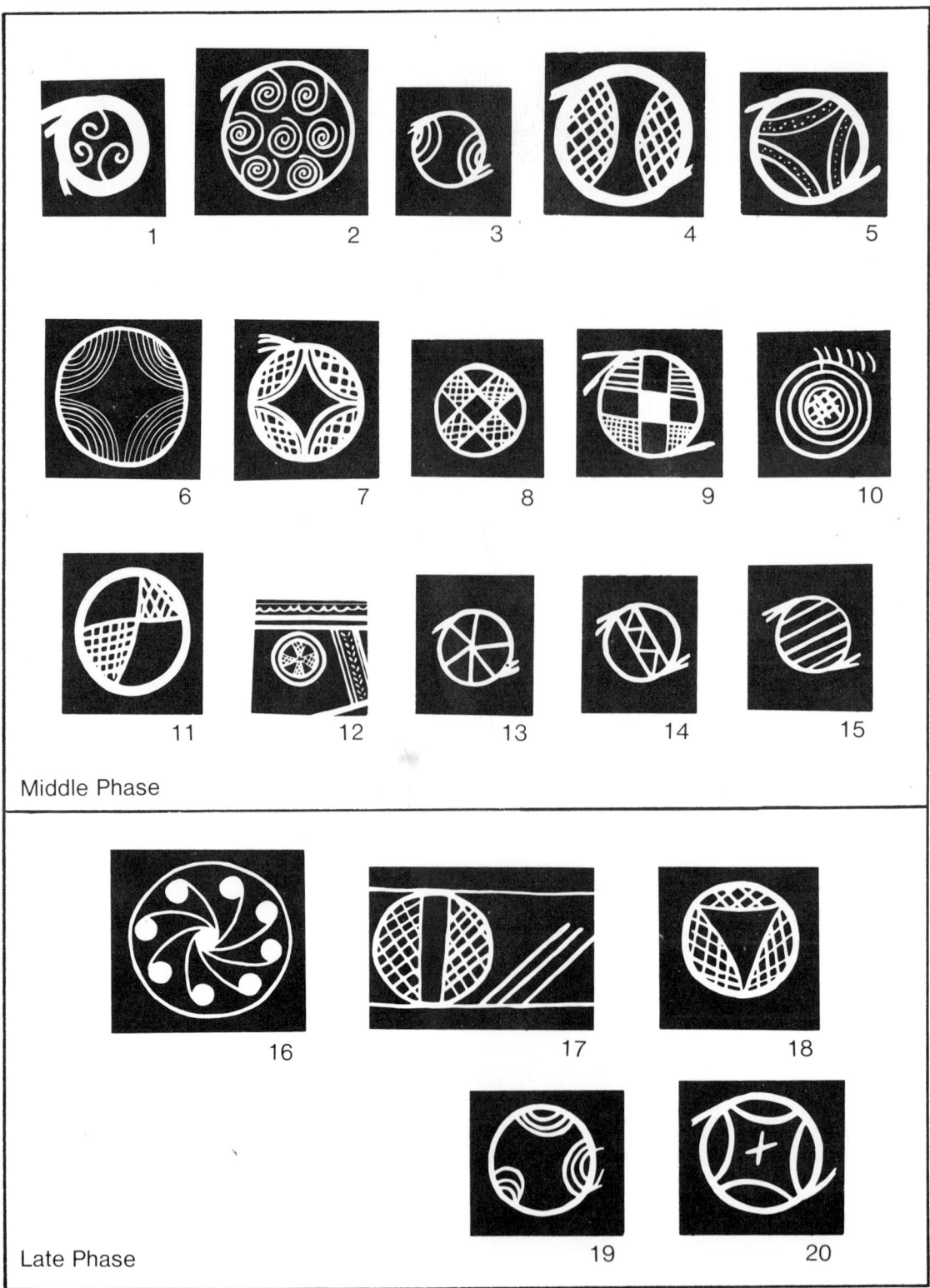

Fig. 3–7. Circles.

THE DECORATIVE MOTIFS   29

11. Triglyphs and Metopes

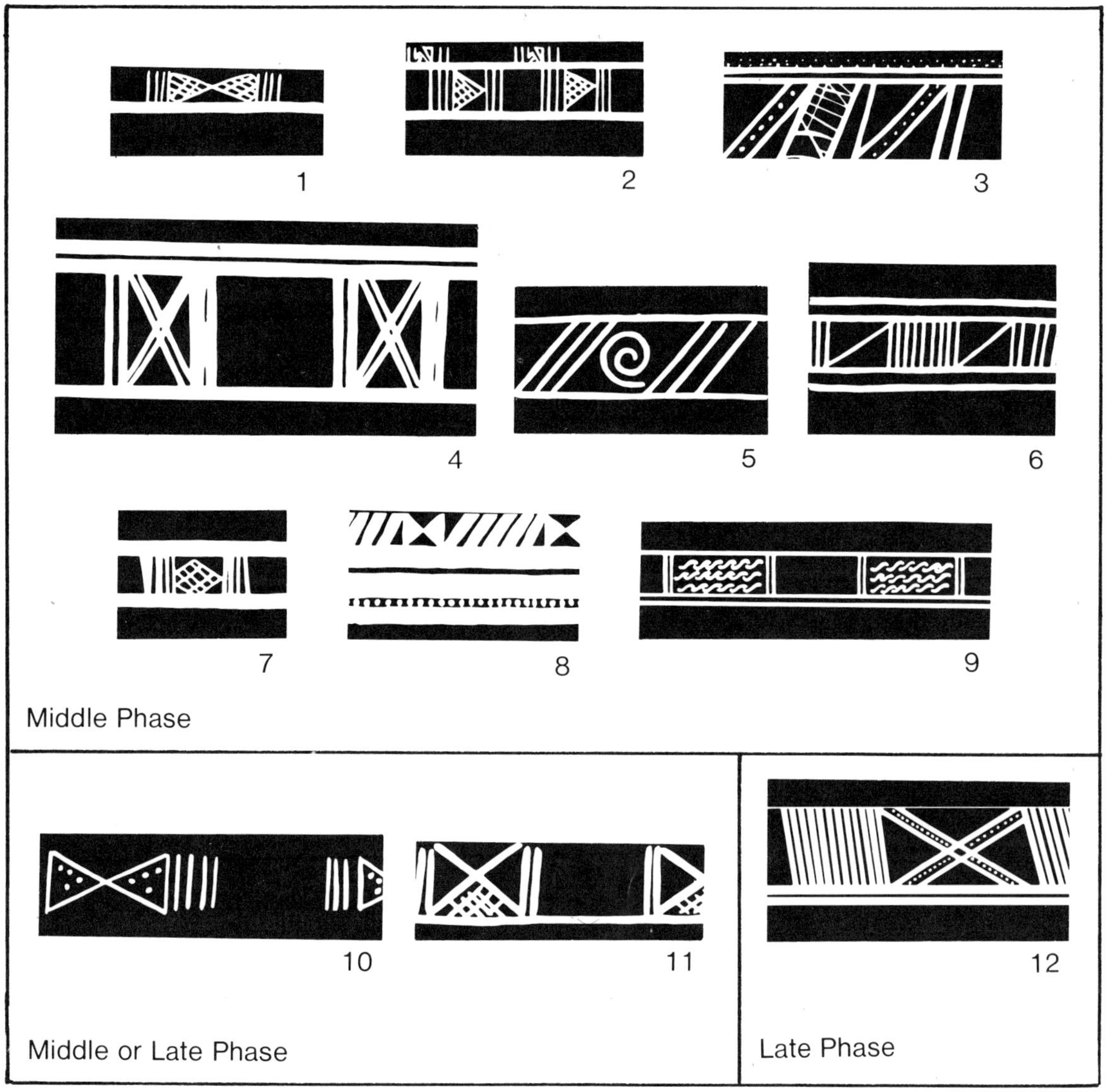

Fig. 3–8. *Triglyphs and Metopes and Zigzags.*

12. Zigzags (cont.)

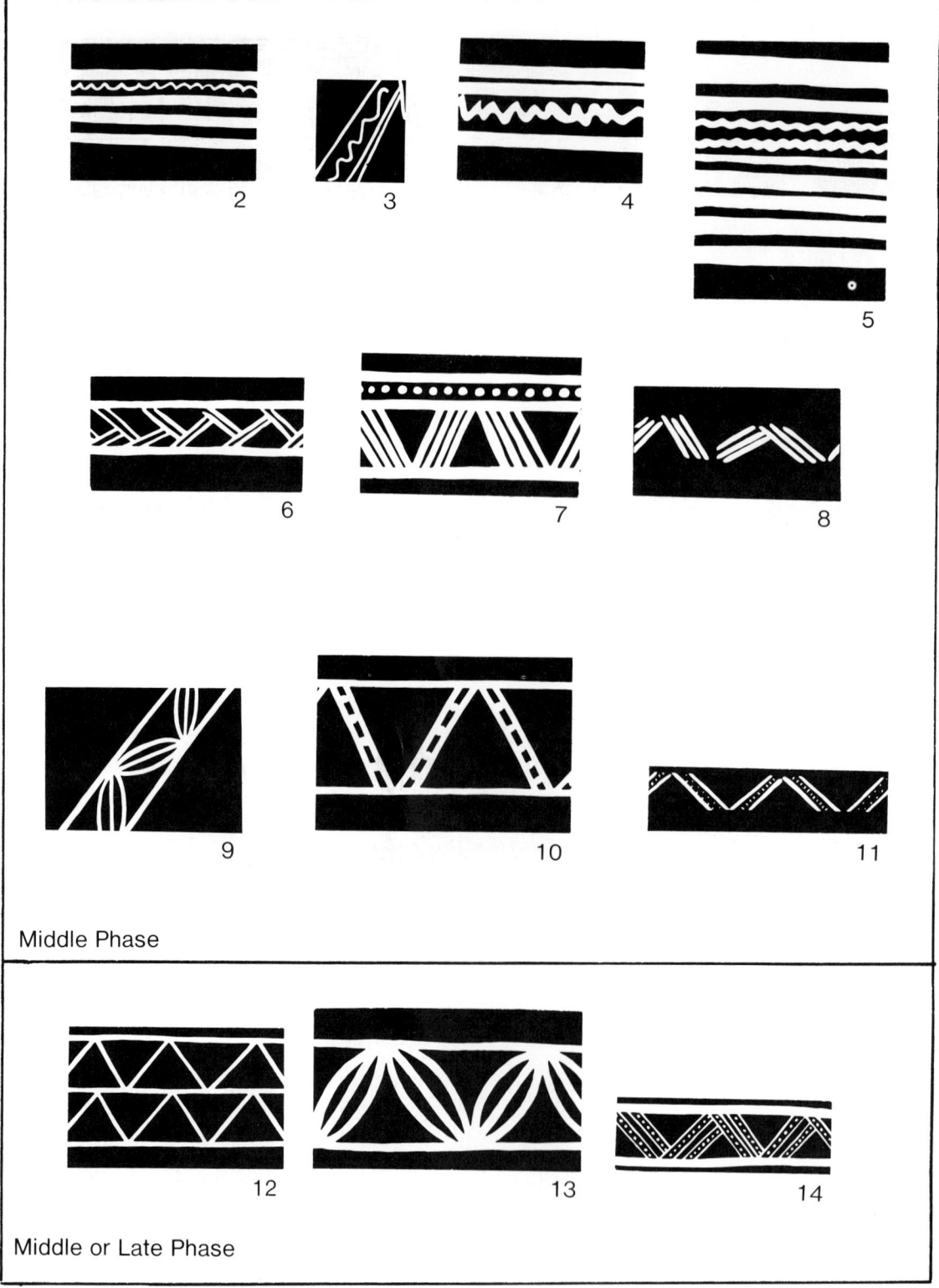

Fig. 3–9. Zigzags (cont.).

THE DECORATIVE MOTIFS

13. Pictorials

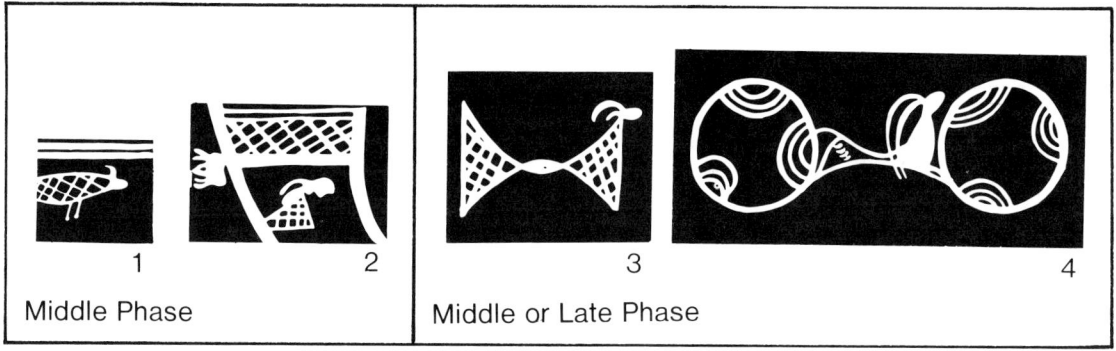

14. Miscellaneous

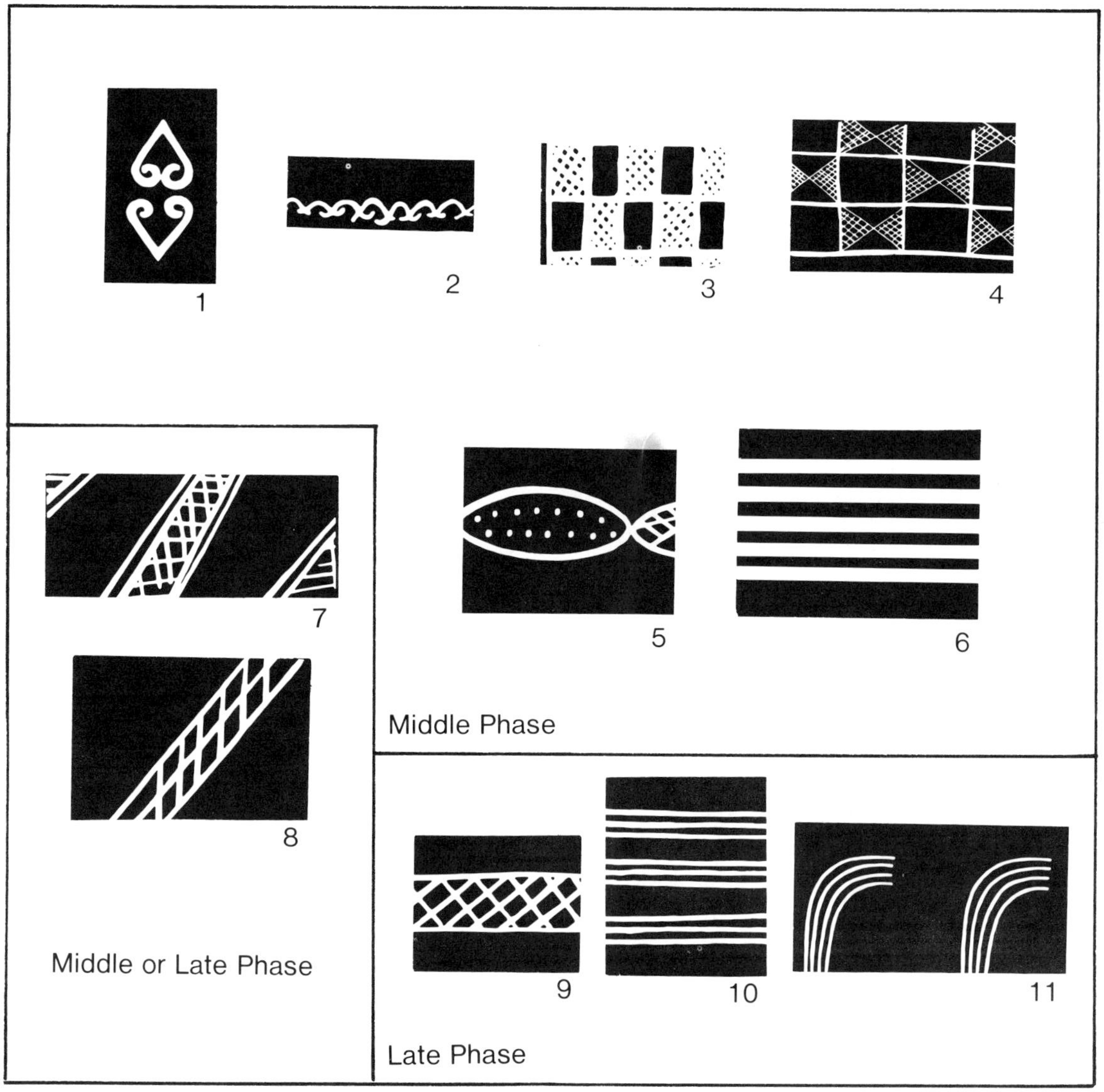

Fig. 3–10. Pictorials and Miscellaneous.

8. J-SPIRALS

J-spirals begin in the Middle Phase. While most examples are joined by connecting lines to form running designs, isolated spirals occur as well. The motif is very characteristic of White-on-dark Ware in eastern Crete, and it continues into later periods as one of the standard Minoan elements (Walberg 1976: Motif 2). Few variations are known in this period.

9. SEMICIRCLES AND CRESCENTS

Designs composed of semicircles or crescents become very popular in the Middle Phase. Many variations exist. The type continues into the Late Phase, sometimes unchanged and sometimes elaborated by the addition of accessory details like dots, hatching, or bands. The motif also continues into Kamares Ware (Walberg 1976: figs. 39–40 Motif 9).

10. CIRCLES

Circle designs are employed singly or with connecting lines in the manner of running spirals (fig. 3–1). They are not known from before the Middle Phase though the lid of a pyxis from Myrtos has radiating lines set within circles. The Middle Phase examples are divided or decorated in various simple ways; in the Late Phase they are more creative. In Kamares Ware circle motifs are often used independently (Walberg 1976: Motifs 1 and 10).

11. TRIGLYPHS AND METOPES

Alternations between X-shaped figures or other elements and small groups of parallel vertical or diagonal lines are called triglyph and metope designs. They are most common in the Middle Phase, though they do continue into the next period. Kamares Ware employs them as well (Walberg 1976: Motifs 32 no. 2 and 33 no. 11).

12. ZIGZAGS

The zigzag band begins in the Early Phase and becomes more popular in the Middle Phase. Many variations exist. Like the band of quirks, it creates an alternating movement that adds a dynamic accent to static shapes. It is popular both as a diagonal and as a horizontal band.

13. PICTORIALS

Pictorialization already begins by the time of the North Trench at Gournia. The agrimi seems to be the most popular motif, and several examples are known with a head or a head and legs added to an otherwise nonobjective figure. By the Late Phase the animal is more lyrical, conceived in its entirety as a pictorial motif. Pictorialization continues into the time of Kamares Ware (Walberg 1976: Motif 26).

14. MISCELLANEOUS

Horizontal bands, crosshatched areas, and many other decorative elements are used for White-on-dark Ware. Since the ornamental repertoire is varied and creative, each new excavation adds several additional motifs; the selection presented here is far from comprehensive.

Sources of Motifs Figured

1. CHEVRONS
   1. Myrtos. Warren 1972: P 675.
   2. Myrtos. Ibid; P 150.
   3. Gournia. Hall 1904–1905: pl. 28, no. 8.
   4. Vasilike. Seager 1906–1907: 122, fig. 5c.
   5. Gournia. Hall 1904–1905: pl. 28, no. 17.
   6. Vasilike. Maraghiannis and Karo 1907–1921: II, pl. 25, no. 5.
   7. Malia. Demargne 1945: pl. 8, no. 8529.
   8. Palaikastro. Forsdyke 1925: 78, no. A 445–15.
   9. Pyrgos Myrtou. Cadogan 1974: fig. 77.

2. TRIANGLES
   1. Aghia Photia. Boyd 1904–1905: pl. 25, no. 3.
   2. Gournia. Hall 1904–1905: pl. 28, no. 16.
   3. Gournia. Ibid., pl. 27, no. 1.
   4. Gournia. Ibid., pl. 27, no. 2.
   5. Gournia. Ibid., pl. 26, no. 1.
   6. Gournia. Ibid., pl. 27, no. 6.
   7. Sphoungaras. Hall 1912: fig. 23F.
   8. Vasilike. Seager 1906–1907: 120, fig. 3a.
   9. Gournia. Hall 1904–1905: pl. 32, no. 3.
   10. Gournia. Ibid., pl. 27, no. 12.
   11. Gournia. Penn no. MS 4615–39.

3. PARALLEL VERTICAL LINES
   1. Myrtos. Warren 1972: P 642.
   2. Palaikastro. Bosanquet and Dawkins 1923: pl. 2h.
   3. Malia. Effenterre and Effenterre 1976: pl. 20A.

4. DIAMONDS
   1. Vasilike. Seager 1906–1907: 121, fig. 4d.
   2. Gulf of Mirabello area. Forsdyke 1925: pl. 6, no. A 436.

5. DOTTED BANDS
   1. Sphoungaras. Hall 1912: fig. 23F.
   2. Gournia. Penn no. MS 4615–23.
   3. Gournia. Penn no. MS 4615–47.
   4. Gournia. Hall 1904–1905: pl. 28, no. 3.
   5. Mokhlos. Seager 1912: fig. 49, no. M 74.
   6. Palaikastro. Sackett, Popham, and Warren 1965: pl. 72e.
   7. Priniatikos Pyrgos. Penn no. MS 4894.

6. WAVY LINES
   1. Palaikastro. Dawkins 1904–1905: 271, fig. 5a.
   2. Gournia. Hall 1904–1905: pl. 28, no. 24.
   3. Gournia Ibid., pl. 28, no. 22.
   4. Gournia. Ibid., pl. 27, no. 11.

7. QUIRKS
   1. Vasilike. Seager 1906–1907: 121, fig. 4d.
   2. Gournia. Hall 1904–1905: pl. 28, no. 20.
   3. Vasilike. Seager 1906–1907: fig. 13.
   4. Vasilike. Maraghiannis and Karo 1907–1921: II, pl. 25, no. 1.
   5. Gournia. Hall 1904–1905: pl. 27, no. 16.
   6. Mokhlos. Seager 1909: 283, fig. 7.

8. J-SPIRALS
   1. Mokhlos. Forsdyke 1925: fig. 96, no. A 451–3.
   2. Gournia. Penn, no. MS 4615–33.
   3. Mokhlos. Seager 1909: 284, fig. 8.
   4. Vasilike. Maraghiannis and Karo 1907–1921: II, pl. 25, no. 10.
   5. Gournia. Hall 1904–1905: pl. 27, no. 18.
   6. Mokhlos. Seager 1912: fig. 49, no. M 60.

9. SEMICIRCLES AND CRESCENTS
   1. Gournia. Hall 1904–1905: pl. 28, no. 9.
   2. Gournia. Ibid., pl. 27, no. 14.
   3. Gournia. Ibid., pl. 31, no. 10.
   4. Gournia. Ibid., pl. 27, no. 15.
   5. Gournia. Ibid., pl. 32, no. 2.
   6. Gournia. Ibid., pl. 27, no. 9.
   7. Gournia. Ibid., pl. 27, no. 10.
   8. Gournia. Ibid., pl. 32, no. 5.
   9. Vasilike. Seager 1906–1907: 121, fig. 4a.
   10. Gournia. Hall 1904–1905: pl. 27, no. 7.
   11. Sphoungaras. Hall 1912: fig. 23c.
   12. Palaikastro. Dawkins 1903–1904: 201, fig. 3a.
   13. Palaikastro. Dawkins 1904–1905: 271, fig. 5d.
   14. Mokhlos. Seager 1909: fig. 13, top row no. 2.
   15. Palaikastro. Sackett, Popham, and Warren 1965: pl. 72d.
   16. Pseira. Seager 1910: 17, fig. 2.
   17. Pseira. Seager 1910: 17, fig. 1.
   18. Palaikastro. Bosanquet and Dawkins 1923: pl. 2g.

10. CIRCLES
    1. Mokhlos. Fairbanks 1928: no. 22.
    2. Gournia. Hall 1904–1905: pl. 29, no. 12.
    3. Gournia. Ibid., pl. 27, no. 23.
    4. Gournia. Penn no. MS 4615–11.
    5. Palaikastro. Forsdyke 1925: 79, no. A 450–2.
    6. Gournia. MMA no. 07.232.162.
    7. Palaikastro. Dawkins 1903–1904: 199, fig. 2f.
    8. Gournia. Hall 1904–1905: pl. 31, no. 9.
    9. Vasilike. Seager 1908: pl. 12, no. 34.
    10. Palaikastro. Dawkins 1903–1904: 199, fig. 2g.
    11. Palaikastro. Ibid., fig. 2d.
    12. Gournia. Hall 1904–1905: pl. 28, no. 2.
    13. Gournia. Ibid., pl 27, no. 20.
    14. Gournia. Ibid., pl. 27, no. 21, right.
    15. Gournia. Ibid., pl. 27, no. 21, left.
    16. Pyrgos, Myrtou. Cadogan 1974: fig. 77 a–b.
    17. Vasilike. Seager 1906–1907: fig. 7.
    18. Malia. Chapouthier, Demargne, and Dessene 1962: pls. 5 and 36, no. 9142.
    19. Malia. Ibid., pl 4D.
    20. Pseira. Seager 1910: 18, fig. 3.

11. TRIGLYPHS AND METOPES
    1. Gournia. MMA no. 07.232.185.
    2. Gournia. Hall 1904–1905: pl. 28, no. 16.
    3. Gournia. Ibid., pl. 28, no. 3.
    4. Gournia. Ibid., pl. 33, no. 4.
    5. Mokhlos. Forsdyke 1925: fig. 96, no. A 451–3.
    6. Palaikastro. Sackett, Popham, and Warren 1965: pl. 72c.
    7. Gournia. Hall 1904–1905: pl. 28, no. 15.
    8. Vasilike. Seager 1906–1907: fig. 4e.
    9. Gournia. Hall 1904–1905: pl. 18, no. 19.
    10. Pseira. Maraghiannis and Karo: 1907–1921: II, pl. 22, no. 3.
    11. Malia. Effentere and Effentere 1976: pl. 20i.
    12. Mokhlos. Seager 1909: fig. 13, top row no. 4.

12. ZIGZAGS
    1. Myrtos. Warren 1972: P 675.
    2. Vasilike. Seager 1906–1907: 121, fig. 46.
    3. Gournia. Hall 1904–1905: pl. 28, no. 14.
    4. Malia. Effentere and Effentere 1976: pl. 20G.
    5. Vasilike. HM no. 5251.
    6. Gournia. Hall 1904–1905: pl. 28, no. 6.

7. Mokhlos. Seager 1912: fig. 49, no. M 74.
8. Gournia. Penn no. MS 4615–15.
9. Gournia. Hall 1904–1905: pl. 28, no. 12.
10. Vasilike. Maraghiannis and Karo 1907–1921: II, pl. 25, no. 11.
11. Gournia. Hall 1904–1905: pl. 28, no. 7.
12. Mokhlos. Seager 1909: 292, fig. 13, third row no. 1.
13. Mokhlos. Ibid., fig. 13, center row no. 4.
14. Mokhlos. Fairbanks 1928: no. 32.

13. PICTORIALS
1. Gournia. Hall 1904–1905: pl. 28, no. 28.
2. Gournia. Ibid., pl. 32, no. 6.
3. Palaikastro. Bosanquet and Dawkins 1923: pl. 2e.
4. Malia. Chapouthier, Demargne, and Dessene, 1962: pl. 4D.

14. MISCELLANEOUS
1. Gournia. Hall 1904–1905: pl. 33, no. 7.
2. Gournia. Ibid., pl. 28, no. 23.
3. Gournia. Hall 1904–1905: pl. 32, no. 10
4. Gournia. MMA no. 07.232.229.
5. Gournia. Hall 1904–1905: pl. 28, no. 5.
6. Vasilike. Seager 1908: pl. 12, no. 24.
7. Mokhlos. Seager 1912: fig. 49, no. M 59.
8. Malia. Demargne 1945: pl. 30, no. 2.
9. Pyrgos, Myrtou. Cadogan 1978: fig. 6.
10. Pyrgos, Myrtou. Ibid., fig. 7 left.
11. Pyrgos, Myrtou. Ibid., fig. 7 right.

Notes

1. The writer would like to thank Gisela Walberg for discussions on the motifs and their development, particularly with references to their relation to Kamares Ware.

References

Bosanquet, R. C. and R. M. Dawkins. 1923. *The Unpublished Objects from the Palaikastro Excavations 1902–1906.* London.

Boyd, H. A. 1904–1905. Gournia. Report of the American Exploration Society's Excavations at Gournia, Crete, 1904. *Transactions of the Department of Archaeology, Free Museum of Science and Art* 1: 177–88.

Cadogan, G. 1974. Myrtos: Pyrghos. *Archaeological Reports for 1973–74:* 37–39.

Cadogan, G. 1978. Pyrgos, Crete, 1970–7. *Archaeological Reports for 1977–78:* 70–84.

Chapouthier, F., P. Demargne, and A. Dessene. 1962. *Fouilles exécutées a Mallia, quatrième rapport: Exploration du palais (1929–1935 et 1946–1960), Études crétoises* 12. Paris.

Dawkins, R. M., 1903–1904. Excavations at Palaikastro III. *BSA* 10: 192–226.

Dawkins, R. M., 1904–1905. Excavations at Palaikastro IV. *BSA* 11: 258–92.

Demargne, P. 1945. *Fouilles exécutees a Mallia: Exploration des nécropoles (1921–1933), Études crétoises* 7. Paris.

Effenterre, H. and M. van, 1976. *Fouilles exécutées a Mallia: Exploration des maisons . . . (1956–1960), Études crétoises* 22. Paris.

Fairbanks, A. 1928. *Catalogue of Greek and Etruscan Vases* I. Cambridge, Mass.

Forsdyke, E. J. 1925. *Catalogue of the Greek and Etruscan Vases in the British Museum.* Vol. I, part I, *Prehistoric Aegean Pottery.* London.

Hall, E. H. 1904–1905. Early Painted Pottery from Gournia, Crete. *Transactions of the Department of Archaeology, Free Museum of Science and Art* 1: 191–205.

Hall, E. H. 1912. *Excavations in Eastern Crete; Sphoungaras.* Philadelphia.

Hawes, H. B. et al. 1908. *Gournia, Vasiliki and other Prehistoric Sites on the Isthmus of Hierapetra, Crete.* Philadelphia.

Maraghiannis, G. and G. Karo. 1907–1921. *Antiquités crétoises* I–III. Vienna and Candia.

Sackett, L. H., M. R. Popham, and P. M. Warren. 1965. Excavations at Palaikastro, VI. *BSA* 60: 248–314.

Seager, R. B. 1906–1907, Report of Excavations at Vasiliki, Crete, in 1906. *Transactions of the Department of Archaeology, Free Museum of Science and Art* 2: 111–32.

Seager, R. B. 1908. Excavations at Vasiliki. In Hawes et al. 1908: 49–50 and pl. 12.

Seager, R. B. 1909. Excavations on the Island of Mochlos, Crete, in 1908. *AJA* 13: 273–303.

Seager, R. B. 1910. *Excavations on the Island of Pseira, Crete.* Philadelphia.

Seager, R. B. 1912. *Explorations in the Island of Mochlos.* Boston and New York.

Walberg, G. 1976. *Kamares. A Study of the Character of Palatial Middle Minoan Pottery.* Uppsala.

Walberg, G. 1978. *The Kamares Style. Overall Effects.* Uppsala.

Warren, P. 1972. *Myrtos. An Early Bronze Age Settlement in Crete.* London.

Zois, A. A. 1968. Der Kamares-Stil. Werden und Wesen. Ph.D. diss., Eberhard-Karls-Universität, Tübingen.

Zois, A. A. 1968B. Ὑπάρχει ΠΜ III 'εποχή; *Πεπράγμενα τοῦ Β' Διεθνοῦς κρητολογικοῦ Συνεδρίου:* 141–56.

4

Analysis of the Shapes

Philip P. Betancourt

The most characteristic shapes of East Cretan White-on-dark Ware are here classified in thirteen groups. While many rarer shapes exist (see Miscellaneous Shapes), the thirteen basic types account for more than 99% of the material in the North Trench at Gournia, regarded as the type-site for the mature phase of the ware, and most other sites seem to be comparable. A tabulation of these shapes with respect to the three chronological phases discussed in chapter 1 (Table 4–I) shows that only a few forms are early or late; most occur in all three periods. The cylindrical cup (Shape 5), the rounded cup with a thin strap handle (Shape 6B), and the carinated cup (Shape 7) are particularly important as they seem to begin with MM IA and are thus diagnostic for the Late Phase.

The classification system is based on several characteristics. Conical shapes are put into three groups: open bowls (Shape 1); cups (Shape 2); and spouted bowls and jars (Shape 3). Cups and bowls with S-shaped profiles are Shape 4. Cylindrical forms, which are less common, include cups (Shape 5), pyxides (Shape 12), and some jars (Shape 11). Among the rounded shapes are cups (Shape 6), jugs (Shape 8), bridge spouted jars (Shape 9), teapots (Shape 10), and some jars (Shape 11). Carinated cups (Shape 7) and lids (Shape 13) also occur. There are, in addition, many miscellaneous shapes: special types of cups and bowls; anthropomorphic and zoomorphic vessels; and other forms.

Information on the relative frequency of the shapes is furnished by the count of Edith Hall, drawn from sherds in the North Trench at Gournia (Table 4–II). Since some sherds were discarded at the time of excavation, and since others have become mixed with other material in the interval since they were studied, it is no longer possible to check the count. Due to the nature of the evidence, the information is somewhat skewed, though it is still highly useful. Shapes which break into many body sherds—jugs (Shape 8), bridge spouted jars (Shape 9) and teapots (Shape 10)—should have a larger relative percentage than the table indicates because body sherds are not readily identified and so cannot be classified. Jug spouts are also excluded, although several examples were noted by Hall (1904–1905: 196–97; 1908). The exclusion of the coarse sherds eliminates all of the jars (Shape 11) and probably most of the shallow bowls (Shape 1). Undecorated shapes, like pithoi and tripod cooking pots, were discarded.

The count was drawn from 200 baskets of excavated pottery (Hall 1904–1905). Three thousand sherds were of fine White-on-dark Ware, and approximately one third of these pieces (889) were identifiable. Only five joins were made among all the sherds, testimony to the fragmentary state of the material.

It is obvious that the pottery from Gournia reflects some local preferences. Cups or bowls and bridge spouted jars make up more than ninety percent of the group. Cups alone are 60.18%. The conical cup or bowl (Shapes 2–3), with 40.72% of the total number of sherds, is by far the most popular type. The rounded cup (Shape 6) comes next, with 6.30%. Fourteen rims of cups with S-shaped profiles (Shape 4) account for 1.57% of the total. The lid (Shape 13) is represented by thiry-six sherds, 4.05%. Even considering the nature of the evidence, several shapes seem particularly poorly represented. Taken together, all shapes except for the cups, lids, and bridge spouted jars comprise less than two percent of the total number of pieces. Clearly the sherds from

TABLE 4-I
The most characteristic shapes of East Cretan White-on-dark Ware

	Early Phase	Middle Phase	Late Phase
Open Shapes			
1. Shallow open bowl	x	x	x
2A. Conical cup, plain	x	x	x
2B. Conical cup, vert. handle		x	x
2C. Conical cup or bowl, frying pan handle	?	x	?
2D. Conical cup, pronounced base		x	?
3A. Spouted, conical bowl	x	x	?
3B. Conical bowl/jar	?	x	x
4. Cup with s-shaped profile	x	x	x
5. Cylindrical cup			x
6A. Rounded cup, plain	x	x	
6B. Rounded cup, thin vert. handle			x
7. Carinated cup			x
Closed Shapes			
8. Jug, raised spout	x	x	x
9. Bridge spouted jar	x	x	x
10. Teapot	?	x	?
11. Jar	?	x	x
12. Pyxis	x	x	x
Other			
13. Lid	x	x	x

Gournia reflect local tastes, needs, and/or sources of supply.

More evidence for the relative abundance of the shapes comes from Ossuary III in the Ellenika Cemetery at Palaikastro where forty-one complete vases and a few fragments were found in a tomb used only in EM III (Table 4–III). The information from here is valuable because it comes from a funeral context and thus complements the domestic material from Gournia (for a brief discussion of the ossuary deposit see chapter 1). As at Gournia, cups are the most common pieces; they make up 75.56% of the total assemblage. Again, the conical cup (Shape 2) is the most common type (plain pieces without handles are 44.44% of the total). Three bridge spouted jars are present (6.67%), and there are two jugs (4.44%). Only one or two examples each of a few other shapes occur.

The relative percentages of the shapes in the North Trench at Gournia and in Ossuary III at Palaikastro suggest that most East Cretan White-on-dark Ware is

TABLE 4-II
Shapes from the North Trench at Gournia

Shape	Rims	Bases	Total	Percent
Open bowl (Shape 1)			1	0.11
Conical cup/bowl (Shapes 2-3)				
Plain base		50		
Pronounced base (Shape 2D)		30		
Plain or pronounced base	262		362	40.72
Rounded cup (Shape 6A)	56		56	6.30
Low cup with wide mouth and defined shoulder (Shape 4)	14		14	1.57
Cup, uncertain type	103		103	11.59
Jug (Shape 8)				several
Bridge spouted jar (Shape 9)			307	34.53
Teapot* (Shape 10)	4		4	0.45
Lid (Shape 13)			36	4.05
Pyxis (Shape 12)			1	0.11
Cylindrical vessel with lid			2	0.22
Openwork vessel			3	0.34
Total			889	99.99
Handles of cups:				
round sections			68	82.93
oval sections			14	17.07
Total			82	100.00

*Not recognized by Hall

designed for pouring and serving liquids. Cups and vessels with spouts (bridge spouted jars, jugs, and teapots) account for all but a tiny fraction of the total number of vases. Most of the ware seems to be a specialized production, filling a cultural need for an attractive ceramic service for liquids. As is to be expected, there are more cups than vessels for pouring. Unfortunately, statistics are not available for other sites, but it is likely that these two deposits are typical.

Besides the general conclusions that emerge from these statistics, one can note that both Gournia and Palaikastro show preferences for specific shapes (note the lids at Gournia and the absence of cups with handles at Palaikastro). Similar patterns seem to occur at other sites, also. At Mokhlos and Vasilike, the rounded cups often have small knobs or handles set low on the body (Shape 6A, nos. 5 and 7–12). Conical cups from Malia, Palaikastro, Mokhlos, and Vasilike occur with frying pan handles (Shape 2C). Most sites with a large body of material have at least a few unusual pieces

TABLE 4-III
Shapes from Ossuary III in the Ellenika Cemetery, Palaikastro

Complete vessels	Total	Percent
Plain conical cup (Shape 2A)	20	44.44
Conical cup, pronounced base (Shape 2D)	3	6.67
Rounded cup (Shape 6A)	7	15.56
"Cup with slightly contracted mouth"	4	8.89
Jug (Shape 8)	2	4.44
Bridge spouted jar (Shape 9)	3	6.67
Jar with two handles (Shape 11)	1	2.22
Pyxis (Shape 13)	1	2.22
Fragmentary vessels		
Open bowl (Shape 1)	1	2.22
Teapot (Shape 10)	1	2.22
Cylindrical jar (Shape 11)	1	2.22
Lid (Shape 13)	1	2.22
Total	45	99.99

(Misc. Shapes, passim). The implication is that East Cretan White-on-dark Ware was made at more than one center, and that different sites were supplied from different sources, some of which might exhibit individual peculiarities in shapes or details.

The Shapes

SHAPE 1. SHALLOW OPEN BOWL

The shallow bowl seems to be directly descended from vessels made in EM IIB (Betancourt et al. 1979: Shape 1). It occurs at many East Cretan sites in White-on-dark Ware, and no stylistic development can be discerned for the duration of this style (compare the example from Myrtos, no. 5, from EM IIB, with the one from Pyrgos Myrtou, no. 8, from MM IA). Some examples have lugs or small handles for lifting or spouts for pouring out the contents. While the regular type has a flat bottom, straight walls, and a conical shape, minor variations like a concave profile for the wall exist as well. The decoration is sometimes placed on a dark band at the rim, but solid painting is also used as the background for the white motifs. Both the rim-band and the solid field can occur on the same bowl, one used inside and the other on the exterior. Spirals (Seager 1909: fig. 8 and fig. 13 second row no. 3, from Mokhlos), wavy or zigzag bands (Hall 1912: fig. 20 lower left, from Sphoungaras), diagonal lines, and many other motifs occur on this shape (see the examples below). Hatched triangles, chevrons, and diagonal lines are especially popular. Although some of the shallow bowls are small, others are more than 25 centimeters in diameter.

Typical examples:
1. Gournia. Stylistically EM III (probably the North Trench). Sherd. Dark band at rim, inside and out. Groups of four diagonal lines, alternating direction. Penn no. MS 4615–15. Fig. 4–1A.
   Silverman 1978: fig. 3, no. 5, and pl. Id, no. 15.
2. Gournia. EM III context (North Trench). Sherd. Large, heavy form. Dark band at rim, on interior; exterior painted dark. Groups of diagonal lines, alternating direction, on rim-band on interior; groups

of diagonal lines, alternating direction, on exterior, at rim. Penn no. MS 4615–16.

Hall 1904–1905; pl. 32, no. 3; Zois 1968B: pl. 15, 98; Silverman 1978: fig. 3, no. 6, and pl. 2a, no. 8.

3. Malia. Stylistically EM III–MM I (probably from the South Houses). Dark band at rim, on exterior; interior painted dark. Chevrons, pendant from the rim, on interior, with the lower one in each group wide; hatching at the corners of the upper chevrons. HM no. 9139. Fig. 4–1B.

Chapouthier, Demargne, and Dessene 1962: pl. 5, below and pl. 36, center left.

4. Malia. Stylistically EM III–MM I. Sherd. Dark band at rim, on interior. Crossed lines with the lower central triangular space cross-hatched, flanked by double lines. MSM.

Effenterre, H. and M. van 1976: pl. 20i.

5. Myrtos. EM IIB context (Period II). Two pairs of triangular lugs on the rim. Chevrons, pendant from rim on interior and exterior. AN (Myrtos no. P 196).

Warren 1972: fig. 51 and pl. 40B–C.

6. Palaikastro. Stylistically EM III–MM I. Sherd. Small coil handles on the rim. Dark band at rim, on interior; exterior painted dark. Groups of short vertical lines alternating with groups of quirks on rimband; groups of diagonal lines, alternating direction, on exterior. BM no. A 445–15.

Forsdyke 1925: 78.

7. Pseira. Stylistically MM I. Dark band at rim, on interior. Isolated individual motifs consisting of crossed lines forming the "butterfly motif" with dots within the triangles, flanked by groups of short vertical lines, on the rim-band. HM no. 5447.

Maraghiannis and Karo 1907–1921: II, pl. 22, no. 3.

8. Pyrgos, Myrtou, MM IA context (Period IIa–b). Whirl motif with lines terminating in dots in tondo; chevrons, pendant from rim, on interior. KSM.

Cadogan 1974: fig. 77; Hiller 1977: pl. 17a.

9. Vasilike. Stylistically EM III–MM I. Sherd. Interior painted dark. Groups of straight lines and bands, on interior. NMC no. 6775.

Blinkenberg and Johansen n.d.: pl. 30, no. 4.

10. Gulf of Mirabello area. Stylistically EM III–MM I. Dark band at rim, on interior; exterior painted dark. Wavy line on interior; pendant hatched triangles on exterior. BM no. A 438.

Forsdyke 1925: 76–77, fig. 94.

SHAPE 2A. PLAIN CONICAL CUP OR BOWL

The conical cup or bowl with a flat base and no handle is a very simple shape. In Crete it begins in EM II and persists until the Late Minoan period. Examples in White-on-dark Ware, usually with thin walls and straight profiles, come from several east Cretan sites. The most common decoration is pendant triangles, either completely hatched or with the hatching only across the corners (to the examples listed below add Seager 1912: fig. 49, nos. M 56, 57, 61, and 63, from Mokhlos; Forsdyke 1925: 78, nos. A 445–6 and 11, from Palaikastro; Bosanquet and Dawkins 1923: fig. 5B, from Palaikastro). They often extend from rim to base. A few other decorations also exist, and one atypical piece (Dawkins 1904–1905: fig. 5a) has panels of dark paint alternating with reserved areas, with the white on the dark panels. The plain cup already appears with the earliest East Cretan White-on-dark Ware (no. 4), and it persists throughout the period. Heights are usually between four and eight centimeters.

Typical examples:

1. Malia. EM III–MM I context (Premier Charnier). Pendant hatched triangles, hatched at the upper corners. HM no. 8656. Fig. 4–1C.

Demargne 1945: pl. 29, no. 8656.

2. Mokhlos. Stylistically EM III–MM I. Pendant hatched triangles. HM no. 5509.

Seager 1912: fig. 49, no. M 62.

3. Mokhlos. Stylistically EM–III–MM I. Tiny knobs on rim. Pendant hatched triangles. MFA no. 09.36.

Fairbanks 1928: 12, no. 25.

4. Myrtos. EM IIB context (Period II). Chevrons, pendant from rim. AN (Myrtos no. P 223).

Warren 1972: fig. 53. Fig. 4–1D.

5. Palaikastro. Stylistically EM III–MM I. Sherd. Diagonal row of quirks flanked by triple lines, with wider diagonal band at side. BM no. A 445–13.

Forsdyke 1925: 78, fig. 96, no. A 445–13.

6. Palaikastro. Stylistically EM III–MM I. Sherd. Pendant hatched triangles. BM no. A 445–2.

Forsdyke 1925: 78, fig. 96, no. A 445–2.

7. Vasilike. Stylistically EM III–MM I. Pendant hatched triangles with the hatching alternating directions on different parts of the triangles. Penn no. MS 4237. Fig. 4–1E.

Betancourt 1983: no. 240.

SHAPE 2B. CONICAL CUP WITH ONE VERTICAL HANDLE

This cup has a conical shape, a straight or nearly straight profile, and one vertical coil or ribbon handle. Of eighty-two handles found in the EM III material in the North Trench at Gournia, sixty-eight were coils and fourteen were thick ribbons (Hall 1904–1905: 105). Thin ribbon handles do not appear until MM I. Several decorations occur on the shape, with pendant hatched triangles (especially those hatched only at the corners) being especially popular. Dimensions are about the same as for the other cups.

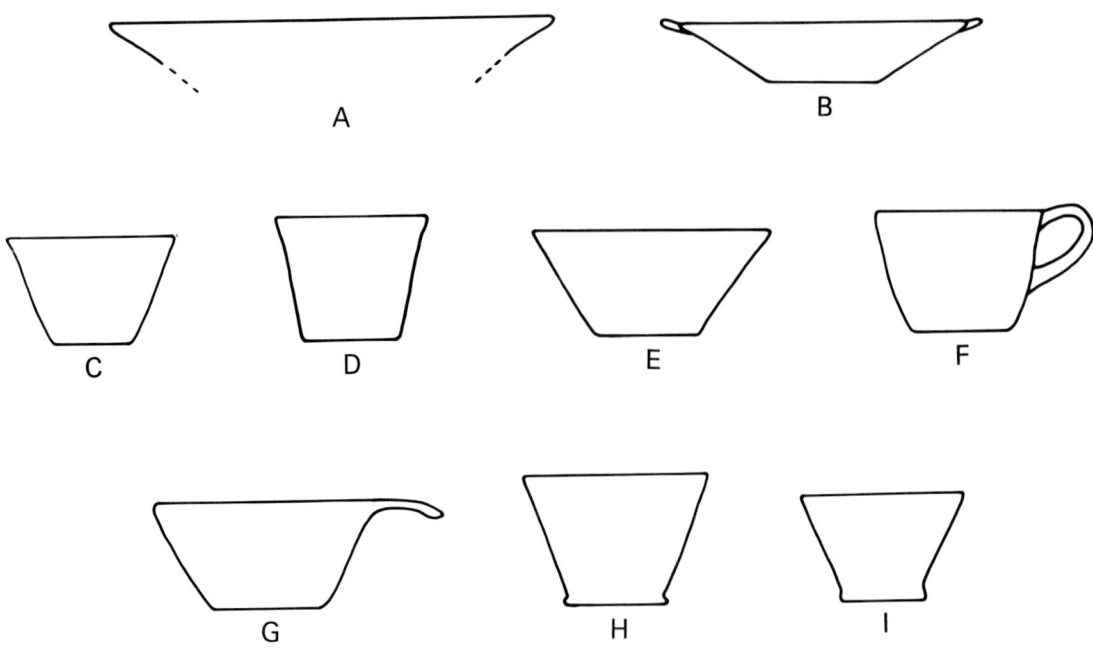

Fig. 4–1. Shapes 1 and 2. Open conical shapes. A. Shape 1 no. 1. B. Shape 1 no. 3. C. Shape 2A no. 1. D. Shape 2A no. 4. E. Shape 2A no. 7. F. Shape 2B no. 2. G. Shape 2C no. 3. H. Shape 2D no. 3. I. Shape 2D no. 4.

Typical examples:

1. Gournia. EM III context (North Trench). Sherd. Pendant triangles, hatched at the corners, above band. HM unnumbered.

  Hall 1904–1905: pl. 26, no. 1; Montelius 1924: pl. 55, no. 1; Müller-Karpe 1974: pl. 380, no. 3; Andreou 1978: fig. 6, no. 11.

2. Gournia. Stylistically EM III (probably the North Trench). Sherd. Thick ribbon handle. Pendant hatched triangles. Penn no. MS 4615–1. Fig. 4–1F.

  Silverman 1978: pl. 2b, no. 6.

3. Malia. EM III–MM I context (Premier Charnier). Pendant triangles, hatched at the corners. HM no. 8674.

  Demargne 1945: pls. 4 and 29, no. 8674.

4. Mokhlos. MM IB context (deposit beneath House D). Pendant hatched arcs at rim, above two bands. HM no. 5575.

  Seager 1909: fig. 13, upper row no. 3; Evans 1921–1935: I, fig. 76, upper center; Hall 1928: fig. 69, top row no. 3.

5. Sphoungaras. Sylistically EM III–MM I. Vertical lines flanking dots on rim; pendant double arcs with dots, between double bands. HM no. 6678.

  Hall 1912: fig. 23B.

SHAPE 2C. CONICAL CUP OR BOWL WITH FRYING PAN HANDLE

Another variation of the small conical vessel uses a horizontally projecting frying pan handle at the rim. Like the other varieties, it has a straight or nearly straight profile and a flat base. It is not common. Pendant hatched triangles are the most usual decoration.

Typical examples:

1. Malia, at Aghia Varvara. Stylistically EM III–MM I. Sherd. Decoration not extant except for lines on handle. MSM.

  Demargne and Gallet de Santerre 1953: pl. 46c.

2. Mokhlos. Stylistically EM III–MM I. Sherd. Pendant hatched triangles. BM no. A 446–1.

  Forsdyke 1925: 79 and fig. 96, no. A 446.

3. Palaikastro. Stylistically EM III–MM I. Pendant hatched triangles. AM no. 742. Fig. 4–1G.

  Unpublished.

4. Vasilike. Stylistically EM III–MM I. Pendant hatched traingles. NMC, no. 6774.

  Blinkenberg and Johansen n.d.: pl. 30, no. 5.

5. Vasilike. Stylistically EM III–MM I. Pendant hatched triangles. HM unnumbered.

Seager 1906–1907: fig. 3a; Maraghiannis and Karo 1907–1921: II, pl. 25, no. 4; Montelius 1924: pl. 56, no. 9; Müller-Karpe 1974: pl. 380, no. 5; Andreou 1978: fig. 6, no. 12.

SHAPE 2D. PLAIN CONICAL CUP WITH PRONOUNCED BASE

A variation of the conical vessel has a well defined base. The shape begins in EM II (no. 3). It is less common than the simpler type, though it occurs at several sites (to the list below add Gournia, Hall 1904–1905: pl. 26, no. 4, and Palaikastro, Bosanquet and Dawkins 1923: pl. 2a). As with the more common design, walls are thin and well formed. Sizes are within the normal range for cups.

Typical examples:
1. Mokhlos. Stylistically EM III–MM I. Pendant hatched triangles, between bands. HM no. 5506.
Seager 1912: fig. 49, no. M 57; Maraghiannis and Karo 1907–1921: II, pl. 10, no. 4; Evans 1921–1935: I, fig. 76, lower row no. 2.
2. Mokhlos. Stylistically EM III–MM I. Dark band at rim. Pendant hatched triangles. HM no. 5510.
Seager 1912: fig. 49, no. M 56; Evans 1921–1935: I, fig. 76, lower row no. 1.
3. Myrtos. EM IIB context (Period II). Chevrons, pendant from rim. AN (Myrtos no. P 227). Fig. 4–1H.
Warren 1968–1969: 35, fig. 49; 1972: 117, fig. 53, and pl. 41F.
4. Vasilike. Stylistically EM III–MM I. Dark bands at rim and base; alternating vertical dark panels and reserved areas. Added white: three thin bands on rim-band; diagonal lines, with some crosshatching, on panels. Penn no. MS 4234. Fig. 4–1I.
Betancourt 1983: no. 239.

SHAPE 3A. CONICAL CUP OR BOWL WITH OPEN SPOUT AND OPPOSED LUG

The small conical vessel with an open spout opposite a lug handle is one of the definitive shapes for EM IIB (Betancourt et al. 1979: Shape II.C.2). It continues to be used in EM III and may be regarded as one of the characteristic shapes for East Cretan White-on-dark Ware. Both shape and decoration are fairly well standardized. Since the walls are rather thick, the vessel is heavy and very stable. The profile is straight or nearly so. The spout is small and open, and the tiny opposed lug is always at the rim. Sometimes one or more grooves help define the base. Pendant hatched triangles are commonly used as decoration. One piece, a rare subtype, is boat shaped (Seager 1906–1907:fig. 5C).

Typical examples:
1. Aghia Photia. EM IIB context with some earlier vases (burial group). Pendant hatched triangles on a mottled slip. HM no. 3760.
Boyd 1904–1905: pl. 25, no. 3; Hawes et al. 1908: color pl. A4; Montelius 1924: pl. 57, no. 6; Lacy 1967: fig. 12a (labeled Gournia); Betancourt et al. 1979: 34.
2. Gournia. Stylistically EM III–MM I. Sherd. Pendant hatched triangles. AN unnumbered.
Soles 1973: figs. 54 right and 56.
3. Malia. EM III–MM I context (Premier Charnier). Lines on interior; pendant hatched triangles on exterior. HM no. 8610.
Demargne 1945: 7 and pls. 3, 4, and 29, no. 8610.
4. Malia. Stylistically EM III–MM I. Sherd. Pendant hatched triangles. MSM no. 60 K 369.
Amouretti 1970: pl. 3, upper right.
5. Myrtos. EM IIB context (Period II). Molded base. Chevrons, pendant from rim. AN (Myrtos no. P 250). Fig. 4–2A.
Warren 1972: 118, fig. 54, and pl. 42C.
6. Palaikastro. Stylistically EM III–MM I. Sherd. Pendant hatched triangles. BM no. A 445–1.
Forsdyke 1925: 78, fig. 96, no. A 445–1.
7. Vasilike. Stylistically EM III–MM I. Pendant hatched triangles. NMC no. 6772.
Blinkenberg and Johansen n.d.: pl. 30, no. 6.
8. Vasilike. Stylistically EM III–MM I. Pendant hatched triangles. NMC no. 6773.
Blinkenberg and Johansen n.d.: pl. 30, no. 7.
9. Vasilike. Stylistically EM III–MM I. Pendant hatched triangles. MMA no. 14.89.3.
Richter 1915: 9, fig. 1; 1917: 9, fig. 2 left; 1930: 9, fig. 2 left.
10. Vasilike. Stylistically EM III–MM IA. Pendant hatched triangles. Penn no. MS 4238. Fig. 4–2B.
Betancourt 1983: no. 242.

SHAPE 3B. CONICAL BOWL OR JAR WITH SPOUT AND TWO HANDLES

The conical vessel with two horizontal coil handles and a single spout seems to be directly descended from a popular EM IIB form (Betancourt et al. 1979: Shapes II.C.3 and II.C.4). In East Cretan White-on-dark Ware the spout is usually open, and the handles are placed high on the body. The profile is nearly straight, but it tends to flare a bit at the rim. A repeated design bounded by bands above and below is the usual scheme of decoration. Heights are usually between 15 and 20 centimeters.

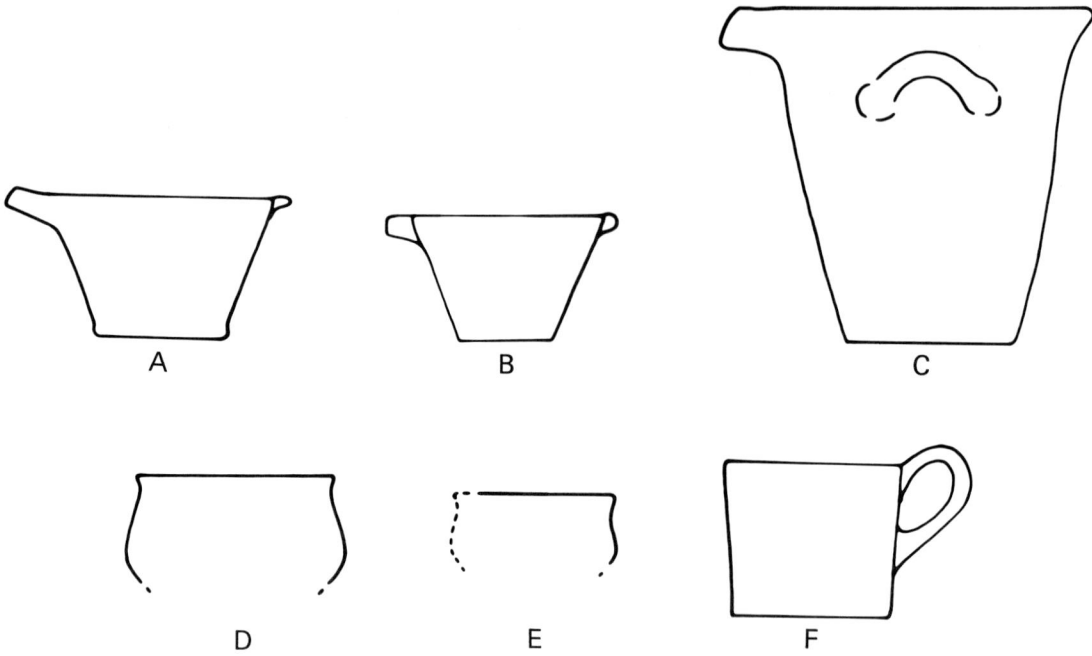

Fig. 4–2. Shapes 3, 4, and 5. Open conical, semiglobular, and cylindrical shapes. A. Shape 3A no. 5. B. Shape 3A no. 10. C. Shape 3B no. 4. D. Shape 4 no. 1. E. Shape 4 no. 3. F. Shape 5 no. 1.

Typical examples:
1. Malia. EM III–MM I context (Premier Charnier). Horizontal, diagonal and vertical bands. HM no. 8519.
   Demargne 1945: pl. 27, no. 8519.
2. Malia. EM III–MM IA context (Premier Charnier). Three bands at rim and at base, with diagonal crosshatched motif between. HM no. 8528.
   Demargne 1945: pl. 30, no. 2.
3. Mokhlos. EM III context (Deposit in Block C). Alternating diagonal lozenges with central lines, with bands above and below. HM.
   Seager 1909: fig. 13, center row right; Evans 1921–1935: I, fig. 76, center left; Hall 1928: fig. 69, center row no. 4; Müller-Karpe 1974: pl. 381, no. 17.
4. Vasilike. EM III context (Well Deposit). Horizontal frieze of chevrons between sets of three bands. HM. Fig. 4–2C.
   Seager 1906–1907: fig. 6; Maraghiannis and Karo 1907–1921: II, pl. 25, no. 5; Montelius 1924: pl. 56, no. 3; Müller-Karpe 1974: pl. 380, no. 2.
5. Vasilike. Stylistically EM III–MM I. Sherd. Groups of three horizontally aligned chevrons between sets of two bands. MHC no. BAI 14–A.
   Foster 1978: no. 33.

SHAPE 4. CUP WITH S-SHAPED PROFILE

This shape, while not common, is important for its later development. It is surely a major ancestor of the semiglobular cup, one of the principal fine ware shapes of the Middle Minoan period. It is present from the beginning of the style.

Typical examples:
1. Myrtos. EM IIB context (Period II). Bowl with S-shaped profile. Chevrons, pendant from rim. AN (Myrtos no. P 150). Fig. 4–2D.
   Warren 1972: fig. 49 and pl. 39D.
2. Myrtos. EM IIB context (Period II). Sherd. Shape and decoration like no. 1. AN (Myrtos no. P 160).
   Warren 1972: 114.
3. Gournia. EM III context (North Trench). Sherd. Groups of chevrons between pairs of bands. MMA no. 07.232.218. Fig. 4–2E.
   Hall 1904–1905: pl. 28, no. 17; Zois 1968: pl. 13, no. 46.

SHAPE 5. CYLINDRICAL CUP

The cylindrical cup has a flat base, vertical sides, and one vertical ribbon handle. It is one of the characteristic shapes for the Late Phase of White-on-dark Ware because it has not been found in any of the deposits from the mature phase. Datable pieces come from Pyrgos and Mokhlos, always associated with MM I pottery. The form continues into later periods as well; the handmade shape is probably the ancestor of the wheelmade straight-sided cup of MM IB and later. As with other shapes from this phase, decoration can cover the entire wall of the vessel. Heights are usually between 6 and 12 cm.

Typical examples:

1. Mokhlos. MM IB context (Deposit beneath House D). Pendant concentric arcs at rim and rising concentric arcs at base. HM no. 5573. Fig. 4–2F.

Seager 1909: fig. 13, top row no. 2; Evans 1921–1935: I, fig. 76, upper right; Hall 1928: fig. 69, top row no. 2; Andreou 1978: fig. 12, no. 2.

2. Pyrgos, Myrtou. MM IA context (Period IIa–b). Three sets of three bands. KSM.

Cadogan 1978: fig. 7, left; Andreou 1978: fig 12, no. 1.

SHAPE 6A. ROUNDED CUP

The cup with a convex profile is one of the most typical shapes of East Cretan White-on-dark Ware. Dozens of examples are known, and it is particularly common in the mature phase of the style. The shape is simple; a flat base and convex sides create a small rounded container. Handles, when present, are small knobs or coils set low on the body. The most common ornament is a repeated design, either placed between bands or just below the rim with bands below. Less often, a design covers more of the field and is repeated around the vessel (no. 3). Sometimes two friezes are used (nos. 1, 6, 8–10, and 12). Most pieces are between 4.5 and 8 centimeters high.

Typical examples:

1. Gournia. EM III context (North Trench). Sherd. Band composed of two rows of dots at rim, above double band; rising arcs with double arcs of dots within on body, above two bands. Penn no. MS 4615–31.

Silverman 1978: fig. 3, no. 2 and pl. ld, no. 1.

2. Malia. EM III–MM I context (Premier Charnier). Horizontal frieze of chevrons, between double bands. HM no. 8529.

Demargne 1945: pls. 8 and 29, no. 8529.

3. Mokhlos. Stylistically EM III–MM IA. Diagonal bands of crosshatching between diagonal bands, covering field from rim to base. HM no. 5511.

Seager 1912: fig. 49, no. M 59; Evans 1921–1935: I, fig. 76, lower row no. 4.

4. Mokhlos. Stylistically EM III–MM IA. Running spirals with triple connecting lines, above three bands. MFA no. 09.555.

Fairbanks 1928: no. 29; Vermeule 1963: fig. 3, lower row no. 3.

5. Mokhlos. Stylistically EM III. Small handles, low on body. Zigzag band at rim; three bands on body. MFA no. 09.556.

Fairbanks 1928: no. 26; Vermeule 1963: fig. 3, lower row no. 1.

6. Sphoungaras. Stylistically EM III–MM IA. Chain motif at rim, above two bands; double rising arcs with double arcs of dots within, and one rising hatched triangle, above two bands. HM no. 6683.

Hall 1912: fig. 23c.

7. Vasilike. EM III context (Well Deposit). Small handles, low on body. Zigzag band at rim, between bands, with two bands below. HM no. 5259.

Seager 1906–1907: fig. 4c; Maraghiannis and Karo 1907–1921: II, pl. 25, no. 9; Andreou 1978: fig. 6, no. 5.

8. Vasilike. EM III context (Well Deposit). Small handles, low on body. Quirks at rim; quirks on lower body; reserved band at center of body. HM no. 5288.

Seager 1906–1907: fig. 4d; Maraghiannis and Karo 1907–1921: II, pl. 25, no. 3; Montelius 1924: pl. 56, no. 6.

9. Vasilike. EM III context (Well Deposit). Small handles, low on body. Frieze composed of four or five diagonal lines alternating with butterfly motif at rim, above two bands; frieze of dots and another band on lower body. HM no. 5290.

Seager 1906–1907: fig. 4e; Andreou 1978: fig. 6, no. 6.

10. Vasilike. EM III context (Well Deposit). Small handles, low on body. Pendant double arcs with dots between on dark band at rim and on lower body, with reserved band at center of cup. HM no. 5291.

Seager 1906–1907: fig. 4a; Maraghiannis and Karo 1907–1921: II, pl. 25, no. 2; Montelius 1924: pl. 56, no. 8; Åberg 1930–1935: IV, fig. 458.

11. Vasilike. EM III context (Well Deposit). Small handles, low on body. Frieze of double quirks with dots within at rim, above three bands. HM no. 5294.

Seager 1906–1907: fig. 4b; Maraghiannis and Karo 1907–1921: II, pl. 25, no. 1; Montelius 1924: pl. 56, no. 4; Pendlebury 1939: pl. 13, no 3f; Matz 1957: pl. 19, above, back row no. 3; Hutchinson 1962: pl. 3, back row no. 3; Schachermeyr 1964: fig. 19, bottom, second from right; Müller-Karpe 1974: pl. 380, no. 4.

12. Vasilike. EM III context (Well Deposit). Small handles, low on body. Linked crosshatched diamonds at rim; running spirals with double connecting lines on lower body; reserved band at center of body. HM no. 5296.

Seager 1906–1907: fig. 4f; Maraghiannis and Karo 1907–1921: II, pl. 25, no. 8; Montelius 1924: pl. 56, no. 5; Pendlebury 1939: pl. 13, no. 3e.

SHAPE 6B. ROUNDED CUP WITH THIN VERTICAL HANDLE

The cup with a convex profile and a vertical ribbon handle is a late manifestation in East Cretan White-on-dark Ware. A very common shape, it begins in the style's Late Phase and continues into later periods. It is probably the ancestor of the graceful Middle Minoan semiglobular cup, needing only the wheelmade

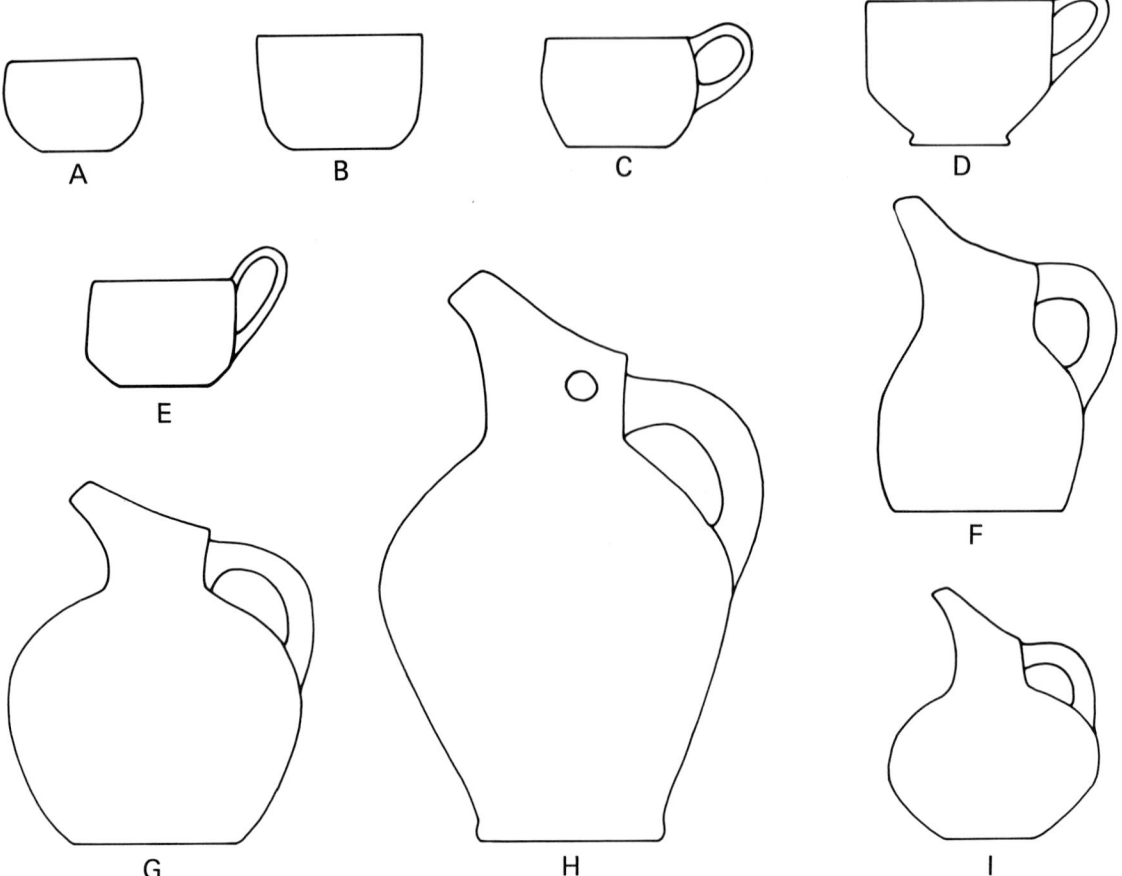

Fig. 4–3. Shapes 6, 7, and 8. Open rounded and carinated shapes and jugs. A. Shape 6A not cat. (Mokhlos, MFA 09.557). B. Shape 6A not cat. (Vasilike, MHC BAI 14–B). C. Shape 6B no. 1. D. Shape 7 no. 1. E. Shape 7 no. 2. F. Shape 8 no. 7. G. Shape 8 no. 3. H. Shape 8 no. 1. I. Shape 8 no. 8.

S-shaped profile to attain its mature form. Decorations vary. Ornaments which cover the entire field are more popular than in earlier times (nos. 1–3). Heights are usually between 5 and 10 centimeters.

Typical examples:
 1. Priniatikos Pyrgos. Stylistically MM I. Motifs consisting of two diagonal lines of dots bounded by double lines, with two bands above and below. Penn no. MS 4894. Fig. 4–3C.
  Betancourt 1983: no. 19.
 2. Pseira. Stylistically MM I. Large pendant arcs containing band of dots bounded by bands above and below. MMA no. 14.89.4.
  Richter 1915: 9, fig. 2; 1917: 9, fig. 2 right; 1930: 9, fig. 2 right; 1953: pl. 2b.
 3. Pyrgos, Myrtou. MM IA context (Period IIa–b). Triple band at rim; quadruple plume design on body. KSM.
  Cadogan 1978: fig. 7, right.

SHAPE 7. CARINATED CUP

The carinated cup has a cylindrical upper section and a conical lower section with a rounded carination near the midpoint of the body. It is a late shape, both handmade and wheelmade, which begins in MM I. Sizes are comparable to the other cups.

Typical examples:
 1. Palaikastro. Stylistically MM I–IIA. Pendant arcs with quirks and radiating line motifs inside. HM no. 3375. Fig. 4–3D.
  Bosanquet and Dawkins 1923: pl. 4f; Hutchinson et al. 1939–1940: pl. 14j.
 2. Vasilike. Stylistically MM I. Bands on upper body. Penn no. MS 4231. Fig. 4–3E.
  Betancourt 1983: no. 245.
 3. Isthmus of Ierapetra. Stylistically MM I. Pendant arcs with groups of concentric circles within. BM no. A 441.
  Forsdyke 1925: 77, fig. 95.

SHAPE 8. JUG WITH RAISED SPOUT

The jug with a flat base, one handle, and a raised spout is one of the most common Early and Middle Minoan shapes (for EM IIB examples, the direct antecedents of the White-on-dark Ware shapes, see Betancourt et al. 1979: Shape VIII). Most of the jugs in East Cretan White-on-dark Ware have a globular body, but slimmer examples also occur, especially in the Late Phase. Considerable variation exists in the body shape, even within specific periods (see the examples in fig. 4–3). The main decoration is usually on the shoulder. While a horizontally arranged repeat pattern is the most common scheme, a few vases have larger motifs placed diagonally across the vessel (nos. 1–2). As early experiments with torsional effects that emphasize the flow of motion around a curved surface, they play an important role in the development of Middle Minoan pottery. By the end of the style one can distinguish an increased proportion of late motifs like simple bands (no. 7). Sizes vary from miniatures to pieces more than 25 centimeters high.

Typical examples:
1. Mokhlos. EM III context (Deposit in Block C). Lines on spout; two bands on lower neck; diagonal band of quirks, between double bands; three bands on body. HM no. 5449. Fig. 4–3H.
Seager 1909: fig. 13, lower row no. 3; Hall 1928: fig. 69, lower row no. 3; Pendlebury 1939: pl. 13, no. 4e.
2. Mokhlos. EM III context (Deposit in Block C). Small plastic "eyes" at sides of spout. Lines on spout; band of dots between bands at base of neck; diagonal band of quirks between bands on shoulder; four bands on body. HM no. 5468.
Seager 1909: figs. 7 and 13, lower row, no. 2; Montelius 1924: pl. 57, no. 10; Hall 1928: fig. 69, lower row, no. 2; Pendlebury 1939: pl. 13, no. 4c; Andreou 1978: fig. 6, no. 17.
3. Mokhlos. EM II–III context (Tomb V). Small plastic "eyes" on sides of spout. Three lines on spout; band at base of neck; running spirals with wide connecting lines on shoulder; three bands on body. HM no. 5471. Fig. 4–3G.
Seager 1912: figs. 18 and 19, no. Va; Evans 1921–1935: I, fig. 76, right upper center; Montelius 1924: pl. 57, no. 12; Hall 1928: fig. 45, upper left; Pendlebury 1939: pl. 13, no. 4a; Schachermeyr 1955: fig. 74, no. 2; Zervos 1956: fig. 138, right; Marinatos and Hirmer n.d.: fig. 8, below; Lacy 1967: fig. 11b; Branigan 1970: pl. 5b, right; Marinatos 1973: fig. 8, below; Müller-Karpe 1974: pls. 371, no. 16 and 381, no. 16.
4. Mokhlos. EM III context (Deposit in Block C). Bands on spout; bands on neck and base of neck; running spirals with triple connecting lines containing dots on shoulder; three bands on body. HM no. 5472.

Seager 1909: figs. 6 and 13, center row no. 1: Montelius 1924: pl. 57, no. 11; Hall 1928: fig. 69, center row no. 1; Andreou 1978: fig. 6, no. 18.
5. Mokhlos. Stylistically EM III–MM I. Horizontal band at base of neck; circles containing two or three spirals, connected by one or two diagonal lines; three bands on body. MFA no. 09.552.
Fairbanks 1928: no. 22.
6. Palaikastro. Stylistically EM III–MM I. Sherd. Horizontal frieze of chevrons between bands on shoulder; bands on body. FM no. 07.1.46.
Lamb 1936: pl. 4, no. 20.
7. Palaikastro. Stylistically MM I–II. Bands on spout; bands at base of neck; bands on body. HM no. 3332. Fig. 4–3F.
Dawkins 1902–1903: fig. 5, lower row no. 3; Maraghiannis and Karo 1907–1921: I, pl. 35, no. 6; Bossert 1923: fig. 143a.
8. Sphoungaras. Stylistically EM III. Bands on spout; bands at base of neck; rising triangles and arcs composed of triple rows of dots on shoulder; two bands on body. HM no. 6680. Fig. 4–3I.
Hall 1912: fig. 23F.
9. Vasilike. MM IB context (House B). Dark paint on rim, shoulder, and bottom of body. Two bands at base of neck; opposed crosshatched semicircles, alternating with diagonal lines, on shoulder; two bands below shoulder zone. HM no. 5272.
Seager 1906–1907: fig. 7; Montelius 1924: pl. 56, no. 2; Åberg 1930–1935: IV fig. 460; Schachermeyr 1964: fig. 19, upper right; Müller-Karpe 1974: pl. 380, no. 1; Betancourt 1977: ill. 1K; Andreou 1978: fig. 13, no. 8.

SHAPE 9. BRIDGE SPOUTED JAR

The bridge spouted jar with a convex profile and two horizontal handles is common. It appears in the earliest deposits containing White-on-dark Ware (nos. 4–5), and it persists to the end of the style, with just about every settlement with EM III or MM I pottery in eastern Crete yielding examples (besides the examples below, for Gournia see Hall 1904–1905: pls. 29–30; for Palaikastro see Bosanquet and Dawkins 1923: pl. 2g; for Pseira see Kaiser 1976: pl. 3, no. 7; for the Trapeza Cave see Pendlebury, Pendlebury, and Money-Coutts 1935–1936: 47 and pl. 8, no. 212; for Vasilike see Seager 1906–1907: pl. 30a; 1908: pl. 12, no. 34). The form directly continues the tradition of EM IIB, with no change in the shape (see Betancourt et al. 1979: 39, Shape V.C.1).

Several subvarieties exist. Sometimes the body is globular (no. 3), but it may also be tall (Seager 1906–1907: pl. 30a). The decoration is usually confined to the upper shoulder. It often consists of simple geometric patterns repeated around the vase, with the

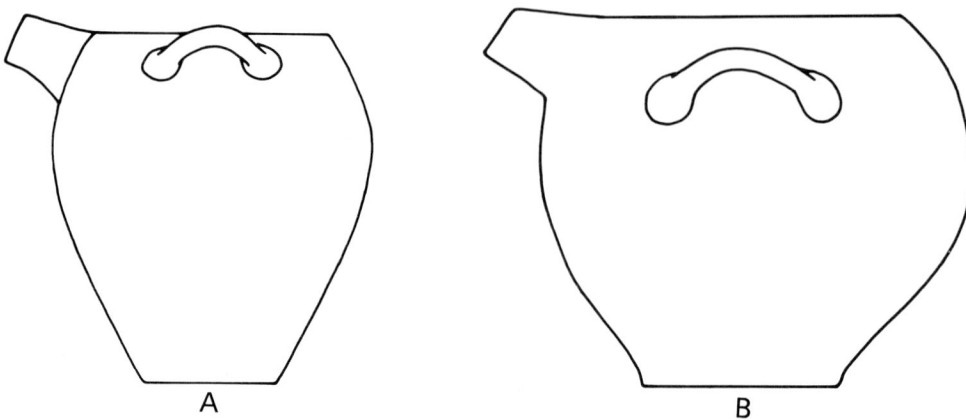

Fig. 4–4. Shape 9. Bridge spouted jars. A. Shape 9 no. 2. B. Shape 9, shape restored from sherds.

frieze usually set off by bands. Heights are usually between 10 and 20 centimeters.

Typical examples:

1. Gournia. EM III context (North Trench). Sherd. Circles with crosshatched sections, connected by multiple connecting lines. Penn no. MS 4615–11.

Hall 1904–1905: pl. 29, no. 2; Zois 1968: pl. 13, no. 60.

2. Malia. EM III–MM I context (Premier Charnier). Band on rim; diagonal zigzags flanked by double lines on shoulder, above three bands; groups of three quirks on lower body, above band. HM no. 8492. Fig. 4–4A.

Demargne 1945: pl. 29, no. 8492.

3. Malia. Stylistically EM III–MM I (probably from the South Houses). Dark paint on upper part only. Band on rim; circles containing triangles, with the outer crescent spaces crosshatched, connected by multiple connecting lines, above two bands; lines on spout. HM no. 9142.

Chapouthier, Demargne, and Dessene 1962: pls. 5 and 36, no. 9142.

4. Myrtos. EM IIB context (Period II). One vertical handle opposite the spout. Chevrons, pendant from rim, on one side; zigzag between bands on opposite side. AN (Myrtos no. P 675).

Warren 1972: 152, fig. 87, and pl. 65A.

5. Myrtos. EM IIB context (Period II). Two clay "eyes" at base of spout. Horizontal bands on upper body; bands down neck. AN (Myrtos no. P 665).

Warren 1972: 151.

6. Pseira. Stylistically EM III–MM I. Sherd. Two rows of dots at rim, above double band; rising arcs with double arcs of dots within, above band. AK no. 2856.

Kaiser 1976: pl. 3, no. 8.

SHAPE 10. TEAPOT

The teapot, an EM II shape that continues into the period of White-on-dark Ware, is perhaps the most distinctive and aristocratic of the style's shapes (for the earlier tradition see Betancourt et al. 1979: Shape X). A base is usually present, though a rarer variation without a base also exists (nos. 1–2). As with earlier examples, the spout may be extraordinarily long. Shorter spouts also occur, and it is this type which continues into later times. The main zone of decoration is usually on the upper shoulder, continuing across the spout. Accessory ornament may be placed on the lower body. The shape is not uncommon, and it is known from many east Cretan sites (to the list below add Maraghiannis and Karo 1907–1921: II, pl. 22, no. 6, from Pseira; Forsdyke 1925: 79, no. A 450–2, from Palaikastro; Penn no. MS 4615–32, from Gournia). Heights vary widely, from less than 10 centimeters to more than 20 centimeters.

Typical examples:

1. Mokhlos. Stylistically EM III–MM I. No base; long spout. Two bands with dots between them on neck; groups of diagonal lines, alternating direction, on shoulder; four bands below; pendant double arcs on lower body. HM no. 5473.

Seager 1912: fig. 49, no. M 74; Maraghiannis and Karo 1907–1921: II, pl. 10; Pendlebury 1939: pl. 13, no. 4b.

2. Vasilike. Stylistically EM II–MM I. No base; long spout; horns on side of spout. Bands on upper body and on spout. HM no. 3737.

Seager 1908: pl. 12, no. 24.

3. Vasilike. EM III–MM IA context (Seager's Period IV). Base; long spout. Two bands on upper shoulder; double quirks on shoulder and spout; two bands on lower shoulder; pendant triple arcs with

dots between them on lower body; base not preserved. HM no. 5249. Fig. 4–5A.

Seager 1906–1907: fig. 13; Maraghiannis and Karo 1907–1921: II, pl. 25, no. 12; Evans 1921–1935: I, fig. 76, above left; Fimmen 1924: fig. 69; Pendlebury 1939: pl. 13, no. 3d; Schachermeyr 1955: fig. 74, no. 1; Zervos 1956: fig. 137, right; Matz 1957: pl. 19, above back row no. 2; Hutchinson 1962: pl. 3, back row no. 2; Schachermeyr 1964: fig. 17e; Lacy 1967: fig. 11a; Schachermeyr 1967: pl. 27e; Müller-Karpe 1974: pl. 381, no. 7; Andreou 1978: fig. 7, no. 1.

4. Vasilike. Stylistically EM III–MM I. Base; long spout. Two bands with dots between them on neck; running spirals on upper shoulder; three bands with band of dots between the upper two on lower shoulder; pendant double arcs with zigzag between them on lower body; rising hatched triangles on base. HM no. 5250.

Maraghiannis and Karo 1907–1921: II, pl. 25, no. 10; Zervos 1956: fig. 138, left; Branigan 1970: pl. 5b, left; Davis 1977: fig. 62.

SHAPE 11. JAR

Jars used for storage or burial are sometimes decorated with white linear ornament. Mouths are usually wide, and handles are small. Friezes in which individual motifs alternate or repeat are the most common decorations. Heights are above 20 centimeters.

Typical examples:
1. Gournia. Stylistically EM III. Sherd. Flat, thickened rim and straight wall. Bands below rim. ERM no. P–531. Fig. 4–5B.
Unpublished.
2. Pakheia Ammos. Stylistically EM III–MM I. Convex profile and two horizontal coil handles; mouth fitted for a lid. Dark band on body. Groups of vertical lines. HM no. 7371.
Seager 1916: pl. 2, no. 1b; Betancourt 1977: ill. 4A.
3. Pakheia Ammos. Stylistically EM III–MM I. Convex profile and two horizontal coil handles. Upper part dark painted. Rising triple triangles containing circles with two crosshatched semicircles, above two bands. HM no. 7375. Fig. 4–5C.
Seager 1916: pl. 11, no. XI–C.

SHAPE 12. PYXIS

Pyxides are not common. They exist in several varieties, with the examples listed here being typical.

Typical examples:
1. Gournia. EM III context (North Trench). Sherd. Cylindrical shape with a groove to accommodate a lid; two horizontal handles. Panels of doubled crossed lines, between pairs of bands. MMA no. 07.232,71. Fig. 4–5E.
Hall 1904–1905: pl. 33, no. 4; Evans 1921–1935: I, fig. 80a, no. 11; Zois 1968: pl. 16, no. 113.
2. Myrtos. EM IIB context (Period II). Pyxis, cylindrical shape on three feet; feet continue up the sides as ribs and terminate in reels below the rim. Vertical lines on exterior, with bands at rim and base. Low conical lid with radiating lines crossed by three concentric circles (catalogued below). AN (Myrtos no. P 642). Fig. 4–5D.
Warren 1972: 149, fig. 84, and pl. 62A.

SHAPE 13. LID

Thirty-six fragments of lids come from the North Trench at Gournia (Hall 1904–1905: 197), and occasional examples come from other sites, also. Two varieties are known, a flat disc (nos. 3–4) and a type with an edge (nos. 1–2). While they usually have central handles, some have no handles at all, and some pieces from Gournia have handles at the sides. If the lid is flat, decoration is placed only on the top, but if it has an edge this portion is decorated as well. Sizes vary, with most pieces having a diameter of less than 15 centimeters.

Typical examples:
1. Gournia. Stylistically EM III (probably the North Trench). Sherd. Flat top; nearly vertical edge; handle not extant. Rising hatched triangles on edge; decoration on top not extant. Penn no. MS 4615–34. Fig. 4–6A.
Silverman 1978: fig. 3, no. 22 and pl. 2a, no. 13.
2. Gournia. Stylistically EM III (from Deposit B). Sherd. Flat top; nearly vertical edge; horizontal handles at edge. Rising hatched triangles on edge; crosshatched motifs on top, only partly preserved. Penn no. MS 4615–39.
Silverman 1978: fig. 3, no. 21 and pl. 2a, no. 12.
3. Eastern Crete (perhaps Gournia). Stylistically EM III. Sherd. Flat top; no edge. Groups of opposed diagonal lines. ERM no. P–518.
Unpublished.
4. Myrtos. EM IIB context (Period II). Low conical shape; no knob. Radiating lines crossed by three concentric circles. AN (Myrtos no. P 642). Fig. 4–6B.
Warren 1972: fig. 84 and pl. 62A.

MISCELLANEOUS SHAPES

At its height White-on-dark Ware makes up more than 90% of the fine decorated pottery at some sites. It is thus inevitable that a wide range of shapes should exist: some are known from only one example; others are favorites at one or two sites but do not occur gen-

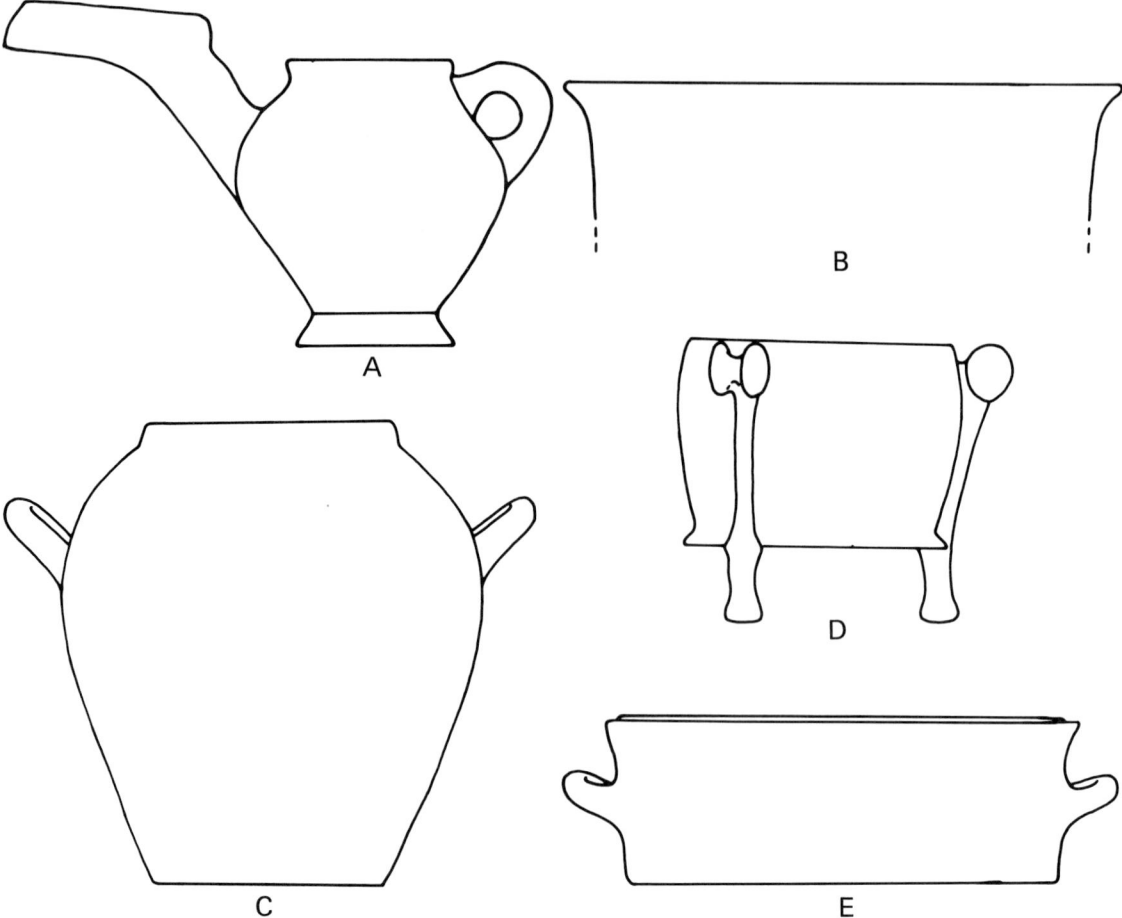

Fig. 4–5. Shapes 10, 11, and 12. Teapots, jars, and pyxides. A. Shape 10 no. 3. B. Shape 11 no. 1. C. Shape 11 no. 3. D. Shape 12 no. 2. E. Shape 12 no. 1.

erally; still others exist from several places but are not common enough to be regarded as characteristic of the ware as a whole. The list below is by no means exhaustive; it is simply intended as a cross section of the many miscellaneous shapes used for the ware. Cups include a conical shape with two opposed horizontal handles (no. 1) and a type with a spout (nos. 2 and 9). The jug with a small pulled out spout (no. 3) and the amphora (no. 4) are rare shapes. A few zoomorphic (no. 7) and anthropomorphic (nos 5–6) figures also exist (to the female figures listed below add Pendlebury, Pendlebury, and Money-Coutts 1935–1936: 94 and pl. 13, no. 1001). Also worthy of mention are the openwork stand (Hall 1904–1905: 197 and pl. 33, no. 7) and the boat-shaped bowl (Seager 1906–1907: fig. 5C), examples of the creative range of individual potters.

Typical examples:

1. Malia. EM III–MM I context (Premier Charnier). Conical cup or bowl with horizontal handles set below the rim. Crossed diagonal lines. HM no. 8549. Fig. 4–6C.

    Demargne 1945: pl. 30, no. 1.

2. Mokhlos. Stylistically EM III–MM I. Cup or bowl with convex profile and spout. Diagonal lines alternating with groups of vertical lines, between several bands. HM no. 5502.

    Seager 1912: fig. 49, no. M 49.

3. Palaikastro. EM III context (Deposit in Delta 32). Jug with trefoil mouth. Pendant concentric arcs on shoulder; groups of vertical lines below and band on body. HM.

    Dawkins 1903–1904: 201, fig. 3a.

4. Mokhlos. EM II–III context (Tomb XXI). Amphora. Groups of diagonal lines, alternating direction, between bands. HM no. 5500. Fig. 4–6D.

    Seager 1912: fig. 46, no. XXI, 5: Pendlebury 1939: pl. 13, no. 4d.

5. Malia EM III–LM I context (Second Charnier).

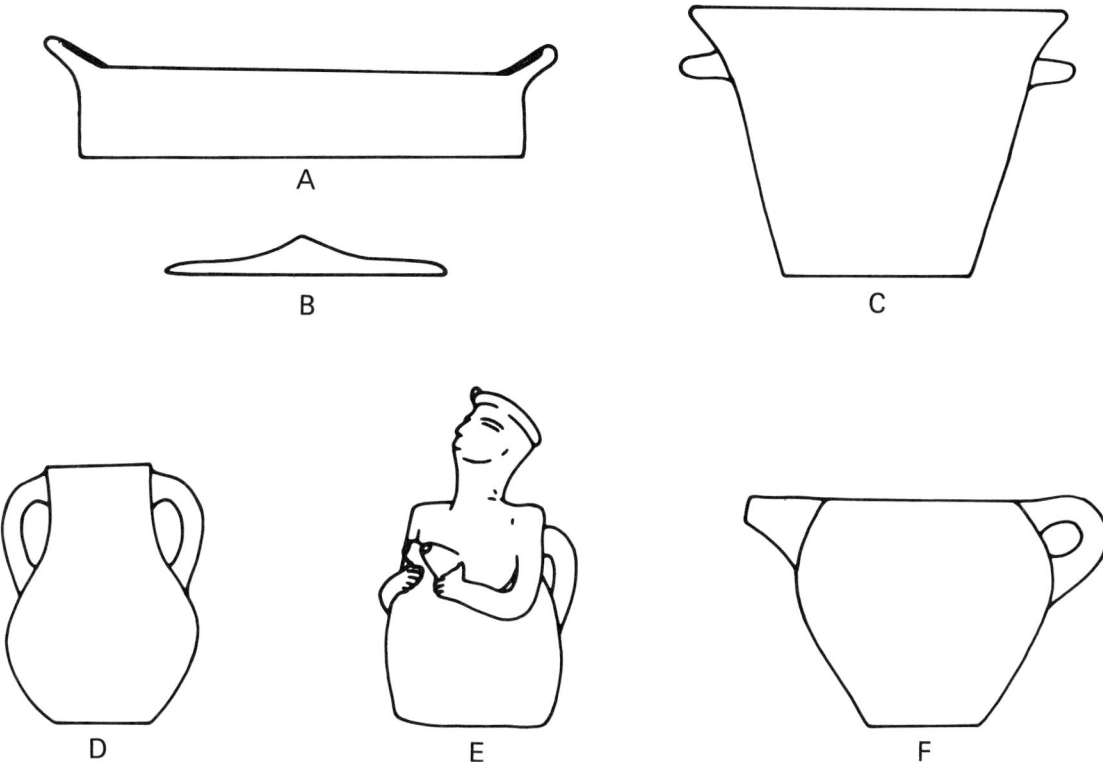

Fig. 4–6. Shape 13 and misc. shapes. A. Shape 13 no. 1. B. Shape 13 no. 4. C. Misc. shapes no. 1. D. Misc. shapes no. 4. E. Misc. shapes no. 6. F. Misc. shapes no. 8.

Female figure; vessel with vertical coil handle at back and openings in top of head and at breasts; abstract form with long skirt; angles at sides (elbows?); schematized, modeled head; hands under breasts; incisions on head; punctations on arms; bands on head; circles for eyes; bands on neck; vertical zigzags between bands on body; quirks between bands on lower body; hatching between diagonal bands on hem of skirt. HM no. 8665.

Demargne 1945: pls. 31–32, no. 8665; Zervos 1956: fig. 116; Demargne 1964: figs. 99–100; Platon 1974: pl. on p. 125, left.

6. Mokhlos. Mixed EM II–MM context (Tomb XIII). Female figure; vessel with vertical coil handle at back and openings in top of head and at breasts; modeled head; rectangular body; arms against torso with hands holding breasts. Band of quirks between double bands on upper torso; zigzags between double bands alternating with vertical double spirals flanked by vertical double bands on lower part of body, probably representing the woman's clothing. HM no. 5499. Fig. 4–6E.

Seager 1912: figs. 32, no. XIIIg and 34; Maraghiannis and Karo 1907–1921: II, pl. 10, no. 6; Dussaud 1914: fig. 274; Evans 1921–1935: I, fig. 84 and II, fig. 153: Zervos 1956: figs. 186–87; Marinatos and Hirmer n.d.: fig. 10, above; Marinatos 1973: fig. 10, above; Müller-Karpe 1974: pl. 368, no. 31; Edey 1975: p. 33, center right.

7. Pyrgos, Myrtou. MM IA context (Period IIa–b). Askoid rhyton in the form of a bird with spread wings; openings in beak and back of neck. Crossed triple lines on neck; triple chevrons on top of body; crosshatched areas on wings. KSM.

Cadogan 1974: fig. 79; Hiller 1977: pl. 17b; Cadogan 1978: fig. 6.

8. Gulf of Mirabello area. Stylistically EM III–MM I. Bridge spouted jug with wide mouth. Dark paint on upper part only. Band of lozenges, crosshatched, between sets of two bands. BM no. A 436. Fig. 4–6F.

Forsdyke 1925: 76 and pl. 6, no. A 436.

9. Gulf of Mirabello area. Stylistically EM III–MM I. Cup with rounded profile with two vertical handles and an open spout. Linked spiral-coils between bands on body. BM no. A 437.

Forsdyke 1925: 76, fig. 93.

References

Åberg, N. F. 1930–1935. *Bronzezeitliche und früheisenzeitliche chronologie.* Stockholm.

Amouretti, M.-C. 1970. *Fouilles exécutées a Mallia, Le centre politique II, La crypte hypostyle, Études crétoises* 18. Paris.

Andreou, S. 1978. Pottery Groups of the Old Palace Period in Crete. Ph.D. diss., University of Cincinnati.

Betancourt, P. P. 1977. Some Chronological Problems in the Middle Minoan Dark-on-Light Pottery of Eastern Crete. *AJA* 81: 341–53.

Betancourt, P. P. 1983. *Minoan Objects Excavated from Vasilike, Pseira, Sphoungaras, Priniatikos Pyrgos, and Other Sites. The Cretan Collection in the University Museum, University of Pennsylvania,* vol. I. Philadelphia.

Betancourt, P. P., T. K. Gaisser, E. Koss, R. F. Lyon, F. R. Matson, S. Montgomery, G. H. Myer, and C. P. Swann. 1979. *Vasilike Ware. An Early Bronze Age Pottery Style in Crete.* Göteborg.

Blinkenberg, Chr. and K. F. Johansen. n.d. *CVA Denmark 1, Copenhagen, National Museum,* fasc. 1.

Bosanquet, R. C. and R. M. Dawkins. 1923. *The Unpublished Objects from the Palaikastro Excavations 1902–1906.* London.

Bossert, H. T. 1923. *Altkreta.* Berlin.

Boyd, H. A. 1904–1905. Gournia. Report of the American Exploration Society's Excavations at Gournia, Crete, 1904. *Transactions of the Department of Archaeology, Free Museum of Science and Art* 1: 177–88.

Branigan, K. 1970. *The Foundations of Palatial Crete.* New York and Washington.

Cadogan G. 1974. Myrtos: Pyrghos. *Archaeological Reports for 1973–74:* 37–39.

Cadogan, G. 1978. Pyrgos, Crete, 1970–7. *Archaeological Reports for 1977–78:* 70–84.

Chapouthier, F., P. Demargne, and A. Dessene. 1962. *Fouilles exécutées a Mallia, quatrième rapport: Exploration du palais (1929–1935 et 1946–1960), Études crétoises* 12. Paris.

Christopoulos, G. A. et al. 1974. *History of the Hellenic World, Prehistory and Protohistory.* University Park, Pennsylvania.

Davis, E. N. 1977. *The Vapheio Cups and Aegean Gold and Silver Ware.* New York and London.

Dawkins, R. M. 1902–1903. Excavations at Palaikastro II. Sections 5–8. *BSA* 9: 290–328.

Dawkins, R. M. 1903–1904. Excavations at Palaikastro III. *BSA* 10: 192–226.

Dawkins, R. M. 1904–1905. Excavations at Palaikastro IV. *BSA* 11: 258–92.

Demargne, P. 1945. *Fouilles exécutées a Mallia: Exploration des nécropoles (1921–1933), Études crétoises* 7. Paris.

Demargne, P. 1964. *Aegean Art. The Origins of Greek Art.* London.

Demargne, P. and H. Gallet de Santerre. 1953. *Fouilles exécutées a Mallia, Exploration des maisons. . . , Études crétoises* 9. Paris.

Dussaud, R. 1914. *Les Civilisations Préhelléniques.* Paris.

Edey, M. A. 1975. *Lost World of the Aegean.* New York.

Effenterre, H, and M. van. 1976. *Fouilles exécutées a Mallia, Exploration des maisons . . . (1956–1960), Études crétoises* 22. Paris.

Evans, A. J. 1921–1935. *The Palace of Minos at Knossos.* London.

Fairbanks, A. 1928. *Catalogue of Greek and Etruscan Vases* I. Cambridge, Mass.

Fimmen, D. 1924. *Die kretisch-mykenische Kultur.* Leipzig and Berlin.

Forsdyke, E. J. 1925. *Catalogue of the Greek and Etruscan Vases in the British Museum.* Vol. I, part I, *Prehistoric Aegean Pottery.* London.

Foster, K. P. 1978. The Mount Holyoke Collection of Minoan Pottery. *Temple University Aegean Symposium* 3: 1–30.

Hall, E. H. 1904–1905. Early Painted Pottery from Gournia, Crete. *Transactions of the Department of Archaeology, Free Museum of Science and Art* 1: 191–205.

Hall, E. H. 1908. Early Minoan III Ware from the North Trench. In Hawes et al. 1908: Appendix E, 57.

Hall, E. H. 1912. *Excavations in Eastern Crete; Sphoungaras.* Philadelphia.

Hall, H. R. 1928. *The Civilization of Greece in the Bronze Age.* London.

Hawes, H. B., B. E. Williams, R. B. Seager, and E. H. Hall. 1908. *Gournia, Vasiliki and other Prehistoric Sites on the Isthmus of Hierapetra, Crete.* Philadelphia.

Hiller, S. 1977. *Das minoische Kreta nach den Ausgrabungen des letzten Jahrzehnts.* Vienna.

Hutchinson, R. W. et al. 1939–1940. Unpublished Objects from Palaikastro and Praisos. II. *BSA* 40: 38–59.

Hutchinson, R. W. 1962. *Prehistoric Crete.* Harmondsworth, Middlesex, and Baltimore.

Kaiser, B. 1976. *CVA Germany* 40, *Bonn, Akademisches Kunstmuseum,* fasc. 2. Munich.

Lacy, A. D. 1967. *Greek Pottery in the Bronze Age.* London.

Lamb, W. 1936. *CVA Great Britain* 11, *Cambridge, Fitzwilliam Museum,* fasc. 2. Oxford, London, and Paris.

Maraghiannis, G., and G. Karo. 1907–1921. *Antiquités crétoises* I–III. Vienna and Candia.

Marinatos, S. 1973. *Kreta, Thera und das mykenishche Hellas.* Munich.

Marinatos, S. and M. Hirmer n.d. [1960]. *Crete and Mycenae.* New York.

Matz, F. 1957. *Kreta, Mykene, Troja.* Stuttgart.

Montelius, O. 1924. *La Grèce préclassique.* Stockholm.

Müller-Karpe, H. 1974. *Handbuch der Vorgeschichte* III. Munich.

Pendlebury, J. D. S. 1939. *The Archaeology of Crete.* London.

Pendlebury, H. W. and J. D. S., and M. B. Money-Coutts. 1935–1936. Excavations in the Plain of Lasithi. I. The Cave of Trapeza. *BSA* 36: 5–131.

Platon, N. E. 1974. The Pre-Palace Minoan Period. In Christopoulos et al. 1974: 116–30.

Richter, G. M. A. 1915. Greek Prehistoric Art. *Bulletin of the Metropolitan Museum of Art* 10: 8–11.

Richter, G. M. A. 1917. *Handbook of the Classical Collection.* New York.

Richter, G. M. A. 1917. *Handbook of the Classical Collection.* New York.

Richter, G. M. A. 1953. *Handbook of the Greek Collection. Metropolitan Museum of Art.* New York.

Schachermeyr, F. 1955. *Die ältesten Kulturen Griechenlands.* Stuttgart.

Schachermeyr, F. 1964. *Die minoishce Kultur des alten Kreta.* Stuttgart.

Schachermeyr, F. 1967. *Ägäis und Orient.* Vienna.

Seager, R. B. 1906–1907. Report of Excavations at Vasiliki, Crete, in 1906. *Transactions of the Department of Archaeology, Free Museum of Science and Art* 2: 111–32.

Seager, R. B. 1908. Excavatons at Vasiliki. In Hawes et al. 1908: 49–50 and pl. 12.

Seager, R. B. 1909. Excavations on the Island of Mochlos, Crete, in 1908. *AJA* 13: 273–303.

Seager, R. B. 1912. *Explorations in the Island of Mochlos.* Boston and New York.

Seager, R. B. 1916. *The Cemetery of Pachyammos, Crete.* Philadelphia.

Silverman, J. S. 1978. The Gournia Collection in the University Museum; A Study in East Cretan Pottery. Ph.D. diss., University of Pennsylvania, Philadelphia.

Soles, J. S. 1973. The Gournia House Tombs. Ph.D. diss., University of Pennsylvania, Philadelphia.

Vermeule, C. C. III. 1963. *Greek Etruscan and Roman Art. The Classical Collections of the Museum of Fine Arts. Boston.* Boston.

Warren, P. M. 1968–1969. Myrtos. *Archaeological Reports for 1968–69:* 34–35.

Warren, P. 1972. *Myrtos. An Early Bronze Age Settlement in Crete.* London.

Zervos, C. 1956. *L'Art de la Crète. Néolithique et minoenne.* Paris.

Zois, A. A. 1968. Ὑπάρχει ΠΜ ΙΙΙ ἐποχή; *Πεπράγμενα τοῦ Β' Διεθνοῦς Κρητολογικοῦ Συνεδρίου:*141–56.

Part III

5

Physical Characteristics of the Fabric, Slip, and Paint

Frederick R. Matson

Introduction

These comments on the physical characteristics of the White-on-dark pottery are made after examining five sherds in nondestructive detail.[1] Small chips removed from these sherds were studied under a Scanning Electron Microscope at The Pennsylvania State University. A total of twenty-seven sherds from the collection of the University Museum of the University of Pennsylvania were later examined as thin sections (prepared by G. Myer) and as smoothly ground cross sections, viewed under a binocular microscope.

It would be presumptious to characterize the range of physical properties of the Gournian White-on-dark Ware of EM III times in a quantitative sense on the basis of this sampling. Since this is a chronologically important collection of rare sherds, however, observations should be made, and they may serve as a background study for those concerned with the analyses of ceramic materials from current excavations. In preparing this report I have had the opportunity to read in manuscript other chapters in this book and have indicated where I have made use of them.

General comments are first offered on the body, the slip, and the paint decoration of the EM III White-on-dark pottery from Gournia before reporting on the study by Scanning Electron Microscope. Comments are also presented on vessel forming and firing.

The University Museum catalogue numbers of the sherds examined in greatest detail and the vessel shapes from which they came are:

MS 4615-11. Bridge spouted jar (Appendix no. 20)
MS 4615-17. Conical cup (Appendix no. 6)
MS 4615-28. Bridge spouted jar (Appendix no. 30)
MS 4615-40. Thin body sherd, probably from a cup (Appendix no. 18).
MS 4615-47. Rounded cup (Appendix no. 17)

Only the identifying sherd numbers 11 through 47 will be used in this report.

Fabric

A smoothly ground sherd edge, preferably one that is aligned with the vertical axis of the original vessel and is normal to the sherd surfaces, provides a useful section through the body for the observation of its color and inclusions. After the final dressing of the cut and ground edge with 600 mesh silicon carbide or a similar abrasive powder on a glass plate, the newly prepared surface, especially the pores which trap abrasive grains, can be cleaned by immersing the sherd in the water-filled tank of a small ultrasonic cleaner. It is then ready for examination with a hand lens or under a binocular microscope. Sometimes a slightly dampened surface shows more detail than one that is dry. A selection of cross sections is shown in pl. 4.

The color of the fired clay body of the Gournian sherds ranges from tan to reddish brown, with gradations occurring from the surfaces to the core. In terms of the Munsell soil color names they would include a range in the Yellow-Red Hues from yellow or very pale brown to red and dark red. A range of gray shades occurs in the bodies of vessels that had been subjected to predominately reducing conditions during firing and possibly in the destruction by fire of houses which contained them. Miss Hall (whom I pleasantly knew in my student days as Mrs. Edith Hall Dohan) reported that "The clay of which this ware was made shades from a buff to a brick-red color according to the firing.... Occasionally a gray clay with black particles is found" (Hall 1908: 57).

Some of the sherds have a body that is mottled with spotty red areas peppered against a pale brown background. A mottled appearance at transitional firing temperatures with respect to color development and an occurrence of pale brown surfaces enclosing a reddish brown core are characteristic of calcareous clays that contain a fair amount of iron. At higher firing temperatures the core would also become pale brown in color. The presence of salt in many calcareous clays can cause pale brown bodies to develop at lower temperatures than would otherwise be likely (Matson 1971: 66–70). The salt, particularly sodium chloride, can be introduced if sea water is used at coastal sites to make the clay plastic. This is done today in the Lebanon and parts of Spain. Salt concentrations can accumulate in surface clay deposits that were readily available to ancient potters if they took clay from ploughed fields.

Inclusions

The fired clay bodies of the sherds contained many inclusions of rock and mineral fragments (see pl. 4). These are often termed *tempering materials* in archaeological reports, but until one is familiar with the texture of the clays, sands, gravels, and weathered rocks near the site where the potsherds were excavated it is better not to imply, at first glance, that the potter added aplastic materials to the clay when it was being prepared for the production of pottery. Therefore the term *inclusions* will be used in this report except where the tempering procedure is specifically considered. The shape of some holes shows that plant fragments had been included in the paste. They may indicate that a small amount of dung was added to the clay to make it more plastic. There are several ethnographic accounts of this practice.

Both a freshly fractured edge and a smoothly ground edge of a sherd are useful sources of information with respect to the nature, size, shape, and abundance of inclusions that may be in the body. On freshly fractured edges individual grains often protrude from the matrix and can be readily examined. Such grains can easily be removed with tweezers and a teasing needle, crushed and identified in powder form under a petrographic microscope or by means of X-ray diffraction.

The inclusions recognized in the five Gournian sherds during the detailed study of the fractured and smoothly ground edges are described below. If one is not certain, it is much better to speak of *white* inclusions rather than term them quartz, flint, feldspar, etc. or *black* ones rather than suggesting a specific dark-colored mineral. Precise identifications must be based on the study of petrographic thin sections, etc. and are not essential for the first characterization of the sherds. False attributions based on impressions rather than mineralogical identifications may be grossly misleading. The inclusions recognized in the examination of the sherd edges at magnifications up to 27 times are:

1. Milky white subrounded to subangular grains ranging in diameter from microscopic up to 1 mm or a little larger in diameter. These are identified as plagioclase feldspar by thin section analysis (by G. Myer). They are the dominant inclusions present.

2. White subrounded to subangular grains which are identified in thin sections as quartz.

3. Many glossy black grains identified as hornblende. They are closely identified with the milky white grains from a rock formation. Since hornblende contains a significant amount of iron, it is likely that the original grains, before they were fired in the pottery, were lighter in color. Oxidizing and reducing atmospheres to which the pottery was exposed in the hearth or kiln would differentially develop the deeper colors. The black grains are less than 1 mm in diameter.

4. Biotite mica, usually as very small reflecting particles, is present. Occasionally flake packets up to 1 mm in diameter can be seen.

5. Rock fragments consisting of two or more of the above minerals. These fragments indicate that the inclusions all come from the same original rock source. Like the individual mineral grains, they are usually under 1 mm in diameter.

6. Red siltstone fragments with fracture indications of a laminated structure. Such a structure is normal in sedimentary deposits. The grains contain

minute black particles. Grains up to 2 mm in size appear in a few sherds, and occasionally they may be up to 3 mm in length. These fragments, large and small, are angular in shape. This indicates that they had been crushed before being included in the clay matrix, for they would be abraded into subrounded shapes in natural deposits. It is likely that they were added by the potter as a tempering material. They may well have been the dregs remaining when an iron-rich siltstone was crushed to prepare materials for the dark slip used on the pottery. The slip surface is peppered with very fine granules which indicates that it had been prepared by grinding or pulverizing a source material. The process was observed and photographically recorded at the pottery-making village of Rachaiyah al Fakhar in the southern part of the Lebanon in 1955 and 1964. The first color of these ferruginous inclusions that are seen in the paste of the Gournian pottery varies according to the thermal and atmospheric conditions to which it was exposed in the hearth or kiln, but it may be characterized as 2.5YR 4–6/6, light red to dark red.

7. Darker red lumps, rounded to subrounded in form. These inclusions, ranging in size range to 2 mm, and very rarely to 3 mm, vary in color from sherd to sherd. They are usually darker in color than the siltstone grains (5YR 4–6/3–4, light reddish brown to reddish brown). They can easily be crushed or abraded, and they consist of numerous minute grains with a micaceous appearance. Examination by thin section (by G. Myer) indicates they were probably in a plastic state when the clay was plastic. Since they apparently vitrify at a slightly lower temperature than the paste as a whole, in some sherds they are vesicular.

8. Chaff-dung voids. Not all holes in potsherds are the result of air occlusions in incompletely wedged clay. They may well be voids left when organic materials burned out during the firing of the pottery. If so, there should be confirmatory evidence on the sherd surfaces in depressions where organic materials had once been. A small amount of dung can serve as an excellent plasticizer in clay. Droppings of ruminants contain exceptionally fine short-stemmed chaff, quite unlike that from threshing floors. In the preparation of clay for the production of very thin-walled vessels, the inclusion of a little dung may be advantageous. This has been discussed in ceramic ethnoarchaeological studies (London 1981). Of the five sherds studied in detail for this report, one, no. 17, a conical cup possibly formed in a mold, shows possible traces of needlelike holes in the black slip. A few appear on the interior surface that had been wet-smoothed. The ground edge of the sherd contains many very fine holes and a few longitudinal holes. Could the inclusion of organic material in the paste have enhanced the reducing conditions to which this vessel had been exposed during firing? No conclusion is possible from the examination of but one sherd of this type.

The intentional tempering of the potter's clay with rock detritus (present in stream beds or crushed by the potter) seem likely because the mineral grains are fairly uniform in size and are most abundant in the thicker-walled vessels. Field studies in the area near Gournia would be needed to resolve this problem more effectively (see Chap. 19). The intentional inclusion of the siltstone grains, grading in size from very fine to 3 mm, is possible if, as seen above, one considers the use of the residue from slip preparation. The grain size distribution of the material, judging from the examination of the sherds at low magnification, differs from that of the white and black grains.

Assuming that the inclusions were intentionally added to the clay by the potter, one may estimate the proportions of the two ingredients. Some years ago standard clay briquettes were prepared and fired that contained from five to fifty percent rock by weight. The rock, weathered granite, was of controlled grain size (Matson 1937: 101–102). Using these standards, it is estimated that Gournian sherds 11, 17, and 28 contain about 20% tempering material, while 40 and 47 have but 10%, but it must be emphasized that these are but approximations.

Slip

The dark slip, which is too often described as black, ranges from dark reddish brown to gray or very dark gray in the Munsell system of soil color names. They are low Value and Chroma colors of the 5 Yellow-Red Hue. About half of the twenty-seven sherds examined under a binocular microscope showed some glossy sheen, reflecting light, that indicates a degree of vitrification. Crazing cracks range from slight to extreme, perhaps due to the shrinkage of the slip during drying after application. Firing shrinkage might also be a factor. There was no consistent pattern. On some sherds flakes of the slip curled up around their edges, something like the drying of a mud flat. This could have occurred during the drying of the slip and might suggest that the bond between the unfired slip and body could have been better. The vessel may have been too dry when the slip was applied. The slip is not completely smooth, but contains

TABLE 5-I
Chemical compositions of Gournian EM III and MM sherds

	EM III			MM		
	Body	Dark Slip	White Paint	Body	Dark Slip	White Paint
SiO_2	39.2%	32.9%	36.5%	40.6%	29.0%	35.0%
Al_2O_3	21.6	31.6	25.6	23.8	36.0	28.2
Fe_2O_3	9.8	12.0	9.6	9.2	13.9	10.1
CaO	11.9	8.3	13.2	15.0	8.4	14.5
MgO	11.1	7.3	8.5	5.8	3.2	3.1
Na_2O	1.9	1.8	1.5	0.9	1.7	1.7
K_2O	2.3	3.4	2.0	2.3	5.1	3.5

many fine granules. This suggests that it was prepared by grinding up a raw material, possibly red siltstone as has been suggested in the discussion of inclusions. The SEM photographs show that the slip was far from uniform in quality and was by no means glass-like. The slip on sherd no. 17, fired under reducing conditions, had a much more consolidated surface than some of the other sherds, but it was not glossy.

The chemical analysis of the EM III slip (see Table 5–I) shows that it contains a little less clay and more MgO than does the MM slip. The relative amounts of Al_2O_3, Fe_2O_3 and K_2O are related to the proportion of red clay in the body. The MgO content could again, like the body composition, be related to the inclusions present. It must also be kept in mind as a possibility that the slip could have been prepared from a washed body clay; this process would have removed the major mineral inclusions, other than the clay itself. However, the abundant fine granules seen in the slip do not support this suggestion. Since red siltstone occurred at or near the site, judging from the inclusions in the sherds, it could have been ground to prepare pigment for the decoration of textiles, the human body, ornamental objects, and, of course, the pottery.

Paint

The paint which is conveniently termed white is actually very pale brown in Munsell color. It is in the high Value and low Chroma area of the 10 Yellow-Red Hue. It is granular and is not well preserved in parts of the designs that were painted on the pottery. Miss Hall observed that "The white paint used for the design is sometimes so fugitive that it could be rubbed away with the stroke of a hand, although in general it is more stable than the white paint of the Middle Minoan Period. It frequently has a yellowish tinge" (Hall 1908: 57). In chemical composition (Table 5–I) the paint resembles that of the body but, as might be expected, is richer in CaO.

It is possible that a local marl was used as the "white" pigment, and that it was applied *after* the pottery had been fired. When the decoration is studied under a binocular microscope, it can be readily seen that in the spots where the paint no longer exists, the dark slip is usually *not* discolored, but agrees in color with the surrounding unpainted slipped areas. This certainly indicates that the decoration was a postfiring application. One may compare it with the application of stucco, also a calcareous marl, in the Early Minoan walls at Vasilike. Heaton characterizes it as "dirty yellow in colour and very hard and tenacious, affording an excellent protective finish to the friable sun-dried brick or loose rubble of which the buildings were constructed." He astutely suggested that "the plaster was prepared by mixing lime with a clay of the type known to mineralogists as zeolite . . . the hardness being due not so much to the carbonation of the lime as to the subsequent combination between the two materials with the formation of silicates of lime and alumina" (Heaton 1911: 698). A possible alternative to an unfired white paint, suggested in Chapter 8, involves a second, low firing which would drive off water but would not be high enough to discolor the underlying dark slip.

One might well consider the painted decoration on the pottery as a stucco decoration, for Early Minoan craftsmen carried out more than one kind of activity within the family or village group, much as people do today. One might go a step further and consider the idea that the application of a red clay to pottery in Neolithic and Early Minoan times is analogous to the coating of stucco and plaster walls and floors with a red pigment. Many examples might be cited both on Crete and on mainland Greece, but one will suffice. Pendlebury says in discussing EM II houses and Seager's work at Vasilike, "Above a stone base the walls were constructed of sun-dried bricks tied together vertically and horizontally with wooden beams. The whole was covered with rough line plaster and a fine surface wash of deep red, which formed a stucco as hard as cement and was really a structural feature" (Pendlebury 1954: 27). An Early Minoan householder could build and stucco walls, make pottery, plough fields, and carry out many other of life's activities at different times of the year!

Scanning Electron Microscope (SEM) Studies

Freshly fractured chips broken from the edges of sherds, coated with gold, and then examined in a vacuum at high magnifications can at times provide useful information that may be of help in better understanding the physical and mineralogical characteristics of the pottery being studied. SEM photographs are of value in assessing the nature and state of the slip and clay structure and the appearance of inclusions that through the chance of fracture are present in the chip's surface. For a thorough study in an archaeological ceramics project such as this, clays from the site should be collected, prepared, fired under controlled oxidizing and reducing atmospheric conditions to several increasingly higher temperatures, and then sampled for SEM examination. The results of such tests would help in the interpretation of the potsherd SEM explorations, but unfortunately the precise clays used by the potters at Gournia have not been identified (see Chap. 15).

The SEM photographs it is possible to include in this report on plates 5–7 show the appearance at a selected spot with increasing magnification of the body and slip of sherds 11 and 17, and the body and inclusions of sherds 28 and 40. In general, the center of the frame at the lower magnification will fill the entire frame at the next higher magnification. One must be cautioned that in viewing SEM photographs, the whiter edge areas do not indicate reaction zones or a change in constitution, but usually represent the luminescence from the electrical charge that builds up most rapidly on the sharper and thinner edges.

Plate 5 A, B, C: The fabric of sherd 11 at magnifications of 30, 1000, and 2500 ×.

5 A. Fractured edge of the sherd. Slipped surface is at the top of the frame. Note that the holes in the body often have rectangular corners and convex or concave sides. These are not the characteristic shape of air pockets and could be due to the poor wedging of a not too plastic clay body. Inclusions in the upper right and lower left areas of the frame shrank during firing, leaving a thin air envelope between them and the matrix. They may be fragments of siltstone or of the darker red grains.

5 B. Characteristic sintering of clay platelets in a calcareous body fired to moderate temperatures. Cleavage faces of hornblende or chloritic grains appear in the center of the frame. A vesicular structure due to thermal decomposition is evident.

5 C. Detail of vesicular structure. Characteristic cleavage angles of 124° and 56° can be seen. They are especially clear in the area between the two largest bubbles.

Plate 5 D, E, F: Dark slipped surface of sherd 11 at magnifications of 180, 2500, and 7500 ×.

5 D. The slipped area is above a diagonal line from the lower left to the upper right corners of the frame. Below this line is the fractured edge of the chip. The slip has some smooth flat areas, but it is largely granular or sintered in nature.

5 E. The irregular surface can be seen at this higher magnification to have many regions of overlapping platelets. These platelets are probably the sintered powder obtained by grinding red siltstone. The slipped surface can hardly be termed vitrified.

5 F. The angular nature of the platelets at 7500 × magnification and the irregular course of the crack attest to the lack of vitrification. A conchoidal fracture would be the expected form in a more glassy slip.

Plate 6 A, B, C: Dark slipped surface of a cup, sherd 17, that was fired under reducing conditions. Magnifications of 100, 1000, and 10,000 ×.

6 A. Reasonably smooth slip surface at slightly less magnification than that of sherd 11 seen on plate 5D. Reducing conditions aided better vitrification. The slip on both sherds showed slight crazing under a binocular microscope. That of 17 had developed some shrinkage cracks with the result that there was slight flaking of the surface. It was more glossy and more finely scoraceous than 11.

6 B. Slipped surface (lower left and bottom of the frame). The core can be seen at the top of the frame to have been quite vitrified at the spot examined, with round gas holes developing.

6 C. The slip at a magnification of 10,000 × shows a unified vitreous structure within discrete areas. The edges of the platelets are subrounded.

Plate 6 D, E, F: Fabric of thin body sherd no. 40. Magnifications of 30, 1250, and 5000 ×.

6 D. Minute inclusions of two kinds are common. The dark ones are more globular in shape, suggesting that they approached their melting point during the firing of the sherd. The remnants of a large oval and laminated (sedimentary) grain are at the bottom of the frame.

6 E. The vesicular structure is apparent. Very fine grained reaction products are on the surfaces of the clay platelets. At the right center the scoraceous nature of the vitrifying clay is evident from the multitude of minute gas holes.

6 F. Cleavage plates of hornblende that have begun to decompose. This thermal decomposition can be seen both as a channel in the outer plate and at its lower left edge. Many cleavage markings are on its surface. A cluster of hornblende platelets is visible near the upper left corner. Their upper ends rest like a deck of cards on the large decomposing plate.

Plate 7 A, B, C: Bridge spouted jar, sherd no. 28, at magnifications of 30, 500, and 3000 ×. The sherd contains many red angular inclusions that have a laminated structure.

7 A. An overlapping combination of two prints shows much of the edge of the sherd chip. Many relatively large and almost rectangular inclusions in the matrix show a lamellar sedimentary origin and contain few cracks parallel to the plane of deposition. These are probably red siltstone inclusions. The more granular nature of the surrounding clay body is apparent. The abundant flattened holes in the matrix may represent voids left when organic materials burned out, rather than air pockets.

7 B. The upper portion of this frame can be recognized in pl. 7A as the base of the conchoidally fractured chip in the top center of that frame. This chip is a portion of a red siltstone inclusion. At a magnification of 500 × it can be seen to be partly vitrified. It is interesting to note the individual platelets in the lower portion of the frame that were freed when the fracture occurred as the chip was removed from the sherd for SEM study.

7 C. The clay platelets at a magnification of 3000 × show considerable coalescence, rounded edges, and possibly reaction products on their surfaces that developed during firing.

Plate 7 D, E: Additional inclusions in sherd no. 28. Magnifications of 700 and 1500 ×.

7 D. Two ovoid grains with scaley surfaces appear in the upper right corner. They are probably red clay pellets, and show some shrinkage away from the clay matrix. A stack of hornblende plates can be recognized at the lower left. The clay body does not appear to be as advanced in its incipient vitrification as is that of the red clay inclusion seen in pl. 7B.

7 E. At this higher magnification the platelets of weathered and probably thermally decomposing hornblende can be observed in both a face and an end view that would interest mineralogists. Cleavage traces at the characteristic 124° are quite evident on the major plate.

Production

The manufacture of pottery during EM III is of technological interest, for its study may provide clues indicating some of the steps along the way toward the later Cretan and Greek ceramic achievements. Some observations relating to the selection and preparation of the raw materials for the body, slip, and paint have already been offered. Further and possibly more specific comments will appear in other chapters. Notes relating to the forming and firing of the Gournian White-on-dark Ware will conclude these comments on the physical characteristics of this pottery.

The handmade fashioning of the vessels in this group was noted by Miss Hall, who reported that "The ware seems to have been hand-made. At least there are no certain traces of the wheel either on the bottom fragments or the inner surfaces of fragments from the sides of vases. The lines, on the contrary, are disjoined, as if the revolution of the vase had been slow, and the transition from neck to rim as in the amphora-like vessels is gradual, not sharp. The shapes, however, are regular, and sometimes, especially in the case of cups, are fashioned of very thin clay" (Hall 1908: 57). These observations, made about seventy-five years ago, are accurate and valid today.

Some form of mold may have been used by the potters for the initial forming of the vessel base and lower walls. Experience and skill are needed to make vessels such as the thin-walled conical and rounded cups that form the dominant EM III ware at Gournia. Could stone bowls, common at that time, have served as molds? A ball of clay could have been worked in a stone bowl until the vessel walls were of the proper thinness. Ash could have been sprinkled on the interior of the bowl so that the clay would not adhere to it firmly. As the clay began to dry, it would shrink and draw away from the mold and could be removed. This might have been an early form of mass production.

The interior shape and dimensions of Early Minoan stone bowls from Myrtos were compared with the vessel forms and dimensions of pottery cups from the same site in order to test this suggestion. The scales of the excellent drawings in Warren's two volumes were adjusted so that direct comparisons could be made (Warren 1969; 1972). It would be tedious to report in detail on this fascinating excursus, but in brief, one can find striking similarities in dimensions between the interior of several of the stone vessels (such as the Bird's Nest Bowls, Blossom Bowls, and other selected bowls, cups, and jars) and those of the Period II ceramic bowls. The shapes of the rims should not be emphasized, for they can readily be finished by the potter in several ways once the major vessel form has been established and is sufficiently dry to permit manipulation. The dimensions found to be most useful in this matching game were the interior basal and rim diameters and the interior heights of the stone vessels, compared with the exterior basal and rim diameters and vessel height of the pottery cups. One certainly cannot insist that stone bowls were used as molds. Wooden and clay vessels and even baskets could have been used to help form the bottoms and lower wall areas of the thin cups, which would be difficult to manipulate while the clay was plastic. Coil building on a basal pat would be a useful process for the larger thicker-walled vessels.

To test this suggestion of the use of molds, I examined the exterior surfaces of the five Gournia sherds I had available for detailed study, although rim sherds are not ideal for this purpose. It was assumed that traces of the shape and possibly texture of the supporting mold wall might be retained as a negative cast on the exterior surfaces of early pottery. The sherd surfaces were examined under a binocular microscope in a dark room using a narrow beam of light from an intense source. The sherds were manipulated so that the light struck the several parts of their surfaces at raking angle. This accentuated surface markings and provided suggestive clues. The data obtained are far from definitive, but the detailed notes from the extended observation of the surfaces are on file should a similar study be undertaken for an appropriate early site from which a sizable number of sherds can be studied. The cup sherds, nos. 17 and 40, had unusually smooth exterior surfaces. Only brush marks from the application of the slip were visible. Rounded cup sherd no. 47 had very faint traces of a herringbone weave in bands 3 mm in width that might suggest a mat impression. Bridge spouted jar sherds nos. 11 and 28 had inclusions protruding from their exterior surfaces which could indicate that the clay was pressed against a soft or resilient surface as the vessel was formed. Surface smoothing during the finishing process might abrade away fine soft clay particles, leaving such protrusions. Twine impressions were clearly visible below the exterior rim of no. 11. They suggest the use of a basket or a piece of coarse fabric to support the vessel wall while its interior surface was being worked. These comments are only suggestive, but indicate that similar more extensive studies for suitably designed purposes might be considered.

Firing

Little information is yet available about Early Minoan kilns, but the present archaeological interest in small village site studies and a concern for excavated details not directly concerned with house plans may result in the recognition of more hearth or kiln sites. It is indeed difficult to attribute them to pottery production because sherds and kiln debris are usually lacking. However, this is often true of the areas around the kilns of village potters today. They are completely cleaned out soon after the firing has been completed. Only if a kiln is unexpectedly abandoned before it is completely emptied can one expect to obtain sure evidence of the use of the structure and its date.

A Neolithic kiln excavated by D. M. Robinson's crew at Olynthus fifty-three years ago was published by G. E. Mylonas. In his clear report he identifies a small red-burned basin with four channels as a kiln (Mylonas 1929: 12–19). Other early Aegean kilns are listed by J. M. Cook (1961), and Costis Davaras (1973; 1980) has recently published a detailed analysis of a round kiln he excavated in 1978 near Palaikastro on the eastern coast of Crete. In the light of the available kiln evidence, which he thoroughly summarizes, he assigns his kiln to Middle Minoan III–Late Minoan I before the LM IB destruction of the town. The kiln has no hearth, but it contains "a large well-cut shelf round the circumference of the chamber but stopping short each side of the entrance" (Davaras 1980: 120). He suggests that the pottery was placed on this shelf during the firing of the ware. If so, this is a major technological step from the firing of pottery in a hearth surrounded by fuel toward the use of a kiln chamber with a perforated floor to support the ware and a firing chamber for the fuel beneath it. The shelf structure would be most interesting to consider with respect to the amount of pottery that could be fired at one time and the effect of variation in firing conditions on the vessels, with one side exposed to the flames and the other near the chamber wall.

The range in firing temperatures of a ware depends on a great many factors related to the kiln design, the fuel used, the duration of the firing, and the manner in which the ware has been loaded in the kiln. A hearth like that at Neolithic Olynthus, a Palaikastro shelf support, and a simple updraft kiln with a hearth will produce different effects and temperature distributions. The techniques for estimating the firing temperatures of individual sherds are developing rapidly, as Maniatis demonstrates in Chapter 9. Maniatis estimates, based on SEM studies, that the firing temperatures of five of the eight sherds he tested ranged from 850° to 1050° C. Such a distribution would be normal for much of the pottery of the ancient Near East (Matson 1971).

Another approach is that of Barron, who presents a good discussion of firing temperatures from the standpoint of a professional potter. He measured the change in porosity of several sherds from Myrtos when they were refired at increasingly higher temperatures and concluded that "None of these sherds were fired above 1000° C and some were considerably lower than this. 9 out of 14 were probably fired below 880° C" (Barron 1972: 336).

As more physical scientists become interested in archaeometric problems it should be possible to develop a cooperative program between them and the archaeologists responsible for excavating and publishing pottery. If the problems are clearly defined before the work is undertaken, and acceptable samples can be obtained for study, the results should contribute not only to our knowledge of technological ceramic development, but also to our better understanding of the people who made and used the pottery.

Notes

1. Thanks are extended to The Pennsylvania State University for assistance and facilities in the research presented here.

References

Barron, P. 1972. Attempt to determine the Firing Temperature of Pottery Sherds. In Warren 1972: 333–40.

Cook, R. M. 1961. The double stoking tunnel of Greek kilns. *BSA* 56: 64–67.

Davaras, C. 1973. Μινωική κεραμεική κάμινος εἰς Στύλον Χανίων. *Arch Eph*: 75–80.

Davaras, C. 1980. A Minoan Pottery Kiln at Palaikastro. *BSA* 75: 115–26.

Hall, E. H. 1908. Early Minoan III Ware from the North Trench. In Hawes et al. 1908: 57.

Hawes, H. B., B. E. Williams, R. B. Seager, and E. H. Hall. 1908. *Gournia, Vasiliki and other Prehistoric Sites on the Isthmus of Hierapetra, Crete*. Philadelphia.

Heaton, N. 1911. Minoan Lime-Plaster and Fresco Painting. *JRIBA* 18: 697–710.

London, G. 1981. Dung-tempered clay. *JFA* 8: 189–95.

Matson, F. R. 1937. Pottery. In *The Younge Site, an Archaeological Record from Michigan*, by Emerson F. Greenman. Occasional Contributions from the Museum of Anthropology of the University of Michigan No. 6: 99–124.

Matson, F. R. 1971. A Study of Temperatures used in Firing Ancient Mesopotamian Pottery. In *Science and Archeology*, ed. Robert H. Brill, 65–79. Cambridge, Mass.

Munsell Soil Color Charts, 1975 edition. Baltimore.

Mylonas, G. E. 1929. *Excavations at Olynthus. Part I. The Neolithic Settlement*. Baltimore.

Pendlebury, J. D. S. 1954. *A Handbook to the Palace of Minos at Knossos with its Dependencies*. London.

Warren, P. 1969. *Minoan Stone Vases*. London.

Warren, P. 1972. *Myrtos. An Early Bronze Age Settlement in Crete*. London.

6

Ceramic Petrography

George H. Myer

Sherds from the following sites were examined by petrographic thin section (for individual descriptions of the sherds see the Appendix). With the exception of Group 2, all are of White-on-dark Ware.
1. Gournia, EM III (31 samples)
2. Gournia, MM I–III (16 samples)
3. Mokhlos, EM III (7 samples)
4. Vasilike, EM III (6 samples)
5. Priniatikos Pyrgos, MM I (1 sample)
6. East Crete, EM III (1 sample)
7. Knossos, EM III (2 samples)

Where insufficient material was available for conventional sample preparation, the sherd chip was encapsulated in epoxy resin before the sawing and grinding. The resulting thin sections were studied under a polarizing microscope. Artificial samples manufactured from east Cretan clays were also made, fired to 800° C, and examined as thin sections. For comparison purposes, small chips from four sherds from Gournia were powdered and analyzed by X-ray diffraction analysis (Penn MS 4615–10, 13, 16, and 47). Only quartz and plagioclase were present in sufficient quantities to yield distinctive X-ray patterns.

1. Gournia, EM III

Since Gournia is the type site for White-on-dark Ware from eastern Crete, a group of 31 sherds was examined from this site. All sherds contained inclusions, with some material apparently added as temper to the raw clay. These inclusions make the hardness of the fabric variable, in the range of 2–3 on Moh's scale. Both color and degree of vitrification also vary considerably, with most sherds in the range of the Munsell Yellow-Red Hues from yellow to very pale brown to red. Reduced sherds are more gray. Slight swirls and waves, as if two clays of different colors were imperfectly mixed, are visible in some samples. Colors of individual sherds are given in the catalogue of analyzed sherds in the Appendix.

The inclusions are of considerable interest (Table 6–1). Their shapes are mostly in the subrounded to subangular range, with sizes from microscopic to half a centimeter. Particles include quartz, plagioclase, hornblende, and sometimes biotite. Olivine has been recognized in four samples. Rock fragments (cryptocrystalline quartz, particles containing two or more of the above minerals and pale colored claystone and siltstone) may also be present. While fragments appear even in the finest cups, in general the larger vessels (especially the bridge spouted jars) are coarser than the small shapes. This situation indicates a deliberate tempering of the clay body, but the presence of fine particles of the same minerals in the cups (and even in the dark slip) shows that at least some of the same minerals were obviously present in small amounts even when no tempering was intended.

The mineral inclusions are compatible with a residual clay soil profile developed on a metamorphic calc-silicate rock formation. Similar inclusions have been noted in pottery from nearby Vasilike, from EM IIB (by Myer, in Betancourt et al. 1979: 5 Table I). The shapes of some of the particles allow the possibility that the material was partly crushed before being added to the clay body, but most particles are completely natural, with very slightly rounded contours.

TABLE 6-I
Inclusions larger than 10 micrometers in sherds from EM III Gournia

Museum	Number	Quartz	Plagio-clase	Biotite	Yellow-Red Hornblende	Yellow-Green Hornblende	Rock Frags.	Olivine	Average size of temper in micrometers
Penn	MS 4615-6	X	X	X	X	--	X	--	50-250
	MS 4615-7	X	X	--	X	--	X	--	50-200
	MS 4615-8	X	X	X	--	--	X	--	50-200
	MS 4615-9	X	X	--	X	--	X	--	50-100
	MS 4615-10	X	X	--	X	--	X	--	50-200
	MS 4615-11	X	X A P	X	X	--	X	X	50-250
	MS 4615-12	X	X A P	--	X	--	X	--	50-200
	MS 4615-13	X	X P	X	--	X	X P	--	50-500
	MS 4615-15	--	--	--	--	--	--	--	--
	MS 4615-16	X	X A P	X	X	X A	X P	--	200-500
	MS 4615-17	X	X	--	X	--	X	--	50-200
	MS 4615-18	X P	X P	X	X P	--	X P	--	200-500
	MS 4615-20	X P	X A P	X	X P	--	X P	--	50-250
	MS 4615-21	X P	X A P	X	--	--	X P	--	50-250
	MS 4615-22	X P	X P	X	X P	--	X P	--	50-200
	MS 4615-23	X P	X P	X	X	--	X P	--	50-250
	MS 4615-24	X	X A P	X	X P	X	X P	X	50-250
	MS 4615-25	X	X P	X	X	--	X P	X	200-700
	MS 4615-26	X P	X P	X	X P	X	X P	--	50-250
	MS 4615-27	X	X A P	X	X P	--	X P	--	50-250
	MS 4615-29	X	X	X	X S	--	X	--	50-250
	MS 4615-31	X	X	X	X S	X	X	--	50-200
	MS 4615-32	X	X P	--	--	--	X	--	50-500
	MS 4615-33	X P	X A P	X	X S P	--	X P	--	200-500
	MS 4615-34	X	X P	X	X P	--	X	X	50-200
	MS 4615-35	--	--	--	--	--	--	--	--
	MS 4615-37	X P	X A P	X	X S	X	X P	--	50-200
	MS 4615-39	X	X P	X	X	--	X P	--	50-200
	MS 4615-43	X	X A P	X	X	--	X P	--	50-200
	MS 4615-44	X	X P	X	X	X	X P	--	50-200
	MS 4615-47	X	X P	X	X S	X	X P	--	50-500

Key: A – Altered S – Strongly Pleochroic P – Plentiful X – Present -- Absent

The Gournian clay body also includes clay lumps. They are rounded to subrounded in shape, with a color that is usually red to black. Their texture is rougher than the matrix, and they have usually shrunk slightly with firing, so that they have pulled away from the surrounding clay. In some cases they are vesicular, indicating their vitrification temperature is lower than that of the matrix. The rounded contours and an occasional deformation indicate they were in a plastic state when the vases were made. Their usual color, redder than the matrix, suggests a higher iron content than the surrounding clay fabric. The high iron content can explain the vitrification because under reducing conditions iron oxide acts as a flux, lowering the melting temperature.

Tests with east Cretan clays show that lumps like those in the Gournian fabrics are formed when two dissimilar clays are partially mixed, especially when one of them is a terra rossa, the iron rich red lateritic soil found throughout much of the region of the

TABLE 6-II
Inclusions in MM I–III sherds from Gournia

Museum No.	Quartz	Plagio-clase	Bio-tite	Yellow-red Hornblende	Yellow-green Hornblende	Rock Frags.	Aver. size of temper in micrometers
Gournia (MM I-III)							
Group 2 A							
Penn MS 4628-6	X	--	--	--	--	--	--
Penn MS 4628-9	X	X	--	--	--	--	--
Penn MS 4628-13	X	X	--	--	--	--	--
Penn MS 4628-15	X	X	--	--	--	--	--
Penn MS 4628-20	X	X	--	--	--	--	--
Penn MS 4628-21	X	X	--	--	--	--	--
Penn MS 4628-22	--	--	--	--	--	--	--
Penn MS 4700-1	--	--	--	--	--	--	--
Penn MS 4700-3	--	--	--	--	--	--	--
Penn MS 4700-5	--	--	--	--	--	--	--
Penn MS 4700-10	X	X	--	--	--	--	--
Group 2 B							
Penn MS 4628-19	X	X	--	--	--	--	20-40
Group 2C							
Penn MS 4628-3	XP	XP	X	--	--	X	50-150
Penn MS 4628-7	X	X	--	X	--	X	200-400
Penn MS 4628-14	X	X	--	--	X	--	200-400
Penn MS 4700-9	X	X	X	--	X	X	150-400

For the key see Table 6-I.

Isthmus of Ierapetra and elsewhere in Crete (see Chap. 15). Since the two clays do not blend uniformly, small terra rossa lumps become suspended in the more uniform matrix. Firing tests of clay bodies made from terra rossa and white east Cretan marine clays resulted in fabrics similar to those in the Gournian sherds.

The dark slip varies from 20 to 50 micrometers in thickness. It is dense and finer than the matrix, but it sometimes includes small fragments of quartz or plagioclase. It adheres well to the underlying clay, much better than the white paint (for the white paint see Chaps. 5 and 8).

One can thus conclude that the potters at Gournia used a minimum of three materials for their clay bodies, two clays (with one probably being a terra rossa) and a tempering material composed of stone particles. The temper was probably found as a coarse sand, and it was only slightly crushed before being added to the pottery.

2. *Gournia, MM I–III.*

A group of Middle Minoan samples from Gournia provides a useful comparison with the EM III material from the same site. While many of the later sherds are not as closely datable as the EM III ones, they are all clearly later than the first group, coming from MM IB to MM III. Both cups and larger shapes are represented in the second group. All of the sherds were chosen (by P. Betancourt) as representative of local

TABLE 6-III
Inclusions in EM III sherds from Mokhlos

Museum No.	Quartz	Plagio-clase	Bio-tite	Yellow-red Horn-blende	Yellow-green Hornblende	Rock Frags.	Aver. size of temper in micro-meters
3. Mokhlos							
Group 3A							
MFA 09.557	—	—	—	—	—	—	—
09.575bisAp1	—	—	—	—	—	—	—
Group 3B							
MFA 09.575	X	X	—	—	—	—	50-120
Group 3C							
MFA 09.573	XP	XP	XP	—	XP	XP	250-400
09.574	XP	XP	XP	—	XP	XP	250-400
09.575bisAp2	XP	XP	XP	—	XP	XP	250-400
09.575bisAp3	XP	XP	—	—	XP	XP	100-200

Gournian MM pottery. They are all covered with dark slip with decoration in white or white and red paint.

The samples may be divided into three groups on the basis of fabric (Table 6–2):
2A. Untempered.
2B. Containing fine inclusions, possibly deliberate additions.
2C. Stone tempered.

All samples have clay lumps of the type found in EM III, and most have tiny fragments of quartz and/or plagioclase. The matrix is composed of microcrystalline particles, mostly under 20 micrometers in size, with irregular to rectangular shapes having interlocking boundaries with crystalline phases varying both in refractive index and in pleochroism (some highly pleochroic and with strong absorption color and others lightly colored in the yellows and yellow-reds). Some phases may be iron oxide/hydroxide; others may be hornblende. Air voids, which occur in all samples, are irregular or flattened parallel to the slip. The dark slip has less variation than in EM III.

It is very regular, about 20 micrometers thick, and dense.

Groups 2 and 3 have inclusions of the same minerals used as temper in EM III. Temper shapes vary considerably within each sherd, from rounded through subrounded and subangular to angular, but the range is well within the EM III range for this site. No cryptocrystalline quartz or pale siltstone was noted. Sample MS 4700–9 contains epidote particles.

In general, the Middle Minoan samples represent a definite shift in ceramic technology at Gournia. The potters now distinguish between a fine, untempered fabric for some small shapes and coarser clay bodies with stone particles for larger vessels (shapes of sherds are noted in the Appendix). The EM III fabric technology has been retained only for the larger shapes, while a new, untempered body is adopted for the fine wheelmade pieces. The dark slip is also more uniform in thickness from sample to sample, and perhaps more standardized measures (like dipping?) were employed in its application.

3. Mokhlos, EM III

Seven samples from Mokhlos were examined. While their basic fabric is not unlike the EM III fabric from Gournia, only some of the sherds are tempered.

The samples from Mokhlos consist of both tempered and untempered fabrics (Table 6–III):
3A. Untempered.
3B. Containing fine inclusions, possibly deliberate additions.
3C. Stone tempered.

The matrix is similar to that of the pottery from Gournia. It contains clay lumps and voids, often flattened parallel to the slip. The dark slip, measurable

TABLE 6-IV
Inclusions in EM III sherds from Vasilike

Museum No.	Quartz	Plagioclase	Biotite	Yellow-red Hornblende	Yellow-green Hornblende	Rock Frags.	Aver. size of temper in micrometers
Vasilike							
Penn MS 4234	X	X	--	X	--	--	10-30
Penn MS 4236	X	XAP	XP	XP	XP	XP	350-400
Penn MS 4237	--	XAP	X	XP	XP	XP	200-250
Penn MS 4238	X	XAP	XP	X	--	XP	100-250
MHC BAI 14A	X	XAP	XP	XP	XP	XP	100-600
MHC BAI 14B	X	X	X	X	X	X	10-50

on two sherds, is 50 micrometers thick. When included particles are present, they are rounded to subrounded to subangular, within the range of the Gournian pottery. Except for the absence of yellow-red hornblende, which may not be significant for such a small sample, the tempered pottery from Mokhlos cannot be distinguished from that of Gournia. Untempered sherds, however, are rare in the EM III samples from Gournia which have been examined here.

4. Vasilike, EM III

Samples from Vasilike were analyzed by the same methods used for the pottery from Gournia. The small group (six samples) included both fine grained cups (Penn MS 4234 and MHC BAI 14B) and coarser bowls and other shapes (remaining samples). The results are presented in Table 6–IV.

Many similarities exist between the White-on-dark Ware of Vasilike and Gournia. The groups have the same ranges in hardness, texture, color, thickness, and types of slips. Rounded clay lumps occur in all samples examined. Voids (air pockets), usually irregular and flattened, also occur in both groups. As at Gournia, the main nonplastic inclusions at Vasilike are quartz, plagioclase feldspar, biotite, hornblende, and rock fragments made up of smaller pieces of two or more of these minerals. The samples all belong to the same ware on mineralogical as well as on stylistic grounds.

TABLE 6-V
Inclusions in sherds from Priniatikos Pyrgos, East Crete, and Knossos

Museum No.	Quartz	Plagioclase	Biotite	Yellow-red Hornblende	Yellow-green Hornblende	Rock Frags.	Aver. size of temper in micrometers
Priniatikos Pyrgos (MM I)							
Penn MS 4894	--	X	--	X	--	X	100-250
East Crete (EM III)							
Penn 60-19-14	XP	XP	--	--	XP	XP	200-500
Knossos (EM III)							
AM AE 752	--	--	--	--	--	--	--
AM AE 753.4	--	--	--	--	--	--	--

Some differences, however, exist. No olivine was noted in the samples from Vasilike, and the rock fragments from there did not include cryptocrystalline quartz or pale-colored siltstone. One sample from Vasilike had quartz with acicular inclusions, a feature not seen in any of the Gournian sherds (Penn MS 4238). In addition, the inclusions at Vasilike are clearly more angular than at Gournia. While the range at each site is sufficient to create some overlap, so that a few individual samples are generally similar, the greater angularity at Vasilike sets the group as a whole somewhat apart. The most likely conclusion is that the stones used for temper at Vasilike were crushed more completely than those used at Gournia, and this difference plus the small variation in the rock fragments suggests the two groups do not come from the same manufacturing source.

The EM III smples from Vasilike are very similar to EM IIB samples of Vasilike Ware from the same site (Myer in Betancourt et al. 1979:5). Both the tempering material and the overall appearance of the fabric in thin section suggest a similar type of clay body. It would seem that the late Early Minoan clay bodies at Vasilike were prepared in traditional ways, with generally similar results from EM IIB to III.

5. *Priniatikos Pyrgos, MM I*

One sample from a rounded cup with handle from Priniatikos Pyrgos was available for study. The matrix, with clay lumps indicating a blending of clays, is typical of east Cretan pottery at this period. Very few inclusions were present (Table 6–V). Many of them were angular, indicating crushing, and they were most likely added as temper. No quartz was noted, but a substantial number of the particles were hornblende (more than in the other sherds examined). The sherd is thus quite different from the other east Cretan groups. Slip was not present on the sample.

6. *East Crete, EM III*

One sherd from an unidentified site in eastern Crete was examined. It came from a conical bowl (Table 6–V). The fabric is within the range of EM III Gournia. It was fired high enough for the clay lumps to become vesicular from initial vitrification, and so the sample is a little harder and more compact than usual. Inclusions, which are numerous, include quartz, plagioclase, hornblende, and rock fragments containing more than one of these minerals. Some of the particles are angular enough to indicate crushing. The dark slip is 20 micrometers thick.

7. *Knossos, EM III*

Knossos, in north central Crete, is the most important site from Bronze Age Crete. Two samples of its White-on-dark Ware were studied by petrographic thin section. Both were of fine grained pottery, typical of EM III–MM I Knossian fine ware. The results are shown in Table 6–V.

The Knossian fabric is very different from that of the analyzed pottery of eastern Crete. It is uniform and fine grained, composed of particles of several materials from under 40 micrometers to under 1 micrometer in size. No clay lumps or coarse tempering materials are present. The color is more pale than is usual for eastern Crete, and the hardness is about 2 by Moh's scale. Dark slip is visible on one thin section (AM no. AE 752). It is 40 micrometers thick, anisotropic, with tiny particles included in it.

The White-on-dark Ware of Knossos is easily distinguished from that of the north coast of the Isthmus of Ierapetra. Knossian clay bodies used for the samples analyzed were obviously prepared differently from those of Gournia, Vasilike, Priniatikos Pyrgos, and Mokhlos, and the absence of clay lumps suggests that the Knossian potters did not use a blend of the same clays used at the eastern sites. Certainly stone temper was not added to the sherds examined, although eastern Cretan pots in this size range would often have been tempered at this period. The differences are sufficient to regard the Knossian samples as examples of a different fabric.

Conclusions

The pottery from the north coast of the Isthmus of Ierapetra is part of a regional style which may be distinguished on the basis of distinctive clay bodies as well as by style. The fabric contains clay lumps which probably indicate a blending of clays, presumably a white marine clay and an iron-rich terra rossa (for the practice in modern times see Chaps. 17 and 18). In addition, tiny fragments of quartz and plagioclase may often be recognized in the untempered fabric. Other particles in the matrix in the under 20 micrometer range were not identifiable.

To this matrix the potters added a number of coarser stone tempers. Since the composition and/or shape of the temper varies from site to site, one can make some distinctions between the productions at different locations: at Gournia the EM III temper may include cryptocrystalline quartz or pale claystone or siltstone fragments; at Vasilike the particles are crushed more thoroughly than at Gournia; at Priniatikos Pyrgos the temper includes an abundance of hornblende. These and other local differences probably indicate a series of local manufacturing centers rather than a single source for the pottery examined here.

The extent of the east Cretan region which has been isolated here is not known. It certainly does not extend to Knossos in central Crete where the untempered fabric is very different and may not have been blended as in the east.

7

Mössbauer Investigation of the Fabric

N.-H. J. Gangas and Th. Bakas

Mössbauer spectroscopy is a relatively recent addition to the various physical techniques used in archaeometry (Kostikas et al. 1976). This technique is based on the recoiless nuclear resonance of gamma rays. The effect was discovered in 1958 by R. Mössbauer and allows us to measure the energy of a nuclear state with the extreme accuracy of $1:10^{12}$. Thus, information about the chemical valence, the crystallographic environment, the magnetic state, and the dynamics of the Mössbauer atom in a solid matrix can be obtained.

Iron is present in clays in amounts up to about 15%. Thus, the isotope ^{57}Fe (2% atomic abundance), which is the most widely used Mössbauer nucleus, presents a sensitive probe for investigating the physical and chemical state of the iron phases in clay as well as their transformations upon firing the clay to pottery. On the basis of the knowledge gained from such studies (Coey 1980; Maniatis et al. 1981), it is now possible to use Mössbauer spectra of ancient pottery sherds to obtain information about the firing atmosphere and temperature and the refractory properties and other characteristics of the clay used.

In the present work[1] we present the results of a Mössbauer investigation of the fabric of sherds from the following fragments:

Penn no. MS 4615–26. Bridge spouted jar, from Gournia. See Appendix, no. 28 (pl. 19).

Penn no. MS 4615–27. Bridge spouted jar, from Gournia. See Appendix, no. 29 (pl. 19).

Penn no. 60–19–14. Open bowl, from eastern Crete. See Appendix, no. 75. (pl. 22).

Powder samples of mass thickness ~80 mg/cm² were prepared from the middle region of the sherd cross section, thus avoiding contributions from the outer and inner surfaces of the ware. Mössbauer spectra were obtained for sample temperatures from 4.2 K up to 300 K. Spectra at room temperature (~300 K) were also obtained for powder samples prepared after refiring at two temperatures (900° C and 1100° C) solid pieces of the sherds in air. The refiring, for four hours, was performed in order to determine roughly the temperature at which these sherds were fired and get some information about the refractory properties of the clays used (see below).

The measurements were carried out in transmission geometry using a constant acceleration spectrometer and a ^{57}Co in Rh-matrix gamma-ray source. Representative Mössbauer spectra of the sherds are shown in figure 7–1. Each spectrum measured in the present work has been analyzed by computer fiting routines which calculated theoretical spectra comprising the contributions of up to five iron sites of paramagnetic and/or magnetic type. Each site of the former type contributes a doublet of absorption lines to the Mössbauer spectrum, while the latter type contributes a sextet of lines (see stick diagrams in fig. 7–1).

Results on the Samples

The Mössbauer parameter values determined from the above analysis allowed the identification of the different iron phases present in each of the three pottery sherds. These results, presented in the form of the diagrams of figure 7–2, are described and discussed below:

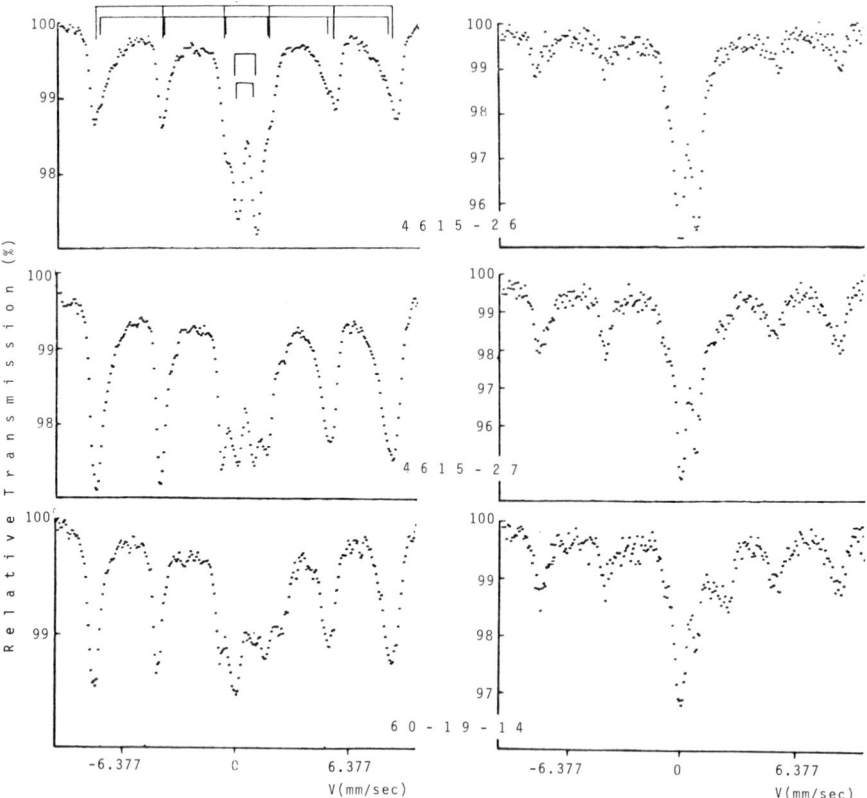

Fig. 7–1. Mössbauer spectra of the as received samples at 4.2 K (left column) and 74 K (right column). The stick diagrams on the upper left spectrum represent the positions of two sextets and two doublets required to fit this spectrum. The other spectra of this figure required other combinations of sextets and/or doublets.

Sherd MS 4615–26 (fig. 7–2a) About 40% of the iron in the fabric occurs as paramagnetic trivalent iron (Fe^{3+}) ions, while the rest is in the form of magnetically ordered Fe_2O_3. These oxide particles normally contribute a sextet of absorption lines in the Mössbauer spectrum. If, however, their size is less than about 500 Å = 0.0005 micrometers, they show paramagnetic behavior, and thus, a doublet appears in the spectrum instead of a sextet whenever the sample temperature exceeds a certain value which is proportional to their volume. Therefore, the sharp decrease observed in fig. 7–2a between 4.2 K and 74 K in the amount of the sextet component reveals that about half of the Fe_2O_3 particles of this sherd are in the form of very fine particles of about 50Å diameter. From these findings it follows that the atmosphere was oxidizing during most of the firing cycling and the clay used had a major part (~40%) of its total iron as trivalent (Fe^{3+}) ions bonded in the structure of the clay mineral platelets.

Sherd MS 4615–27 (fig. 7–2b): The amount of the iron ions bonded in the clay structure is, in this case, only 20%. Half of these ions are divalent (Fe^{2+}). This fact and the presence of magnetite (Fe_3O_4) as the major oxide-phase indicate that a reducing atmosphere prevailed during the firing cycle. We may also note that about half of the trivalent iron oxides (Fe_2O_3) are in the form of very fine particles.

Sherd 60–19–14 (fig. 7–2c.): A large portion (~35%) of the total iron of this sherd, too, is structural, as trivalent (Fe^{3+}) and divalent (Fe^{2+}) ions. The field of the magnetically stable oxides consists of about equal amounts of hematite (α-Fe_2O_3) and magnetite (Fe_3O_4) particles. The Fe_2O_3 particles showing superparamagnetic behavior are about 50 Å in diameter. They represent only ~15% of the total iron. From these findings we deduce that the reducing atmosphere was not extended during the firing cycle and the clay mixture is probably different from the mixtures used for the production of the previous two sherds.

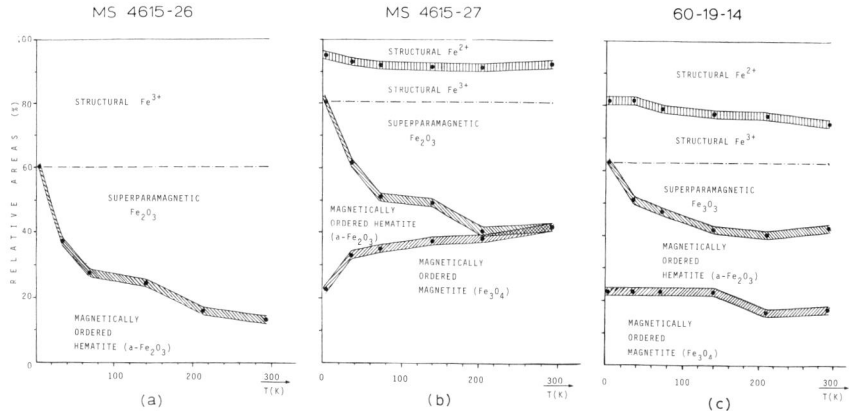

Fig. 7–2. Relative areas of spectral components plotted versus measuring temperature of the samples: (a) MS 4615–26; (b) MS 4615–27 and (c) 60–19–14. The thickness of the boundaries separating the regions of the various spectral components corresponds to two standard deviations in the values for the areas. The dots represent these values at the temperature points measured. The boundaries infer a straight line continuation from each point measured to the next one.

Results on the Refired Samples

In comparing the Mössbauer spectra of the sherds as received and the refired samples (fig. 7–3), we note that the spectral shapes changed when the refiring temperature reached 1100° C. Therefore, it can be concluded (Bakas et al. 1980; Maniatis et al. 1982) that the firing temperature of all three sherds is less than 1100° C and greater than 900° C. Moreover, in the spectra of the Gournian sherds MS 4615–26 and 27 refired at 1100° C, we note a substantial increase of the sextet type contribution, while for sherd 60–19–14 this increase is not as pronounced. Thus, the two Gournian sherds show refractory properties typical of noncalcareous clays. It is known (Maniatis et al. 1981) that when such clays are fired in air at high temperature, the iron oxide particles do not dissolve into crystalline phases of the clay matrix, while the developing glassy state favors the growth of the iron oxides at the cost of the structural iron of the initial clay matrix.

Scanning Electron Microscopy (SEM) examinations performed for these three sherds by Maniatis gave firing temperature estimates in agreement with the limits set by the present work. The characteristics of the sherd structure found by SEM as well as chemical data lead, however, to the conclusion that all sherds should behave as calcareous (i.e., one expects that at a temperature of ca. 1080° C most of the oxide particles will dissolve into the crystalline phases developing from 850° C). This prediction is, however, in contradiction with the findings presented above from the Mössbauer data of the sherds as received and the refired Gournian samples. Similar discrepancies have been observed in a few cases in studies of modern fired clays (Maniatis et al. 1981), but they are not yet fully understood.

Conclusions

On the basis of the results presented above, the following conclusions can be drawn:
  a) All three fragments examined belonged to pottery wares fired around 1000° C.
  b) The firing atmospheres were different among the three sherds. While for MS 4615–26 atmosphere was purely oxidizing, MS 4615–27 was fired under totally reducing circumstances, and 60–19–14 was fired in a partially reducing atmosphere.
  c) The two Gournian sherds (MS 4615–26 and MS 4615–27), as judged from their large fraction of very fine iron oxide particles and their refiring behavior, are similar to each other but different from sherd 60–19–14.

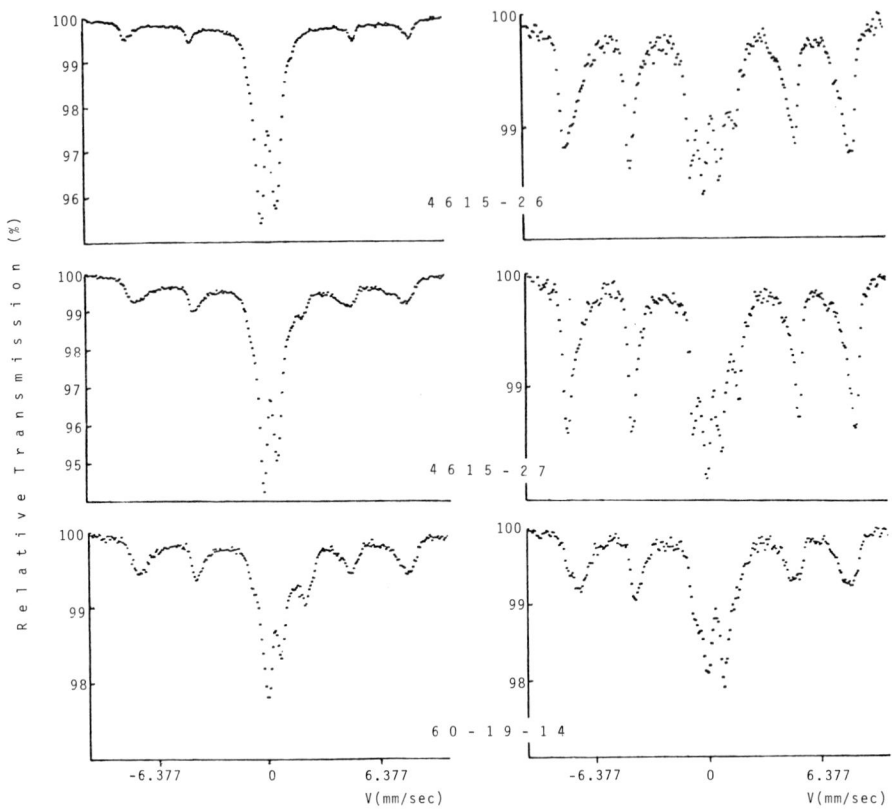

Fig. 7–3. Mössbauer spectra of the as received samples (left column) and the samples refired at 1100°C (right column). The spectra were obtained at 293 K.

Notes

1. The authors thank Dr. Y. Maniatis for the SEM examination of the samples and for fruitful discussions.

References

Bakas, Th., N.-H. Gangas, and M. J. Aitken. 1980. Mössbauer Study of Glozel tablet 198b1. *Archaeometry* 22, 1: 69–80.

Coey, J. M. D., 1980. Clay Minerals and their transformations studied with Nuclear Techniques. *Atomic Energy Review* 18: 73–124.

Kostikas, A., A. Simopoulos, and N.-H. Gangas. 1976. *Applications of Mössbauer Spectroscopy* vol. I, ed. R. L. Cohen, 241–60. New York.

Maniatis, Y., A. Simopoulos, and A. Kostikas. 1981. Mössbauer Study of the Effect of Calcium Content on Iron Oxide Transformations in Fired Clays. *Journal of the American Ceramic Society* 64: 263–9.

Maniatis, Y., A. Simopoulos, and A. Kostikas. 1982. The Investigation of Ancient Ceramic Technologies by Mössbauer Spectroscopy. In *Archaeological Ceramics*, eds. J. S. Olin and A. D. Franklin, 97–107. Washington, D.C.

8

Studies on the Gournian White Slip

Philip P. Betancourt, Thomas K. Gaisser,
Frederick R. Matson, George H. Myer,
Charles P. Swann, and Robert G. White

Pale colored linear designs are a defining characteristic of East Cretan White-on-dark Ware. Their color, which differs very slightly from piece to piece, is usually very pale brown to pink, in the high Value and low Chroma area of the Munsell 10YR series. The thickness varies from a little less than 20 to about 120 micrometers, with most samples falling in the 20–25 micrometer range. In the period considered here, the white is always applied on top of the dark-firing background slip rather than directly onto the clay body. Its texture looks even to the unaided eye, with a surface that is matte rather than vitreous.

The Gournian pigment from EM III has been examined by several analytical techniques to ascertain its composition and characteristics. Its hardness, checked by means of a conventional scratch test under a low power binocular microscope (10×) is about 2, making it a softer than the dark slip or the fabric. It does not show a reaction with hydrochloric acid, indicating that the calcium it contains is not in the form of a carbonate. While it does not adhere really well to the underlying darker surface, it does not rub off with normal handling. Where it has chipped away, the dark surface very rarely shows a slight matte discoloration from a reaction where the pale pigment protected the lower slip during firing (for example, Penn no. MS 4615–40). On most sherds, however, no discoloration at all is visible where the white has chipped away.

When seen as transparent thin sections with polarized light microscopy, the white slip is consistently transparent and anisotropic. Bubbles (spherical voids) were noted in one sample (Penn no. MS 4615–25). In all cases, the slip consists of several optically distinct phases. A majority of the material is a matrix of submicroscopic texture. It is anisotropic, and its higher index of refraction is parallel to the surface of the slip. The second largest proportion consists of particles averaging .5 micrometers in size, with a higher refractive index than the matrix. Most of these particles are elongated, with their longest dimension often parallel to the surface of the slip. They are anisotropic and have their higher index parallel to the elongation. Some of them may be lepidocrocite. A third phase consists of subhedral to euhedral grains with a reddish yellow color, identified as lepidocrocite by their optical properties. They range from submicroscopic to ca. 5 × 10 micrometers in size and are usually situated with their long axes parallel to the slip's surface. Their index of refraction is lower than that of the matrix. A fourth phase consists of angular transparent fragments up to 10 micrometers in size. They are anisotropic and birefringent and so may be feldspar or quartz. Since no feldspar cleavage is visible, quartz is the more likely identification.

White paints on Minoan pottery have been investigated in a number of previous studies. On the basis of X-ray fluorescence analysis, Farnsworth and Simmons suggested that two Middle Minoan sherds with white painted decoration used a clay with a low iron

TABLE 8-I
Elemental percentages (by weight) for the white slip on sherds from Gournia

	Na	MgO	Al_2O_3	SiO_2	CaO	Fe_2O_3
MS 4615-6	1.35	9.10	25.79	39.77	11.53	9.34
MS 4615-7	0.96	7.07	24.13	28.32	17.76	11.43
MS 4615-8	1.50	9.71	26.48	37.60	12.31	8.68
MS 4615-9	0.99	8.21	28.95	35.73	11.13	10.95
MS 4615-10	0.00	6.90	28.99	39.48	7.71	10.79
MS 4615-11	1.36	5.16	22.65	33.13	21.00	5.41
MS 4615-12	1.60	7.44	30.10	35.00	9.14	11.90
MS 4615-13	0.73	6.45	28.37	34.55	16.78	9.19
MS 4615-15	1.06	7.41	25.11	41.09	9.95	9.97
MS 4615-16	– –	7.44	22.32	41.00	13.85	10.08
MS 4615-17	2.85	8.70	28.80	43.76	8.82	2.25
MS 4615-18	1.39	8.95	31.59	35.23	6.40	11.95
MS 4615-20	2.23	8.72	25.11	39.23	10.77	9.55
MS 4615-21	2.06	8.24	28.48	33.16	14.98	10.06
MS 4615-22	1.22	7.89	25.73	35.76	14.61	10.65
MS 4615-23	1.99	7.38	27.48	37.51	12.36	9.16
MS 4615-24	1.79	8.18	19.89	41.30	12.89	10.75
MS 4615-25	1.69	7.15	27.96	36.53	12.63	9.46
MS 4615-26	1.42	9.14	25.08	39.08	9.82	11.78
MS 4615-27	1.58	7.63	26.10	37.11	13.06	9.47
MS 4615-29	2.17	9.02	25.62	40.57	9.24	8.47
MS 4615-31	1.30	6.51	24.55	41.47	10.90	9.83
MS 4615-32	1.12	8.28	23.34	38.61	14.00	10.88
MS 4615-33	1.62	27.66	24.63	30.36	5.33	7.33
MS 4615-34	2.30	6.63	25.37	32.96	20.92	8.14
MS 4615-35	1.82	13.04	20.05	40.02	13.40	8.29
MS 4615-37	1.71	6.38	25.23	30.20	17.30	9.47
MS 4615-39	1.30	7.24	25.17	37.04	15.52	9.94
MS 4615-43	1.36	7.90	27.78	34.45	11.90	12.72
MS 4615-44	1.45	9.06	24.66	40.00	12.33	9.76
MS 4615-47	1.56	7.06	28.82	38.68	8.82	9.57

content (1963: 396). By using the XRF–XRD method, Stos-Fertner, Hedges, and Evely concluded that huntite was used as a white pigment at Knossos in EM III and in MM times and that a light firing clay (meta-kaolinite after firing) was present on a Late Minoan sherd (1979: 192–93 and Table I). The most thorough studies of Minoan pigments, however, are by Noll (Noll, Holm, and Born 1971: 617–18; Noll 1977: 21; 1982: 190–93, with additional references). From the presence of significant percentages of magnesium and silicon and from the observation of the structure with the Scanning Electron Microscope, he has identified the presence of talc on some sherds (protoenstatite after firing; this is perhaps the same Mg-rich substance identified as huntite by Stos-Fertner, Hedges, and Evely). Noll's most recent work clearly

TABLE 8-II
Elemental percentages (by weight) for MS 4615-13

	Na	Mg	Al	Si	S	Cl	K	Ca	Ti	Fe
White	1.1	4.9	23.2	43.3	0.4	1.5	2.2	14.0	0.7	8.9
Dark	0.6	5.1	25.9	35.4	0.3	1.5	2.0	7.7	1.6	19.9
Dark	--	3.8	25.8	35.1	1.2	1.0	5.4	9.0	1.2	17.4
Dark	0.6	5.0	25.5	36.4	0.3	1.5	1.9	7.6	1.6	19.6

isolates two groups of white pigments used in the Early and Middle Bronze Ages, one using talc and the other employing a calcium silicate (1982: 190–93 and fig. 22). He suggests that the talc white is palatial while the calcium silicate white was used in provincial workshops, including some (like Miletos) outside of Crete.

The research presented here fits well with the conclusions of Noll. Elemental compositions of selected elements for 31 samples from EM III Gournia are shown in Table 8–I. The samples were analyzed by proton microprobe (PIXE), using the method described in chapter 11. Pigments were analyzed on the sherds, and as a control a small chip of white was removed from MS 4615–13 (pl. 18 no. 5) and analyzed separately. The results for all elements, demonstrate the essentially similar nature of the two analyses. As is to be expected, minor variations result from any analysis of heterogeneous materials such as ancient pottery.

The figures in Table 8–I indicate that the white pigment at Gournia is most likely a calcium silicate. Only one sample, MS 4615–33, has a high enough Mg content to suggest the possibility of talc or huntite. In all other cases the compositions compare favorably with those of Noll for calcium silicates from other Minoan sites, and this conclusion is compatible with the physical characteristics.

In addition, a chip of white slip was removed from MS 4615–13 for analysis by energy dispersive spectroscopy. Analysis was performed at the Electron Microscopy Central Facility, Laboratory for Research in the Structure of Matter, University of Pennsylvania, by Robert White, using a windowless detector. The resolution of the instrument was 150 e.s., and the beam voltage was 18 k.v. All spectra were collected for 200 seconds; the semiquantitative computer routines were Frame NBS for the ZAF corrections.

Results for the white slip, with three analyses of the dark background slip from the same sherd, are presented in Table 8–II. The three analyses of the dark slip are taken from different parts of the same sample.

The elemental percentages are quite compatible with the results obtained from the proton microprobe, allowing for differences in the methodology, the heterogeneous nature of the sample, and the difference in expression (elemental for the energy dispersive spectroscopy; as oxides for the proton microprobe).

Of particular interest is the relatively high percentage of iron, a finding which also agrees with the analyses of Noll. In fired pottery iron usually oxidizes and produces a darker color than is found in the white to off-white paint of White-on-dark Ware. To ascertain the effect of heat on the pigment, a small chip was removed from MS 4615–13 and refired in a kiln in an oxidizing atmosphere to 800° C. It experienced a very slight color change, visible only under 10 × magnification, suggesting it had not previously been fired this high.

Three possibilities exist for the application of the white:

1. It is an unfired calcium silicate, applied after firing.
2. It is a low fired pigment. The pottery was fired twice, once for the body and dark slip and a second time (at a much lower temperature) for the white pigment.
3. The pottery is fired only once with the white applied before the firing.

Points in favor of an unfired pigment include the lack of discoloration under the white paint on most sherds, because fired pottery should produce discolorations. The slight change in the color of the white paint when it was test fired could point in the same direction, but a low previous firing (below 800° C) is also possible, and the color change was so minimal it could even be the result of contamination after burial. In favor of a firing of some type is the firm nature of the white surface (since heating drives off water and helps fix the pigment to the underlying surface). The evidence is not really definitive, and the authors are divided in their conclusions on which theory is most likely.

References

Farnsworth, M., and I. Simmons. 1963. Coloring Agents for Greek Glazes. *AJA* 67: 389–96.

Noll, W. 1977. Techniken antiker Töpfer und Vasenmaler. *Antike Welt* 8, no. 8: 21–36.

Noll, W. 1982. Mineralogie und Technik der Keramiken Altkretas. *Neues Jahrbuch für Mineralogie. Abhandlungen* 143: 150–99.

Noll, W., R. Holm, and L. Born. 1971. Chemie und Techniken altkretischer Vasenmalerei vom Kamares-Typ. *Die Naturwissenschaften* 58: 615–18.

Stos-Fertner, Z., R. M. E. Hedges, and R. D. G. Evely. 1979. The application of the XRF—XRD method to the analysis of the pigments of Minoan painted pottery. *Archaeometry* 21: 187–94.

9

Firing Conditions of White-on-dark Ware from Eastern Crete

Yannis Maniatis

Introduction

The examination of ancient pottery under the Scanning Electron Microscope (SEM) provides very useful information about ancient ceramic technology (Maniatis and Tite 1981). First, the internal morphology developed by the clay during firing can be readily and directly investigated, and the degree of vitrification (amount of glass), pore structure, and crystalline phases which characterize the initial clay and its refractory properties can be assessed. Second, by refiring pieces of the pottery in a laboratory furnace at different temperatures and after reexamination of fresh fractured surfaces under the SEM, the temperature at which an increase in the amount of glass or a change in the microstructure occurred can be observed. This provides the maximum temperature at which the ware could have been fired initially. By coordinating this information with the type of clay and its refractory properties, the lower limit and therefore the firing temperature ranges used in antiquity can be estimated. The method thus provides information on the firing temperatures and internal morphology (type of clay used) as well as on the manufacturing procedures and level of technology.

Experimental Techniques and Results

Fresh fractured surfaces of pottery samples (approximately 5 mm × 5 mm) were obtained and coated with a thin layer of gold in an evaporator to make the surfaces sufficiently conducting. The samples were then examined under a Cambridge–150 Scanning Electron Microscope at the Department of Physics of the Agronomy School at Athens.

All the pottery samples studied in this work were manufactured from calcareous clays, that is, clays containing more than 6% CaO. This is evident from the internal morphology which is characteristic of calcareous clays and also from the analyses of other workers on the same material. The presence of Ca as fine grained and evenly distributed calcite in the clays significantly affects the development of vitrification (Tite and Maniatis 1981). When present, a distinct cellular vitrification microstructure (pl. 8C and D) is formed at about 850° C in an oxidizing atmosphere, and this structure remains essentially unchanged for ca. 200° C until a firing temperature of about 1050° C is reached. When fired above ca. 1050° C, the amount of glass in these calcareous clays increases rather rapidly (pl. 8E and F), and a totally vitrified microstructure is formed by about 1150° C. In con-

TABLE 9-I
Firing conditions of East Cretan White-on-dark Ware

Sample	Atmosphere[1]	Vitrification stage[2]	Approx. Firing Temperature
2 MS 4615-11	O	V_c	850-1050°C
3 MS 4615-13	O	V_c	850-1050
4 MS 4615-26	O	V_c	850-1050
5 MS 4615-31	O/R	V_c	850-1050
6 MS 4615-47	O	V_c	850-1050
7 BAI-14-A	O/R	V_c/V_c+	1000-1080
8 MS 4615-27	O/R	V_c/V_c+	1000-1080
1 60-19-14	O/R	V_c+	1050-1100

[1] O: Oxidizing
O/R: Oxidizing/Reducing

[2] V_c: Characteristic cellular
V_c+: Coarse vitrified cellular
V_c/V_c+: Intermediate stage

trast, in clays not containing calcite, the amount of glass present increases progressively from about 800° C to 1000° C at which point a total vitrification stage is achieved. The reasons for the difference in refractory properties between calcareous and non-calcareous clays are described in Tite et al. 1982 and Tite and Maniatis 1975. The difference is due to the fact that in calcareous clays calcium aluminosilicate microcrystalline phases are formed which inhibit the development of glass in the temperature range of about 850–1050° C, producing the characteristic stable microstructure.

The results obtained from the White-on-dark pottery from Crete are summarised in Table 9–I. The atmosphere of the kiln is indicated by the color of the finished product. As can be seen, most samples developed the characteristic cellular calcareous microstructure (V_c) or a slightly more advanced one. Only one sherd exhibits a clearly advanced vitrification stage definitely above the characteristic pattern. For those sherds exhibiting the characteristic cellular microstructure, a firing temperature range of ca. 850–1050° C has been assigned. This ca. 200° C range cannot be narrowed down because, as described earlier, the microstructure within this temperature range remains unchanged. To test the stability of the microstructure, all the sherds were refired to 1000° C in a laboratory electrical furnace and then reexamined under the SEM. The microstructure remained unchanged. The intermediate stage (V_c/V_c+) has been assumed for those sherds exhibiting a slight advance in the amount of glass in certain areas, but the characteristic calcareous microstructure is still quite evident. Therefore, an overlapping temperature range of ca. 1000–1080° C has been assigned for these sherds. Finally, a temperature range of 1050–1100° C has been assigned for 60-19-14 because the characteristic microstructure has been definitely altered producing a coarser more glassy internal morphology throughout the clay body. This sherd has certainly been fired above the ca. 850–1050° C range, but it has not reached the total vitrification stage usually obtained at ca. 1150° C.

Conclusions

In conclusion, one can clearly see that calcareous clays were used for all the samples studied. They were probably natural calcareous clays containing fine calcite grains which would react readily with the clay minerals and result in the production of the characteristic cellular calcareous microstructure upon firing (for east Cretan clay sources see Chap. 15). Although the temperatures were in general in the 850–1050° C range, in some cases the firing evidently exceeded 1000° C or even 1050° C, and though the use of calcareous clays may depend on their availability, it is interesting to discuss the major advantages produced by their use. With these clays a fair amount of vitrification is produced. It remains stable at ca. 200° C (ca. 850–1050° C) whereas with non-calcareous clays the extent of vitrification increases progressively with increasing firing temperature. Therefore, if the stronger and more durable pottery associated with an extensive vitrification structure is being produced, the control of the firing temperature needed to achieve a consistent quality is less critical in the case of calcareous as opposed to non-calcareous clays. Also, calcareous clays tend to produce a less dense and more porous fabric when fired to the extensive vitrification stage. Since this fabric is more resistant to thermal and mechanical shock, it can be used in more versatile ways. Furthermore, the thermal expansion coefficient of a calcareous clay body is similar to the expansion coefficient of the black vitrified slip (Noll et al. 1975). The danger of cracking on cooling is thus decreased, and this may be another reason for using these clays (as was evidently the case with Attic pottery).

Finally, the dark brown colored clay bodies in a number of the sherds indicate some degree of reduction. Thus, either the ventilation of the kiln did not always produce a fully oxidizing atmosphere, or the sherds were fired in an oxidizing-reducing-oxidizing cycle to produce the black slip. Either conclusion is possible from the available evidence.

References

Maniatis, Y. and M. S. Tite. 1981. Technological Examination of Neolithic–Bronze Age Pottery from Central and Southeast Europe and from the Near East. *Journal of Arch. Science* 8: 59–76.

Noll, W., R. Holm, and L. Born. 1975. Painting of Ancient Ceramics. *Angewandte Chemie, International Edition* 14: 602–19.

Tite, M. S., Y. Maniatis, N. D. Meeks, M. Bimson, M. J. Hughes, and S. C. Leppard. 1982. Technological studies of Ancient Ceramics. In *Early Pyrotechnology*, eds. T. A. Wertime and S. F. Wertime. Washington, D. C.

Tite, M. S. and Y. Maniatis. 1975. Scanning Electron Microscopy of Fired Calcareous Clays. *Transactions, British Ceramic Society* 74: 19–22.

10

Porosity Studies

Nicholas Hartmann

Introduction

The porosity of a ceramic object is the proportion of empty space contained within a unit volume of material. It is determined by many factors including the type or types of clay used, the nature, size, and shape of the included particles, the materials (if any) added as temper, the presence or absence of fluxing agents (which can lower the vitrification temperature), the inclusion of organic matter (which can burn away and leave cavities), the amount of air trapped in the clay during preparation, and the conditions during firing (cf. Matson 1940: 469). The most important of the firing conditions is the degree of vitrification which is, in turn, a function of temperature, kiln atmosphere, fluxing, firing time, and other variables. Given the complexity of this situation, it is unlikely that primitive potters ever gained an overall understanding of the process. However, many variables can be controlled, and potters were therefore probably able to learn, by trial and error, to exert some control over the porosity of their vessels.

The advantage of being able to manufacture porous or impervious vessels at will lies in the different characteristics of the two types of finished product: fired vases can range from highly porous pieces which will not hold liquid to virtually impermeable containers with a smooth and lustrous surface. The greatest advantage of the more porous vessels is that water vapor and other gases can pass more readily through the clay. Therefore, porous vessels do not warp or crack so readily while drying, are not so likely to break during firing, and can withstand greater thermal shock during use. On the other hand, both practical and aesthetic considerations tend to favor smooth, dense pottery for use as tableware.

The primary aim of this study[1] was to characterize the fine EM III pottery of Gournia in terms of its porosity. This information was then used in an effort to determine whether the EM III potters made any effort to control the porosity of their vessels in order to suit them to particular uses. In order to answer this question, an attempt was made to correlate the observed porosity of each sherd with the shape (and therefore the assumed function) of the vessel from which it came.

Theory

True porosity (P_t) is "the ratio of the volume of the open and sealed pores to the bulk volume of the material" (Norton 1968: 472). However, determination of the true porosity requires that a portion of the test piece be reduced to powder. Since this would have involved unacceptable damage to the sherds in question, the value determined in this case was *apparent porosity* (P_a), which is "the ratio of the volume of the open pores to the bulk volume of the material."

TABLE 10-I
Values for saturated weight in air, dry weight in air, saturated weight in water,
and apparent porosity for EM III sherds

Sherd No.	weights in grams			P_a, %
	W_{sa}	W_{da}	W_{sw}	
MS 4615-6	5.32	4.37	2.70	36.24
-7	8.37	6.84	4.23	35.97
-8	4.17	3.56	2.19	30.93
-9	6.94	5.78	3.54	34.19
-12	7.33	6.00	3.71	36.88
-15	12.36	10.20	6.36	35.95
-17	8.96	7.84	4.58	25.61
-18	21.96	18.44	11.35	33.20
-20	18.16	14.94	9.38	36.66
-21	20.07	17.65	10.55	25.43
-22	10.31	8.41	5.17	37.08
-23	22.82	19.27	11.97	32.75
-24	38.65	32.00	20.39	36.40
-25	28.15	23.23	14.40	35.79
-28	26.41	22.20	13.99	33.94
-29	8.45	6.76	4.36	41.16
-31	13.34	10.83	6.75	38.15
-32	9.63	9.07	5.14	12.50
-33	24.24	20.59	12.75	31.80
-35	12.00	8.95	5.59	47.51
-37	11.69	9.36	6.00	40.91
-39	25.00	20.28	12.86	38.89
-40	3.65	3.07	1.82	31.62
-43	19.72	16.38	10.04	34.51
-44	21.79	17.82	11.18	37.42
-47	5.96	4.79	3.04	39.94

Method

The sherds were first placed in a beaker of distilled water which was, in turn, placed in a vacuum chamber under 15–20 in. of vacuum for about three days, or until lowering of the pressure to 25 in. produced no further bubbles. Each sherd was then weighed while suspended in water (W_{sw}), and then removed from the water, patted dry, and quickly weighed in air (W_{sa}). The sherds were allowed to dry for a few days at room temperature, then placed in a 108° C oven for 24 hours, and further dried in a vacuum desiccator over calcium chloride for 24 hours, to ensure that all residual moisture had been driven out of the open pores. The dry weight in air (W_{da}) was then measured for each sherd. A Mettler H16 analytical balance was used for all of the above weight determinations.

Apparent porosity was calculated using the formula:

$$P_a = \frac{W_{sa} - W_{da}}{W_{sa} - W_{sw}} \times 100$$

which is a dimensionless percentage.

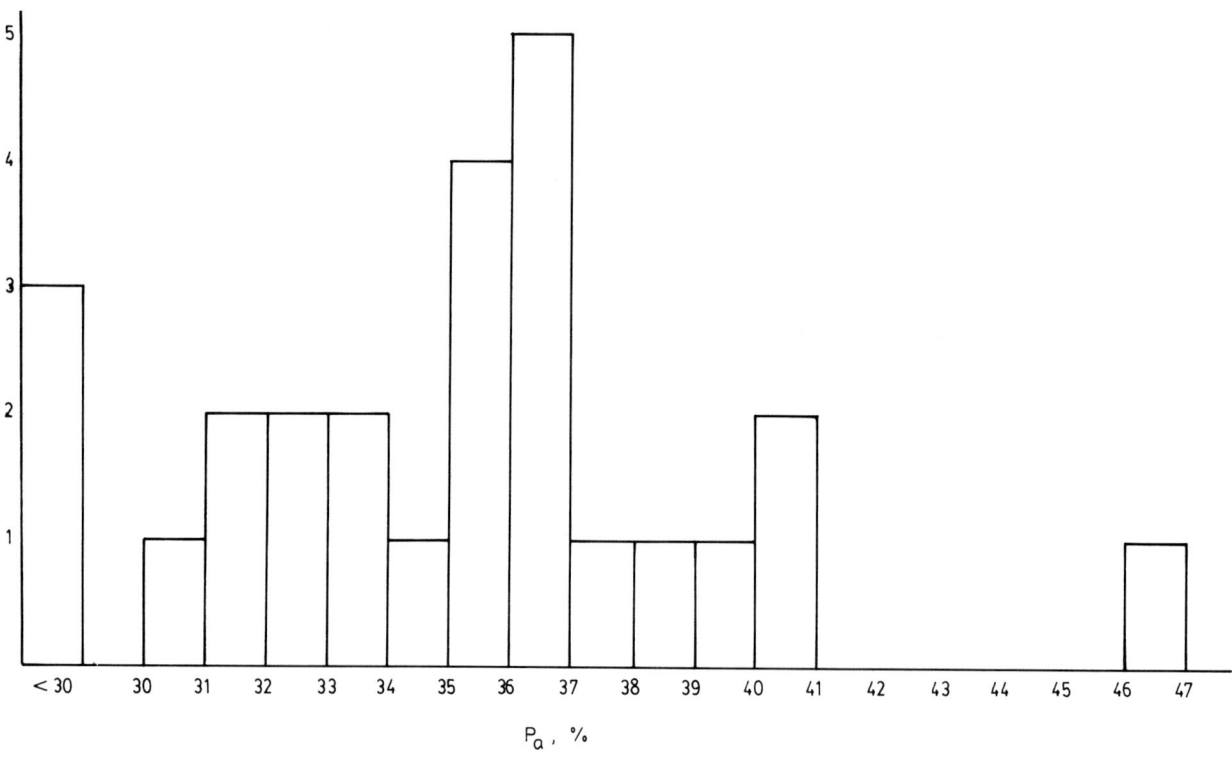

Fig. 10–1. Apparent porosity (P_a) values, displaying as a histogram.

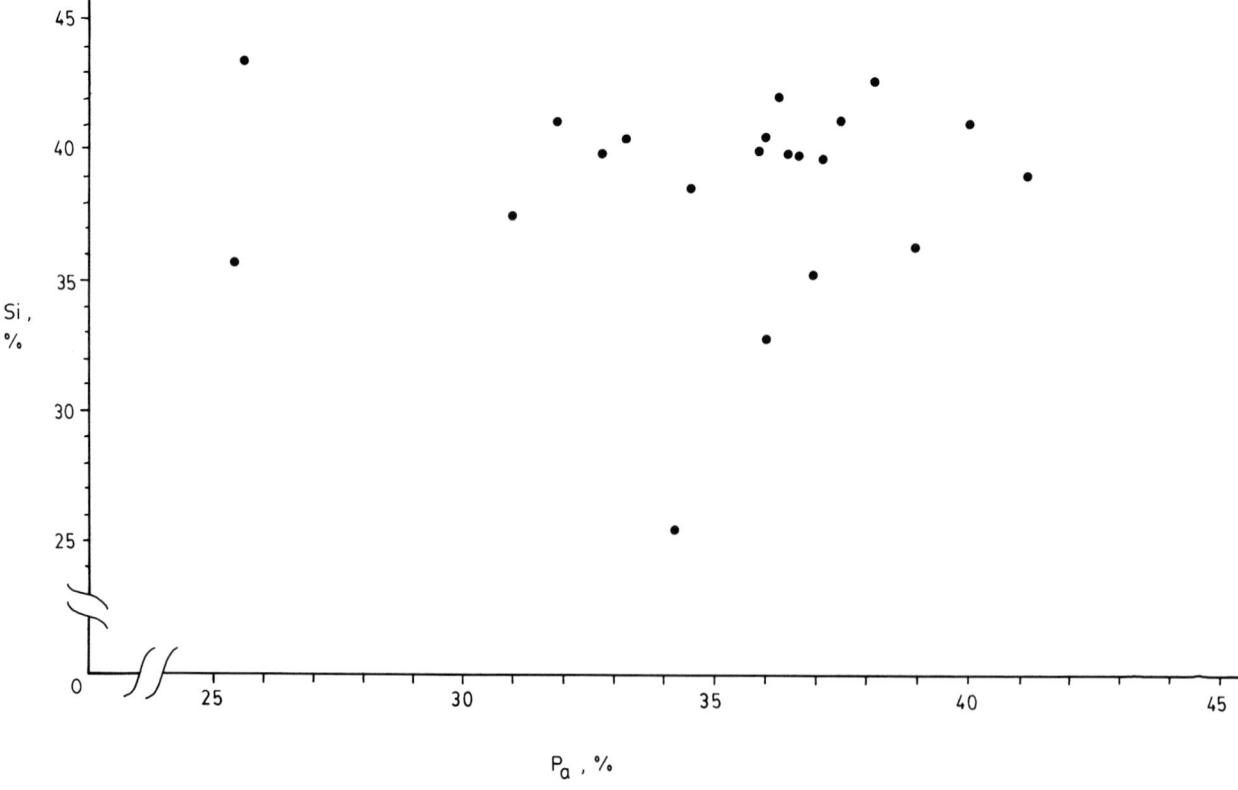

Fig. 10–2. Apparent porosity (P_a) plotted as a function of Si content (determined as SiO_2). Nos. 28, 32, 35, 37, 40 not plotted.

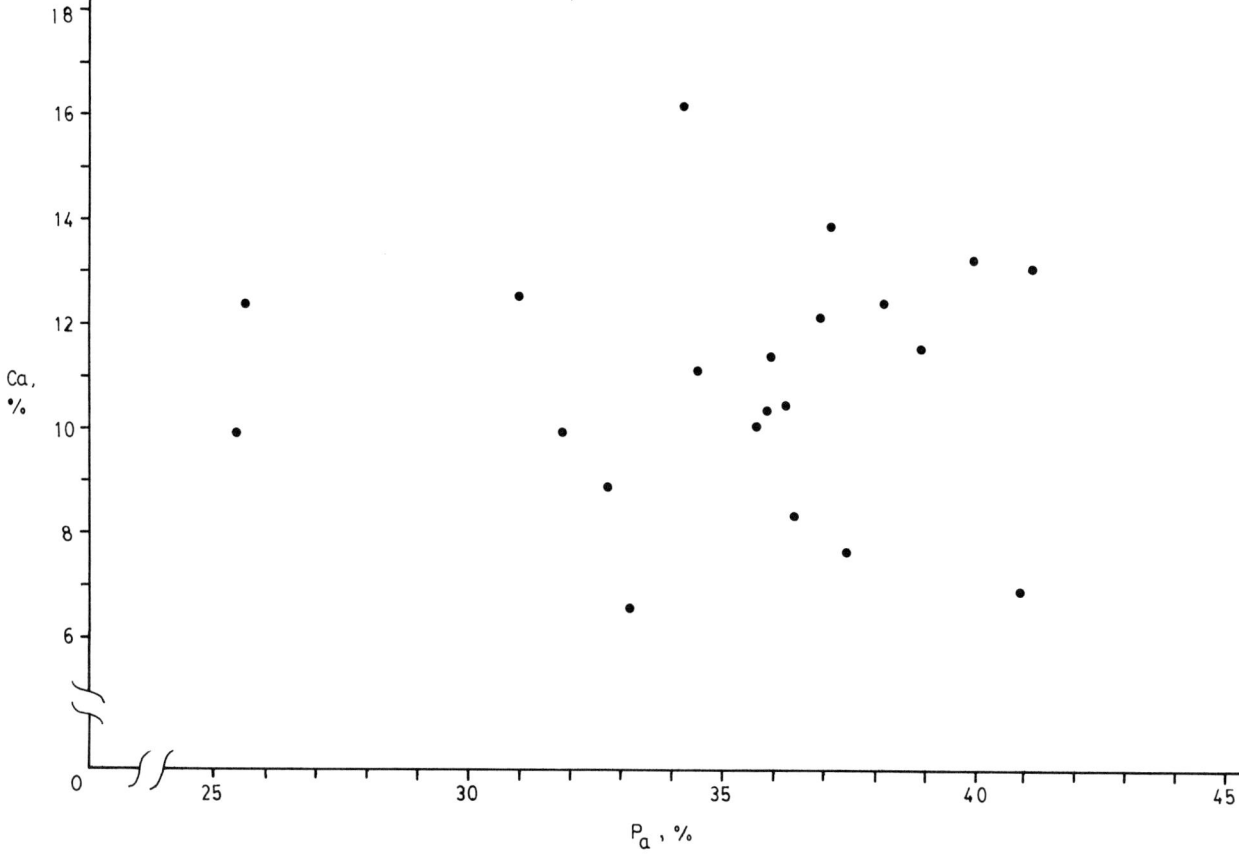

Fig. 10–3. Apparent porosity (P_a) plotted as a function of Ca content (determined as CaO). Nos. 7, 28, 32, 35, 40 not plotted.

Error Sources

The following are the major sources of error in measurement of the various parameters; where it could be determined, the probable magnitude of the error is also mentioned:

1. Presence of calcareous accretions on most of the sherds. This accretion has a different specific gravity and porosity from the sherd itself, which will have altered the reading to an unknown degree.
2. Variation in the amount of water adhering to the sherd during measurement of W_{sa}. In an experiment in which various amounts of water were left adhering to the sherd during this weighing, the maximum weight variation of the sample was less than 1%.
3. Insufficient dessication of the sherds before measurement of W_{da}.
4. Insufficient saturation before measurement of W_{sa} and W_{sw}. A sample of sherds tested showed that saturation for 30 hours rather than the 48–72 hours actually used yielded values only 2–3% lower.

Results

Table 10–1 shows the values obtained for the various parameters measured, and the calculated apparent porosity, for each of the 26 EM III sherds studied. Values were measured and calculated to a precision of 0.0001 gm but were rounded off to 0.01 gm for the table.

Figure 10–1 shows the apparent porosity values displayed as a histogram. The histogram shows that

TABLE 10-II
Average apparent porosities for 26 EM III sherds grouped according to vessel shape

Cups (12 sherds)		Larger Shapes (14 sherds)			
Rounded Cups (8) nos. MS 4615-6, 7,8,9,31,35,40,47	Conical Cups (4) nos. MS 4615-12, 17,29,37	Shallow bowl (1) no. MS 4615-15	Lid (1) no. MS 4615-39	Teapots (2) nos. MS 4615-32,43	Bridge spouted jars (10) nos. MS 4615-18, 21,22,23,24,25,28, 33,44
36.82 ± 10.28%	36.14 ± 7.29%	35.95%	38.89%	23.51 ± 15.56%	34.05 ± 3.62%
34.93 ± 10.28%		30.02 ± 6.76%			

as a group the Gournian sherds are relatively porous; about half of the samples fall within the range 35–40%. The full range of porosity is much wider, and there is only a weak clustering of values around 36–37%. It is thus evident that the potters produced vessels with a wide latitude in this characteristic.

Figures 10–2 and 10–3 show the apparent porosity values for each sherd plotted against its percentage content of Si and Ca, as determined by Gaisser and Swann (see Chap. 11). Since the Si content partly reflects the amount of sandy material in the fabric, and since $CaCO_3$ acts as a fluxing agent, the percentage of these elements might affect porosity. However, cross-plotting of apparent porosity and Si and Ca content shows no clustering or linear relationship. This lack of correlation indicates that the differences found within the range of these sherds does not materially affect the porosity.

Since potters might adjust the porosity for shapes used for different functions (for example, making larger shapes more porous), an effort was made to correlate the apparent porosity of each sherd with the shape of the vessel from which it came. The results, in the form of average porosities for each general shape, are given in Table 10–2. There is no striking difference in porosity between the two larger groups, cups and larger shapes; in fact, the porosity of the larger shapes is, if anything, slightly lower. In each case, however, the spread of the data is so large that the difference between the two groups is probably without significance. Therefore, it appears that the EM III potters whose work is represented by this group of sherds did not make an effort to tailor the porosities of these vessels to particular functions.

The only correlation that can in fact be made between apparent porosity and other experimental data concerns vitrification. The majority of the EM III sherds analyzed may be regarded as slightly vitrified on the basis of visual examination through a low-power binocular microscope. These sherds have porosities above 30%. Two sherds, nos. MS 4615–17 and 21, are moderately vitrified, and their porosities are respectively 25.61% and 25.43%. Finally, no. MS 4615–32 is highly vitrified, and its measured apparent porosity is 12.50%. As expected, increased vitrification does reduce the porosity by sealing off pores within the clay body. Whether this effect was deliberately produced in the case of the Gournian sherds, and if so, why low porosity was needed for the particular vessels involved cannot at present be determined. It seems unlikely, however, that the low porosity of these sherds was intentional.

Notes

1. It is my pleasure to thank Dr. Robert Heimann of the Institute of Materials Research, McMaster University, for practical and theoretical advice; and Dr. Stuart Fleming, Scientific Director of the Museum Applied Science Center for Archaeology, University Museum, for generously allowing me to use laboratory materials and facilities.

References

Matson, F. R. 1940. Porosity Studies of Ancient Pottery. *Papers of the Michigan Academy of Science, Arts and Letters* 26: 469–77.

Norton, F. H. 1968. *Refractories: Production and Properties.* 4th ed. New York.

11

Proton Microprobe Analysis of White-on-dark Ware

T. K. Gaisser and C. P. Swann

Introduction

The use of proton induced X-rays (PIXE) for the study of archaeological artifacts began with the work of Folkman (1975) and Ahlbert et al. (1976). Since then a number of other reports have appeared, the most recent being those of Fleming and Crowfoot-Payne (1979) on Egyptian bronzes, Duerden et al. (1979) on obsidians from the Pacific region, and Betancourt et al. (1979) on Vasilike Ware. All but the last of these studies were performed with the sample in vacuum with the spatial resolution being defined by the beam size. The system being discussed in this report makes use of an external beam generated by passing the protons through a pinhole. The advantages of such a technique have been discussed by Grodzins et al. (1975) and later by Cookson (1979).

The proton probe is complementary to other methods of elemental analysis such as neutron activation and electron microscopy. With an external beam, it has the distinct advantage of allowing one to deal with almost any size sample, studying any particular surface region of interest. Furthermore, no sample preparation is required beyond simple cleaning, so damage to the sample is negligible. Some radioactivity can be induced by the 2 MeV beam, but for the beam currents used (nanoamperes) such radioactivity is minimal. It is, of course, true that the chemical form is not determined by this method. In some cases the chemical combination in which an element occurs is obvious, but in other cases other techniques must be applied.

The remainder of this report will be divided into four parts. The first will deal with the technique itself including a description of the Bartol-Delaware proton probe. Next we will summarize our results for the basic group of thirty-one samples of EM III pottery from Gournia. We then compare the basic group to four other groups from other periods and locations in Crete, and we conclude with a brief discussion of the results.

Proton Probe

There are many reports in the literature which describe the various types of ion probe systems. That of Cookson (1979) is probably the most comprehensive and includes a very thorough list of references. The Bartol-Delaware microprobe itself has been described elsewhere (Fou et al. 1979; Van Patter et al. 1980). For the purposes of this paper only a brief description will be given, with the emphasis on aspects important to the present studies.

The source of exciting protons is the Delaware TN2000 Van de Graaff accelerator, which can provide protons with energies up to 2.5 MeV. For the present work two energies of 1.3 and 2.0 MeV have been used; the reasons for two separate energies will be given below.

The beam transport consists of initial steering into the magnetic analyzer system followed by focusing of the beam by a pair of magnetic quadrupoles into the final stage of the probe. This stage consists of a 0.5 mm aperture, a 1.25 mm antiscattering aperture, and a graphite tip through which a small hole has been drilled; a 7.5 micrometer Kapton film serves as the vacuum-atmosphere interface. The effect of this film on scattering of the proton beam is negligible for the hole size used in these experiments is approximately 0.45 mm. Much smaller hole sizes are possible for finer spatial resolution, but they have not been used in the present work. The effect of the atmosphere cannot be neglected since the range of 2 MeV protons in air is about 5 cm, and the scatter over this range is significant. To minimize energy loss and scattering, the distance between the Kapton film and the sample under study is kept to a few mm. Within the sample itself the proton range is very limited, the effective depth for an average medium being only 10 to 15 micrometers for 2 MeV protons. Consequently only the surface of the sample is analyzed.

The characteristic X-rays induced by the proton bombardment are observed in a Si (Li) detector with an area of 30 mm^2 and an active depth of 3 mm. In order to get the optimum efficiency the diode must be cooled to the temperature of liquid nitrogen, which requires that the system be in vacuum. A 7 micrometer window acts as the vacuum-atmosphere interface. Because of its absorption, this window itself limits the observable X-rays to those with energies greater than or equal to the characteristic lines of sodium. So only elements beyond sodium in the periodic table are readily observable, and sodium is visible with some difficulty.

The electronics of the detector system is quite standard; it has a measured energy resolution of 160 eV (FWHM) at 5.89 keV with a 10 microsecond pulse-shaping time. The sample is attached to a pair of precision translational stages with 50 mm, 100-turn micrometer heads. The horizontal stage is driven by a stepping motor in 2.5 micrometer steps, whereas the vertical stage is hand operated. This arrangement allows one either to average over a limited region or to scan a region for mapping.

As pointed out above, two separate conditions were established in obtaining the data. First, measurements were made in a helium atmosphere with a proton energy of 1.3 MeV. This lower energy favors the low energy X-rays, i.e., the low Z elements, and the helium atmosphere allows for the observation of Na and Mg. Second, measurements were made in air or a nitrogen atmosphere with different combinations of filters between the sample and the detector; the proton energy was 2.0 MeV. The purpose of the filters is to reduce, selectively, the effect of the most prominent low energy X-rays. This allows a significantly higher beam current to be used without introducing serious problems resulting from high counting rates from the abundant light elements (principally Fe, Ca, and Si) which emit low energy X-rays. The problem being avoided is pile-up of the intense X-rays. This results when two X-rays impinge upon the detector within the resolving time of the electronics. This generates a pulse with an energy equal to the sum of the two incident X-rays, which can obscure the signal from a single high energy X-ray characteristic of a less abundant, heavier element, such as those above iron in the periodic table. In the present study the filter consisted of KCl followed by vanadium.

The goal is to establish actual percentages of the elements observed in the material under study. In principle this could be accomplished by a calculation involving measured cross sections for excitation together with geometry of the target and detector. This would, however, require a precise knowledge of the proton beam current striking the sample, the effective depth of penetration of the beam, and the absorption of the emitted X-rays. We have used the simpler and more reliable procedure of callibration using standards. The standards are prepared with compo-

TABLE 11-I
Composition of the standard

compound	wt.(gm)	compound	wt.(gm)
Na CO	2.0	CrCl	2.0
MgCO	5.0	Fe O	3.5
Al O	4.0	CuO	0.25
H SiO	30.0	ZnO	0.25
S	0.25	Se	0.25
CaCO	6.0	SrO	0.2
TiO	1.0	Bi O	0.5

TABLE 11-II
Average concentrations of elements

	EMIII(31)[b] (Gournia)	MM(16)[c] (Gournia)	Mokhlos(7)[d]	Vasilike(6)[e]	Knossos(5)[f]
Na	1.89+.14 1.76+.10 1.46+.11	.86+.24 1.7+.5 1.7+.3	2.96+.25 3.0+.2 —	1.6+.6 1.8+.5 —	.9+.3 — —
Mg	11.1+.4 7.3+.2 8.5+.7	5.8+.7 3.2+.2 3.1+.3	11.8+.4 6.5+.8 —	6.8+.8 3.7+.7 —	10.6+1.7 — —
Al	21.6+.4 31.6+.7 25.6+.7	23.8+.6 36 + 1 28.2+2.5	23.1+.4 31.6+1.8 —	20.3+.8 34.4+1.6 —	19.1+1.2 — —
Si	39.2+.7 32.9+.7 36.5+.9	40.6+.9 29 + 1 35 + 2	42.8+.8 39.3+.3 —	42.9+.6 37.9+1.6 —	41.0+2.1 — —
S	.46+.26 1.3+.3 1.6+.6	1.0+.3 1.0+.2 1.7+.5	.032+.017 .071+.026 —	1.1+.4 .5+.2 —	1.7+1.4 — —
Cl	.17+.03 .18+.03 .23+.06	.4+.1 .21+.04 .42+.14	.15+.03 .09+.04 —	.5+.4 .3+.2 —	.012+.011 — —
K	2.28+.08 3.37+.20 1.96+.14	2.3+.1 5.1+.5 3.5+.6	2.43+.13 4.50+.20 —	3.8+.4 5.4+.3 —	2.6+.3 — —
Ca	11.9+.7 8.3+.6 13.2+1.1	15.0+1.4 8.4+1.1 14.5+2.2	9.3+.6 4.6+1.3 —	12.3+1.1 4.4+.8 —	16.5+4.2 — —
Ti	.50+.02 .58+.02 .54+.02	.54+.02 .72+.02 .68+.04	.47+.02 .53+.02 —	.56+.07 .57+.07 —	.38+.01 — —
Cr	.48+.04 .26+.03 .48+.04	.21+.03 .12+.01 .21+.03	.10+.03 .08+.04 —	.26+.03 .14+.02 —	.32+.03 — —
Mn	.22+.02 .19+.03 .18+.02	.061+.016 .13+.04 .08+.04	.05+.02 .08+.07 —	.12+.02 .02+.02 —	.06+.05 — —
Fe	9.8+.5 12.0+.3 9.6+.4	9.16+.45 13.9+.5 10.1+1.1	7.6+.4 9.4+.2 —	9.1+.6 10.6+1.7 —	6.6+.4 — —

TABLE 11-II (continued)

	EMIII(31)[b] (Gournia)	MM(16)[c] (Gournia)	Mokhlos(7)[d]	Vasilike(6)[e]	Knossos(5)[f]
Ni	.054+.004 .035+.002 .028+.002	.058+.008 .054+.007 .043+.007	.11+.014 .20+.12 —	.09+.01 .14+.05 —	.12+.03 — —
Cu	.013+.002 .011+.001 .013+.001	.015+.002 .018+.002 .021+.006	.013+.001 .012+.0004 —	.03+.01 .04+.01 —	.006+.003 — —
Zn	.016+.001 .046+.002 .040+.003	.018+.002 .053+.006 .042+.009	.014+.002 .027+.002 —	.29+.24 .035+.007 —	.012+.002 — —
As	.017+.001 .0033+.001 .0032+.001	.0012+.0004 .0027+.0006 .0024+.0006	.0001+.0001 .0005+.0005 —	.0008+.0007 — —	— — —
Pb	.007+.001 .023+.005 .022+.004	.009+.002 .016+.002 .020+.004	.0055+.0007 .007+.001 —	.15+.12[g] .019+.006 —	.004+.003 — —
Rb	.020+.002 .028+.002 .018+.002	.016+.002 .047+.003 .028+.006	.019+.002 .035+.003 —	.028+.002 .043+.001 —	.029+.004 — —
Sr	.045+.005 .039+.002 .048+.003	.042+.003 .050+.006 .006+.010	.035+.004 .031+.005 —	.10+.05 .022+.003 —	.10+.02 — —
Y	.008+.003 .012+.002 .010+.001	.004+.0005 .004+.0008 .006+.001	.0035+.0002 .0086+.0018 —	.004+.001 .0117+.0005 —	.0057+.0008 — —
Zr	.045+.005 .057+.003 .069+.009	.029+.003 .056+.008 .040+.007	.020+.002 .030+.002 —	.016+.003 .028+.003 —	.021+.005 — —

For each element 1st, 2nd, & 3rd lines are for fabric, white slip & dark slip.

[a] This table gives the percentages by weight of elements or, in some cases, assumed chemical combinations. See text. The numbers in parenthesis denote the number of samples in each group.

[b] EM III stands for Early Minoan III from Gournia.

[c] MM is Middle Minoan from Gournia.

[d] From the site at Mokhlos near Gournia, from EM III.

[e] From Vasilike near Gournia and Mokhlos, from EM III.

[f] From Knossos in central Crete, EM III.

[g] This set contains one sample (MS 4234) with an anomalously high concentration of Pb in the fabric.

sition close to that of the material under study to duplicate as closely as possible the absorption of the incident protons and outgoing X-rays. The standard used in this study was prepared in the laboratory by ball-milling commercial compounds. The compounds used and their proportions in the standard are listed in Table 11–I.

Basic Data

The basic data for all five groups of samples are summarized in Table 11–II. Concentrations of twenty-one elements were found in the basic EM III group. These were measured on a freshly broken or clean edge, which represents the fabric, on the dark slipped surface, and, where possible, on the white painted portion of the surface. Inclusions were avoided where possible. Some other elements were occasionally detected in the other groups, as noted below. The results are quoted as percentages by weight. In the case of some of the light elements, the percentages refer to an assumed chemical form: Na as Na_2O, Mg as MgO, Al as Al_2O_3, Si as SiO_2, K as K_2O, Ca as CaO, and Fe as Fe_2O_3. These choices were made for consistency with the form in which concentrations of elements in standard geological samples are presented (Flanagan 1969). The standard error in determination of the average is the root mean square deviation of individual measurements divided by the square root of the number of samples used to determine the average. The statistical uncertainties in determining the concentration of an element in a particular sample are negligible compared to the r.m.s. deviations from the mean. They are also probably negligible compared to variations from place to place on the surface of a given sample.

Inspection of the first column of Table 11–II shows some systematic effects: (1) Mg and Ni are depleted in both surface areas, the white and the dark slip, compared to the fabric, whereas Zn, As, and Pb are enhanced on the surface. The concentration of aluminum increases from fabric to white to dark slip. (2) There is also a group of elements with similar concentration in the fabric and in the white paint, but

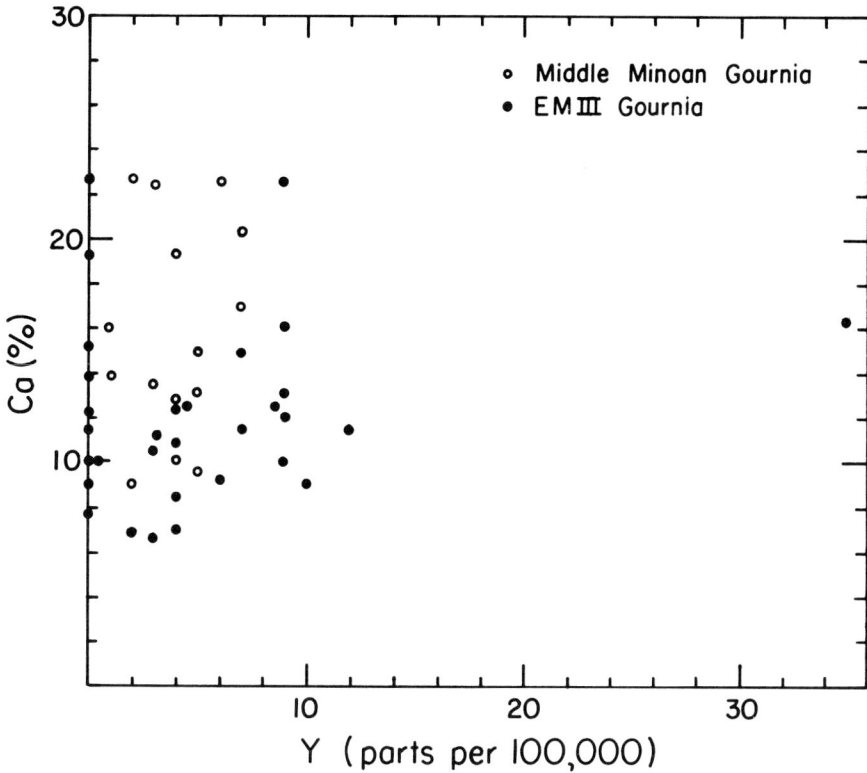

Fig. 11–1. A comparison between Ca and Y from EM III and MM I–III Gournia.

TABLE 11-III
Concentrations relative to the Gournian EM III group

	MM Gournia	EM III Mokhlos	EM III Vasilike	EM III Knossos
Na	−	+		−
Mg	−		−	
Al				
Si		+	+	
K			+	
Ca	+	−		
Ti				
Cr	−	−	−	−
Mn	−	−	−	−
Fe		−		−
Ni		+	+	+
Cu				−
Zn				
As	−	−	−	−
Pb				
Sr				+
Y	−			
Zr	−	−	−	−

with differing concentrations in the dark slip. The elements K, Fe, and possibly Rb are enhanced in the dark slip, whereas Ca and Cr are depleted. Chlorine and sulfur show wide variations with little pattern, and we guess that their concentrations reflect accidents of the history of individual samples (e.g., contamination by sulfur from the atmosphere). We also note that the results for concentration of Zn on the surfaces show much greater scatter than for the fabric.

We have searched through the data to find samples that appear to be anomalous in some way. Four sherds stand out:

MS 4615–39, EM III Gournia. This sample has a very high concentration of Pb in the fabric, white and dark slip—about 15 times the average for the fabric and 6 times higher than the average for the dark slip and white.

MS 4615–21, EM III Gournia. This sample has a similarly high concentration of As—about 20 times normal in the fabric, 10 times normal in the white, and 5 times normal in the dark slip.

MS 4615–7, EM III Gournia. The concentration of sulfur is anomalously high in the fabric (about 15 times normal) and also somewhat enhanced on the surface.

MS 4615–32, EM III Gournia. Both Ca and Cr are significantly enhanced relative to the average in the fabric of this sample.

Comparison to Other Groups

A significant difference among the various groups appears in the concentration of magnesium. EM III Gournia, Mokhlos and probably Knossos have similarly high concentrations of Mg, while the Middle Minoan Gournian group and the Vasilike group have low concentrations of this element.

In addition, certain elements were detected at the level of several parts per ten thousand in the Mokhlos (Ga, Br, and in one case Se), Vasilike (Ga, Br) and Knossos (Br and in one case Sn) groups that were not present at these levels in the Gournian EM III group.

To get an overview of differences among the groups we show in Table 11–III with a + or − sign whether an element is significantly more or less abundant than

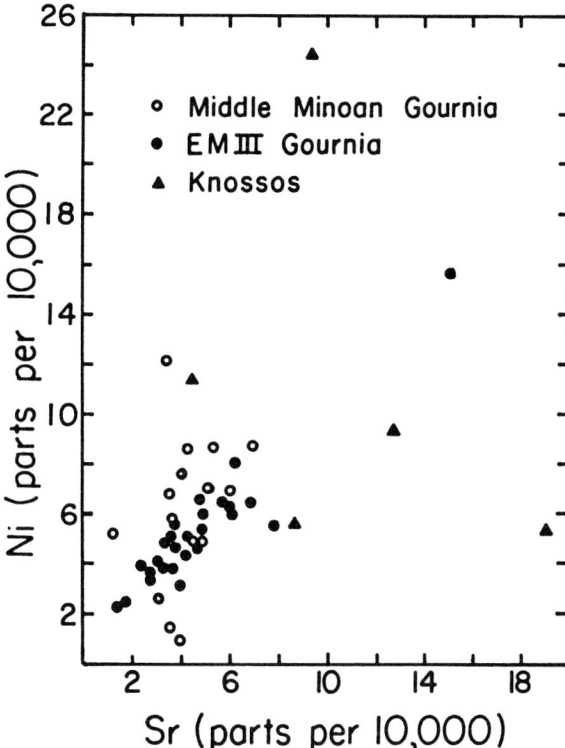

Fig. 11–2. A comparison between Ni and Sr from EM III and MM I–III Gournia.

in the EM III group from Gournia. A blank entry indicates no significant difference. (By "significant difference" we mean more than three standard deviations.)

The most striking feature that emerges from an inspection of Table 11–III is that the Gournian EM III group is significantly enriched in several elements compared to the four other groups. It contains significantly more Cr, Mn, As, and Zr than the others. The comparison shown in Table 11–III was made for the fabric of the samples, so these differences reflect a difference in the composition of the clay rather than in the decorating or painting technique. In particular, we can conclude that the clays of EM and MM Gournia differ significantly.

It is conventional to construct scatter plots of pairs of elements to look for characteristic groupings of compositions from different regions or periods. We show two typical illustrations of this from the present data in figs. 11–1 and 11–2. Fig. 11–1, which shows a comparison of Ca and Y for the two periods from Gournia, illustrates the danger of drawing conclusions about particular samples. Table 11–III shows that the average values for both these elements differ significantly for the Middle Minoan Gournian group from their concentrations in the EM III Gournian group. Yet there is considerable overlap for individuals in the two groups.

The situation is somewhat more favorable in fig. 11–2. The concentrations of Ni and Sr are very closely correlated wtih each other in the EM III Gournian group, and somewhat less so in the Middle Minoan Gournian samples. In contrast, the five samples from Knossos show no correlation between these two elements, and significantly larger concentrations of both elements than most (but not all!) of the Gournian ware.

In view of the high concentration of Sr in the samples from Knossos (see Table 11–III), one can ask whether this can serve to distinguish the clay from Knossos from the others. To answer this, we refer to the more detailed Table 11–II and look at the entry under Sr. We see that the concentration of Sr is significantly higher in the Knossian group than in all other groups except Vasilike. (The Vasilike group did not appear as a "+" in Table 11–III because the large uncertainty of 50% in the average means that this group is not significantly different from the others even though the average is large.) We can now search through the entries for the other elements in Table

11–II looking for some other element that discriminates between Knossos and Vasilike. Zn appears at first sight to differ, but the scatter in the samples from Vasilike is very large, and similarly for Cl, which we do not consider to be significant in any case. The anomaly in Pb for the ware from Vasilike has already been noted in footnote g to Table 11–II. Concentrations of K and Fe are somewhat higher in the Vasilike group, but, on the whole, these two clays appear rather similar. Larger numbers of samples from the Vasilike and Knossos sites would have to be examined to establish differences that may exist among their clays.

We thus consider our most significant result to be the differences established between the EM III Gournian clay and that of the other groups, including the Middle Minoan Gournian samples.

References

Ahlbert, M., R. Akselsson, B. Forkman, and G. Rausing. 1976. Gold traces on wedge-shaped artifacts from the late neolithic of southern Scandinavia analyzed by proton-induced X-ray emission spectroscopy. *Archaeometry* 18: 39–49.

Betancourt, P. P., T. K. Gaisser, F. R. Matson, G. H. Myer, and C. P. Swann. 1979. *Vasilike Ware*, 3–11. Göteborg.

Cookson, J. A. 1979. The production and use of a nuclear microprobe of ions at MeV energies. *Nucl. Instr. and Methods* 165: 477–508.

Duerdon, P., D. D. Cohen, E. Clayton, J. R. Bird, W. R. Ambrose, and B. F. Leach. 1979. Elemental analysis of thick obsidian samples by proton induced X-ray emission spectroscopy. *Analytic Chemistry* 51: 2350–54.

Flanagan, F. J. 1969. U.S. Geological survey standards—II. First compilation of data for new U.S.G.S. rocks. *Geochimica et Cosmochimica Acta* 33: 81–120.

Fleming, S. J. and J. Crowfoot-Payne. 1979. PIXE Analyses of some Egyptian bronzes of the Late Period. *MASCA Journal* 1: 46–47.

Folkman, F. 1975. Analytical use of ion-induced X-rays. *Journal of Phys. E, Scientific Instr.* 8: 429–44.

Fou, C. M., V. K. Rasmussen, C. P. Swann, and D. M. Van Patter. 1979. The Bartol-University of Delaware proton microprobe. *IEEE Trans. (Nucl. Sci.)* N. S. 26: 1378–80.

Grodzins, L., P. Horowitz, and J. Ryan. 1975. The scanning proton microprobe in an atmosphere environment. *Science* 189: 795–97.

Van Patter, D. M., C. P. Swann, and B. P. Glass. 1980. Proton probe analysis of an irghizite and a high-magnesium Java tektite. *Geochimica et Cosmochimica Acta* 45: 229–34.

12

Neutron Activation and Cluster Analyses

George Rapp, Jr. and John A. Gifford

Introduction

Neutron activation analysis (NAA) has been used for trace-element analyses for over two decades. This physical method of analysis allows determination of trace elements in the parts per billion (ppb) range, requiring only 50 mg or less of material. The sample is bombarded by an intense beam of neutrons that generates secondary radioactive nuclei from most metallic elements. Gamma ray emission spectra from these daughter nuclei are characteristic of the elements in the sample, and the intensity of the emissions is a measure of the concentrations of the elements. Instrumental NAA is done without any chemical separation.

Neutron activation analysis has been used extensively in archaeology for provenance studies of copper (Rapp et al. 1980; Fields et al. 1971), obsidian (Gordus et al. 1968; Griffin et al. 1969), flint (de Bruin et al. 1972), turquoise (Sigleo 1975), faience beads (Aspinall et al. 1972), and ceramics (Perlman and Asaro 1969; 1971; Brooks et al. 1975).

The NAA analyses reported here[1] were done at the nuclear reactor facilities at the University of Wisconsin, Madison (Richard Cashwell, director). A thermal neutron flux of about 10^{12} neutrons cm^{-2} sec^{-1} was used. The gamma radiation was counted using a Ge(Li) detector and the spectra were analyzed by Wisconsin's NAA CALC program. For the Gournian sherds of the MS 4615 series (Table 12–I) gold was the only internal standard used. Between the analysis of this series and the remainder of the samples shown in Table 12–I an entirely new standard, the Canadian Reference Soil Sample, was introduced. Although these later analyses are more accurate, they will not be completely comparable to the MS 4615 series, particularly for elements cesium (Cs), lutetium (Lu), scandium (Sc), and thorium (Th).

Analyses of ceramic materials are hampered by inherent inhomogeneities caused by natural or artificial inclusions. Most ancient pottery contains tempering materials as well as a variety of silt- or sand-sized grains of heavy minerals (a class of minerals containing metallic elements) incorporated with the secondary clays. Unless a large amount of material from each ceramic object is finely powdered and homogenized, there can be significant differences in the trace-element abundances among small chips from the same vessel. Because of the limited quantity of sherds available, this project analyzed very small chips from the sherds. Therefore, some differences can be expected among the analyses reported in various chapters in this book, and the range of values reported by each analytical method will be larger than if an homogenized sample had been prepared.

The objectives of this facet of the overall study of East Cretan White-on-dark Ware were to determine (1) if the sherds formed one or more distinct groups on the basis of their trace-element concentrations, and (2) if any of the clays that were collected as potential raw materials could be correlated with the pottery groups on the basis of trace-element concentrations.

TABLE 12-I
Concentrations for 21 elements

TRACE-ELEMENT CONCENTRATIONS (ppm)

SAMPLE	Ag	As	Au	Ba	Ce	Co	Cr	Cs	Eu	Fe	Hg	Ir	Lu	Ni	Sb	Sc	Ta	Te	Th	U	Yb
JAG-1	0.0	7.4	0.0	190.	38.	27.	260.	0.0	0.74	38000	0.0	0.0	0.36	0.	0.0	17	0.0	0.0	6.5	1.6	2.2
JAG-1	0.0	1.3	0.0	175.	45.	51.	240.	0.0	1.2	41000	0.0	0.0	0.39	0.	0.0	18	0.0	0.0	6.0	1.6	1.9
JAG-1	0.0	4.4	0.0	160.	37.	31.	190.	0.0	1.0	29000	0.0	0.0	0.28	0.	0.0	14	0.0	0.05	5.1	3.0	1.9
JAG-1	0.0	8.5	0.01	130.	49.	51.	250.	1.2	1.3	36000	0.0	0.0	0.21	270.	0.0	17	0.0	0.0	7.2	3.2	1.9
JAG-2	0.0	16.	0.0	155.	37.	56.	350.	1.3	0.79	55000	0.0	0.0	0.28	0.	0.0	17	0.0	0.0	6.1	3.3	1.8
JAG-2	0.0	4.4	0.0	120.	47.	47.	330.	0.0	0.67	49000	0.0	0.0	0.24	0.	1.5	17	0.0	0.05	5.9	2.9	1.9
JAG-2	0.0	5.2	0.0	190.	44.	53.	340.	0.0	0.68	54000	0.0	0.0	0.24	0.	0.0	18	0.0	0.0	6.2	2.4	1.9
JAG-2	0.0	5.9	0.0	155.	49.	46.	350.	0.0	0.55	52000	0.0	0.0	0.24	0.	0.0	17	0.0	6.6	6.5	3.8	2.0
JAG-2	0.0	16.	0.01	118.	56.	34.	390.	3.3	0.0	46000	0.0	0.0	0.33	0.	0.0	17	0.0	0.0	6.6	2.2	2.3
JAG-2	0.0	19.	0.01	306.	48.	39.	370.	9.4	0.0	48000	0.0	0.18	0.15	0.	0.0	17	0.0	0.0	5.7	2.7	2.2
JAG-3	0.0	1.2	0.0	150.	27.	29.	190.	0.0	0.72	23000	0.0	0.0	0.40	190.	0.0	11	0.55	0.0	4.1	2.5	1.8
JAG-4	0.0	3.0	0.0	163.	36.	38.	300.	0.0	0.58	32000	0.0	0.0	0.31	190.	0.0	15	0.56	0.0	6.2	3.8	1.7
JAG-4	0.0	0.0	0.0	250.	46.	37.	280.	0.0	0.85	38000	0.0	0.0	0.33	0.	0.0	16	0.0	0.0	6.6	3.5	1.6
JAG-4	0.0	0.0	0.0	140.	41.	56.	290.	0.0	0.85	39000	0.0	0.0	0.31	0.	0.0	17	0.0	0.05	5.9	3.8	1.6
JAG-4	0.0	0.0	0.0	99.	42.	41.	290.	0.0	0.40	38000	0.0	0.0	0.31	0.	0.0	16	0.46	0.0	6.2	3.5	1.6
JAG-4	2.7	9.6	0.0	0.	45.	43.	320.	2.8	0.0	41000	0.0	0.0	0.28	0.	1.7	16	0.86	0.0	5.4	2.5	1.9
JAG-4	0.0	0.0	0.0	271.	51.	42.	330.	0.0	0.0	39000	0.0	0.0	0.31	0.	0.0	16	0.0	6.4	5.6	2.4	1.9
JAG-5A	0.0	8.6	0.0	290.	53.	32.	120.	0.0	1.3	36000	0.0	0.0	0.37	0.	0.0	15	0.0	0.0	8.4	4.7	2.1
JAG-5A	0.0	6.4	0.0	150.	55.	32.	120.	0.0	0.61	30000	0.0	0.0	0.33	0.	0.0	15	0.0	0.0	9.4	2.8	2.1
JAG-5A	0.0	6.4	0:0	260.	55.	30.	120.	0.0	1.1	33000	0.0	0.0	0.36	0.	0.0	15	1.1	0.0	9.9	2.6	2.1
JAG-5A	0.0	4.2	0.0	110.	57.	29.	130.	0.0	0.87	34000	0.0	0.0	0.77	0.	0.0	16	0.0	0.0	9.3	2.9	2.0
JAG-5A	0.0	5.9	0.0	171.	59.	35.	190.	6.0	2.3	43000	0.0	0.0	0.45	0.	0.0	19	0.0	5.4	10	3.2	2.7
JAG-5B	0.0	4.0	0.0	330.	44.	26.	190.	0.0	0.30	30000	0.0	0.0	0.30	0.	1.3	14	1.5	0.0	8.1	2.5	1.8
JAG-5B	0.0	0.0	0.0	170.	48.	26.	180.	0.0	0.77	32000	0.0	0.0	0.34	0.	0.0	14	0.0	0.0	7.8	1.8	1.8
JAG-5B	0.0	0.0	0.0	213.	51.	27.	180.	0.0	0.89	31000	0.0	0.0	0.34	0.	0.0	14	0.0	0.0	6.7	2.1	2.1
JAG-5B	0.0	0.0	0.0	140.	52.	30.	180.	0.0	0.65	32000	0.0	0.0	0.69	0.	0.0	14	0.0	0.0	8.5	3.1	1.8
JAG-5B	0.0	1.9	0.0	350.	50.	19.	210.	3.4	0.0	29000	0.0	0.0	0.31	0.	0.0	15	0.0	0.0	6.7	3.3	1.4
JAG-5C	2.4	3.7	0.0	190.	49.	30.	170.	0.0	0.69	33000	0.0	0.0	0.33	0.	0.0	14	0.62	0.0	8.1	2.6	2.3
JAG-5C	0.0	0.0	0.0	230.	50.	30.	140.	0.0	1.0	32000	0.0	0.0	0.32	0.	0.0	14	0.0	0.0	8.6	2.1	2.0
JAG-5C	0.0	0.0	0.0	68.	52.	30.	140.	0.0	0.95	31000	2.8	0.0	0.35	0.	0.0	14	0.83	0.0	8.9	2.4	2.2
JAG-5C	0.0	0.0	0.0	240.	49.	25.	170.	5.6	1.4	33000	0.0	0.0	0.41	0.	0.0	14	0.0	0.0	9.2	2.0	1.4
JAG-5D	0.0	3.9	0.0	180.	46.	28.	130.	0.0	0.0	29000	0.0	0.0	0.36	0.	0.0	13	0.0	0.0	7.9	3.7	1.9
JAG-5D	0.0	0.0	0.0	160.	49.	27.	120.	0.0	0.42	29000	0.0	0.0	0.28	0.	0.0	13	0.71	0.0	9.4	3.0	2.0
JAG-5D	0.0	0.0	0.0	120.	53.	26.	130.	0.0	0.62	30000	0.0	0.0	0.30	0.	0.0	13	0.0	0.0	8.9	2.5	1.7
JAG-5D	0.0	3.5	0.0	0.	49.	15.	130.	3.9	1.2	26000	0.0	0.01	0.29	0.	0.0	12	0.0	0.0	6.7	2.5	1.7
JAG-6	0.0	21.	0.01	330.	100.	43.	130.	0.0	0.42	58000	0.0	0.0	0.56	0.	0.0	23	0.0	0.0	19.	3.8	3.9
JAG-7	2.0	3.0	0.0	87.	38.	38.	230.	0.0	0.35	36000	0.0	0.0	0.36	0.	0.61	16	0.0	0.0	6.3	2.6	1.8
JAG-7	0.0	0.0	0.0	130.	50.	40.	270.	0.0	0.53	40000	1.5	0.0	0.58	0.	0.0	18	0.0	0.0	6.7	1.6	2.0
JAG-7	0.0	0.0	0.0	130.	50.	40.	270.	0.0	0.53	40000	0.0	0.0	0.58	0.	0.0	18	0.0	0.0	6.7	1.6	2.0
JAG-7	0.0	0.0	0.0	0.	51.	37.	310.	5.5	0.0	37000	0.0	0.0	0.17	0.	0.0	17	0.0	0.0	6.8	1.6	1.7
JAG-7	0.0	0.0	0.0	400.	62.	53.	370.	5.9	0.0	47000	0.0	0.0	0.39	0.	0.0	20	0.0	0.0	8.0	2.6	2.2
JAG-8A	0.0	6.2	0.0	180.	44.	30.	250.	0.0	0.0	32000	0.0	0.0	0.33	0.	0.0	14	0.0	0.0	7.6	2.6	2.2
JAG-8A	0.0	0.0	0.0	110.	50.	31.	160.	0.0	0.65	33000	0.0	0.0	0.48	0.	0.0	15	0.0	0.0	7.8	2.9	2.1
JAG-8A	0.0	0.0	0.0	130.	49.	30.	180.	0.0	0.71	36000	0.0	0.0	0.60	0.	0.0	15	0.0	0.0	7.6	2.3	1.7
JAG-8A	0.0	6.9	0.0	250.	46.	26.	170.	5.4	0.59	25000	0.0	0.0	0.33	0.	0.0	14	0.0	0.0	8.1	2.3	1.4
JAG-8A	0.0	0.0	0.0	230.	36.	22.	180.	1.3	0.0	27000	0.0	0.01	0.42	0.	0.99	14	0.0	0.0	7.2	1.8	1.7

TABLE 12-I (continued)

TRACE-ELEMENT CONCENTRATIONS (ppm)

SAMPLE	Ag	As	Au	Ba	Ce	Co	Cr	Cs	Eu	Fe	Hg	Ir	Lu	Ni	Sb	Sc	Ta	Te	Th	U	Yb
JAG-8B	0.0	7.7	0.0	320.	44.	37.	100.	0.0	0.0	40000	0.0	0.0	0.34	0.	0.0	18	0.0	0.0	6.9	2.5	2.0
JAG-8B	0.0	0.0	0.0	0.	46.	39.	98.	0.0	0.72	44000	1.7	0.0	0.59	0.	0.0	18	0.0	0.0	6.4	1.8	2.0
JAG-9	0.0	2.4	0.0	250.	84.	26.	79.	1.1	0.0	30000	0.0	0.0	0.48	0.	0.0	16	3.0	0.0	14	4.7	2.9
JAG-9	0.0	0.0	0.0	150.	80.	35.	70.	0.0	0.23	31000	2.4	0.0	0.57	0.	10.0	16	0.0	0.0	15	3.7	3.0
JAG-10	0.0	3.5	0.0	150.	46.	53.	410.	0.0	0.49	37000	0.0	0.0	0.33	220.	0.0	19	2.0	0.0	7.8	3.8	2.8
JAG-10	0.0	4.0	0.0	130.	56.	52.	410.	0.0	1.1	41000	2.2	0.0	0.40	0.	0.0	20	0.0	0.0	7.7	4.0	2.3
JAG-10	0.0	3.8	0.0	330.	57.	50.	460.	0.0	0.82	40000	1.8	0.0	0.39	0.	0.0	20	0.0	0.0	8.8	2.6	2.3
JAG-10	0.0	3.8	0.0	200.	56.	62.	420.	0.0	0.86	40000	0.0	0.0	0.36	0.	10.0	20	0.0	0.0	8.3	2.9	2.2
JAG-10	0.0	2.8	0.0	0.	60.	52.	410.	3.8	2.0	37000	0.0	0.0	0.20	0.	10.0	19	0.0	0.0	8.0	2.6	1.6
JAG-11	0.0	0.0	0.0	99.	18.	21.	160.	0.0	0.19	13000	0.0	0.0	0.17	0.	0.0	6.9	0.0	0.0	2.6	2.1	1.1
JAG-12	2.1	9.1	0.0	290.	69.	29.	70.	0.0	1.0	34000	0.0	0.0	0.48	0.	10.0	17	2.1	0.0	11	3.3	2.2
JAG-12	0.0	0.0	0.0	200.	56.	23.	57.	0.0	1.1	26000	0.0	0.0	0.33	0.	0.0	14	0.0	0.0	9.1	2.4	2.2
JAG-12	0.0	0.0	0.0	240.	61.	23.	60.	0.0	0.83	26000	0.0	0.0	0.40	0.	0.0	14	0.0	0.0	9.2	2.5	2.3
JAG-12	0.0	0.0	0.0	250.	72.	29.	68.	0.0	1.1	35000	0.0	0.0	0.50	0.	2.9	17	1.2	0.0	11	4.5	2.7
JAG-12	2.0	9.2	0.0	310.	76.	13.	81.	0.0	0.67	28000	0.0	0.01	0.19	0.	0.0	16	1.0	0.0	12	3.5	2.4
JAG-13	0.0	4.9	0.01	120.	47.	22.	110.	0.0	0.20	30000	0.0	0.0	0.34	0.	0.0	12	0.0	0.0	7.0	4.3	1.7
JAG-13	0.0	4.7	0.0	190.	51.	24.	67.	0.0	0.72	29000	0.0	0.0	0.37	0.	0.0	12	0.0	0.0	8.0	2.3	2.1
JAG-13	0.0	4.4	0.0	230.	36.	21.	74.	0.0	0.72	28000	0.0	0.0	0.29	0.	0.0	13	0.0	4.5	7.4	3.0	1.7
JAG-13	0.0	4.9	0.0	210.	47.	19.	77.	0.0	0.72	29000	0.0	0.0	0.34	0.	0.0	13	0.0	0.0	7.0	2.9	1.8
JAG-13	0.0	8.2	0.01	0.	41.	14.	81.	1.7	0.48	24000	0.0	0.01	0.29	0.	0.0	12	0.96	0.0	7.8	3.3	1.7
JAG-14	0.0	0.0	0.0	130.	25.	26.	140.	0.0	0.68	16000	0.0	0.0	0.22	120.	0.0	8.0	0.0	0.0	3.6	2.1	1.0
JAG-14	0.0	0.0	0.0	0.	36.	20.	150.	0.0	0.52	23000	2.6	0.0	0.14	0.	0.78	10	0.0	0.0	4.3	2.4	1.1
JAG-14	0.0	0.0	0.0	0.	40.	25.	160.	0.0	0.84	23000	2.5	0.0	0.24	0.	0.0	11	0.0	0.0	5.1	2.9	1.3
JAG-14	0.0	2.9	0.01	93.	39.	24.	170.	4.6	0.0	21000	0.0	0.0	0.13	0.	0.0	10	0.55	0.0	4.6	1.7	1.3
JAG-15	0.0	0.0	0.01	180.	21.	19.	140.	0.0	0.77	19000	0.0	0.0	0.20	0.	0.0	7.9	0.0	0.0	2.9	2.6	1.0
JAG-15	0.0	0.0	0.0	0.	20.	20.	150.	0.0	0.74	19000	0.0	0.0	0.14	0.	0.0	8.2	0.39	0.0	3.0	1.6	1.2
JAG-15	0.0	0.0	0.0	0.	25.	22.	160.	0.0	0.71	21000	1.3	0.0	0.15	0.	0.0	8.8	0.0	0.0	3.1	0.73	1.3
JAG-15	0.0	0.0	0.0	98.	27.	15.	170.	0.0	0.28	19000	0.0	0.0	0.10	0.	0.0	7.9	0.57	0.0	3.4	1.4	1.1
JAG-16A	0.0	7.7	0.0	220.	49.	33.	200.	0.0	0.49	38000	0.0	0.0	0.40	0.	0.0	17	0.53	0.0	8.8	2.6	2.1
JAG-16A	0.0	0.0	0.0	150.	56.	34.	200.	0.0	0.66	40000	0.0	0.0	0.39	0.	0.0	17	0.0	0.0	8.9	2.5	2.3
JAG-16A	0.0	0.0	0.0	140.	54.	35.	200.	0.0	0.0	41000	0.0	0.0	0.38	0.	0.0	17	0.93	0.0	7.9	2.6	2.1
JAG-16A	0.0	12.	0.0	110.	58.	34.	210.	1.5	0.83	39000	0.0	0.0	0.16	0.	0.0	16	0.0	5.5	7.9	0.57	1.9
JAG-16A	0.0	5.1	0.01	270.	57.	33.	210.	2.1	0.84	39000	0.0	0.01	0.21	0.	0.54	16	0.0	0.0	8.6	2.2	2.3
JAG-16B	0.0	6.6	0.00	230.	54.	36.	190.	0.0	0.37	35000	0.0	0.0	0.36	140.	0.0	16	0.0	0.0	8.4	3.3	1.9
JAG-16B	0.0	1.8	0.0	160.	60.	41.	200.	0.0	1.5	40000	2.3	0.0	0.40	0.	0.0	17	0.0	0.0	8.4	2.1	2.4
JAG-16B	0.0	2.1	0.0	140.	65.	43.	200.	0.0	0.70	40000	0.0	0.0	0.43	0.	0.0	17	0.0	0.0	8.4	2.1	2.4
JAG-16B	0.0	3.5	0.0	210.	52.	41.	180.	0.0	0.51	39000	1.8	0.0	0.85	0.	0.0	17	0.0	0.0	8.4	1.4	1.9
JAG-16B	0.0	5.3	0.0	260.	54.	32.	200.	5.6	0.0	36000	0.0	0.0	0.40	160.	10.0	16	0.84	0.0	9.5	2.9	2.0
JAG-16B	0.0	12.	0.01	430.	57.	37.	200.	3.9	0.0	35000	0.0	0.0	0.45	0.	0.0	16	0.86	0.0	10.	3.5	2.3
JAG-17	0.0	17.	0.0	75.1	34.	13.	190.	0.0	0.94	17000	0.0	0.0	0.54	0.	0.90	10	0.66	6.6	3.7	6.9	2.8
JAG-17	0.0	6.8	0.0	99.1	29.	19.	210.	0.0	0.83	17000	0.0	0.0	0.26	0.	1.0	11	1.3	0.0	3.2	9.6	2.4
JAG-17	0.0	12.	0.0	87.1	25.	18.	210.	0.0	0.72	19000	0.0	0.0	0.21	0.	1.3	12	0.0	0.0	3.7	8.5	2.9
JAG-17	0.0	12.	0.0	0.1	29.	12.	220.	2.6	0.0	16000	0.0	0.0	0.26	0.	0.88	11	0.0	0.0	4.4	7.4	2.5
JAG-17	0.0	6.8	0.0	0.1	29.	3.9	200.	3.9	0.62	13000	0.0	0.13	0.25	0.	0.0	12	0.80	25.	3.8	6.2	3.3

TABLE 12-I (continued)

TRACE-ELEMENT CONCENTRATIONS (ppm)

SAMPLE	Ag	As	Au	Ba	Ce	Co	Cr	Cs	Eu	Fe	Hg	Ir	Lu	Ni	Sb	Sc	Ta	Te	Th	U	Yb
Penn 60-19-14	0.0	0.0	0.01	330.	60.	86.	360.	0.0	1.4	67000.	0.0	0.0	0.51	0.	6.2	30.	0.0	0.0	15.	.17	2.6
Penn MS 4628-3	0.0	0.0	0.0	490.	100.	110.	580.	0.0	0.0	58000.	2.2	0.0	0.44	0.	0.0	28.	1.3	0.0	18.	0.0	1.1
Penn MS 4628-6	3.5	0.0	0.0	0.	69.	100.	490.	0.0	0.53	80000.	0.0	0.0	0.54	290.	0.0	34.	0.0	0.0	16.	0.0	2.4
Penn MS 4628-7	0.0	0.0	0.0	560.	75.	110.	400.	0.0	1.1	80000.	0.0	0.0	0.70	600.	0.0	37.	0.0	0.0	15.	0.0	3.3
Penn MS 4628-9	0.0	0.0	0.0	0.	54.	83.	450.	0.0	1.2	68000.	0.0	0.0	0.31	0.	0.0	27.	1.4	0.0	12.	3.6	2.5
Penn MS 4628-13	0.0	0.0	0.0	250.	95.	40.	88.	0.0	0.41	48000.	0.0	0.0	0.59	0.	1.6	18.	.94	0.0	16.	0.0	3.2
Penn MS 4628-14	0.0	0.0	0.0	870.	130.	42.	120.	0.0	0.68	54000.	0.0	0.0	0.52	0.	1.5	24.	1.7	0.0	21.	5.7	3.4
Penn MS 4628-15	0.0	0.0	0.0	850.	61.	87.	450.	0.0	1.1	79000.	0.0	0.0	0.56	250.	0.0	34.	.78	0.0	14.	0.0	1.8
Penn MS 4628-19	0.0	0.0	0.0	550.	87.	39.	95.	0.0	0.0	49000.	0.0	0.0	0.44	0.	2.3	18.	0.0	0.0	16.	3.4	2.3
Penn MS 4628-20	0.0	0.0	0.0	0.	87.	66.	380.	0.0	0.62	56000.	0.0	0.012	0.29	0.	0.0	26.	1.0	0.0	16.	2.8	2.3
Penn MS 4628-21	0.0	0.0	0.0	0.	93.	62.	83.	0.0	0.77	47000.	0.0	0.0	0.98	0.	4.1	20.	0.0	0.0	15.	0.0	3.4
Penn MS 4628-22	0.0	0.0	0.0	0.	67.	100.	450.	0.0	0.54	82000.	0.0	0.0	0.30	0.	4.2	37.	0.0	0.0	16.	0.0	1.4
Penn MS 4700-1	0.0	0.0	0.0	330.	66.	77.	410.	0.0	1.3	69000.	0.0	0.0	0.52	420.	07.8	30.	.64	0.0	13.	1.3	2.3
Penn MS 4700-3	0.0	0.0	0.0	430.	82.	39.	190.	0.0	0.0	49000.	0.0	0.0	0.34	0.	0.0	21.	.58	0.0	13.	3.6	2.4
Penn MS 4700-5	0.0	0.0	0.0	0.	71.	83.	420.	0.0	0.0	65000.	0.0	0.0	0.28	0.	0.0	29.	0.0	0.0	13.	0.0	2.3
Penn MS 4700-9	0.0	0.0	0.03	690.	66.	65.	410.	0.0	1.2	70000.	0.0	0.0	0.56	350.	0.0	29.	.67	0.0	14.	4.0	2.2
Penn MS 4700-10	0.0	0.0	0.0	50.	78.	110.	440.	0.0	0.82	73000.	0.0	0.0	0.23	320.	3.9	29.	2.1	0.0	12.	0.0	2.5
AM AE 753.4	0.0	0.0	0.0	730.	65.	95.	530.	0.0	0.0	75000.	0.0	0.0	0.49	0.	0.0	33.	.97	0.0	13.	0.0	2.3
AM 1938.421	0.0	0.0	0.0	0.	67.	97.	480.	0.0	1.1	71000.	0.0	0.0	0.30	0.	0.0	32.	0.0	22.	13.	0.0	2.0
AM 1938.821	8.5	0.0	0.0	370.	63.	130.	540.	0.0	0.89	77000.	0.0	0.0	0.02	0.	18.	33.	0.0	0.0	14.	0.0	0.0
Penn MS 4894	0.0	0.0	0.0	290.	60.	88.	410.	0.0	0.0	76000.	0.0	0.0	0.24	0.	10.	33.	0.0	0.0	15.	6.1	3.0
MHC BAI-14-B	0.0	0.0	0.0	410.	63.	77.	450.	0.0	1.3	63000.	0.0	0.013	0.49	580.	0.0	25.	0.0	0.0	13.	0.0	2.1
Penn MS 4237	0.0	39.	0.0	140.	48.	76.	350.	0.0	1.8	66000.	0.83	0.0	0.53	180.	0.0	32.	0.0	0.0	11.	0.0	2.4
Penn MS 4236	0.0	0.0	0.17	390.	51.	77.	250.	0.0	0.0	59000.	0.0	0.0	0.47	0.	0.0	28.	0.0	0.0	10.	0.0	3.1
Penn MS 4238	0.0	0.0	0.0	450.	46.	93.	290.	0.0	0.0	65000.	2.0	0.0	0.29	0.	0.0	28.	0.0	0.0	11.	0.0	2.2
Penn MS 4234	0.0	6.0	0.0	1300.	75.	100.	430.	0.0	0.0	76000.	1.2	0.02	0.36	310.	0.0	31.	1.3	0.0	16.	0.0	2.2
MHC BAI-14-A	0.0	0.0	0.0	600.	64.	71.	260.	0.0	0.0	68000.	0.0	0.0	0.72	260.	9.9	27.	.41	0.0	13.	2.6	3.0
AM AE.752	0.0	0.0	0.01	920.	62.	140.	520.	0.0	1.4	77000.	0.0	0.0	0.40	340.	0.0	34.	1.2	0.0	14.	1.8	1.5
AM AE.1672	0.0	0.0	0.0	430.	79.	140.	540.	0.0	0.0	73000.	0.0	0.0	0.39	340.	0.0	32.	0.0	0.0	13.	0.0	2.8
MFA 9.557	0.0	76.	0.0	420.	63.	110.	500.	0.0	0.0	90000.	0.0	0.0	0.50	340.	0.0	35.	.71	0.0	14.	0.0	2.6
MFA 9.573	0.0	0.0	0.0	1000.	75.	67.	350.	0.0	1.3	67000.	4.9	0.0	0.92	460.	0.0	30.	1.5	0.0	12.	0.0	3.5
MFA 9.574	0.0	0.0	0.0	350.	46.	93.	350.	0.0	0.53	71000.	0.0	0.0	0.50	640.	0.0	31.	0.0	0.0	10.	0.0	2.0
MFA 9.575	0.0	0.0	0.0	450.	77.	120.	450.	0.0	0.0	90000.	0.0	0.0	0.51	0.	0.0	36.	0.0	0.0	16.	0.0	2.9
MFA 575.2	0.0	0.0	0.0	1400.	90.	170.	720.	0.0	0.0	120000.	0.0	0.0	1.1	820.	0.0	53.	0.0	0.0	21.	0.0	1.8
MFA 9.66	0.0	0.0	00.2	0.	48.	75.	270.	0.0	0.85	55000.	0.0	0.0	0.33	310.	4.4	22.	0.0	0.0	11.	0.0	2.0
MFA 575.3	0.0	0.0	0.0	0.	66.	120.	460.	0.0	0.87	84000.	0.0	0.0	0.0	0.	0.0	35.	1.4	0.0	16.	0.0	2.9
AM 9.334	0.0	0.0	00.4	440.	55.	120.	440.	0.0	0.0	83000.	0.0	0.0	0.67	0.	5.0	36.	0.0	0.0	14.	6.5	1.8

The Analyses

Table 12–I presents the results of the analyses of the sherd and clay samples. The 22 members of the JAG series are clays from potential source localities in the Isthmus of Ierapetra (see Chap. 15). Most of these were reanalyzed from two to five times; all the results are listed here. The thirty samples from the University of Pennsylvania numbered in the MS 4615 series (MS 4615–2 through MS 4615–47) are from Gournia and are Early Minoan III in date. This is the type-site for East Cretan White-on-dark Ware. The sherds formed a tight stylistic group. There was some variation in coarseness, with cups being finer textured than jars. The group probably represents a narrow span of time (see Chap. 2).

The seven samples designated MFA and AM sample 9.334 are from the island of Mokhlos, 13 km northeast of Gournia. They also form a tight stylistic group of the Early Minoan III period. The four samples labeled MS 4234, 6, 7, and 8, and the two with the BAI prefix are from EM III deposits at nearby Vasilike. For comparison, the three samples with the AE prefix and the two in the 1938 series are from EM III levels at Knossos in central Crete. The sample designated MS 4894 is from Priniatikos Pyrgos, on the north coast near Gournia and Vasilike.

The sixteen samples of the MS 4628 and MS 4700 series are from Middle Minoan levels at Gournia. This group ranges widely in style and date within Middle Minoan, i.e., it lacks the homogeneity of the EM III group. All sherds are listed in the Appendix.

Because of the lack of duplicate analyses and the "mid-stream" change in standards, the results in Table 12–I are given to only two significant figures.

In order to make our analytical data more comparable to published trace-element data on Bronze Age pottery from the Aegean area, we analyzed five

TABLE 12-I (continued)

TRACE-ELEMENT CONCENTRATIONS (ppm)

SAMPLE	Ag	As	Au	Ba	Ce	Co	Cr	Cs	Eu	Fe	Hg	Ir	Lu	Ni	Sb	Sc	Ta	Te	Th	U	Yb
Penn MS 4615-2	0.0	1.5	0.58	92.	26.	36.	220.	6.9	0.27	36000.	0.0	0.0	160.	0.	0.0	5.6	0.0	5.6	4.6	1.5	2.9
Penn MS 4615-6	0.0	5.0	0.41	180.	29.	36.	270.	8.0	0.78	47000.	0.0	0.0	210.	170.	0.0	6.4	0.0	0.0	6.2	1.7	3.1
Penn MS 4615-7	0.0	4.1	0.54	260.	31.	29.	270.	9.0	0.0	45000.	0.0	0.0	180.	9.2	0.0	6.4	0.36	0.0	6.7	4.0	4.3
Penn MS 4615-8	0.0	4.1	0.37	240.	33.	28.	220.	13.	0.0	46000.	0.0	0.0	170.	190.	0.0	6.4	0.66	0.0	6.5	2.6	3.5
Penn MS 4615-9	0.0	0.0	0.99	170.	32.	50.	280.	13.	0.27	46000.	0.0	0.0	200.	180.	0.0	6.8	0.0	0.0	6.2	0.8	4.0
Penn MS 4615-10	0.0	0.0	0.27	290.	29.	25.	230.	8.3	0.34	40000.	0.0	0.0	170.	84.	0.0	5.6	0.0	0.0	5.7	2.6	2.9
Penn MS 4615-11	0.0	0.0	0.94	140.	18.	34.	170.	7.0	0.0	29000.	0.0	0.0	110.	86.	1.2	4.6	0.0	0.0	3.3	1.2	2.1
Penn MS 4615-12	0.0	0.0	0.23	150.	29.	26.	220.	0.0	0.0	43000.	0.0	0.0	180.	96.	0.0	6.1	0.0	0.0	5.4	1.2	3.3
Penn MS 4615-13	2.0	13.	0.45	320.	27.	37.	290.	3.9	0.54	43000.	3.2	0.0	190.	110.	1.1	6.0	0.62	0.0	5.3	1.7	3.6
Penn MS 4615-15	0.0	0.0	0.45	100.	19.	28.	160.	9.1	0.0	28000.	0.0	0.0	120.	110.	0.0	3.9	0.0	0.0	4.5	2.2	2.3
Penn MS 4615-16	0.0	1.8	0.19	270.	26.	34.	250.	8.1	0.0	42000.	1.9	0.0	180.	0.	0.0	6.0	0.0	0.0	4.9	1.9	3.3
Penn MS 4615-17	0.0	0.0	1.8	0.	31.	47.	270.	9.4	0.34	40000.	1.9	0.013	150.	150.	0.77	5.8	0.76	0.0	6.0	1.8	3.3
Penn MS 4615-18	0.0	0.0	0.34	210.	32.	24.	220.	9.8	0.74	42000.	0.0	0.0	180.	0.	0.0	5.9	0.0	0.0	5.5	2.9	3.1
Penn MS 4615-19	0.0	4.6	0.36	260.	33.	39.	280.	7.6	0.24	50000.	0.0	0.022	220.	130.	0.54	7.3	0.0	0.0	6.9	3.1	4.1
Penn MS 4615-21	0.0	21.	2.1	460.	28.	50.	230.	14.	0.0	51000.	0.0	0.0	220.	100.	1.5	6.9	0.0	0.0	5.9	1.9	3.3
Penn MS 4615-22	0.0	3.3	0.52	0.	18.	20.	160.	7.0	0.18	25000.	0.0	0.0	130.	0.	0.43	3.6	0.0	0.0	3.2	0.0	1.8
Penn MS 4615-23	0.0	7.8	2.0	200.	33.	37.	290.	10.	0.47	51000.	0.0	0.0	240.	0.	0.0	8.2	0.0	0.0	6.6	3.4	5.0
Penn MS 4615-23	2.1	3.0	0.32	400.	31.	47.	280.	13.	0.30	51000.	3.5	0.0	180.	75.	0.0	7.9	0.0	0.0	6.5	2.4	4.4
Penn MS 4615-26	0.0	6.3	0.47	330.	31.	41.	270.	9.9	0.0	49000.	3.0	0.0	250.	99.	0.36	7.6	0.0	0.0	4.6	2.0	4.4
Penn MS 4615-27	0.0	0.0	0.28	0.	24.	24.	180.	8.6	0.17	36000.	0.0	0.0	170.	150.	0.0	5.7	0.87	0.0	6.0	2.1	3.4
Penn MS 4615-29	0.0	4.6	0.70	400.	31.	40.	300.	9.6	0.65	47000.	1.0	0.0	190.	110.	1.1	7.1	0.0	0.0	6.5	2.2	4.6
Penn MS 4615-31	0.0	3.5	0.57	160.	34.	39.	300.	9.6	1.1	48000.	2.4	0.0	230.	110.	0.77	7.0	0.0	5.9	6.6	2.7	4.7
Penn MS 4615-32	0.0	4.9	0.82	290.	36.	45.	240.	16.	0.50	47000.	3.0	0.0	240.	0.	1.1	7.3	0.0	0.0	48.	2.2	4.4
Penn MS 4615-33	0.0	2.6	0.33	290.	27.	34.	240.	7.3	0.95	47000.	2.0	0.0	240.	0.	0.5	6.4	0.0	8.6	4.7	1.7	4.6
Penn MS 4615-34	0.0	0.0	7.4	0.	28.	76.	240.	16.	0.0	39000.	0.0	0.0	210.	0.	2.7	5.6	0.0	0.0	7.8	0.0	4.0
Penn MS 4615-35	0.0	0.0	0.71	440.	36.	29.	320.	11.	0.64	50000.	0.0	0.0	250.	180.	0.0	6.6	1.8	0.0	7.8	2.7	3.1
Penn MS 4615-36	0.0	4.2	0.79	180.	35.	41.	310.	13.	0.21	55000.	0.0	0.0	200.	120.	0.0	7.7	0.98	0.0	6.6	2.5	4.3
Penn MS 4615-39	0.0	0.0	0.34	150.	32.	44.	300.	6.6	0.75	47000.	0.0	0.0	230.	100.	0.0	6.9	0.47	0.0	7.1	2.5	4.0
Penn MS 4615-40	0.0	2.9	1.4	150.	33.	49.	320.	12.	0.0	50000.	3.1	0.0	220.	0.	0.0	7.4	0.0	0.0	6.0	1.9	3.6
Penn MS 4615-41	0.0	0.0	0.55	180.	27.	41.	270.	10.	0.35	48000.	2.9	0.0	200.	160.	0.0	6.9	0.38	0.0	6.3	1.3	4.1
Penn MS 4615-44	0.0	2.7	0.34	220.	31.	41.	300.	11.	0.45	51000.	2.3	0.0	220.	79.	1.9	7.7	0.0	0.0	6.6	2.2	4.1
Penn MS 4615-45	3.9	7.0	0.26	170.	26.	45.	270.	9.3	0.0	53000.	0.0	0.0	230.	0.	0.0	8.1	0.56	0.0	7.1	3.7	4.2
Penn MS 4615-47	0.0	7.3	0.60	430.	33.	41.	300.	11.	0.0	53000.	3.4	0.0	240.	90.	1.3	7.4	0.0	0.0	5.9	3.2	3.7

standard materials and recalculated our analytical values for the eight elements (Ba, Ce, Co, Cr, Eu, Fe, Sc, Th) that were common to our data set and the values for the standards. Four of the standards are from the U.S. Geological Survey: AGV–1, G–2, GSP–1, PCC–1. The fifth standard is the basic reference material for many eastern Mediterranean pottery analyses, the AP standard of Perlman and Asaro.

The element concentrations for the U.S.G.S. standards (calculated from the oxide values in Abscal et al. 1974: Table 1) and the AP standard (Perlman and Asaro 1971: Table 13.3) were compared with our concentration values; a correction factor representing the mean ratio of the two values for each standard was calculated, and element concentrations of all clay and sherd samples were multiplied by the corresponding correction factors. Corrected values of the eight elements for all clay and sherd samples are listed in Table 12–II.

Formation of Clusters

With the element concentrations for two types of samples (clays and sherds) from known localities, we used a numerical clustering technique to confirm or modify these empirical groups. Ideally there should exist some correlations of the archaeological/geological groups with the clusters calculated from trace-element concentrations.

The numerical approach chosen for this study was K-means cluster analysis, an iterative clustering technique with reallocation capability. (See Doran and Hodson 1975: 180–85 for a general discussion of the application of K-means procedures to archaeological data sets.) The most important advantage of K-means clustering over the hierarchical aggregative techniques more often used in NAA data analysis (e.g., Bieber et al. 1976; Attas et al. 1977) is its capability to continuously review cluster membership and to reallocate members by an optimizing criterion. In PKM, the K-means program used here (University of California 1979), the reallocation algorithm mini-

TABLE 12-II
Corrected concentrations for eight elements

TRACE ELEMENTS (ppm)

SAMPLE	Ba	Ce	Co	Cr	Eu	Fe	Sc	Th
JAG-1	126.	36.6	19.4	156.	.369	27000.	10.2	3.04
JAG-2	135.	41.3	22.2	238.	.241	37400.	10.2	2.97
JAG-3	117.	23.5	14.3	123.	.208	174.00	6.75	1.20
JAG-4	135.	38.5	20.8	197.	.228	27900.	9.42	2.97
JAG-5A	144.	48.8	15.8	90.2	.402	26100.	9.42	4.67
JAG-5B	180.	43.2	12.2	123.	.214	22600.	8.64	3.75
JAG-5C	135.	44.1	14.3	98.4	.348	24400.	8.64	4.31
JAG-5D	117.	43.2	11.5	82.0	.241	20900.	7.85	4.03
JAG-6	260.	88.3	21.5	82.0	.147	43600.	14.1	1.91
JAG-7	126.	44.1	20.1	189.	.161	29600.	11.0	3.39
JAG-8A	135.	39.4	13.6	123.	.235	22600.	8.64	3.82
JAG-8B	251.	39.4	18.6	65.6	.255	31300.	11.0	3.32
JAG-9	153.	72.3	15.1	49.2	.080	22600.	9.42	7.07
JAG-10	153.	47.9	26.5	279.	.342	29600.	11.8	4.03
JAG-11	79.	16.0	10.8	107.	.067	9590.	4.24	1.06
JAG-12	207.	58.2	11.5	44.3	.328	21800.	9.42	5.16
JAG-13	144.	38.5	10.0	53.3	.462	20900.	7.61	3.68
JAG-14	88.	30.0	11.5	107.	.241	15600.	5.97	2.19
JAG-15	108.	20.7	9.3	107.	.208	14800.	5.02	1.56
JAG-16A	135.	47.9	16.5	139.	.248	29600.	10.2	4.17
JAG-16B	180.	49.8	18.6	131.	.241	27900.	10.2	4.38
JAG-17	69.	25.4	7.90	172.	.275	12200.	6.83	1.84
Penn MS 4615-2	83.0	24.4	25.8	180.	.181	31300.	4.40	4.60
Penn MS 4615-6	162.	27.2	25.8	221.	.523	40900.	5.02	6.15
Penn MS 4615-7	233.	29.1	20.8	221.	0.0	39200.	5.02	6.72
Penn MS 4615-8	216.	31.0	20.1	180.	0.0	40100.	5.02	6.50
Penn MS 4615-9	153.	30.0	35.9	230.	.181	40100.	5.34	6.22
Penn MS 4615-10	260.	27.2	17.9	189.	.228	34800.	4.40	5.66
Penn MS 4615-11	126.	16.9	24.4	139.	0.0	25200.	3.61	3.25
Penn MS 4615-12	135.	27.2	18.6	180.	0.0	37400.	4.79	5.44
Penn MS 4615-13	287.	25.4	26.5	238.	.362	37400.	4.71	5.30
Penn MS 4615-15	90.	17.8	20.1	131.	0.0	24400.	3.06	4.45
Penn MS 4615-16	242.	24.4	24.4	205.	0.0	36600.	4.71	4.88
Penn MS 4615-17	0.0	29.1	33.7	221.	.228	34800.	4.55	6.01
Penn MS 4615-18	189.	30.0	17.2	180.	.496	36600.	4.63	5.51
Penn MS 4615-19	233.	31.0	28.0	230.	.161	43600.	5.73	6.86
Penn MS 4615-21	413.	26.3	35.9	189.	0.0	44400.	5.42	5.87
Penn MS 4615-22	0.0	16.9	14.3	131.	.121	21800.	2.83	3.18
Penn MS 4615-23	359.	29.1	33.7	230.	.201	44400.	6.20	6.58
Penn MS 4615-26	296.	29.1	29.4	221.	0.0	42700.	5.97	6.50
Penn MS 4615-27	0.0	22.5	17.2	148.	.114	31300.	4.47	4.60
Penn MS 4615-29	359.	29.1	28.7	246.	.436	40900.	5.57	6.01
Penn MS 4615-31	144.	31.9	28.0	246.	.737	41800.	5.50	6.50
Penn MS 4615-32	260.	33.8	32.3	197.	.335	40900.	5.73	6.58

TABLE 12-II (continued)

Penn MS 4615-33	260.	25.4	24.4	197.	.637	40900.	5.02	48.1
Penn MS 4615-34	0.0	26.3	54.5	197.	0.0	34000.	4.40	4.67
Penn MS 4615-35	395.	33.8	20.8	262.	.429	43600.	5.18	7.78
Penn MS 4615-36	162.	32.9	29.4	254.	.141	47900.	6.04	7.78
Penn MS 4615-39	135.	30.0	31.5	246.	.503	43600.	5.42	6.58
Penn MS 4615-40	135.	31.0	35.1	262.	0.0	43600.	5.81	7.07
Penn MS 4615-41	162.	25.4	29.4	221.	.235	41800.	5.42	6.01
Penn MS 4615-44	198.	29.1	29.4	246.	.302	44400.	6.04	6.29
Penn MS 4615-45	153.	24.4	32.3	221.	0.0	46200.	6.36	6.65
Penn MS 4615-47	386.	31.0	29.4	246.	0.0	46200.	5.81	7.07
Penn 60-19-14	260.	52.6	43.0	238.	.503	50500.	18.1	5.87
Penn MS 4628-3	395.	89.2	53.1	385.	0.0	43600.	17.3	9.19
Penn MS 4628-6	269.	61.0	50.9	328.	.188	60100.	21.2	8.48
Penn MS 4628-7	449.	66.7	53.1	271.	.395	60100.	22.8	7.07
Penn MS 4628-9	0.0	47.9	41.6	303.	.436	50500.	16.5	5.80
Penn MS 4628-13	198.	83.6	20.1	59.0	.147	36600.	11.0	7.78
Penn MS 4628-14	700.	113.	20.8	81.2	.248	40100.	14.9	10.6
Penn MS 4628-15	682.	53.5	43.0	303.	.395	59200.	21.2	6.86
Penn MS 4628-19	440.	77.0	19.4	63.1	0.0	36600.	11.0	7.78
Penn MS 4628-20	0.0	77.0	33.0	254.	.221	42700.	15.7	7.78
Penn MS 4628-21	0.0	81.7	30.8	55.8	.275	34800.	11.8	7.78
Penn MS 4628-22	0.0	59.2	50.2	303.	.194	61900.	22.8	7.78
Penn MS 4700-1	269.	58.2	38.0	279.	.469	52300.	18.1	6.58
Penn MS 4700-3	341.	72.3	19.4	131.	0.0	36600.	12.56	6.43
Penn MS 4700-5	0.0	62.9	41.6	279.	0.0	48800.	18.1	6.72
Penn MS 4700-9	548.	58.2	32.3	271.	.436	53100.	18.1	6.93
Penn MS 4700-10	0.0	68.5	54.5	295.	.295	54900.	18.1	5.94
MHC BAI-14-B	332.	55.4	38.0	303.	.469	47000.	14.9	6.43
Penn MS 4237	108.	42.3	38.0	230.	.650	49700.	19.6	5.44
Penn MS 4236	314.	45.1	38.0	172.	0.0	44400.	17.3	4.95
Penn MS 4238	368.	40.4	45.9	189.	0.0	48800.	17.3	5.44
Penn MS 4234	1080.	66.7	51.6	287.	0.0	57500.	18.8	7.78
MHC BAI-14-A	485.	56.3	35.1	172.	0.0	51400.	16.5	6.43
AM AE.753.4	593.	57.3	47.3	353.	0.0	56600.	20.4	6.43
AM 1938.421	0.0	59.2	48.0	320.	.395	53100.	19.6	6.43
AM 1938.821	296.	55.4	62.4	361.	.322	58400.	20.4	6.93
AM AE.752	736.	54.5	71.0	344.	.503	58400.	21.2	6.93
AM AE.1672	350.	43.2	67.4	361.	0.0	54900.	19.6	6.43
Penn MS 4894	233.	52.6	43.7	271.	0.0	57500.	20.4	7.78
MFA 9.557	341.	55.4	52.3	336.	0.0	68000.	21.2	6.93
MFA 9.573	799.	66.7	33.0	230.	.469	50500.	18.1	5.94
MFA 9.574	278.	40.4	45.9	230.	.188	53100.	18.8	4.95
MFA 9.575	359.	67.6	59.5	295.	0.0	68000.	22.0	7.78
MFA 575.2	1170.	79.8	86.0	484.	0.0	87200.	32.2	10.6
MFA 9.66	0.0	42.3	37.3	180.	.308	40900.	13.4	5.44
MFA 575.3	0.0	58.2	59.5	312.	.315	62700.	21.2	7.78
AM 09.334	350.	48.8	57.4	295.	0.0	62700.	22.0	6.93

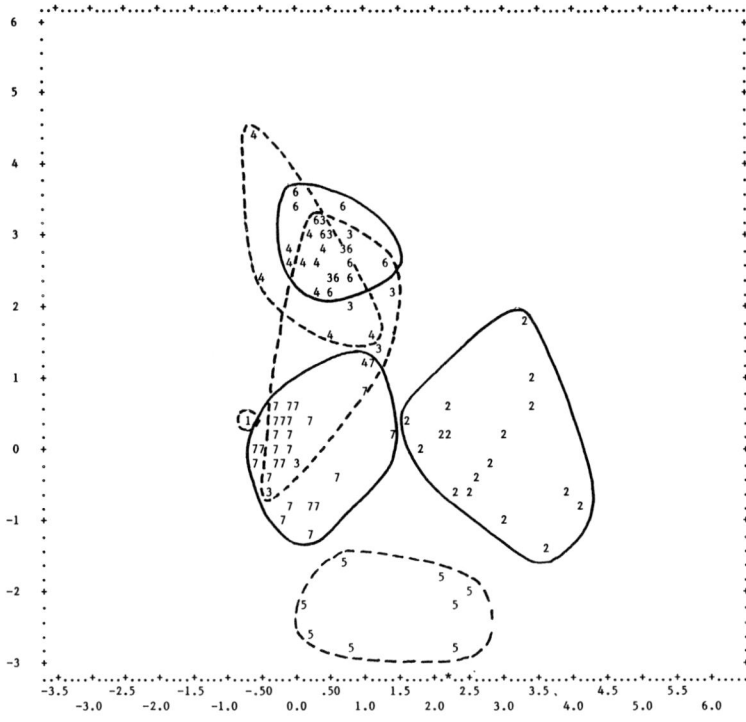

Fig. 12−1. Sherd samples, K-means clustering (K = 7, 1 iteration) based on eight elements (Ba, Ce, Co, Cr, Eu, Fe, Sc, Th). Scatter plot of the seven clusters projected from eight dimensions on to the plane defined by the centroids of the three most populous clusters (4, 6, and 7). See Table 12−IV for cluster membership.

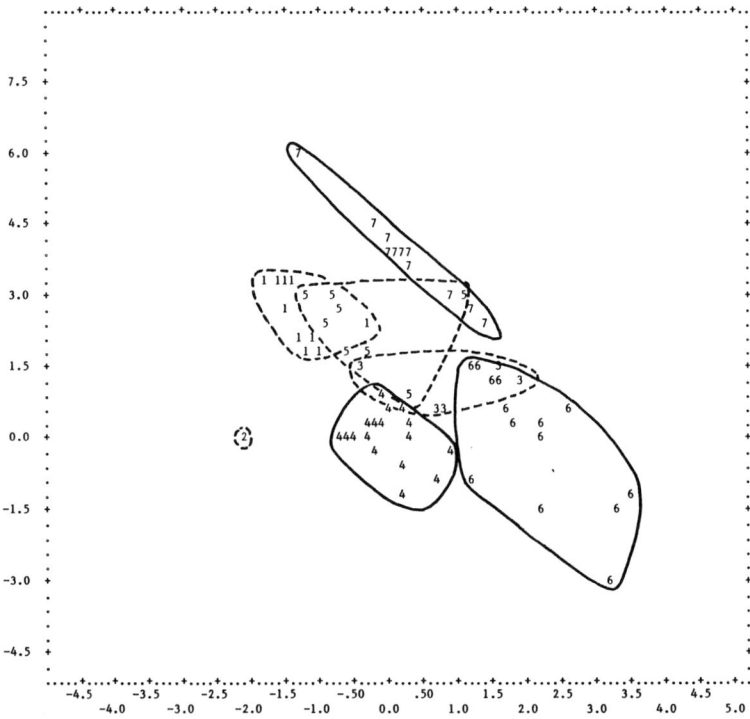

Fig. 12−2. Clay samples plus all sherds, K-means clustering (K = 7, 5 iterations) based on eight elements (Ba, Ce, Co, Cr, Eu, Fe, Sc, Th). Scatter plot of the seven clusters projected from eight dimensions on to the plane defined by the centroids of the three most populous clusters (2, 6, and 7). See Table 12−V for cluster membership.

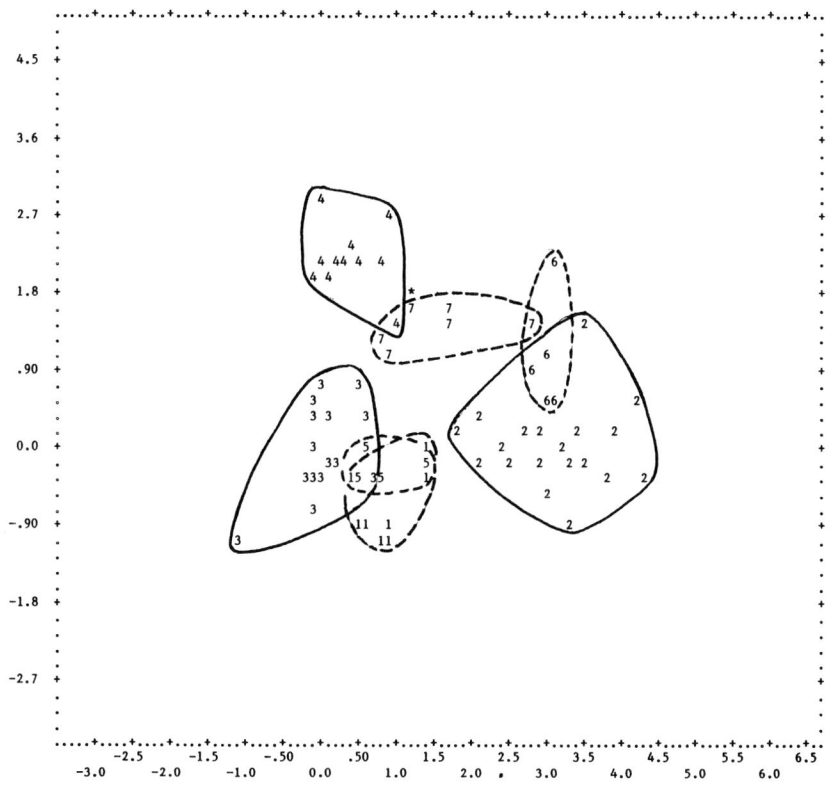

Fig. 12–3. Clay samples plus sherds from Gournia and Vasilike, K-means cluster analysis (K = 7, 3 iterations) based on eight elements (Ba, Ce, Co, Cr, Eu, Fe, Sc, Th). Scatter plot of the seven clusters projected from eight dimensions on to the plane defined by the centroids of the three most populous clusters (2, 3, and 4). See Table 12–VI for cluster membership.

mizes the Euclidean distance between the members of a given cluster and the cluster centroid. Initially, all samples are members of a single cluster (i.e., K = 1); this is subsequently subdivided until the final number of clusters specified by the user is attained. Samples are then iteratively reallocated to the cluster whose centroid is closest to them. The optimum K-number for any clustering operation was determined both quantitatively, by finding the K-number with the smallest mean of average intracluster Euclidean distances, and qualitatively, by examining the scatter plot of the orthogonal projection of samples into the plane defined by the centroids of the three most populous clusters (figs. 12–1 to 12–3). All the various clay and sherd data sets to be described were tested with K = 5, 6, 7, and 8.

We note that the original element concentration values in ppm were adjusted in two ways prior to clustering. First, all zero values were replaced by 0.02 ppm, then all values were normalized by the function f(x) = log 100x to 4 decimal places.

Results of K-Means Clustering

We analyzed the following four data sets by K-means cluster analysis:
 A. All clay samples
 B. All sherd samples
 C. All clay plus sherd samples
 D. All clay samples plus sherds from Gournia and Vasilike

1. Clustering of all clay samples

Table 12–III details the cluster memberships and sample distances from centroids of the six clusters identified. The six geological groups represented by the clay samples (see Chap. 15, Table 15–I) are fairly well distinguished in the clusters, with only clay sample #11 forming a unique outlier group. In particular,

TABLE 12-III
Clay samples, K-means clustering based on eight elements

Sample	Identification	Dist.	Sample	Identification	Dist.
Cluster #1			Cluster #4		
4	Makrilia, upper	0.70	11	Ammoudares	0.00
2	Makrilia, upper	0.99			
16A	Makrilia, upper	1.01	Cluster #5		
7	Makrilia, lower	1.08	14	Ammoudares	0.94
1	Makrilia, upper	1.15	15	Ammoudares	1.11
16B	Makrilia, upper	1.26	3	Makrilia, upper	1.54
10	Makrilia, upper	1.53	17	Pakhia Ammos	1.70
Cluster #2			Cluster #6		
8B	Makrilia, lower	1.33	5C	Makrilia, lower	0.58
12	Phothia	1.33	8A	Makrilia, lower	0.91
			5D	Makrilia, lower	0.95
Cluster #3			5A	Makrilia, lower	1.17
6	Phothia	2.28	5B	Makrilia, lower	1.27
9	Phothia	2.28	13	Phothia	1.75

samples from the upper and lower member of the Makrilia Formation are separated into clusters 1 and 6. These results at least lend credence to the geological framework described in Chapter 15.

2. Clustering of all sherd samples

When sherds only were subject to K-means clustering, it was found that seven clusters produced the most internally consistent and archaeologically interpretable grouping (Table 12–IV). The stylistic homogeneity and presumed narrow time span represented by the EM III Gournian sherds is well reflected in their exclusive composition of clusters 4 and 6. Cluster 2 consists of a single sherd outlier of the EM III group, while cluster 3 comprises MM Gournian sherds. The remaining three clusters (1, 5, 7) are heterogeneous and comprise sherds from all five sites; however, no sherds from Gournia appear in cluster 7. The appearance of MM Gournian sherds in clusters 1, 3, and 5 may reflect the fact that while this material is fine ware, it does not constitute as stylistically homogeneous a group as the EM III Gournian sherds (see below).

Figure 12–1, a scatter plot of the seven clusters projected from eight dimensions into two dimensions, illustrates the integrity of the EM III Gournian sherd group (clusters 4 and 6) and its clear separation from most of the nonlocal sherd groups (clusters 1 and 7). (Note in this and the following figures that the program is not capable of identifying individual samples on the plot, only their cluster membership.)

3. Clustering of all clay and sherd samples

We next combined the two previous data sets to determine if some relationship might appear between clay samples and sherds from the Isthmus of Ierapetra versus sherds from outside this area. Table 12–V summarizes the results of this clustering run, with K = 7. In no instance does a clay sample appear in a cluster with sherds *other than* from EM III Gournia (clusters 5 and 7), or MM Gournia (cluster 2). Sherds from this site are compositionally more similar to the clay samples than those from other sites.

Cluster 7 shows a weak grouping of all the EM III Gournian sherds with some clay samples from the upper member of the Makrilia Formation, while cluster 2 shows a relationship among some MM Gournian sherds, almost all the clay samples from the Makrilia Formation, and clay samples from the Phothia Formation. Cluster 5 shows a mixture of EM III Gournian sherds plus clays from the Ammoudares Formation, the Pakheia Ammos Formation, and one from the Makrilia Formation. Clusters 3, 4, and 6 are exclusively heterogeneous mixtures of sherds, with some Gournian sherds appearing in all three.

The two-dimensional relationship of all seven clusters is illustrated in figure 12–2. Clusters 4 and 6 (containing few sherds from the Ierapetra region) are distinct from clusters 2, 5, and 7, which contain only sherds from Gournia plus clay samples.

4. Clustering of all clay samples plus Ierapetra region sherds

The final analysis involved a clustering run of all twenty-two clay samples plus the sherd samples from Gournia (EM III and MM) and from EM Vasilike. It was our intention here to discriminate more finely among sherds and potential clay sources from the area where both were found.

Table 12–VI lists the membership of the seven clus-

TABLE 12-IV
Sherds, K-means clustering

Sample	Identification	Dist.	Sample	Identification	Dist.
Cluster #1			**Cluster #5**		
Penn MS 4700-1	MM Gournia	0.48	AM 1938.421	Knossos	0.64
Penn MS 4628-15	MM Gournia	0.52	Penn MS 4700-10	MM Gournia	0.81
Penn 60-19-14	East Crete	0.63	Penn MS 4628-9	MM Gournia	0.87
MHC BAI-14-B	Vasilike	0.84	Penn MS 4628-22	MM Gournia	1.05
Penn MS 4628-7	MM Gournia	0.85	MFA 575.3	Mokhlos	1.29
Penn MS 4700-9	MM Gournia	0.87	Penn MS 4628-20	MM Gournia	1.38
MFA 9.573	Mokhlos	1.10	Penn MS 4700-5	MM Gournia	1.74
AM 1938.821	Knossos	1.15	MFA 9.66	Mokhlos	1.85
Penn MS 4237	Vasilike	1.18			
Penn MS 4628-6	MM Gournia	1.24	**Cluster #6**		
MFA 9.574	Mokhlos	1.31	Penn MS 4615-15	EMIII Gournia	0.73
AM AE.752	Knossos	1.38	Penn MS 4615-12	EMIII Gournia	0.99
			Penn MS 4615-8	EMIII Gournia	1.30
Cluster #2			Penn MS 4615-7	EMIII Gournia	1.31
Penn MS 4615-33	EMIII Gournia	0.00	Penn MS 4615-26	EMIII Gournia	1.44
			Penn MS 4615-2	EMIII Gournia	1.50
Cluster #3			Penn MS 4615-21	EMIII Gournia	1.56
Penn MS 4628-13	MM Gournia	0.82	Penn MS 4615-45	EMIII Gournia	1.67
Penn MS 4628-19	MM Gournia	1.30	Penn MS 4615-47	EMIII Gournia	1.90
Penn MS 4628-14	MM Gournia	1.61	Penn MS 4615-40	EMIII Gournia	1.90
Penn MS 4628-3	MM Gournia	1.99	Penn MS 4615-15	EMIII Gournia	2.19
Penn MS 4628-21	MM Gournia	2.55	Penn MS 4615-11	EMIII Gournia	2.42
			Penn MS 4615-27	EMIII Gournia	2.55
Cluster #4			Penn MS 4615-34	EMIII Gournia	2.80
Penn MS 4615-44	EMIII Gournia	0.46	Penn MS 4615-22	EMIII Gournia	3.93
Penn MS 4615-29	EMIII Gournia	0.48			
Penn MS 4615-6	EMIII Gournia	0.49	**Cluster #7**		
Penn MS 4615-41	EMIII Gournia	0.49	Penn MS 4234	Vasilike	0.53
Penn MS 4615-23	EMIII Gournia	0.55	Penn MS 4894	Priniatikos Pyrgos	0.59
Penn MS 4615-39	EMIII Gournia	0.60	AM 09.334	Mokhlos	0.60
Penn MS 4615-19	EMIII Gournia	0.62	AM AE.753.4	Knossos	0.65
Penn MS 4615-32	EMIII Gournia	0.67	MFA 9.557	Mokhlos	0.82
Penn MS 4615-31	EMIII Gournia	0.69	MFA 9.575	Mokhlos	0.94
Penn MS 4615-9	EMIII Gournia	0.80	AM AE.1672	Knossos	1.14
Penn MS 4615-13	EMIII Gournia	0.85	Penn MS 4238	Vasilike	1.71
Penn MS 4615-35	EMIII Gournia	1.14	MHC BAI-14-A	Vasilike	1.71
Penn MS 4615-36	EMIII Gournia	1.14	Penn MS 4628-3	MM Gournia	1.89
Penn MS 4615-10	EMIII Gournia	1.48	Penn MS 4236	Vasilike	2.21
Penn MS 4615-18	EMIII Gournia	1.53	MFA 575.2	Mokhlos	3.02
Penn MS 4615-17	EMIII Gournia	2.51			

ters formed, and figure 12-3 illustrates the scatter plot of these samples. Note that the integrity of cluster 2 from the previous run is maintained here; certain of the MM Gournian sherds continue to be associated (albeit as outliers) with clay samples of the Makrilia and Phothia Formations. However, the EM III sherd group (clusters 3 and 4) is no longer associated with any clay samples. (One EM III sherd appears with clays of the Ammoudares and Pakhia Ammos Formations in cluster 6, but it is clearly an outlier.) The only other association of clay and sherd samples appears in cluster 1, with samples 2 and 10 (Makrilia Formation, upper member), but these are again outliers at the greatest distance from the cluster centroid.

In comparing cluster memberships among the three data sets of Tables 12–IV, V, and VI, three recurrent groups emerge:

1. MM Gournian sherds (MS 4700–1, MS 4628–15, MS 4628–7, MS 4700–9, MS 4628–6) and Vasilike sherds (BAI–14–B, MS 4237) that are associated with sherds from Mokhlos and Knossos in cluster 1 of Table 12–IV, and not associated with any clays in cluster 6 of Table 12–V, and are only weakly associated with clay samples in cluster 1 of Table 12–VI;

2. A group of MM Gournian sherds (MS 4628–13, MS 4628–19, MS 4628–14, MS 4628–21) that is unmixed in cluster 3 of Table 12–IV, and is as-

TABLE 12-V
Clay samples plus all sherds, K-means clustering

Sample	I.D.	D.C.	Sample	I.D.	D.C.	Sample	I.D.	D.C.
Cluster #1			**Cluster #4**			Penn MS 4237	VAS	1.03
Penn MS 4615-33		0.00	Penn MS 4894	PYRG	0.48	AM AE.752	KNOS	1.07
			AM AE.753.4	KNOS	0.50	MFA 9.574	MOKH	1.14
Cluster #2			AM 09.334	MOKH	0.51			
JAG-5A	MAKL	0.75	Penn MS 4234	VAS	0.51	**Cluster #7**		
JAG-16B	MAKU	0.90	MFA 9.557	MOKH	0.55	Penn MS 4615-19	EMG	0.46
JAG-5C	MAKL	0.98	MFA 9.575	MOKH	0.70	Penn MS 4615-41	EMG	0.67
JAG-16A	MAKU	1.03	AM AE.1672	KNOS	0.97	Penn MS 4615-9	EMG	0.68
JAG-8B	MAKL	1.31	MHC BAI-14-A	VAS	1.33	Penn MS 4615-23	EMG	0.73
JAG-5B	MAKL	1.35	Penn MS 4238	VAS	1.37	Penn MS 4615-44	EMG	0.80
JAG-5D	MAKL	1.36	Penn MS 4628-3	MMG	1.50	Penn MS 4615-36	EMG	0.85
JAG-8A	MAKL	1.37	Penn MS 4236	VAS	1.63	Penn MS 4615-23	EMG	0.87
JAG-12	PHOT	1.75	MFA 575.2	MOKH	2.27	Penn MS 4615-32	EMG	0.96
JAG-7	MAKU	1.78				Penn MS 4615-13	EMG	1.01
Penn MS 4628-13	MMG	1.78	**Cluster #5**			Penn MS 4615-29	EMG	1.02
JAG-9	PHOT	1.78	JAG-14	AMMO	1.45	Penn MS 4615-10	EMG	1.12
JAG-1	MAKU	1.85	JAG-15	AMMO	1.50	Penn MS 4615-6	EMG	1.16
JAG-13	PHOT	2.08	JAG-3	MAKU	1.74	Penn MS 4615-2	EMG	1.18
Penn MS 4700-3	MMG	2.27	JAG-17	PAKH	2.04	Penn MS 4615-39	EMG	1.20
Penn MS 4628-19	MMG	2.40	Penn MS 4615-11	EMG	2.23	Penn MS 4615-35	EMG	1.32
JAG-6	PHOT	2.53	Penn MS 4615-22	EMG	2.35	Penn MS 4615-31	EMG	1.43
Penn MS 4628-14	MMG	2.68	Penn MS 4615-15	EMG	2.35	Penn MS 4615-18	EMG	1.48
Penn MS 4628-21	MMG	3.37	JAG-11	AMMO	2.47	Penn MS 4615-26	EMG	1.52
			Penn MS 4615-27	EMG	2.89	Penn MS 4615-7	EMG	1.59
Cluster #3						Penn MS 4615-47	EMG	1.60
Penn MS 4628-9	MMG	0.91	**Cluster #6**			Penn MS 4615-8	EMG	1.64
AM 1938-21	KNOS	1.10	Penn MS 4628-15	MMG	0.40	Penn MS 4615-16	EMG	1.66
MFA 9.66	MOKH	1.13	Penn MS 4700-1	MMG	0.40	Penn MS 4615-45	EMG	1.67
Penn MS 4700-10	MMG	1.13	Penn 60-19-14	ECRE	0.49	Penn MS 4615-40	EMG	1.67
Penn MS 4628-22	MMG	1.29	MHC BAI-14-B	VAS	0.67	Penn MS 4615-21	EMG	1.68
Penn MS 4628-20	MMG	1.29	Penn MS 4700-9	MMG	0.68	Penn MS 4615-12	EMG	1.73
MFA 575.3	MOKH	1.42	Penn MS 4628-7	MMG	0.72	JAG-2	MAKU	1.96
Penn MS 4700-5	MMG	1.84	AM 1938.821	KNOS	0.88	JAG-4	MAKU	2.07
Penn MS 4615-17	EMG	2.45	MFA 9.573	MOKH	0.92	JAG-10	MAKU	2.14
Penn MS 4615-34	EMG	3.19	Penn MS 4628-6	MMG	0.99			

sociated with clays of the Makrilia and Phothia Formations in cluster 1 of Table 12–V and cluster 2 of Table 12–VI;
3. A group of MM Gournian sherds (MS 4700–10, MS 4628–22, MS 4628–20, MS 4628–9, MS 4700–5) that is never associated with clay samples; it is combined with sherds from EM Mokhlos and Knossos in cluster 5 of Table 12–IV and cluster 3 of Table 12–V, but is independent in cluster 5 of Table 12–VI.

Other than the EM III Gournian sherds (which are already known to represent a homogeneous group), the three groups of MM sherds from Gournia just described represent the only ones of possible archaeological significance. It appears that the MM Gournian sherds of group 2 (above) are associated with clays of the Makrilia and Phothia Formations, whereas the Vasilike sherds are not associated with any clays and the EM III Gournian sherds are only weakly associated with some clays. None of the sherd samples from sites outside the Isthmus of Ierapetra are associated with any of the clay samples.

Many explanations for these associations might be suggested, but the most important unevaluated factor is the possible addition of terra rossa soil sediments to the pottery clays (see Chap. 15). At least this would account for the higher iron concentrations in most of the sherds relative to the clay samples. Presumably trace elements would be introduced into the pottery clay mixture along with the iron of the terra rossa, which could alter significantly the trace element distributions and therefore the cluster memberships and associations.

TABLE 12-VI
Clay samples plus sherds from Gournia and Vasilike, K-means clustering

Sample	I.D.	D.C.	Sample	I.D.	D.C.	Sample	I.D.	D.C.
Cluster #1			**Cluster #3**			**Cluster #5**		
Penn MS 4700-1	MMG	0.41	Penn MS 4615-23	EMG	0.49	Penn MS 4700-10	MMG	0.79
MHC BAI-14-B	VAS	0.44	Penn MS 4615-44	EMG	0.49	Penn MS 4628-22	MMG	0.80
Penn 60-90-14	ECRE	0.48	Penn MS 4615-41	EMG	0.51	Penn MS 4628-20	MMG	1.05
Penn MS 4700-9	MMG	0.61	Penn MS 4615-6	EMG	0.54	Penn MS 4628-9	MMG	1.08
Penn MS 4237	VAS	0.86	Penn MS 4615-29	EMG	0.57	Penn MS 4700-5	MMG	1.72
Penn MS 4628-15	MMG	0.86	Penn MS 4615-39	EMG	0.59			
Penn MS 4628-7	MMG	1.26	Penn MS 4615-32	EMG	0.64	**Cluster #6**		
Penn MS 4628-6	MMG	1.43	Penn MS 4615-19	EMG	0.65	JAG-15	AMMO	0.74
JAG-10	MAKU	1.85	Penn MS 4615-13	EMG	0.76	JAG-14	AMMO	1.12
JAG-2	MAKU	2.24	Penn MS 4615-31	EMG	0.78	JAG-3	AMKU	1.27
			Penn MS 4615-23	EMG	0.78	JAG-17	PAKH	1.41
Cluster #2			Penn MS 4615-9	EMG	0.79	JAG-11	AMMO	1.89
JAG-5A	MAKL	0.65	Penn MS 4615-35	EMG	0.91	Penn MS 4615-22	EMG	3.06
JAG-16B	MAKU	0.84	Penn MS 4615-10	EMG	1.23			
JAG-5C	MAKL	0.88	Penn MS 4615-18	EMG	1.29	**Cluster #7**		
JAG-16A	MAKU	0.95	Penn MS 4615-2	EMG	1.35	MHC BAI-14-A	VAS	0.52
JAG-8B	MAKL	1.22	Penn MS 4615-17	EMG	2.89	Penn MS 4236	VAS	0.94
JAG-8A	MAKL	1.28	Penn MS 4615-33	EMG	3.86	Penn MS 4238	VAS	1.06
JAG-5B	MAKL	1.30				Penn MS 4234	VAS	1.20
JAG-5D	MAKL	1.36	**Cluster #4**			Penn MS 4628-3	MMG	1.82
JAG-1	MAKU	1.71	Penn MS 4615-16	EMG	0.64	Penn MS 4700-3	MMG	1.98
JAG-7	MAKU	1.73	Penn MS 4615-12	EMG	0.86			
JAG-12	PHOT	1.84	Penn MS 4615-7	EMG	0.94			
Penn MS 4628-13	MMG	1.90	Penn MS 4615-8	EMG	0.98			
JAG-9	PHOT	1.92	Penn MS 4615-26	EMG	0.98			
JAG-4	MAKU	1.99	Penn MS 4615-45	EMG	1.07			
JAG-13	PHOT	2.09	Penn MS 4615-21	EMG	1.10			
JAG-6	PHOT	2.52	Penn MS 4615-40	EMG	1.27			
Penn MS 4628-19	MMG	2.61	Penn MS 4615-47	EMG	1.28			
Penn MS 4628-14	MMG	2.77	Penn MS 4615-15	EMG	1.94			
Penn MS 4628-21	MMG	3.56	Penn MS 4615-11	EMG	1.96			
			Penn MS 4615-34	EMG	2.97			
			Penn MS 4615-27	EMG	3.07			

Conclusions

While an unambiguous determination of the compositional groups within and the probable clay sources of the Cretan pottery studied by this project would require a more ambitious analytical program demanding a more complete and more ideal selection of sherd and source materials, the results presented in this chapter illustrate the potential for provenance and for "kinship" studies based on trace-element patterns. However, it should also be noted again that the analytical differences between the MS 4615 series and the remainder of the samples will be due, at least in part, to the change in trace-element standards used by the Wisconsin Reactor Facility.

Notes

1. The neutron activation analyses were done as part of the Reactor Sharing Program under DOE contract E–(11–1)–2144 to the University of Wisconsin Reactor Facility, Richard Cashwell, Director. James Allert provided invaluable assistance with computer analyses of the data. Professor Frank Martin offered important advice on the approach to use for the statistical analyses. Frank Asaro provided a sample of the AP pottery standard, and F. J. Flanagan of the United States Geological Survey kindly provided splits of their standards.

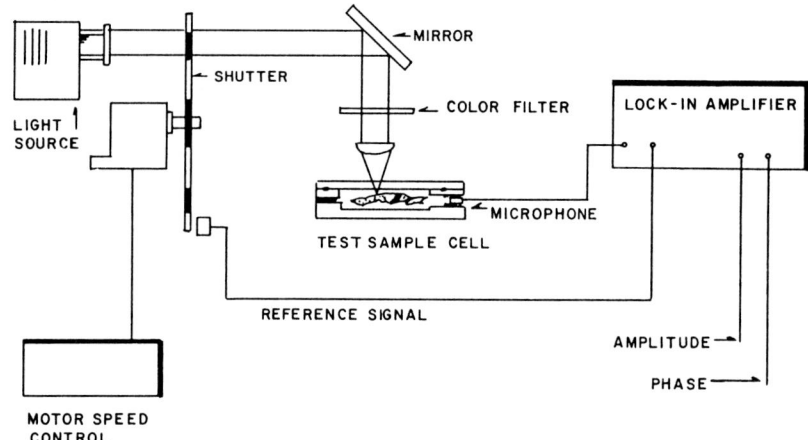

Fig. 13–1. Block diagram of experimental equipment used for photoacoustic measurements. The light source uses a GE Type ELH 300 W projection lamp. The lock-in amplifier is a Princeton Applied Research Model 5204. For the linear PA scan plots the chopping rate was held at 12 Hz.

Acoustic Signal Analysis

The strength of the PA (photoacoustic signal) from a solid is a complex function of interrelated physical and thermal properties of the sample under test. These parameters include: k_s (thermal conductivity), C_s (specific heat), ρ (density), and β (the optical absorption coefficient). In addition, the circumstances of the measurement, such as the strength and color of the light source, f (the chopping or interruption rate), and the residual air volume within the test cell inclosure, all influence the observed PA signal strength. In a homogeneous material, the PA signal is a result of the absorption, in the surface region, of the incident illumination. The resulting temperature changes extend into the body of the material with an exponential decrease in amplitude with depth below the surface as shown in fig. 13–2. A measure of this penetration is provided by the thermal diffusion length (L_s) of a sample (Rosencwaig 1975) where L_s is given by the equation

$$L_s^2 = \frac{\rho\, C_s}{\pi\, f\, k_s} \qquad (1)$$

Since the amplitude of the temperature change results from an integration of the energy input, the relative PA signal produced in any particular case will vary as

$$PA_s \sim f^n \qquad (2)$$

for a sample homogeneous in both color and physical properties, $n = -1$.

Extensive application of the photoacoustic effect has been made in the area of optical absorption spectroscopy for homogeneous materials. Since the PA signal will vary with the wavelength of the illumination, absorbed wavelengths will produce a strong PA response, and reflected ones will produce a weak or zero response.

Examination of Laminar Samples

If a test sample has a distinct surface layer over a thick substrate, then several additional considerations are involved in the production of a photoacoustic signal. If the illumination is absorbed in the upper layer which is substantially thicker than the length L_s then the exponent in formula (2) will be -1, and there will be no observable difference when compared with a nonlayered sample. If, however, the surface layer is thermally thin and optically thick, there will be a redistribution in heating effects. If the thermal properties of the substrate differ from those of the surface layer or there is a discontinuity in the

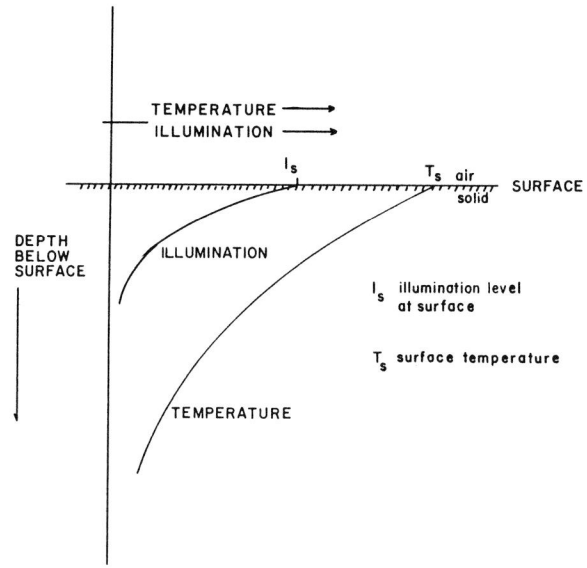

Fig. 13–2. Schematic diagram of the distribution of illumination flux and temperature at and below the sample surface for a thermally homogenous material.

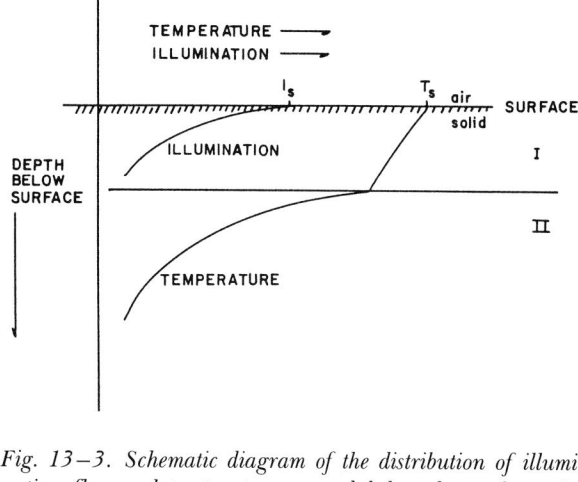

Fig. 13–3. Schematic diagram of the distribution of illumination flux and temperature at and below the surface of a sample in which the surface layer is optically thick (essentially all of the light which is incident on the sample is absorbed in this layer) and thermally thin (heat penetrates to the surface layer-substrate boundary and extends into the substrate material).

heat transfer across the interface, there will be a concentration of heat energy in the surface layer and a temperature distribution profile with depth as shown in fig. 13–3. Under these conditions the sample surface temperature fluctuation amplitude will be larger and the resulting photoacoustic signal stronger. The rate of change of surface temperature as a function of f is also reduced, and n will lie in the range from 0 to -1. Photoacoustic signal measurements were made at several points on the patterned side of a rim sherd from a bridge spouted jar, no. MS 4615–2. PA signal levels are plotted in fig. 13–4 as a function of f (the illumination chopping rate), using a logarithmic frequency scale. In the dark areas marked A and B, the slope of the PA signal strength as a function of frequency corresponds to $n = -1$. This is evidence that the dark surface coloration is thin and tightly bonded to the sherd body. Points C, D, and E on the white pattern area show a frequency dependance corresponding to $n = -.5$ and $-.8$. The difference noted at various positions may relate either to the thickness of the colored layer, its density, or its bonding to the substrate. The low value at C may be due to multiple layers put down in the process of creating the design. Similarly low values of n were also noted at other points where pattern elements converged.

Surface Mapping Observations

If the light level and chopping rate are held at fixed values as the illumination spot position is moved over the sample surface, any changes in the PA signal strength will be due to changes in surface color or in the physical composition of the surface or substrate. Several sherds among those studied in the White-on-dark Ware project were examined in this manner. The results are presented as photoacoustic signal amplitude plots projected along the spot path across the sample as shown in fig. 13–5. In this example the acoustic signal (arbitrary units) is plotted on the x axis and relative spot position on the y axis. Note that zero scale for the PA signal is to the right.

The effect of decoration is shown in fig. 13–6 where distinct changes in surface color result in corresponding changes in the photoacoustic signal. As a consequence of the finite spot size, the edges of the design are smeared, but the two bands traversed are clearly evident. In general, if a surface design is thin and well bonded to the body of the sample, the darker regions, being more absorptive, would produce a stronger PA signal level than the lighter ones.

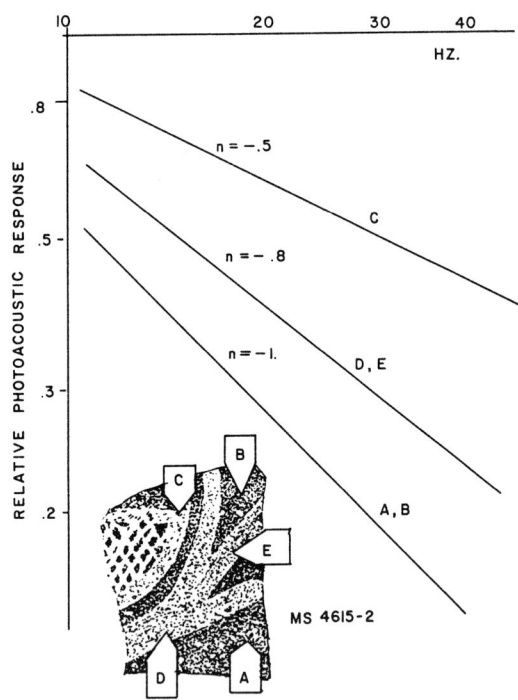

Fig. 13–4. Variation in the photoacoustic signal strength as a function of chopping rate for several illumination spots designated A, B, C, D and E located on the design side surface of sherd MS 4615-2.

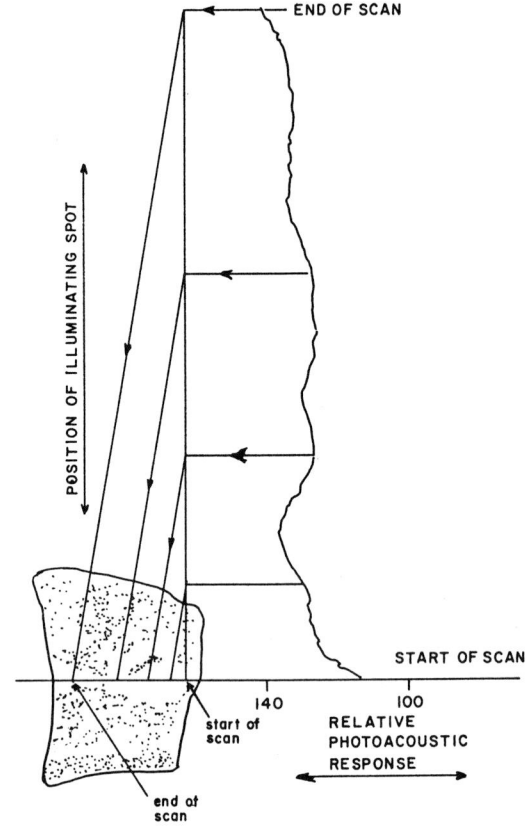

Fig. 13–5. Variation in relative photoacoustic response (fixed chopping rate of 12 Hz) as the illumination spot is moved linearly across the sample surface. This is an example of the graphical construction used in this paper to relate the observed PA signal strength to the corresponding spot position.

This is not the case in sample MS 4615–2 seen in fig. 13–6 where a stronger signal is obtained when the spot is on the light design bands and a weaker signal in the dark background areas. This is the same sherd shown in fig. 13–5. One of the bands scanned is in the region marked "E" in fig. 13–5 and has an n value of −.8. This suggests that since the design is a distinct layer, the energy is concentrated in that layer and not dissipated into the body of the sample causing a higher surface temperature.

A traverse scan of the inside surface of this same sherd is shown in fig. 13–7. The photoacoustic signal, when plotted as a function of position along the scan path, shows two distinctive characteristics: a plateau of nearly constant acoustic response, and a transition region of decreasing response. This same kind of distribution is evident in fig. 13–8 where the scanning path is parallel to that used in fig. 13–7 and adjacent to the opposite edge of the sherd. Linear scans along several other paths have been combined with the previous data to prepare a composite contour map of the relative photoacoustic response for the interior surface of Penn no. MS 4615–2, fig. 13–9. The transition from high to low values of PA response occurs in a well defined band 2 to 3 cm wide located approximately parallel to the rim of the original pottery object. Similar observations have been made on two other bridge spouted jars, MS 4615–28 and MS 4615–45, as shown in fig. 13–10(a) and 10(b).

Examination of these findings has led to the suggestion (made by Betancourt) that this evidence of a distinctive local change in the surface physical and thermal properties may be the consequence of a previously unsuspected burnishing or smoothing operation carried out during the fabrication of the pottery. This hypothesis is supported by visual inspection of selected samples where it proved possible to detect a very faint surface gloss closely corresponding in its location to the previously mapped boundaries of the transition region. A burnishing operation can produce several, possibly significant, physical changes including the exclusion of air bubbles, increase in den-

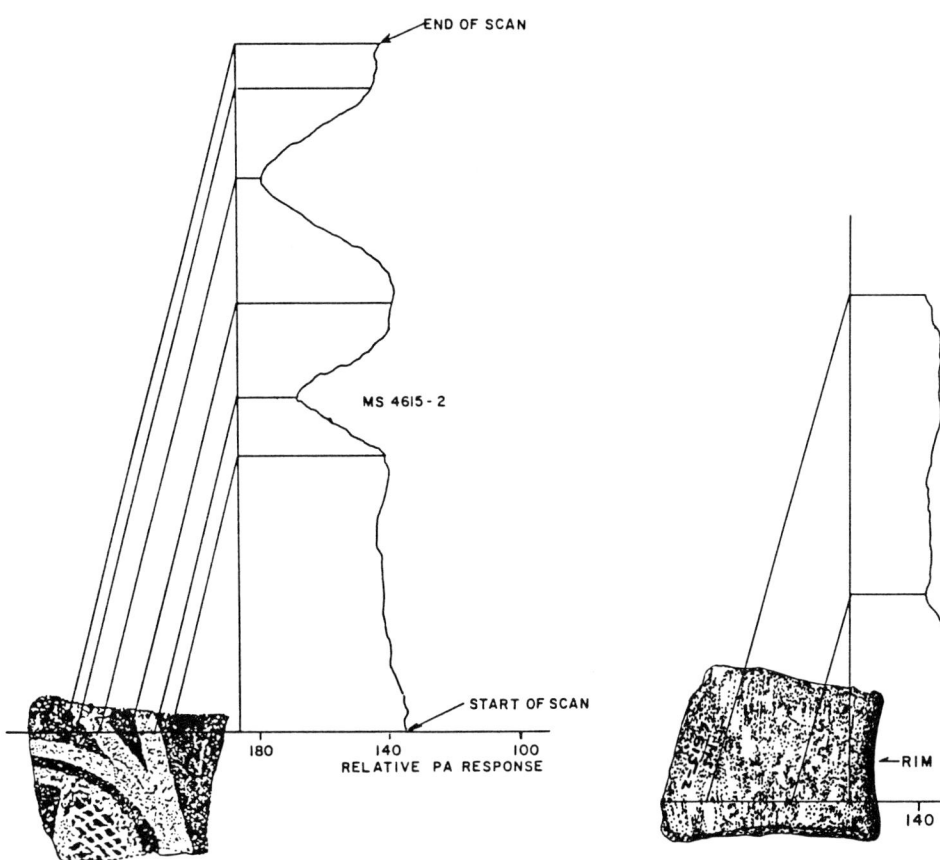

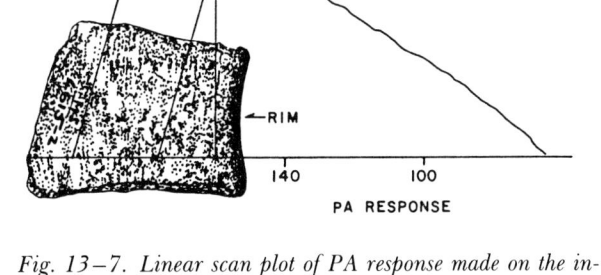

Fig. 13–6. Linear scan plot of PA response made on the design side surface of MS 4615-2.

Fig. 13–7. Linear scan plot of PA response made on the interior surface of MS 4615-2; right side as shown.

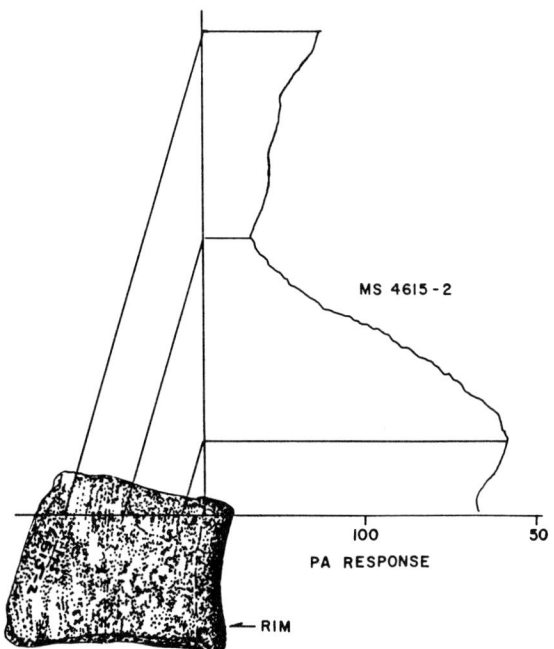

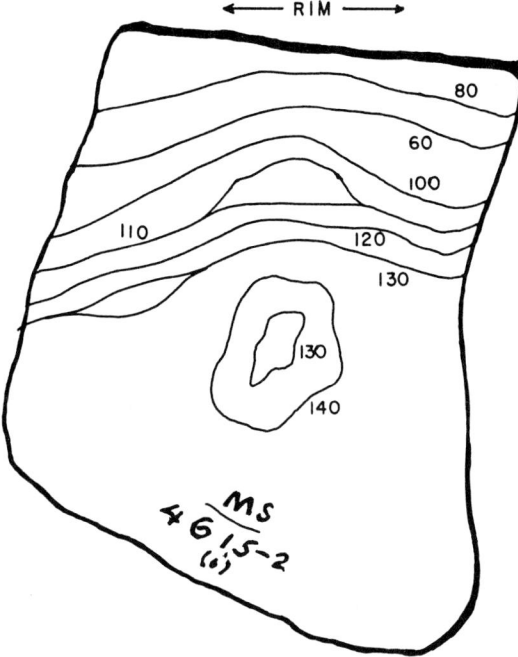

Fig. 13–8. Linear scan plot of PA response made on the interior surface of MS 4615-2.

Fig. 13–9. Map of equal photoacoustic signal strength contours for the interior surface of MS 4615-2.

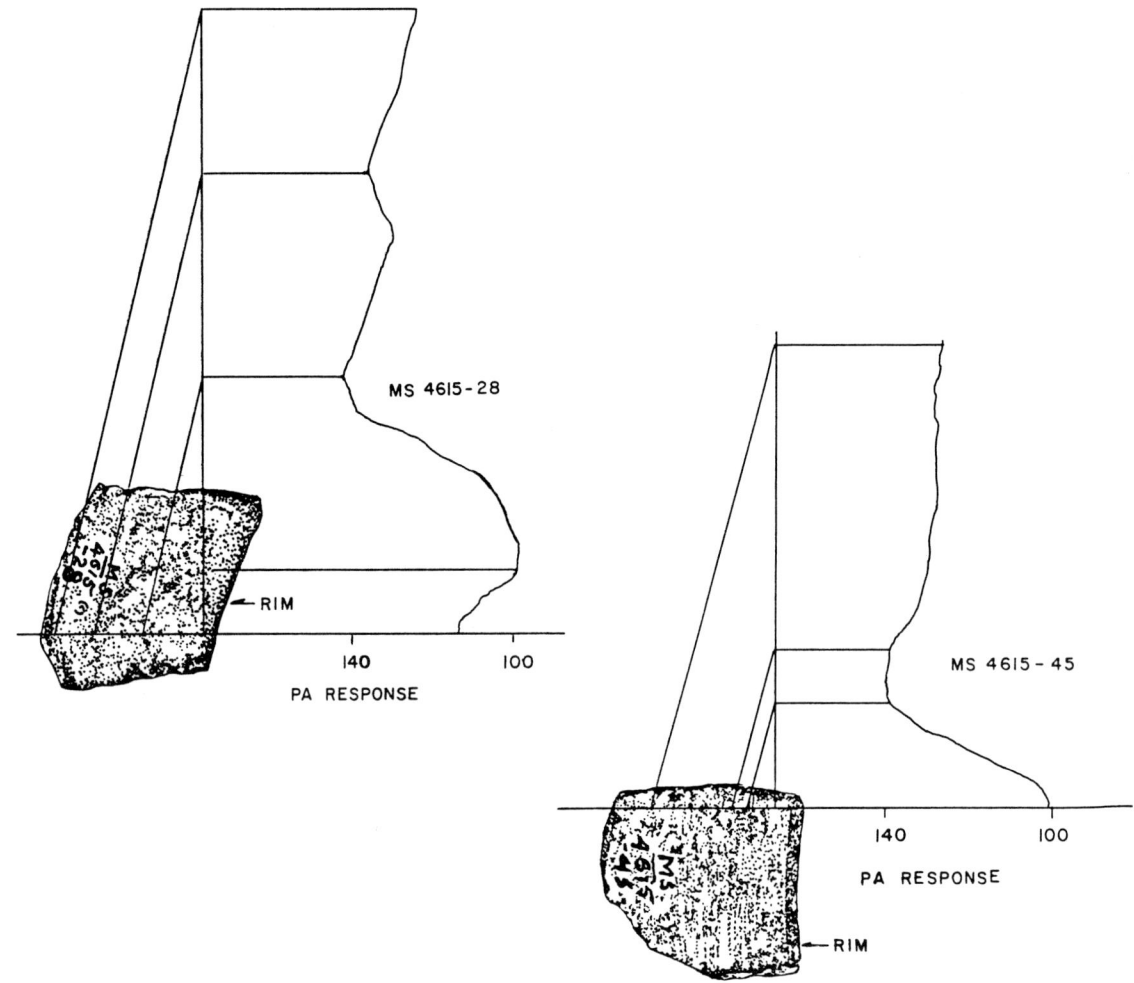

Fig. 13–10. (a) Linear scan plot of relative PA signal on the inside surface of MS 4615-28. (b) Linear scan plot of relative PA signal on the inside surface of MS 4615-45.

sity, and the orientation of grains within the clay. The observed decrease in photoacoustic signal corresponds to a decrease in surface specific heat and/or thermal conductivity. The gradual transitional change in the surface properties suggests the altered surface layer is tapered, increasing in effective thickness toward the rim as might be expected if the forming pressure exerted by the plotter was nonuniform.

In most cases the rear surfaces of these samples had *not* been cleaned. As a further test of these observations the inside surface of two other bridge spouted jars, MS 4615–20 and MS 4615–21, were examined. The former sherd was not cleaned while the latter had been cleaned in the past and evidence of burnishing was detected on close visual examination. The results (fig. 13–11a and b) show that while the rim effect is more clearly defined for the cleaned sample, the photoacoustic effect can penetrate a surface layer accumulation and disclose changes in the ceramic material beneath.

In contrast to these findings are the results seen in fig. 13–12 obtained from a photoacoustic scan examination of the inside surface of MS 4615–36. This sherd is a fragment from a conical cup which lacks the thickened rim section present on the other samples. In this case there is a uniform photoacoustic response over the entire inner surface and no transition region related to the rim edge of the sherd. One would conclude that there was no inner burnishing operation used for this type of vessel or by this potter.

The value of combining photoacoustic examination

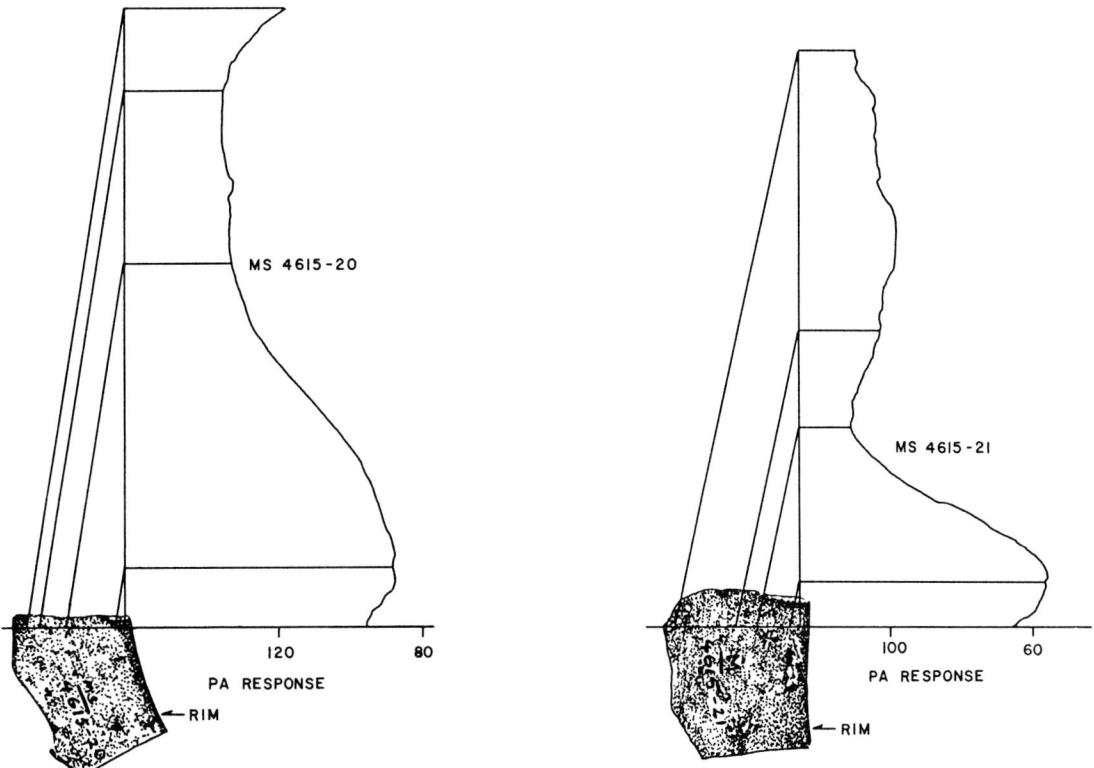

Fig. 13–11. (a) Linear scan plot of relative PA signal on the inside surface of MS 4615-20; a sample left in its original uncleaned condition. (b) Linear scan plot of relative PA signal on the inside surface of MS 4615-21; a sample which has been cleaned.

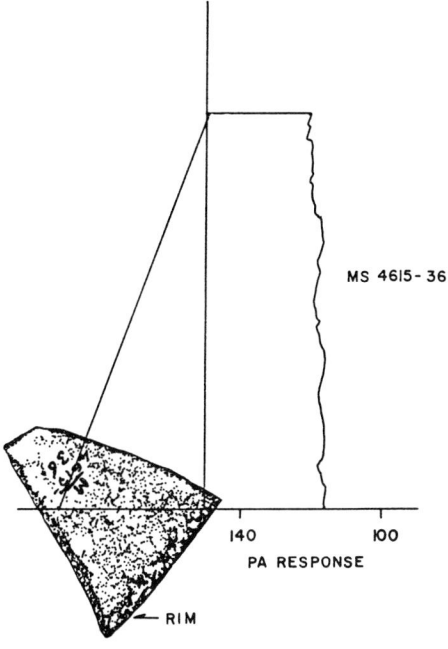

Fig. 13–12. Linear scan plot of the relative PA signal on the inside of MS 4615-36.

with other exploratory techniques is clearly demonstrated in a comparison of the linear PA scan plot made on the decorated surface side of a sherd from a conical cup, MS 4615–10 (fig. 13–13), the composite PA response contour map (fig. 13–14a), and a drawing made from the xeroradiography image of the same sherd (fig. 13–14b). Traverse PA scans of the sherd revealed large variations in photoacoustic response. The composite map shows a well defined region of low values extending away from the rim edge. There is no visual evidence to be seen of a significant difference in the pottery in this region. Xeroradiography, however, shows that an anomaly exists here, visible as air bubbles trapped beneath the surface (see Chap. 14). The air bubbles which appear as dark spots in the xerographic image are aligned with the region of rapid change in PA signal strength. Since the bubbles are evidence of a seam in the pot body, it is possible that the surface changes detected photoacoustically are a consequence of an effort at local smoothing by the potter during the finishing process.

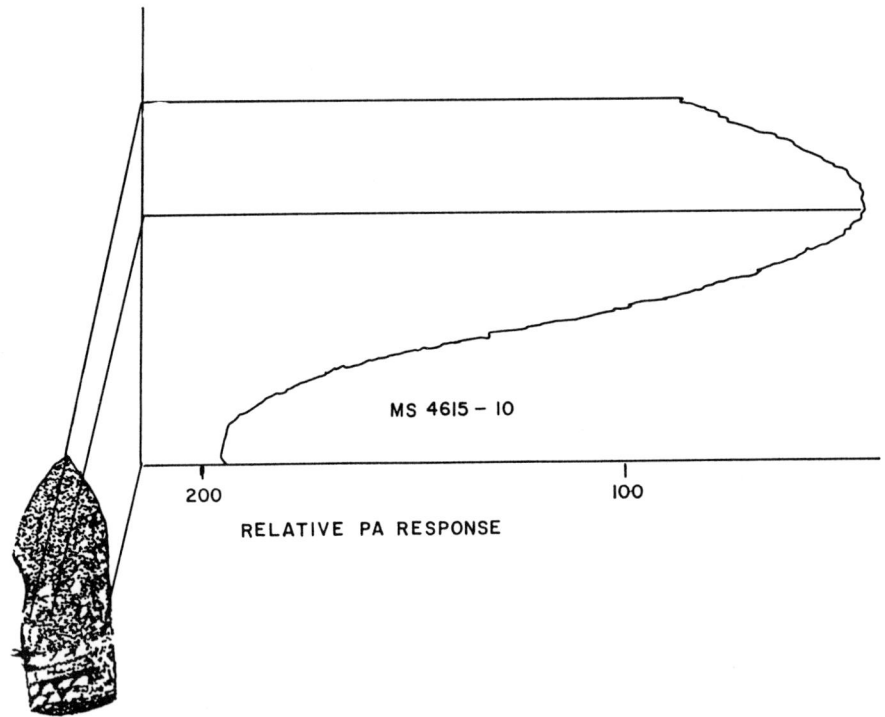

Fig. 13–13. Linear scan plot of relative PA signal on the design side surface of MS 4615-10.

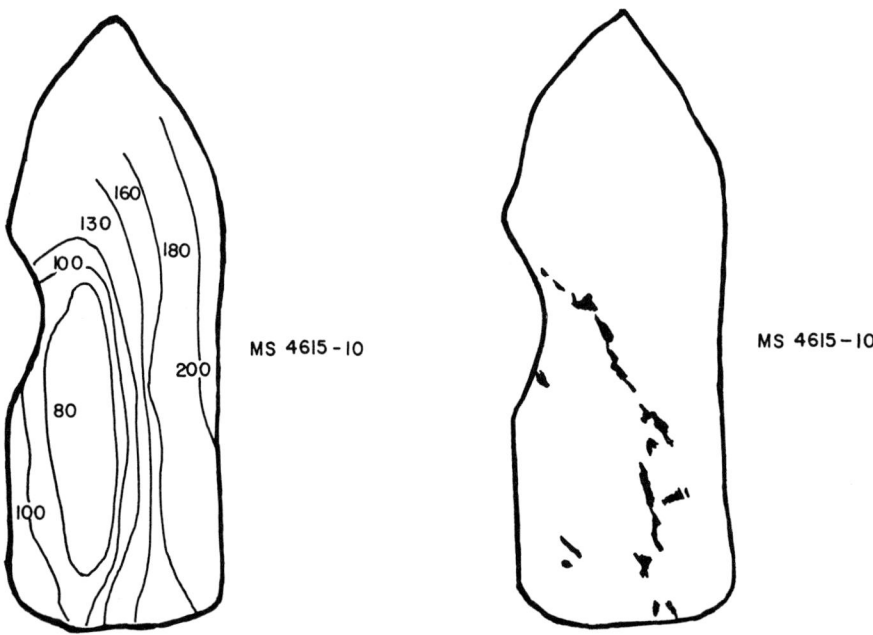

Fig. 13–14. (a) Map of equal PA signal strength contours for the design side surface of MS 4615-10. (b) Drawing of the xeroradiography image of MS 4615-10 showing air bubbles included within the body of the clay.

Conclusion

Photoacoustic techniques can, under suitable conditions, reveal in a nondestructive manner significant surface layer characteristics of ceramic materials. In connection with the East Cretan White-on-dark Ware project, it has been employed to detect changes in the physical properties of the base material hidden under pigment layers or accumulated surface coatings. As with any physical or chemical analytic technique applied to an archaeological investigation, these observations must be made in the context of other parallel studies to which the surface layer characteristics or anomalies can be contributed as another parameter, a physical fingerprint that may assist in determining the source of samples or the technology which created them.

Notes

1. Much of the initial theoretical and experimental work relating to the application of photoacoustic techniques to the examination of ceramic materials was carried out in 1978–1979 at the Research Laboratory of Archaeometry and the History of Art, Oxford University, with the kind permission of Professor E. T. Hall and Dr. Martin J. Aitken. Thanks are due to Dr. Robert Hedges and to the entire RLAHA staff for their courtesy and interest, and to Stacey Frost for archaeological drafting.

References

Bell, A. G. 1881. *Philosophical Magazine* 11: 510.

Frost, A. D. 1982. Photoacoustic Examination of Ceramic Surface Layers. In *Archaeological Ceramics*, ed. J. S. Olin and A. D. Franklin, 155–63. Washington, D.C.

Rayleigh, F. R. S. 1881. The Photophone. *Nature* 23: 274–5.

Rosencwaig, A. 1975. Photoacoustic spectroscopy of solids. *Physics Today* 28: 23–30.

Rosencwaig, A. and A. Gersho. 1976. Theory of photoacoustic effects in solids. *Applied Physics* 47: 64–9.

Tyndall, J. 1881. Action of an Intermittent Beam of Radiant Heat upon Gaseous Matter. *Proceedings of the Royal Society of London* 31: 307–17.

14

Xeroradiography Studies

Robert H. Johnston and Philip P. Betancourt

Xeroradiography is a high resolution X-ray technique developed by the Xerox Corporation.[1] Since it provides electro-photography of great clarity with images based on the density of the material being examined and the techniques employed in the process, it has wide applications in the study of archaeological material (Heinemann 1976; Alexander and Johnston 1982). The technique is non-destructive, and it does not harm the sample.

To observe the internal structure of east Cretan pottery, six sherds of typical White-on-dark Ware were examined by xeroradiography. All date to EM III. The studies had four main goals: 1) an examination of the interior pore space, 2) study of the opaque non-plastic inclusions, 3) the possible detection of joins reflecting the manufacturing process, and 4) a comparative study of the various clay features. None of these goals could be carried out without an X-ray method because they involve an examination of the interior of the clay body.

The research was carried out with the instrument in the Paleoceramic Laboratory at the Rochester Institute of Technology, Rochester, New York. Both positive and negative images were made of the samples, varying the X-ray techniques to reveal as wide a range as possible of the morphological details. The images were studied both as xeroradiographs and as photographically enhanced prints. These prints were prepared using both filters and Xerox technique. Low power binocular microscopy (10 X) was useful for some of the observations, particularly in determining the shapes of the included particles. (A zoom stereo microscope is a most useful tool in the initial examination of ancient ceramic material. Low power magnification is often more useful and easier to obtain than high power microscopy, e.g., the SEM. The use of the Petrographic microscope with thin sections can provide additional data.)

The sherds were chosen to provide a selection of several vase shapes:

1. Bridge spouted jar, from Vasilike, Penn no. MS 4236 (pl. 9A–B).
2. Rounded cup, from Gournia, Penn no. MS 4615–31 (pl. 9C–D).
3–4. Conical cups, from Gournia, Penn nos. MS 4615–10 and MS 4615–13 (pl. 9E–F and 10C–D).
5. Lid, from Gournia, Penn no. MS 4615–39 (pl. 10A–B).
6. Bowl, from Gournia, Penn no. MS 4615–16 (pl. 10E–F).

More specific provenances are not known. Profile drawings (fig. 14–1) illustrate the shapes, and photographs and more detailed descriptions are given in the Appendix. For comparison purposes, a xeroradiograph of a later jug from Pseira (from LM IB) is also presented here (pl. 10G).

The Aplastic Inclusions and Pore Space

A variety of nonplastic inclusions are present in the clay bodies of East Cretan White-on-dark Ware. They apparently come from two sources, the clays used as raw materials and the sand added as temper (for discussion, see Chap. 6). The principal particles are quartz, plagioclase, hornblende, biotite mica, and rock

Fig. 14–1. Reconstructions of shapes of White-on-dark Ware. Scale 1:3. 1. Bridge spouted jar from Vasilike (Penn MS 4236). 2. Cup from Gournia (Penn MS 4615-31). 3. Bowl from Gournia (Penn MS 4615-13). 4. Lid from Gournia (Penn MS 4615-39).

fragments. They are normally rounded to subrounded in shape, with a size ranging from microscopic to .3 cm (with a very few particles being even larger), meaning they come from secondary sources and are tumbled by moving action away from primary sources. Cups have fewer inclusions than the larger shapes, a difference ascribed to the addition of sand as temper for some vessels.

Aplastic inclusions tend to be found in larger sizes in pithoi, cooking pots, and other larger vessels. The use of aplastic additions tends to alleviate stresses and strains in the firing process and counteracts thermal shock in cooking ware. In the vessels examined here, the inclusions will have lessened the likelihood of breakage (for a good recent discussion of the effects of temper see Braun 1982).

The fabric seems to be a rather porous body (for discussion, see Chap. 10), and one result of the more impervious dark slip is to partly counteract this porosity. The xeroradiographs make it possible to examine the pore space and voids with regard to size, shape, frequency, and distribution.

Identifying the inclusions was not a part of this study because this aspect of research can be better accomplished with other methods. The distribution and degree of uniformity within that distribution, however, can be effected with an X-ray technique. This use of xeroradiography needs much more study, but it could become a precise tool in the study of ceramic material (Braun 1982). The distribution of the inclusions is an important characteristic of pottery because it can be a clue to the care used in preparing the clay before working. Long periods of kneading or wedging result in a more uniform clay than is obtained with only a casual mixing of ingredients. If the aplastic particle distribution is uniform enough, its density can be systematized, and the resulting profile can be used as a defining characteristic for particular subclasses. In addition, vessels with unevenly distributed aplastic inclusions should serve as a caution to anyone interested in analysis because clay fabric sampling techniques normally use only a small fraction of a sherd for investigation, and choosing samples from different parts of heterogeneous materials can lead to erratic results.

The xeroradiographs in pls. 9 and 10A–F show typical examples of East Cretan White-on-dark Ware. Since these are positive images, the aplastic inclusions are seen as white dots, while pore spaces and air pockets are dark. On these sherds the pattern of inclusions is far from uniform. The heterogeneity can be seen in the cups, but it is more visible in a large sherd like the fragment of a bridge spouted jar from Vasilike shown in pl. 9A–B. A comparison between the areas labeled X and Y on this sample points up the extreme difference that can exist from one part of a vessel to another. Samples for analysis or petrographic thin sections taken from these two areas would be very dissimilar in appearance and in the percentages of the constituents. The lack of uniformity is so pronounced that the inclusions were not reduced to systematic measurements for characterization purposes (only small sherds from a few vessels were studied, and it was felt that the pattern had too little uniformity for one part of a vase to be used to characterize the entire vessel).

The xeroradiographs were also used to check the shapes of the inclusions as revealed by thin sections. The thin sections suggested that most of the particles in the Gournian sherds were rounded to subrounded, indicating they came from secondary deposits (sand or secondary clay deposits) rather than from crushed stone or some other material which would yield angular fragments with sharp corners (see Chap. 6). Thin sections can only examine a narrow slice through a sherd, but the xeroradiographs of complete sherds show the same shapes. Most inclusions are rounded or subrounded, with only a few angular and subangular ones. One can conclude that most particles dense enough to show up as white dots (i.e., all of those which are stones) had been subjected to some natural abrading and erosion before being included in the paste at Gournia. The sherd from Vasilike (pl. 9A–B) shows more angular shapes among some of the tiny inclusions, but many of the largest ones are well rounded.

The vases also have many tiny random pore spaces and air pockets. They are seen as black dots in pls. 9 and 10, contrasting with the white inclusions and the middle tones of the clay paste. Their outlines are irregular, indicating they are air trapped in the forming process rather than organic matter which burned away leaving cavities. In other words, organic materials (such as straw) were probably not added as temper to these sherds, and the paste consisted of clays and sand.

These studies suggest that the preparation of the clay was casual rather than deliberately ordered. The sand used as temper was not well mixed at all, resulting in a paste that varied in consistency and coarseness even within one vessel. The situation may be contrasted with that of later Bronze Age pottery from eastern Crete (pl. 10G) where the more uniform consistency of the paste indicates a much more careful preparation to give a more homogeneous body. The change in this basic step in pottery making, which occurred after the time of the White-on-dark Ware discussed here, may be at least partly due to the changes that accompanied the introduction of the potter's wheel in MM IB. Throwing requires a different type of clay body from that used in hand methods, and the change in production technique may have caused a change in the craft at other steps in the manufacturing process, including a more systematic approach to the preparation of clay.

Seams Caused by the Manufacturing Process

A xeroradiograph sometimes reveals joins where two slabs or coils of clay are put together. This aspect of the analytical method is especially important for reconstruction of the technology used for White-on-dark Ware because in most cases no seams are visible with the unaided eye; since the ancient potters carefully smoothed all visible surfaces, they removed the obvious traces of their joins.

In pls. 9 and 10A–F the seams are visible as subtle dark lines. The features are shown in drawings as well as photographs for clarification, and the effect of the air pockets at the seams may be better appreciated by comparing it with the continuous black line indicating a crack in pl. 10C–D (labeled B) and the unbroken texture of the wheelmade jug in pl. 10G. As one might expect, the bridge spouted jar has a seam where the spout was added (pl. 9A–B), and the lid has a seam where the edge was joined to the top (pl. 10A–B). While the wall of one of the cups was made from two slabs (pl. 9C–D), the other two cups used only a single slab to reach from base to rim (pls. 9E–F and 10C–D). The joins are not always exactly horizontal or vertical, perhaps because of the working of the vessel as well as because of the original shape of the slabs. The bowl (pl. 10E–F) has no seams preserved on the sherd examined.

The xeroradiographs permit a more thorough reconstruction of the Early Bronze Age potting technology than has been possible before. They show that vessels were built up from strips or slabs of clay of varying width, with each strip probably being long enough to reach all around the vase (note the vertical seam in pl. 9E–F). By adding successive strips, the wall was gradually raised to the desired height. Joins were carefully knitted and smoothed in a slow, laborious process (for additional discussion, see Chap. 16). The method may be seen as a careful hand technique, a meticulous way to produce symmetrical and well-fashioned products.

Notes

1. The study was made possible by a grant from the Xerox Corporation to Dr. Robert H. Johnston, Dean and Professor at the Rochester Institute of Technology in Rochester, New York.

References

Alexander, R. E., and R. H. Johnston. 1982. Xeroradiography of Ancient Objects: A New Imaging Modality. In *Archaeological Ceramics*, ed. J. S. Olin and A. D. Franklin, 145–63. Washington, D.C.

Braun, David P. 1982. Radiographic Analysis of Temper in Ceramic Vessels: Goals and Initial Methods. *JFA* 9: 183–92.

Heinemann, S. 1976. Xeroradiography: a new radiological tool. *American Antiquity* 41: 106–11.

Part IV

15

Clay Sources in the Isthmus of Ierapetra

John A. Gifford and George H. Myer

The thousands of kilograms of clay used to fabricate East Cretan White-on-dark Ware were obtained, most probably, within the area of the Isthmus of Ierapetra. Key archaeological deposits of this pottery span the Isthmus, and, as will be documented here, several potential geological sources of clay exist there as well.

These sources will be discussed within the geological framework of the region. Physical characteristics of grain size and mineralogy will be described, and the accessibility of these sources in the Bronze Age will be briefly considered.

Time Scales and Terminology

From the viewpoint of stratigraphical geology, the Ierapetra region of 4000 years ago was exactly the same as it is today, no new rock units having been deposited in such an insignificant period of time. From an archaeological perspective, some relatively minor geomorphological changes occurring within this time span are important in evaluating resource availability, at least in terms of clay sources.

Minoan (as well as modern) potters in the Ierapetra region utilized clays derived from sediments deposited some 8–10 million years ago when the island of Crete did not exist. In fact, although these sediments reflect (indirectly) the uplift and erosion of bedrock blocks tens of kilometers in areal extent over time periods of millions of years, we are really dealing with a very small area and a very recent period in the geological history of the Mediterranean.

Most of the clays discussed here were laid down during the middle to late Miocene Epoch, between approximately 12 and 6 million years ago. Rocks dating from this time interval have been subdivided into lithostratigraphic units that include, in Europe and the Mediterranean, the Serravallian, Tortonian, and Messenian Stages. The Miocene and the succeeding epoch, the Pliocene, comprise the Neogene—roughly the more recent half of the Tertiary Period.

In the Ierapetra region clay is present in bedrock outcrops of Neogene age not as pure clay strata (which usually represent *primary* clays, residues from the weathering *in situ* of igneous rocks), but rather mixed with sediment grains both larger in size and of different mineralogies than the commonly-held notion of pottery clay. They are therefore *secondary*, or redeposited as sediments in some location other than that where they formed.

In geological usage "clay" refers both to a size range of sediment grains and to several families of minerals—finely crystalline or amorphous hydrous aluminum silicates—that are commonly (though not exclusively) the main mineral constituents of the clay size range. Three size ranges of mineral grains will be discussed here:

sand-size: grains *coarser* than 62.5 micrometers (0.0625 mm)
silt-size: grains *between* 62.5 and 4 micrometers
clay-size: grains *finer* than 4 micrometers

In natural sediments clay minerals are so commonly found mixed with particles of the non-clay minerals calcite and quartz—in both the silt-size and clay-size range—that the resulting sediment has a common generic name: marl. All gradations of marl exist, but sediments containing between 35 and 65% clay minerals (or 65–35% calcite and quartz) are marls *sensu strictu*. Marls are characteristic of sedimentary deposition in quiet, relatively low-energy water environments, either fresh (swamps), brackish (lagoons), or marine (deep-water basins). In addition to the minerals of the clay-size and silt-size fractions, marls contain occasional sand-size grains, as well as (in many cases) microscopic shells of organisms such as ostracods and foraminifers that inhabited the water column above the site of marl deposition. Identification of these microfaunal assemblages included in a marl not only indicates its environment of deposition, but also, thanks to techniques of stratigraphic micropaleontology, allows an estimate to be made of the time of its deposition.

While coarser sediment types often become cemented (lithified) after deposition into siltstones or sandstones, fine-grained marls can be found in the area of the Isthmus of Ierapetra in as soft and unconsolidated a state as when they were deposited, some 8–10 million years ago. Marlstones–argillaceous siltstones—do exist in the Neogene stratigraphy of Crete, but, of course, they are of no interest to potters.

The Neogene Geology of the Isthmus of Ierapetra

The best general treatment of the Neogene geology of the Ierapetra region is Fortuin's excellent synthesis (1977) of his stratigraphical study of the area. His geological map of the Ierapetra region (1:75,000) supercedes the institute of Geology and Subsurface Research *Ierapetra Sheet* (1959, 1:50,000), at least for that time period. He divides the Ierapetra region's Neogene rocks into nine formal units (Fortuin 1977: 20–21 and 128–40) which are, from oldest to youngest:

1. the Mythoi Formation: terrestrial conglomerates eroded from igneous and metamorphic pre-Neogene rocks that formed highlands north of the present Isthmus of Ierapetra. This unit was deposited sometime before the middle Miocene, approximately 12 million years before the present.
2. the Males Formation: also terrestrial conglomerates, but derived from highlands further northeast of the Ierapetra region, and interbedded with sandstones and clayey marls. The upper section of the formation (the Parathyri Member) was deposited in middle to late Miocene time.
3. the Prinia Complex: predominantly coarse breccias and conglomerates containing large masses of pre-Neogene limestones. Also deposited in middle to late Miocene time.
4. the Phothia Formation: conglomerates interbedded with sandy and marly strata, especially toward the top of the section. Deposited in middle to late Miocene time.
5. the Kalamauka Formation: marls and calcareous sandstones (representing turbidites) deposited in a deep marine basin at some time during the middle to late Miocene.
6. the Makrilia Formation: fossiliferous marine marls interbedded with laminated sands, also a deep, low-energy marine shelf environment (possibly similar to that presently at the bottom of the Gulf of Mirabello), deposited in late Miocene time.
7. the Ammoudares Formation: carbonate- and fossil-rich sandstones and marls deposited in a relatively shallow marine environment in late Miocene time.
8. the Myrtos Formation: marl breccia overlain by fossiliferous marls, deposited in early to middle Pliocene time and restricted in its present distribution to the south coast.
9. the Pakheia Ammos Formation: terrigenous clastic deposits overlain by algal limestones, marl breccias, and capped by homogeneous marls. Deposited in shallow to deep brackish and marine environments during the late Miocene and early Pliocene. It has a very limited distribution in the vicinity of the modern town of the same name.

Figure 15–1 shows the distribution of the nine Neogene units in the Isthmus. The most recent of these was deposited some 3–4 million years ago. Between that time and approximately 200,000 years ago, there is essentially no record of sediment deposition in this

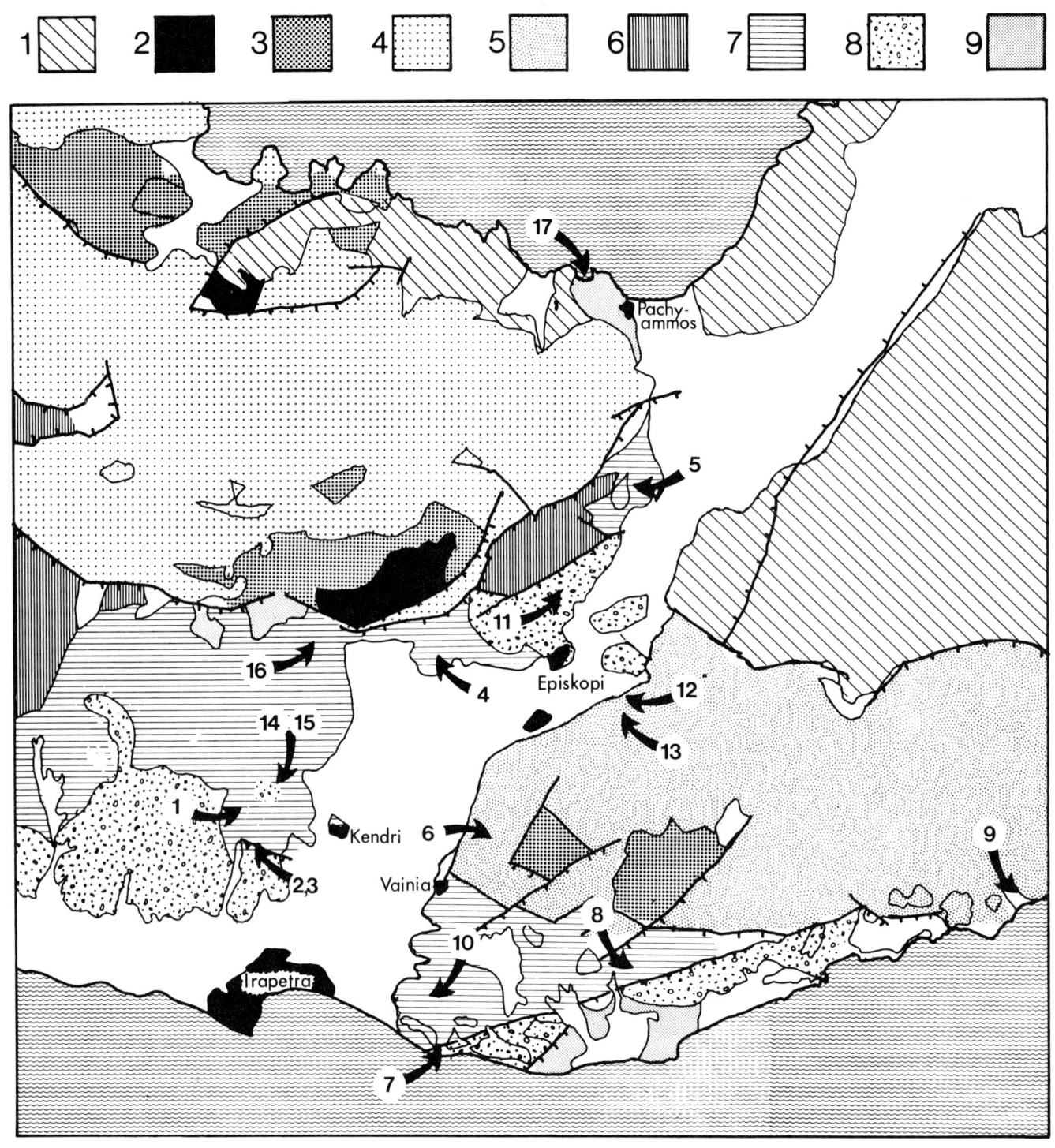

Fig. 15–1. Geological sketch map of the Isthmus of Ierapetra (greatly simplified from Fortuin's 1977 map), with the 17 sample locations of the present study. The geological units are: 1-pre-Neogene rocks; 2-Mithoi Formation; 3-Males Formation; 4-Prinia Complex; 5-Phothia Formation; 6-Kalamavka Formation; 7-Makrilia Formation; 8-Ammoudhares Formation; 9-Myrtos (south shore) and Pakheia Ammos (north shore) Formations. Only major faults (observed and assumed) bounding rock units are shown. Areas in white represent Quaternary sediments.

area. Quaternary marine terraces, talus breccias (pl. 15–1C and D), and colluvium and alluvium represent the most recent deposits in the Pakheia Ammos-Ierapetra depression. They do not contain marl strata, but possess localized deposits of terra rossa, of further importance to archaeologists as the most recent of them is probably only a few thousand years old.

A terra rossa is a red subtropical soil weathered from calcareous parent material (Butzer 1971: 95–96). It contains stable anhydrous iron compounds (such as hematite and goethite) dispersed within colloidal silica. While it is usually decalcified during formation, it may be given secondary calcification after deposition. Many of the terra rossa soils of the Isthmus of Ierapetra are slopewash deposits.

Sampling Procedures

It is clear from Fortuin's stratigraphic sections and from a field survey conducted by J. Gifford and J. Moody (Center for Ancient Studies, University of Minnesota) in June, 1980 that all nine of the Neogene rock units identified in the Ierapetra region contain some marl strata. However, the predominant clastic/ terrigenous nature of the earlier units—the Mithoi and Males Formations and the Prinia Complex—serve both to dilute the occurrence of marl strata in any given outcrop and also to increase the units' resistance to weathering. This results in the present regional topography being highest and roughest where these bedrock types crop out. In fig. 15–1 these areas are seen to be south of Gournia and west of ancient Vasilike.

In contrast, the homogeneous marls of the upper Phothia, the Makrilia, and to a lesser extent the Ammoudares and Pakheia Ammos Formations, are both more common and more accessible in any given outcrop, since these units underlie the subdued and relatively gentle topography that borders the natural cross-Isthmus route along the Pakheia Ammos-Ierapetra depression. Therefore the seventeen marl outcrops surveyed (located in fig. 15–1 and presented as a stratigraphic column in Table 15–I) represent the results of a judgmental sampling strategy that was literally stratified, since it was concentrated in the younger units just mentioned.

It should be noted that there do not appear to be any primary clay deposits in the Ierapetra region; with one exception, all are secondary and occur in the marl strata mentioned above. This is the terra rossa soil sediments, mostly remobilized slopewash deposits, which are found along the northeast border of the depression, especially in the vicinity of the villages of Aghia Marina and Monastiraki. Terra rossa soil sediment has been documented as a component of clay mixtures made by modern potters in the area (see Chap. 18). But the clays of terra rossa sediments are generally so amorphous (non-crystalline) that they cannot be traced to particular geological sources (or geographic localities) by X-ray diffraction analysis.

Of the seventeen localities surveyed for this report, five (nos. 3, 4, 10, 12, and 14) represent outcrops exposed by recent human activities such as road-cuts and agricultural terracing; three of the localities (nos. 5, 13, and 16) are exposures resulting from very recent (probably less than a few centuries old) erosion; and only the remaining half could be regarded as "natural" exposures of marl bedrock that might have also been accessible in the Bronze Age. These include

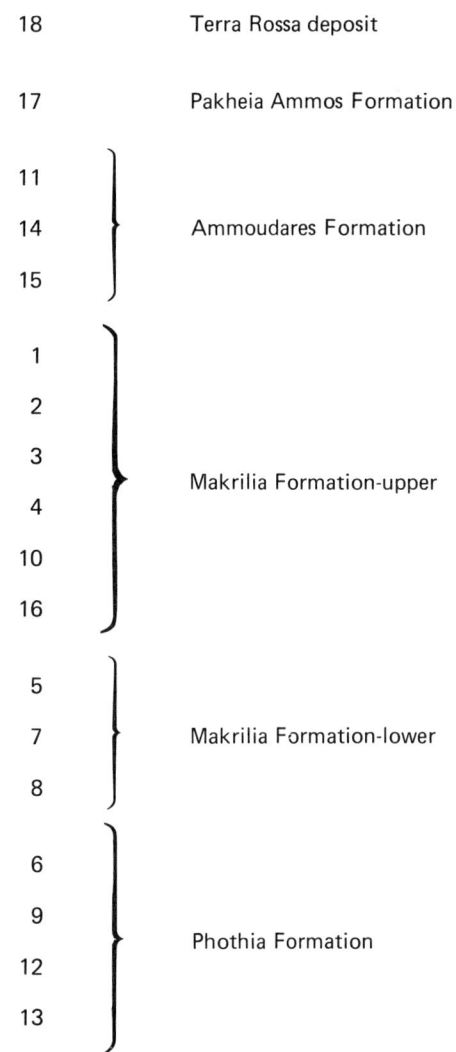

TABLE 15-I
Clay samples presented as a stratigraphic column

18	Terra Rossa deposit
17	Pakheia Ammos Formation
11	
14	Ammoudares Formation
15	
1	
2	
3	
4	Makrilia Formation-upper
10	
16	
5	
7	Makrilia Formation-lower
8	
6	
9	
12	Phothia Formation
13	

TABLE 15-II
Munsell colors and calcium carbonate percentages of marl samples

Sample	Form.	Color (wet)	(dry)	% CaCO$_3$	Sample	Form.	Color (wet)	(dry)	% CaCO$_3$*
1	M	5Y7/4	5Y8/3	44.2	8b	M	5Y6/4	5Y8/3	42.3
2	M	10YR6/6	10YR7/3	43.3	9	Ph	10YR6/4	10YR7/2	44.9
3	M	5Y7/4	5Y8/3	69.1	10	M	5Y6/4	5YR7/2	40.4
4	M	5Y7/3	5Y7/2	49.5	11	A	5Y8/3	5Y8/2	76.5
5a	M	10YR5/2	10YR7/1	42.8	12	Ph	5Y4/1	5Y6/1	44.7
5b	M	2.5Y6/4	2.5Y7/2	46.9	13	Ph	5Y6/4	5Y7/2	57.2
5c	M	10YR5/2	10YR6/2	46.2	14	A	5Y7/4	2.5Y8/2	60.5
5d	M	10YR5/2	10YR6/2	47.8	15	A	5Y8/3	5Y8/2	71.0
6	Ph	5Y5/3	5Y7/3	50.1	16a	M	5Y5/3	5Y7/1	51.7
7	M	5Y6/4	5Y7/2	46.6	16b	M	5Y7/4	5Y8/3	47.1
8a	M	5Y7/3	5Y7/1	51.8	17	P	10YR6/4	10YR7/2	65.6

*Precision of ±5%.

the relatively stabilized gulley at locality 6 (shown in pl. 15–1A), the slowly eroding spurs at locality 8 (pl. 15–1B), and the coastal cliff at locality 17 (pl. 15–10). In contrast, the extensive sequences of homogeneous marls exposed at locality 16 and at locality 5 (pls. 15–16) probably were not exposed in the Bronze Age, but lay below stable, vegetated slopes. These very extensive marl strata could have been accessible by human excavation, if one assumes that Minoan potters actively prospected for what they believed to be "good" clay sources, and occasional clay deposits must certainly have been exposed by excavation for other purposes.

At each of the seventeen localities sampled the marl was collected from 10–20 cm within the deposit, in some cases with corresponding surface samples also collected to determine the effects of weathering on clay mineralogy.

Analyses

Munsell colors (wet and dry) of each sample's clay fraction were determined at the Archaeometry Laboratory, University of Minnesota. The percentages of calcium carbonate present in one gram subsamples of each bulk sample were also established by the pressure-calcimiter method (Allison and Moodie 1965). The results are presented in Table 15–II.

Four samples were grain size-analyzed in detail at the Archaeometry Laboratory, University of Minnesota. Table 15–III summarizes the results. Note that

TABLE 15-III
Descriptive grain-size statistics of four marl samples

Sample	Form.	% sand	% silt	% clay	Median grain size	sed. type
6	Ph	0.7	62.4	36.9	7.3μm.	mud
9	Ph	8.9	70.3	20.8	19.1μm.	mud
12	Ph	1.4	57.9	40.7	5.7μm.	mud
5d	M	1.8	68.1	30.1	7.9μm.	mud

the modal size fraction is *silt*, that the samples are all *mud* from a grain-size standpoint, as well as being *marls* from a mineralogical standpoint.

At the Mineralogical Laboratory of Temple University, 6.3 cm³ of all samples were suspended in 100 ml of distilled water by mixing by paddle followed by ten minutes of ultrasonic vibration. The mixure was poured through a nested set of stainless steel sieves with gradations of 1000, 500, 250, 149, and 74 micrometers. Sufficient water was used to wash through all the sieves with nothing being washed away. The filled beaker was allowed to stand for 22–24 hours, and after this time the less than two-micrometer size fraction was siphoned off leaving a 2 to 74 micrometer silt-size range in the bottom of the beaker for XRD analysis. All particles retained on a particular sieve screen were stored in vials and examined by polarized light microscopy.

Foraminifera tests of various types were observed on the 250 micrometer screens for all samples except nos. 6, 9, 18, and 19. Few mineral fragments were present in this size range. Many minerals were evident on the 74 micrometer screens, including mica, pyroxene, feldspar, and quartz. Heavy mineral fractions were concentrated for further study.

Slurry slides were prepared for each sample from the less than 74 micrometer size range without any grinding. An eyedropper amount of a pasty slurry was placed on a glass slide and allowed to air dry. One other slide was also prepared for each sample for glycolation and then heat treatment (560° C for one hour). Standard 2° 2θ per minute patterns (3° to 70°) were run at 2° per inch with Cu-radiation and a time constant of 0.5 seconds. The diffracted beam was analyzed by a curved crystal graphite monochromator. Instrumental conditions were kept constant and monitored. The resulting patterns (air dried, glycolated, and heat treated) were analyzed for peak positions and shapes. Minerals were identified on the basis of one or more definitive peaks (not necessarily the highest peaks but those which were free from interference from other peaks).

Table 15–IV lists the following dominant minerals by definitive X-ray diffraction peak position: dolomite; plagioclase; calcite; quartz; kaolinite; mica; and zeolites (mordenite and clinoptilolite). These minerals are present in nearly all samples. It has not been possible to quantify the proportions. Substantially less amounts of the following minerals are noted: amphibole (Phothia Formation, sample 9), clinopyroxene (Phothia Formation, samples 9 and 12; Lower Makrilia Formation, sample 5d), gypsum (Phothia Formation, sample 6), potassium feldspar (Phothia Formation, sample 6), chlorite (all samples), and chrysotile serpentine (Phothia Formation, sample 9).

Two special samples, terra rossa and marl over clay (sample 19) have a limited mineral suite in the terra rossa: plagioclase, quartz, kaolinite, mica, and zeolites; and in sample 19, calcite, quartz, mica, and zeolites.

Discussion

Phothia Formation (samples 6, 9, 12, and 13)

All four samples' silt-size fractions show peaks characteristic of dolomite (except no. 6), plagioclase, calcite, quartz, kaolinite, mica, and zeolites. Sample 6 is more crystalline than the other samples of the Phothia Formation. In fact, it is the most crystalline of the clays examined in this study. That this degree of crystallinity developed in the deposit after its deposition (i.e., through diagenesis) is suggested by the complete absence of calcareous microfauna (possibly recrystallized) and the presence in the stratum of authigenic gypsum crystals scattered throughout the marl. The mechanism for such recrystallization may have been a favorable microchemical environment within the sediment some time after its deposition. The significance of identifying such well-crystallized clay in this particular outcrop (pl. 11A) is that it presently serves as a clay source for at least one local potter in the village of Kentri, about 3 km to the west (see Chap. 18).

Makrilia Formation (samples 5, 7, and 8; uppermost section, samples 1–4, 10, and 16)

This formation contains the highest percentage of homogeneous marls to be found in the nine Neogene units of the Ierapetra region. Toward the top of the section, outcrops may expose 10–20 m of such sediments, showing only occasional interbedded siltstones and sandstones (Fortuin 1977: fig. 34).

The fourteen samples collected from nine different exposures of this formation show two groupings of clay mineralogies. Localities 5, 7, and 8 are stratigraphically below the uppermost 30 or so meters of the formation; their XRD patterns show peaks of dolomite (questionable in 7 and 8), plagioclase, calcite,

TABLE 15-IV
Composition of clay samples

Formation	sample no.	dolomite 30.9°	plagioclase 28.0°	calcite 23.0°	quartz 20.8°	kaolinite 12.5°	mica 8.9°	zeolites 6.3°
Pakheia Ammos	17	–	–	x	x	–	x	x
Ammoudares	11	–	x	x	x	x	x	x
	14	x	x	x	x	x	x	x
	15	x	x	x	x	–	–	–
Makrilia, upper	1	x	x	x	x	x	x	x
	2	x	x	x	x	x	x	x
	3	x	x	x	x	x	x	x
	4	x	x	x	x	x	x	x
	10	x	x	x	x	x	x	x
	16A	x	x	x	x	x	x	x
	16B	x	x	x	x	x	x	x
Makrilia, lower	5A	x	x	x	x	x	x	x
	5B	x	x	x	x	x	x	x
	5C	x	x	x	x	x	x	x
	5D	x	x	x	x	x	x	x
	7	?	x	x	x	x	x	x
	8A	?	x	x	x	x	x	x
	8B	?	x	x	x	x	x	x
Phothia	6	?	x	x	x	x	x	x
	9	x	x	x	x	x	x	x
	12	x	x	x	x	x	x	x
	13	x	x	x	x	x	x	x
Terra Rossa	18	–	x	–	x	x	x	x
marl over clay	19	–	–	x	x	–	x	x

quartz, kaolinite, mica, and zeolites. Minor amounts of chlorite were also noted. Four samples were collected down the stratigraphic section exposed in a recently eroded gulley at locality 5 (pl. 11C). All four show the same pattern as sample 5a, reflecting how homogeneous these marls are. At locality 8 (pl. 11B), sample 8a was collected about 10 m stratigraphically above sample 8b; the former shows more amorphous clay peaks than the latter, probably due to extreme weathering above 20 cm depth in the deposit.

The six localities sampled within the uppermost 20 cm section of the Makrilia Formation show the same minerals. The kaolinite peak becomes broader than in the lower formation, and the mica peak becomes sharper.

Ammoudares Formation (samples 11, 14, and 15)

Fortuin (1977: 95) notes the very calcareous nature of this rock unit, in contrast to the underlying formations. Table 15–II confirms this observation. Minerals noted include dolomite (except for no. 11), plagioclase, calcite, quartz, kaolinite (except for no. 15), mica (except for no. 15), and zeolites (except for no. 15).

Pakheia Ammos Formation (sample 17)

Although very limited in areal extent (Fortuin 1977: 119), outcrops of this formation occur closer to Gournia than any other marl-bearing unit. A sea cliff section about 500 m northeast of the archaeological site (it is Fortuin's type-section for the formation) exposes a homogeneous marl stratum near its top (pl. 11D). The sample from this deposit includes calcite, quartz, mica, and zeolites.

Miscellaneous Samples

In the vicinity of sample localities 10 and 17, several discontinuous strata from 1–10 cm thick of a pure, white, powdery substance are interbedded with the homogeneous marl sediments (sample 19). XRD shows both these exposures to be mostly calcite and quartz grains of clay and silt size, along with minor amounts of mica and zeolites.

Analysis of the terra rossa shows that it contains several minerals. These include: plagioclase, quartz, kaolinite, mica, and zeolites. The analyzed composition is thus different from the marls in that it lacks calcite and dolomite. It is also not very plastic and would be unsuitable for ceramics if used alone.

For comparison purposes, four sherds of White-on-dark Ware from Gournia were examined by XRD at the Mineralogical Laboratory, Temple University (Penn nos. MS 4615–10, 13, 16, and 47). Small chips of the clay body were ground to a powder, with an attempt to avoid the nonplastic inclusions which seem to represent the addition of sand as temper. Only quartz and plagioclase were detected in these analyses, as the other minerals were too amorphous for XRD analysis.

Four tests pieces were also made from east Cretan clay, using a combination of sample no. 6 and terra rossa in the following percentages:

1. 100% sample no. 6
2. mostly sample no. 6 with a small amount of terra rossa
3. 50% sample no. 6 and 50% terra rossa
4. 100% terra rossa

The test pieces were fired in a kiln (with an oxidizing atmosphere throughout) to 800° C and were then sampled for analysis by XRD (at the Mineralogical Laboratory, Temple University). Only quartz, calcite, and plagioclase were detected. All other minerals were either destroyed in the firing or were too amorphous to be detected in the fired samples.

As these analyses of ancient sherds and modern test pieces demonstrate, XRD is unsatisfactory for comparisons between fired pottery and raw clays. Its main use is in demonstrating the composition (and with this the characteristics) of the clays available for use.

References

Allison, L. E., and C. D. Moodie 1965. Carbonate. In *Methods of Soil Analysis*, ed. C. A. Black. Part II. Madison, WI.

Butzer, K. W. 1971. *Environment and Archeology. An Introduction to Pleistocene Geography*, 2d ed. Chicago.

Fortuin, A. R. 1977. Stratigraphy and Sedimentary History of the Neogene Deposits in the Ierapetra Region, Eastern Crete. *GUA Papers of Geology* (Amsterdam), series 1, no. 8.

Part V

16

Reconstruction of Potting Techniques and Pyrotechnology

Philip P. Betancourt, Gail Gosser, and Susan Sapareto

Replication studies were conducted at the Tyler School of Art of Temple University. Evidence for this work came from a variety of sources including careful observation of vases and sherds (including cross sections and thin sections), xeroradiography, and several of the analytical studies presented elsewhere in this volume. Replication was done both with modern commercial clays and with clays collected in eastern Crete by P. Betancourt and by J. Gifford.

Materials

The east Cretans used relatively porous clay bodies with many included non-plastics. When fired to a low temperature (see Chap. 9), these clays produced a rather porous, soft fabric. The red to black slip, which partly vitrified in the firing, was colored only by iron. Observations of its characteristics (Chaps. 5–6) suggest an iron-rich clay or clay mixture, probably containing a high percentage of terra rossa, or a ground siltstone. The white was probably also a naturally occurring clay.

Tests were made with several clay bodies. According to the ceramic petrography (Chaps. 5–6), the east Cretan bodies were made from at least three ingredients; blends composed of white, fine-grained marine clay and terra rossa are the most likely material used at Gournia and elsewhere, and stone particles were sometimes added as well. A similar conclusion is suggested by the usual practices of traditional potters in this region today (for Thrapsano see Chap. 17, and for Kentri see Chap. 18), as these craftsmen also mix a highly plastic white clay with a red soil. Mixtures of Cretan calcareous marine clays with iron-rich terra rossa produce workable clay blends. The marine clays are so plastic they do not perform well when pure; they are much more satisfactory when tempered with the less plastic lateritic red soil. The addition of sand-sized particles produces an even coarser and more porous body, useful for the making of larger shapes. The result is a body with good resistance to thermal and mechanical shock. The potter thus has a large margin of error in the case of too rapid heating or cooling when the vessels are being fired, or with too rapid drying before firing.

The dark-firing slip requires a careful preparation. Surfaces with the same luster and appearance as White-on-dark Ware can only be achieved with an iron-rich, low-fired, partly sintered slip. This type of engobe is generally similar to the slips used in Classical Greece for black-figured and red-figured pottery, in the Roman world for terra sigillata, and in several other parts of the ancient world for dark or red surfaced pottery (for discussion see Noble 1965; Noll, Holm, and Born 1975; Winter 1978; Noll 1977; 1982). Modern potters usually call this slip by its Roman name, terra sigillata. It is prepared from clays with a high iron content by a process that removes the coarser particles, leaving only the finest platelets for use as the slip. For the benefit of potters who may wish to duplicate the process, several modern recipes are presented here (for discussion and for other recipes see Alexander 1978):

1. "Roman terra sigillata" (Cone 011)
Osage clay (dry, crushed) .... 690 grams
Calgon water softener.................. 15 grams
Distilled water .... 3 liters

2. "Alfred terra sigillata" (Cone 07)
Red clay (dry, crushed)................ 300 grams
Calgon water softener.................. 1.5 grams
Distilled water .... 0.7 liter

3. "Swiss terra sigillata" (Cone 07)
Red clay (dry, crushed)................ 680 grams
Sodium hydroxide..................... 1.95 grams
Distilled water .... 3 liters

4. "Red Art terra sigillata" (Cone 06)
Red Art Clay (a commercial brand
  name, Cedar Heights Corporation)
  (dry, crushed) .... 4 kilograms
Calgon water softener.................. 4.5 grams
Distilled water .... 16 liters

The water softener is dissolved in hot water, the clay is added, and the clay mixture is stirred well and allowed to settle for two or three days. A glass jar for settling is ideal. Three distinct layers will form. The top layer of water is syphoned off, and the second layer is removed and used for the slip. Repeating the settling process will insure that only the finest particles are retained. For best results, the clay may be ground after levigation, either with a mortar and pestle or in a ball mill. Some potters prefer to use the syphoned water, which still has particles in the under two-micrometer range suspended in it, boiling the water until it thickens sufficiently for use as a slip. While this is not necessary for surfaces such as those used for White-on-dark Ware, it yields a more lustrous firing slip and is recommended for those who wish to duplicate higher gloss slips (as in Attic Black Figure and Red Figure). Burnishing the surface, which also enhances the luster, is used for some of the very earliest East Cretan White-on-dark Ware (see Chap. 2), but is not a regular feature of the style.

The slip is best applied to leather hard vessels to help reduce the shrinkage problem. In the firing, the fineness of the slip and its high illite content will cause it to vitrify before the more porous body, and the included iron will create the red to brown to black surface, depending on the composition and the kiln atmosphere.

Reduction during the firing is crucial to the proper vitrification of the slip. It was demonstrated some years ago (Hoffman 1962) that a reducing atmosphere in the kiln will cause iron rich illitic clays to vitrify at a temperature that is approximately 100° C lower than an oxidizing atmosphere. The difference, caused partly by the Fe^2 ions and partly by the high potassium content of the illite (which act as fluxes), gives a substantial margin of error during the firing, but it means that for optimum results the kiln must be blocked and a reducing atmosphere induced at the peak temperature. The iron rich illite is the dominant factor in the vitrification, masking the effect of increased glassification caused by fine size alone. Thus an important objective of the levigation is the sorting out of the illite particles, which are among the smaller constituents of the pure clay. Since the best results are obtained by reducing atmospheres, the dark color of the slip on most of the White-on-dark Ware is more than a casual stylistic preference; it is the result of the technology, perhaps representing a conscious attempt to vitrify the slip as much as possible.

Satisfactory experimental slips were made by using the same clays as the bodies as well as by using different clays. The advantage of using one blend for both body and slip is that it minimizes the shrinkage differential, resulting in less cracking and flaking. A considerable variety in the appearance of ancient fabrics and surfaces suggests that the materials were never completely standardized, with potters following a generally accepted procedure within limits that allowed substitutions of both materials and relative percentages of the ingredients.

While the modern tests only provide some general correspondences for ancient methods, several circumstances must be similar in order to achieve proper results. Ancient potters must have prepared their slips by some means which would retain only the smallest particles, and grinding and/or levigation are the surest and simplest ways to produce this result. A suitable deflocculant (the counterpart of the water softener used in modern recipes) can be made by soaking wood ash in water. Settling tanks have not been identified in the archaeological record, but there is no reason to assume they were not used. Grinding to achieve an even finer slip than is possible with settling alone is also extremely likely, and it is possible the slip was made from an illitic siltstone, crushed into powder and then levigated (as suggested in Chap. 5).

Potting Techniques

White-on-dark Ware was made by hand with the occasional aid of a turntable or handheld tool. The technique was successful, and most surviving vases are attractive, with uniformly thick walls and invisible or nearly invisible seams. Vessels are smooth and regular, showing a high level of potting skill as well as a keen appreciation of well-made pottery.

Xeroradiography indicates the use of clay slabs up to several centimeters high (Chap. 14). These slabs required careful work to join them together and to make the walls even and obliterate the seams. For shapes with thickened lips, such as bridge spouted jars, an extra strip was needed at the rim (detectable in pl. 12A by the difference in the coarseness of the clay). The forming process, with a large amount of wet working, resulted in different profiles on the interior and exterior of vessels, especially near the base (pl. 12B). Elongation of air bubbles parallel to the surface of the walls (pl. 12B) is a good indication of this type of process. The smoothing was apparently sometimes aided by a support on the outside of the walls (compare the "Knuckling" and "Rib" operations at Thrapsano, Chap. 17). Traces of a tool held against the outside wall are sometimes visible (pl. 12D), and some vases may have been fashioned with support from a section of basket, a broken sherd, or some other material (see discussion in Chap. 5).

The following steps are suggested as the most likely stages in the manufacture of a cup:

1. A small ball of clay is flattened with the palm of the hand (pl. 13A). It is either attached directly to a turntable or some other support (in this case a flat, broken sherd), or it is first placed on sand and then put on the support. Placing the slab on sand first, a process attested from a surviving base (see Chap. 19), would prevent the vessel from sticking so tightly that it would be deformed when it was pulled off the support after completion.

2. A thick coil is made by rolling a piece of clay between the hands. It is then flattened to make a slab.

3. The perimeter of the base is moistened with water, and the slab is pressed down onto the edge of the disc with a turning motion (pl. 13B). A pressing, pinching, and rotary movement seems to work well.

4. The excess of the slab is cut or pinched off, and the seam is pressed together.

5. The seam inside the vessel where the slab joins the base is secured with a sponge or damp fingers.

6. With the fingers on the outside of the cup supporting the wall, the clay is smoothed upward with the thumb while the pot is rotated (pl. 13C). The wall will start to assume a convex profile. To straighten it, the fingers and thumb can be reversed. It is at this stage that a piece of fabric or some other support may be useful if held against the outside wall, particularly on larger vases.

7. When the wall is the desired thickness and height (pl. 13D), the rim can be smoothed with a sponge or the fingers.

8. The dark-firing slip is applied at the leather hard stage (pl. 13E).

9. The white decoration is brushed on (pl. 13F).

Even, symmetrical vessels can be produced with this method if the potter is skillful. Molds, as suggested by Matson in Chapter 5, are unnecessary. Careful observation of the same sherds studied by Matson failed to show any trace either of mold marks or basket impressions, and the senior author of this chapter feels it is unlikely they were used for these vessels.

Since the forming technique was meticulous, it was not especially fast. Experiments with the making of a simple rounded cup (as in pl. 13) suggest 20–30 minutes to fashion this type of vessel. Speed would, of course, improve with practice, but even at this pace a steady worker could make two to three cups per hour, or about twenty in an eight hour day. A week's work would produce almost a hundred and fifty, and a longer work day could raise the number to two hundred. Another three or four days would add the necessary pouring vessels, lids, and other shapes, and the firing could be done in three days, allowing the first day to repair the local kiln and the other two for firing and cooling. Two experienced workers and an assistant could probably supply a household's fine ware needs for an entire year with about two weeks of work.

The speed of manufacture is particularly important in any reconstruction of the ancient production. If Myrtos is regarded as a typical EM settlement, one can assume only a few households in a community (Warren 1972). Such small habitation sites could never have supported permanent full time workshops. Before the increase in Minoan population that seems to have occurred about MM I, one must assume some different model—a seasonal production, a household industry which worked only when the need arose, or a regional production seem the most likely candidates.

Firing Tests

To better understand the ancient technology, a small kiln was built and experiments were conducted with both oxidizing and reducing atmospheres. The goal of these tests was to produce a pale tan body, a good black slip, and clean white decoration with no discoloration.

A finely levigated slip, prepared as described above, will yield a satisfactory red to black surface. The color results from the firing, with reducing conditions creating black surfaces, oxidizing conditions producing red, and partial reduction resulting in browns and tans. Since the fine particles start to vitrify and begin the sintering process, the surface becomes smooth, with a soft luster. With oxygen present during the firing (an oxidizing atmosphere), the iron in the slip and the body unites with it to form red ferric oxide (Fe_2O_3). If too little oxygen is present (a reducing atmosphere), either ferrous oxide (FeO) or magnetite (Fe_3O_4) form. Both are black. Intermediate stages produce mixtures which may appear brown. The crucial property of the slip is its ability to vitrify before the clay body. By sintering, it can trap the black oxides within a glassy, airtight surface so that even if the more porous body reoxidizes, the slip will remain dark.

Evidence for the ancient firing conditions comes from several quarters. The presence of a surface sheen on many sherds (see Chap. 5) indicates a probable contact with ashes during the firing, implying that the fuel was not far from the stacked vessels. Mössbauer spectroscopy indicates a high enough percentage of trivalent iron in one of the sherds examined to prove that it was in an oxidizing atmosphere during most of the firing cycle (Chap. 7). Since some of the White-on-dark Ware vessels are large, one could not fire even a moderate load of pottery in an oxidizing atmosphere without using a kiln chamber. This situation rules out banked hearths, covered stacks of vessels over a fire, and other systems which would yield reduced or mostly reduced atmospheres. The most likely system seems to be a small kiln with the fuel added either at the entrance or in a connecting chamber.

For experimental purposes, a brick kiln of 20 cubic inches was constructed. Propane gas was used as the primary fuel, and wood was added as an accessory fuel to produce the necessary reduction. The best results were obtained if an oxidizing atmosphere was maintained to cone 06 (999° C). Wood was then introduced continuously, creating a smokey, reducing atmosphere for up to one hour. The heat was then shut off and all openings were closed off. The kiln required four to five hours to cool, and during this time it reoxidized through the casual introduction of a little oxygen.

The firings produced a fine textured, lustrous black surface on a pale clay body. Experiments with the identical clay for both body and slip yielded good results, as did tests with different clays. Reduction time was found to be a crucial factor in producing acceptable results. Good white lines (for the decoration) were achieved with a variety of materials, including dolomite and several white-firing clays, but the results were not uniform, and some materials flaked badly.

In general, the technology is not complex, but it needed a high degree of skill to achieve good results. Oxidizing and reducing cycles would occur as a natural consequence of periodically adding fuel, so that the process, once mastered, would be easy to duplicate. Moderately good results may be achieved within a relatively wide latitude of both clay preparation and firing conditions, as well as with different raw materials. The various surfaces observed in White-on-dark Ware (dull to lustrous; red to brown to black; durable to crazed) suggest that the general level of skill varied greatly from piece to piece. Evidently the tradition did not maintain the interest or skill to duplicate the results exactly every time a vase was made. The modern experiments suggest that a high level of pyrotechnic skill was achieved on a regular basis, with mastery of clay preparation, vessel manufacture, and kiln construction and use.

References

Alexander, B. 1978. CeramActivities. Terra Sigillata. *Ceramics Monthly* 26, no. 1: 89–91.

Hofmann, U. 1962. The Chemical Basis of Ancient Greek Vase Painting. *Angewandte Chemie, International Edition* 1: 341–414.

Noble, J. V. 1965. *The Techniques of Painted Attic Pottery.* New York.

Noll, W. 1977. Techniken antiker Töpfer und Vasenmaler. *Antike Welt* 8, no. 8: 21–36.

Noll, W. 1982. Mineralogie und Technik der Keramiken Altkretas. *Neues Jahrbuch für Mineralogie. Abhandlungen* 143:150–99.

Noll, W., R. Holm, and L. Born. 1975. Painting of Ancient Ceramics. *Angewandte Chemie, International Edition* 14: 602–19.

Warren, P. M. 1972. *Myrtos. An Early Bronze Age Settlement in Crete.* London.

Winter, A. 1978. *Die antike Glanztonkeramik, praktische Versuche.* Mainz.

Part VI

17

Thrapsano, Village of Jar Makers

Maria Voyatzoglou

Traditional Ceramics In Modern Greece

The Workshops

Greek pottery workshops have functioned in a similar way for centuries. Until recently, they produced large quantities of ceramic wares, operating in many coastal and inland villages to fill the needs of a population that was basically agricultural. Fewer workshops operate today, but in some areas a few potters still maintain the age-old practices. In a typical workshop, the members of one or more families produce and sell their wares within their own village or in the surrounding area. Functioning independently, the shop is not a part of any guild or organization. It is usually organized on the patriarchal family system—the potter-craftsman is the father while other members of the family are his assistants. Usually the sons learn the craft in order to succeed their father, carrying on the tradition from one generation to the next.

The raw materials are easily obtainable. Except for the tools, the kiln, and the working space, ceramics requires only clay, water, and fuel. Potters do not pay for using water, and they can excavate their own clay and cut their own fuel (dry brushwood and firewood). The materials, however, need to be carried to the working place.

A traditional Greek potter's workshop is a plain installation. It is often set in the open, with a covered place being used only where a kick-wheel is placed. The preparation of the clay, the kneading, the drying, and the firing are all generally done out of doors. Often the wooden kick-wheel (with an iron bearing) is made by the potter himself.

The most common type of firing chamber is an updraft kiln. This is a tall cylindrical or square building, built partly beneath the surface of the earth. The fuel is separated from the vessels by a built-in perforated floor. The upper part of the kiln either communicates directly with the open air (the kiln being covered only during the firing), or it has a vaulted, permanent roof. Kilns are built by the potters themselves.

Local Centers of Production in Traditional Ceramics[1]

A center of production is a place where a number of potter's workshops operate at the same time, producing a large quantity of ceramic vessels. While each workshop has its own production, they all work within the same tradition. Their raw materials also have a common origin.

The different workshops at one center produce the same ware, but they are not interrelated as a community. Rather than being organized into a guild, they function independently in the same way as the isolated potter's workshop.

The pottery is not always sold for money. Very often, especially in earlier times, it was bartered for other goods (cereals, pulses, or oil). Usually the potter negotiates directly for the exchange of his production, but sometimes a retailer is needed, especially when a large shipment is to be carried and sold beyond the center's immediate area.

Comparatively few centers produce a "special artifact."[2] This is a vessel with a form that is considered typical for the center producing it, often modeled with a special technique. Examples of "special artifacts" are:

Center of Production	Special Artifact	Local Name
Siphnos	cooking dish	τσικάλι
Aigina	pitcher	σταμνί
Lesbos	pitcher	κουμάρι
Thrapsano, in Crete	jar	πιθάρι
Koroni, in the south Peloponnese	jar	τζάρα

In these examples the "special artifact" is not the only product of the center, but it is made in greater numbers than any other artifact in the production. It is often exported more widely than other products of the center (for a brief discussion and some examples see Casson 1938).

Social and Professional Structure

In modern Greece, traditional pottery is the output of craftsmen who are farmers during the greater part of the year. The farmer-potter works in ceramics only during the three summer months; with this seasonal production, he can cover all the pottery needs of the agricultural community. This type of seasonal work is possible because of the type of cultivation that is practiced: olive trees; vineyards; small areas of cereals (barley, wheat, and oats); and some beans and pulses (beans, broad beans, lentils, and chick peas). Because of the seasonal nature of this type of agriculture, the farmer can earn a supplementary income, dividing his year's time between working in the fields and working in his pottery. Poor owner in both cases, he has to stretch his personal activity in order to cover his family's needs around the year.

Traditional Greek pottery is generally a thrown earthenware (see the production at Kentri, Chap. 18). It is normally fired only once. While an endless variety of thrown forms exists, and while many of these shapes are common throughout the country, the same vessel may have slightly different dimensions in different centers. In addition, potters working at the same center may vary the proportions of a particular type of vase. This situation is understandable and to be expected as there are no strict rules for the shaping, and each potter is guided by his own sense of proportion. In addition, aesthetic and technical experimentation are completely foreign to the traditional potter. Through his craft, the potter transmits to his pot an unconscious, yet vigorous sense of life; the resulting form is a human record.

Definition of the Ventema and Organization of the Guild at Thrapsano

The Guild

Thrapsano (Θραψανό), a village of about 1500 inhabitants, is located in the province of Pediada, about thirty kilometers southeast of Herakleion. Until recent years, about half the male population of the village were potters who made and sold a type of large jar called a πιθάρι (the most detailed description of the Thrapsano potters is Voyatzoglou 1972; see also Xanthoudides 1927; Casson 1938: 468; Hampe and Winter 1962: 4–11; Voyatzoglou 1973; 1974). Every May, several teams of potters would leave Thrapsano to make and sell jars in other parts of Crete during the three summer months. This system of producing and selling jars is called the Ventema (βεντέμα), and the jar makers are called the Ventemaroi.

The Ventema begins on May 21 and lasts until September 14. Both dates are Orthodox holidays marking the beginning and the end of summer. The departure of the groups of jar makers from Thrapsano was treated as a festival, and the guilds separated as soon as they came out of the village, with each team taking a different direction to reach its destination. Each team, or guild, stayed at the same location all summer, setting up its workshop to make jars and then selling them to the inhabitants of the neighboring district. About thirty to thirty five guilds used to set out from Thrapsano in the past, totaling about two hundred men. While only a few guilds still participate, they still carry on the system.

Each guild has six members:

1. The Master (ὁ *Μάστορας*) is the head of the guild and the main craftsman. He picks the other members of the team and is also the business manager for the group.

2. The Second Master (ὁ *Σοτομάστορας*) is the technical assistant to the Master.

3. The Wheeler (ὁ *Τροχάρης*) turns the hand operated turntable. He is also the kiln man (ὁ *Καμινάρης*), setting the wares in the kiln and regulating the duration and intensity of the firing.

4. The Clay Man (ὁ *Χωματάς*) pounds and sieves the dry clay.

5. The Wood Cutter (ὁ *Ξυλάς*) cuts faggots for the firing and loads the bundles of wood on the pack animals.

6. The Carrier (ὁ *Κουβαλητής*) transports the wood and the dry clay from their source, loaded on the Master's animals. He also takes the jars to the buyer's house, two on each pack animal.

The Installation

The Master negotiates the renting of a field where the workshop can be set up. Ideally, the location would offer the three essential raw materials required for the work: clay, water, and fuel. The men then build a kiln or repair an old one and put up a hut made of tree branches where they can have their meals and take a rest. Of all the work involved in ceramics, only the kneading can be done inside the hut. The turntables are put up in the open, and the men work in the sun so that the sections of the jars will dry quickly (see the discussion below). Prospective buyers also meet the craftsmen in the open. Except for the Carrier, everyone has his own pack animal to carry his tools and his personal articles.

The Daily Work Schedule

The work begins early in the morning, at about 4:30 AM. First, the men prepare the dry clay brought in by the Carrier the evening before. Then, if there was a firing the previous day, they unload the kiln. Work on the turntables lasts from about 6:00 AM until around 5:00 PM. Ten to sixteen jars are made in one day, but no jars are made on kiln firing days. On these days the kiln is loaded about 10:00 or 11:00 AM, and the firing begins in the early afternoon. It lasts until the jars are mature, which takes four or five hours. This means that the firing ends about sundown.

The work is interrupted for several breaks. Those who work in the open workshop have a snack at about 9:00 in the morning and another at noon. The three who work away from the workshop take dry food with them for lunch and return to the installation in the evening so that everyone can eat the evening meal together. The most common dish is a soup made of broad beans, served in a single deep vessel which the men all share in common.

Finances

The guild keeps a common cash account, a kind of pool for money received and expenses paid. This account takes care of the rent for the field and the cost of food and drink. The Master transacts all the guild's business. It is he who rents the field, sells the ware to the buyers, and sees to the production in general.

A personal account for each member of the guild is also kept, and a daybook is maintained with both collective and individual expenses. At the end of the Ventema, the profits are shared on the basis of these entries. Each member's share is determined by long standing tradition:

Master	1½ parts
Second Master	1½ parts
Wheeler and Kiln Man	1¼ parts
Clay Worker	1 part
Wood Cutter	1 part
Carrier	½ part (he takes one part if he has his own pack animal)

Institutional and Professional Framework

Of the six members of the guild, only three (the Master, Second Master, and Wheeler/Kiln Man) are actually craftsmen; the other three (the Clay Man, Wood Cutter, and Carrier) are assistants. The Master is the principal figure in the team. He is directly responsible for the technical processes, performing the main operations in the shaping of the jars. Besides deciding where the workshop will be set up, negotiating for its installation, and dealing with the sale of the production, he is responsible for the members' social behavior. The jar makers, being strangers outside their own village, have to follow certain social obligations. In case of any misunderstanding with the residents of the nearest village, it is the Master who speaks for the members of the guild. He also coordinates the workshop's production, keeping an eye on the work of every member so that the completion of the jars will not be delayed. Like the responsibilities of the Master, the duties of the other members of the guild are codified within the system of the Ventema. The principles of the Ventema, a moral as well as a professional code, are accepted by everyone in Thrapsano (not just by the jar makers.)

Technique

Clay Sources and Clay Preparation

The blending of clays is common in ceramic art. In general, the choice of the dry clay determines the form of the clay body, and it, in turn, is related to the form of the shaped artifact. Hard clay, composed of coarse particles, gives a porous surface which allows the water of the clay to evaporate faster during the drying and firing. Such a hard clay is needed for the modeling of the Thrapsaniot jars.

Within the area covered by the Ventema, clay sources have usually been located already by older jar makers—they are known, more or less, by everyone connected with the craft. The clay needed for jars is not the common red earthenware clay that is so well known all over Greece. Jar clay, found in many places throughout Crete, is a hard, refractory clay, plastic enough for working, darker in color than the common red earthenware clay of Greece. It is not used by itself. The kind of jar clay excavated determines the proportions of its blending with two other kinds of clay, one more plastic and one more refractory. The most common blend is eight parts of jar clay to two parts of refractory clay. There is no rule for the ratio of water to dry clay, but because of the climate, the resulting body must be very moist so that the kneading can be done rapidly.

The process is:

1. The blend is prepared of dry clays, after they have been pounded and sieved.
2. The kneading is done directly with the two ingredients, clay and water.
3. The clay is then used immediately (the storing of clay is unknown among the jar makers).

The process of preparing the clay seems to have been determined by the working conditions of the Ventema. The jar clay does not need to be carried by the potters because clay sources are already known, and clay can be secured at the source which is nearest the installation. Choosing the proper clay is a responsibility of the Master.

A parallel situation exists among potters from Siphnos who travel to other islands and to coastal communities on the Greek peninsula during the three summer months. Like their Thrapsaniot colleagues, they carry their tools but not clay. Thus, while they are away from their own island they cannot produce the "special artifact" of Siphnos, the cooking dish.

The Kneading

About 60 kgs of clay are required for one jar with a capacity of 100 liters. In other words, 600 kgs of clay must be prepared for one day's work (i.e., for ten jars).

The kneading is done inside the hut, the only covered place in the jar maker's installation. On the evening before it is to be kneaded, the dry, powdered clay blend is spread on the hut's earth floor. At dawn the next day, water is poured into a depression at the center of the powder, and the process of kneading begins. Four members of the guild participate: the Master; the Second Master; the Wheeler; and the Clay Man.

Kneading is done with the feet, with the process

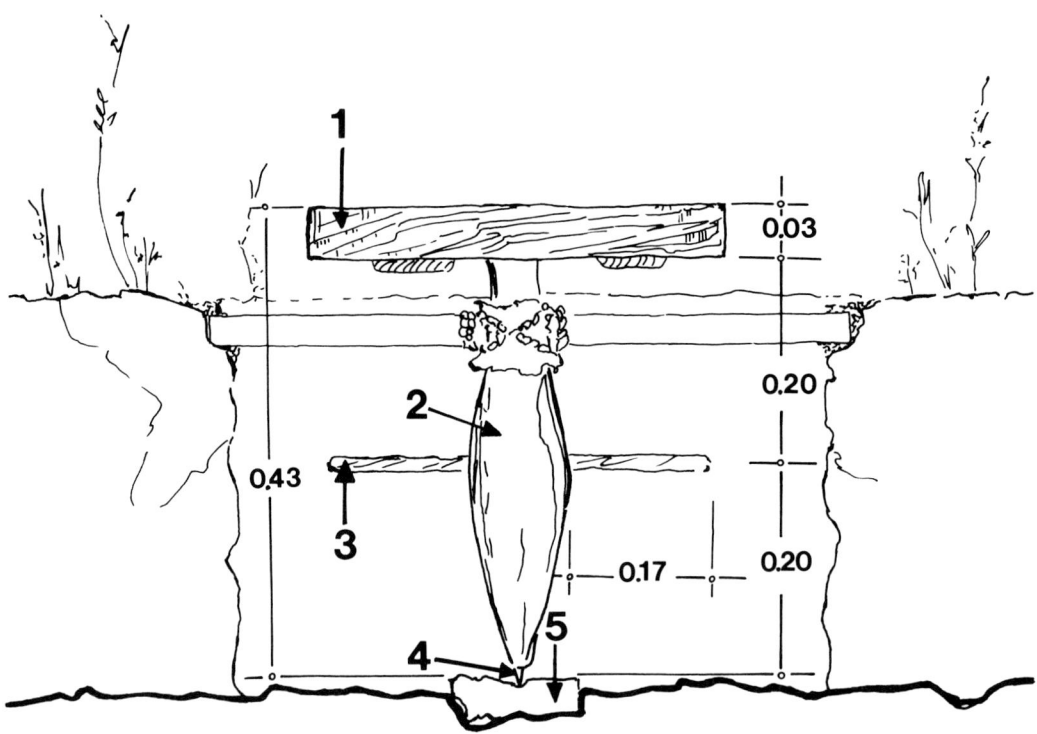

Fig. 17–1. The turntable, elevation. 1. Disc, of wood (κεφαλαρά). 2. Axle, of wood (ἀδράκτι). 3. Handles to rotate the wheel (περόνες). 4. A nail used as the point of rotation (μοχλός). 5. Stone with a socket for rotation (πλιθί).

repeated four times. Each time, the clay is either gradually consolidated into one lump at the center of the hut, or it is separated into several small lumps at the periphery of the floor. In between, the clay is divided into small lumps by hand, and each lump is turned upside down and then transported either to the periphery or to the center of the hut. The principal work of kneading is all done with the feet, while the hands assist by moving the clay about. Finally, the kneaded clay lies in a large vaulted lump at the center of the hut. The Second Master then presses the three fingers of his right hand onto the surface of the clay vault, forming a cross, while uttering the wish, "May the Cross help us." He then throws the small piece of clay left in his hand (called "leaven") at the middle of the impressed cross. The process of kneading is now finished.

Kneading clay and kneading dough appear as two similar processes. Apart from the verbal metaphor[3] or words like "knead" and "leaven," an impressed cross is also used on loaves of bread. The natural elements of water and fire stand at the beginning and end of both processes.

Production on the Turntables

The jars are made on low, hand operated turntables, with a separate wheel (τροχί) used for each jar. The turntables are operated by the Wheeler who rotates them for the Master but does not take part in the shaping of the jars themselves.

The construction of the turntable is important to the final form of the jar (fig. 17–1). A wooden axle (τὸ ἀρδάκτι) with an iron pivot (ὁ μοχλός) is used as the vertical spindle. It stands in a socket made from a stone or an iron slab (τὸ πλιθί), with the upper end in the center of a wooden disc (κεφαλαρά) which acts as the wheel head. Axle and wheel head stand upright with the aid of the crossbar (τὸ σταυροσάνιδον), a horizontal brace fixed to the sides of the "wheeler trench." The crossbar has a square incision at the center, and the rotating axle, wrapped in a piece of felt dipped in oil, fits inside this incision (fig. 17–2). Two small wooden wedges are lodged into the straight side of

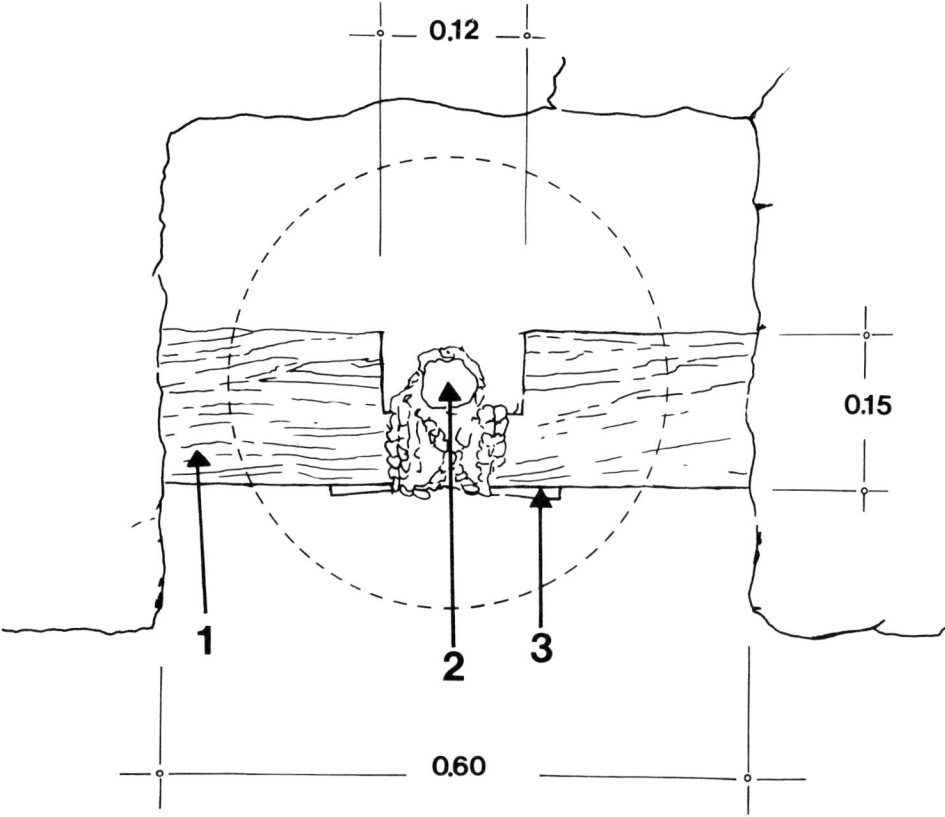

Fig. 17–2. The turntable, plan. 1. Crossbar (σταυροσάνιδο). 2. A piece of wool is impregnated with oil to help the rotation (μποξάς). 3. Wedges (κατίνες).

the crossbar, opposite the square incision. Since the felt lessens the friction, it aids the rotation of the axle. Small handles, to turn the wheel, are made by passing a piece of wood through the axle. In order to fix the turntables in place and secure a seat for the Wheeler, the jar makers dig a long rectangular trench (the "wheeler trench"). It is widened by digging small square spaces (τροχολάκκοι) on one side, at intervals of about half a meter (see pl. 14A and D). The turntables are set up in these spaces, and a stretch of solid ground is left between them. Since one jar is made on each turntable, a separate space is needed for each jar. Usually twelve jars constitute a day's work.

Making a jar requires close cooperation between Master and Wheeler. The Wheeler squats crosslegged in the "wheeler trench," facing the turntable and turning it with his hands. By pushing and pulling the two handles, he produces a nearly continuous rotation. The Master sits on the ground opposite the Wheeler, at a higher level. He finishes the "planting" and the "first brim" while sitting on the ground, he uses a stool (about 15 cm high) for the "round brim,"

and he stands up to shape the "lip." He moves from right to left, from turntable to turntable, carrying his stool, a bucket of water, and his tools. At the same time, the Wheeler moves in the trench; he crawls on his soles and palms, following the movement of the Master, so that they can each work at the same turntable.

The jar is not made directly on the wheel head, but on a separate ceramic disc, called a bat (ἡ πλάκα). The bat always has a larger diameter than the wheel head (about 45 cm as opposed to 40 cm). It is fixed to the wheel head with a coil or with lumps of moist clay and is kept in place by the weight of the jar. Bats are made on a kickwheel (τροχός), on an even larger bat (the use of bats at Thrapsano is not limited to the jar makers, as the Thrapsaniot potters use them as well).

Jars are made from six superimposed strips of clay smoothed with the help of the rotating turntable. As the first step, the Second Master pushes his palm through the moist clay, cutting off lumps of clay. Holding a lump between his palms, he quickly moves his hands back and forth, rolling it into a coil. Each coil is made from the same amount of clay (four to five kilograms). Two or three coils make up one 12 cm high strip in the final form of the jar, that is, one "brim."

Each brim represents one stage in the process of shaping a jar. When a brim has dried sufficiently, it is ready to receive the next higher cylinder, so that sections are added about an hour apart. Usually a jar has six brims. Each one has its own size, proportions, and name: the "planting" (φύτεμα); the "first brim" (πρώτη στομωσά); the "round brim" (στρογγυλὴ στομωσά); the "straight brim" (ντρέτη στομωσά); the "big brim" (μεγάλη στομωσά); and the "lip" (χείλωμα). An additional strip of clay, called a "belt" (ζωνάρι) is added where two brims are joined.

All the brims are added while the jar is on the turntable, which is rotated clockwise or counterclockwise by the Wheeler, depending on the operation then in progress. To begin, the Second Master sprinkles the bat with clay flour. He then takes a ball of clay and flattens it on the bat with his palm, making a disc about 43–45 cm in diameter and 1–1.5 cm thick. This is the base of the jar. The first strip, the "planting," is placed at the periphery of the base while the wheel is rotated counterclockwise. Since the Second Master does not work with the Wheeler, he manipulates the clay with his hands while he rotates the wheel with his right foot.

The operations required for each brim are:

1. "Dressing," fig. 17–3 (Second Master without a Wheeler)

The Second Master holds a coil in his left hand and lets only one end touch the lower brim (or the base, in the case of the first coil). With his right hand, he sticks the moist coil onto the dry edge of the lower brim, pressing it into the inner surface of the jar with his bent index finger. The movement of the index finger is diagonal and downward. The inner surface of the brim is finished when the turntable comes full circle. At a second full circle, the outer surface is finished.

2. "Milking," fig. 17–4 and pl. 14C (Second Master without a Wheeler)

The left hand palms the coil, pushing the clay to the periphery of the brim, while the bent index finger and the thumb of the right hand lift the clay upward.

3. The "String," fig. 17–5 (Master and Wheeler)

The Master presses the outer surface of the brim with a piece of string. This is done at the point where it meets the new coil, with the string passing around the jar two or three times.

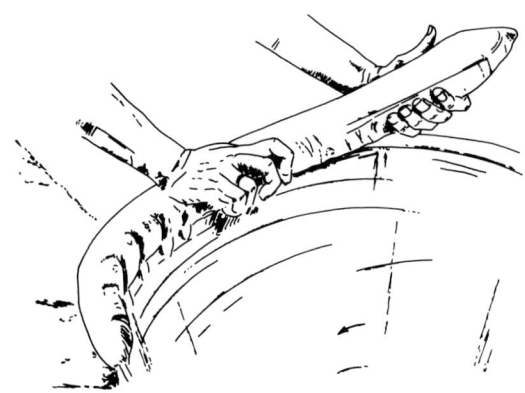

Fig. 17–3. The "Dressing" operation.

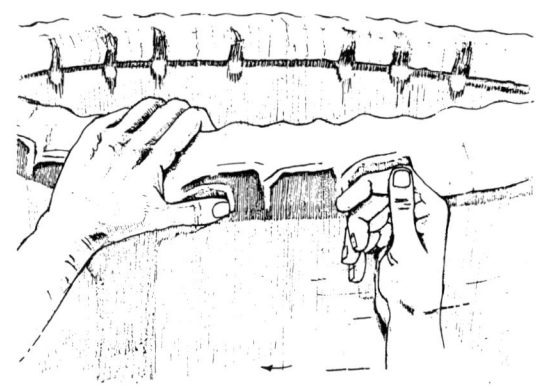

Fig. 17–4. The "Milking" operation.

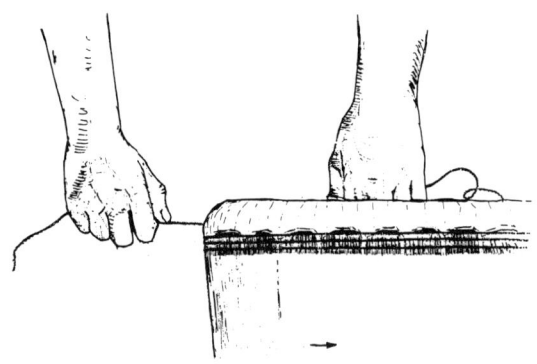

Fig. 17–5. The "String" operation.

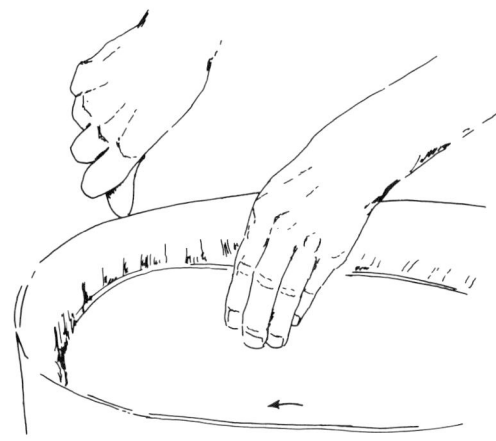

Fig. 17–6. The "Pulling" operation.

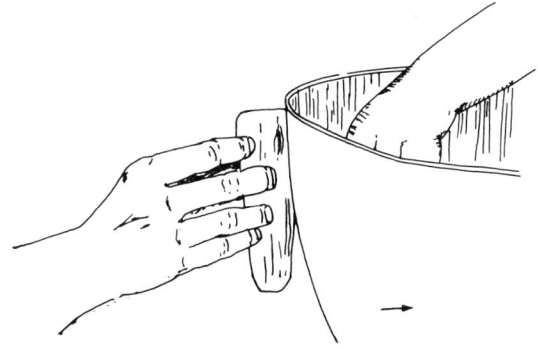

Fig. 17–9. The "Rib" operation.

Fig. 17–7. Levelling the clay between the fingers.

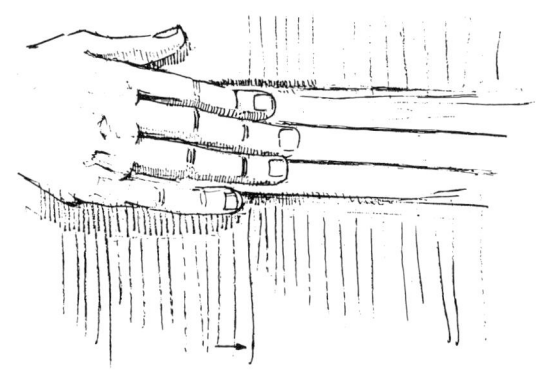

Fig. 17–10. Applying the "Belt".

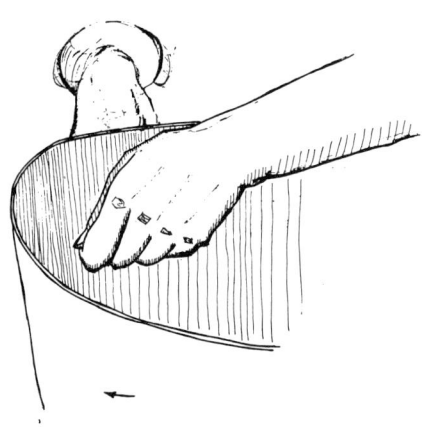

Fig. 17–8. The "Knuckling" operation.

4. The "Pulling", fig. 17–6 and pl. 14B (Master and Wheeler)

The Master takes a wet sponge and wrings it over the coil which has been attached by the Second Master. He then palms the coil and smooths it until it forms a perfect circle.

5. Leveling the clay between the fingers, fig. 17–7 (Master and Wheeler)

The coil is leveled and centered with the fingers, so that it begins to assume the shape of a thick wall.

6. "Knuckling," fig. 17–8 (Master and Wheeler)

The wall of clay is held between the two bent index fingers and is pulled upward, making it thinner. The Wheeler then unsticks the end of the string as the wheel turns, and the Master pulls it off.

7. The "Rib," fig. 17–9 (Master and Wheeler)

Table 17–I. Operations in the making of one strip.

Operation	Movement of the hands	Result	Movement of the turntable	Operator
Dry Movements				
"Dressing"	Horizontal	Fixing the coil on the brim	Counterclockwise	Second Master without Wheeler
"Milking"	Horizontal	Fixing the coil on the brim	Counterclockwise	Second Master without Wheeler
"String"	Horizontal	Resistance to centrifugal force	Clockwise	Master and Wheeler
Wet Movements				
"Pulling"	Horizontal	Equal division of clay	Clockwise	Master and Wheeler
"Leveling"	Horizontal between fingers	Making wall even and final line of coil horizontal	Clockwise	Master and Wheeler
"Knuckling"	Upright	Raising clay upward and making wall thinner	Clockwise	Master and Wheeler
"String"	Horizontal	Removed	Clockwise	Master and Wheeler
"Rib"	Upright	Making wall thinner while shaping the curve	Clockwise	Master and Wheeler
"Second Rib"	Upright	Giving final form to curve (Necessary only for concave wall)	Clockwise	Master and Wheeler

The Master holds a wooden rib against the outer wall of the brim, supporting it while he performs the "knuckling" operation. The wall now begins to assume a convex shape.

8. The "Second Rib" (Master and Wheeler)

The previous operation is repeated, so that the wall takes its final shape.

Table 17–I shows the sequence of operations in schematic form. They are the same for each brim, for all the jars in the series. In general, the horizontal operations fix or center the clay while the upright operations (except in the case of the "Second Rib") help pull the clay upward. For wet movements, the left hand operates inside the form while the right hand operates outside it. The clay is fixed by means of dry movements; it is pulled upward and shaped by means of wet movements.

Immediately after the "Second Rib," the Second Master prepares a small quantity of clay and sets the turntable in motion with his foot. Bending the fingers of his right hand, he presses this "belt clay" exactly over the place where one strip meets the other (fig. 17–10). He then steps aside for the Master and Wheeler. By pressing with a wet sponge, the Master straightens the clay and forms two parallel grooves.

The craftsmen use the same process to make the successive strips, gradually building up the form of the jar. Table 17–II shows the time table for one jar. Because the vessels are made in a series of 10–16 at a time, in the beginning the bottom of the first jar is set in place by the Master, while the bottom of the second jar is set in place by the Second Master. In other words, the two men work side by side at the same time, at the same stage of construction (Stage I). The "Second Rib" and the "Belt" are made in immediate succession (though not at every stage of the operation). As soon as Operation IIa is ended with the last jar of the series, the craftsmen do the "Second Rib." They then make the "Belt" beginning again with the first jar of the series. Only then does the interval of drying begin. Drying is a complete break between each two brims.

After the lip is completed, the jar is fully formed. Three handles are then attached, and three crosses are added, impressed between the handles. A simple decoration is beaten onto the "Belts".

Table 17–II. Time table for one jar.

Strip to be Shaped		Operation	Operator	Approx. Time in Minutes
"Planting"	I.	"Pressing"	Second Master	2
		"Milking"	Second Master	
	II. a.	"Pulling"	Master and Wheeler	5
		"Knuckling"		
		"Rib"		
	b.	"Second Rib"	Master and Wheeler	2
Drying				60 interval
"First Brim"	I.		Second Master	5
	II. a.		Master and Wheeler	5
	b.		Master and Wheeler	2
	III.	"Belt"	Second Master and	
			Master and Wheeler	1
Drying				60 interval
"Round Brim"	I.		Second Master	5
	II. a.		Master and Wheeler	5
	b.		Master and Wheeler	2
	III.		Second Master and	
			Master and Wheeler	1
Drying				60 interval
"Straight Brim"	I.		Second Master	5
	II. a.		Master and Wheeler	5
	b.		Master and Wheeler	2
	III.		Second Master and	
			Master and Wheeler	1
Drying				60 interval
"Big Brim"	I.		Second Master	5
	II. a.		Master and Wheeler	5
	b.		Master and Wheeler	2
	III.		Second Master and	
			Master and Wheeler	1
Drying				60 interval
Lip	I.		Second Master	5
	II. a.		Master and Wheeler	5

The Drying

The jars are not taken off of the turntables until the next day, by which time they are set. The craftsmen loosen the bats and remove both the jars and their bats from the turntables, transferring them to the ground alongside the "wheeler trench." They are left there to dry for twenty-four hours while a new series is made on the wheels. Every morning the men move the older jars a little farther away from the trench, so that the series next to the Wheeler is always the most recent one.

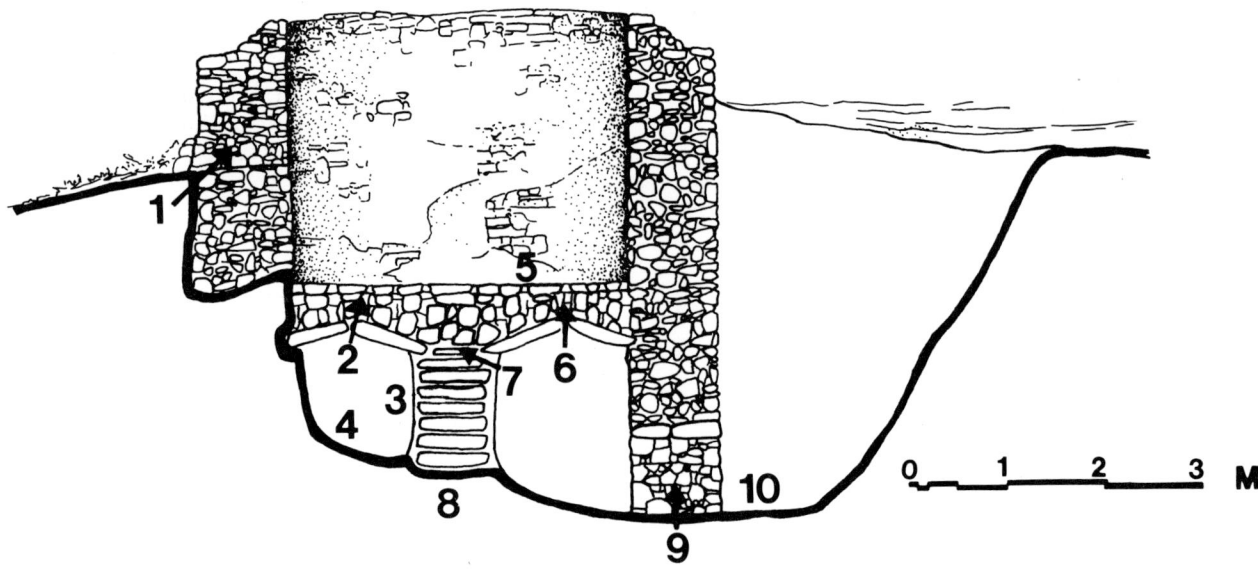

Fig. 17–11. Elevation of the kiln. 1. Door for loading. 2. Perforated kiln floor. 3. Layer of clay to protect the column. 4. Firing chamber. 5. Surface of the kiln floor. 6. Upper point of the vault. 7. Column for support, of stone. 8. Central support rests on the floor of the firing chamber. 9. Door for stoking the fire. 10. Access to the door.

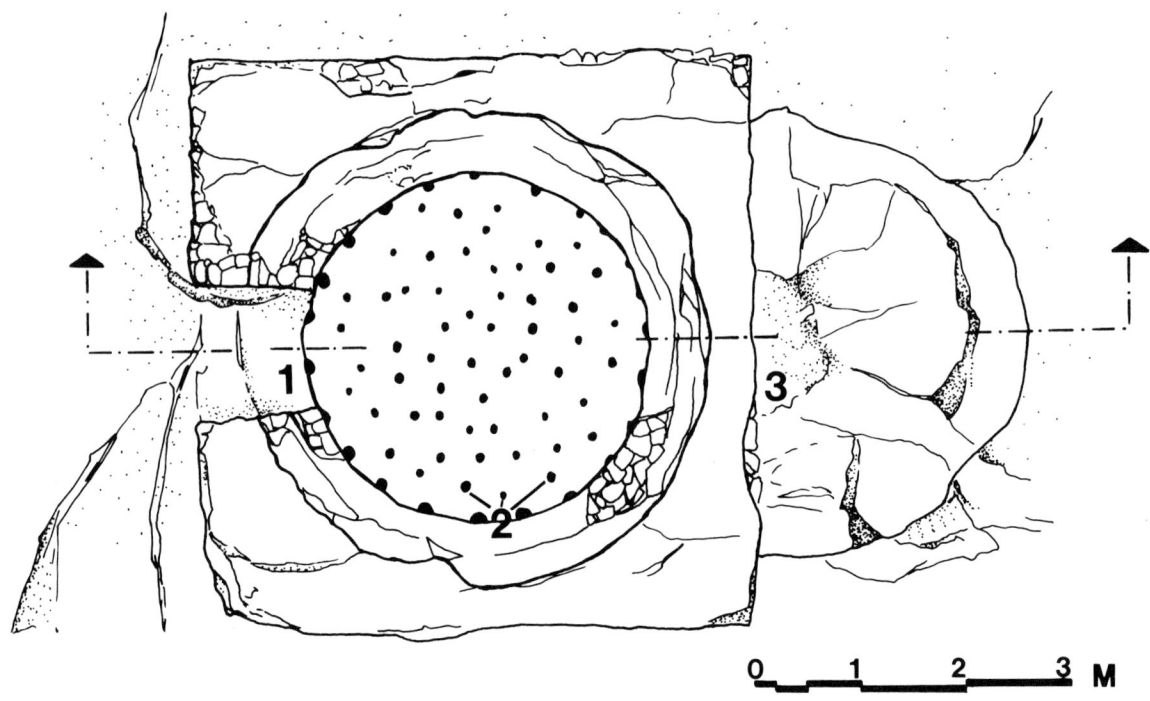

Fig. 17–12. Plan of the kiln. 1. Door for loading. 2. Perforations in the floor (larger at the periphery to aid the draft here). 3. Door for stoking the fire.

The Firing

The Thrapsaniot potters use an updraft kiln, a type found all over Greece (figs. 17–11 and 17–12). It is built as a cylindrical form, open at the top with no permanent roof, and so must be partly covered during the firing. Today this is accomplished with galvanized iron sheets, placed loosely to let the smoke out. They are put on the built walls of the kiln, and sherds are used to keep them in place.

All the members of the guild help stack the kiln. They carry the jars from the drying place and pack them in two horizontal circles inside the chamber, and the Kiln Man then builds the kiln door and the fire hole out of mud bricks and mud. He works by himself during the whole process of the firing.

The schedule for stacking, firing, and unloading a kiln holding twenty-four jars is:

First Day (work always begins about 10:00 AM)

10:00–10:50 AM	Transferring the jars and setting them in the kiln.
10:50–11:10 AM	Building the kiln door.
11:10–11:15 AM	Covering the top of the kiln.
(break for lunch)	
3:20–7:15 PM	Firing the kiln.

Second Day (work always done at daybreak, after the kneading)

5:00–5:30 AM	Emptying the kiln.

Evolution of the Ceramic Art

Before World War II, thirty to thirty-five teams of jar makers produced about 15,000 jars annually. All of this output was sold in the Cretan market because the jars were needed in all Cretan villages for storing oil, cereals, and other items. The jars were able to fill this need quite well.

Jar making was regarded as a seasonal occupation. Little labor is required for the cultivation of olive trees throughout the major part of the year because olives are picked and pressed during November and December. Cereals are plowed and sowed in October and November. Although some harvesting and threshing needs to be done during the summer, this was done by the wives of the jar makers so that their husbands could go on the Ventema. During that period the men earned more than they would have working as farmers. Since they did not earn a whole year's living expenses during the Ventema, they had to work in their fields for the rest of the year. In addition, some of the jar makers would produce some thrown pots (such as jugs and pitchers), working as potters in the proximity of the village.

After World War II living conditions in Greece changed, especially in regard to the agricultural economy. In the region of Thrapsano, for example, the cultivation of cereals has been nearly abandoned and vineyards (which require much more care) have increased in numbers. In addition, urbanization and industrialization have made it easier to earn a living in the cities, lowering the population of many agricultural villages. New containers of metal, plastic, and other materials have lessened the need for clay vases. These developments have had a profound effect on the production of traditional ceramics.

During the decade 1950–1960, the Greek centers of production underwent a fundamental change, with responses to the new conditions taking several forms. In a few cases, a minimum production is still to be found in two or three of the workshops of a center, with a small output to meet the reduced needs (as, for example, at Kentri). In a majority of cases, however, the center no longer functions at all.

Today, most pottery in Greece is made in permanent workshops which operate throughout the year and are run by professional potters. Obviously, there is no comparison between a modern ceramic workshop and a traditional one. The modern shop is usually located near some urban center, and it produces decorative rather than utilitarian artifacts. Both the product and the technology have now been altered. Most of the products are glazed, twice-fired wares. The clays are standardized industrial materials, and the same raw materials are often used by workshops operating in different parts of the country. The change is complete, affecting the whole process of making the wares as well as the resulting products.

In Thrapsano, however, there is no such evolution. Here the craft is dying out toward a complete extinction. The jar makers and potters who are left in the village still work in the traditional way; one cannot find any evidence for a change in the ceramic technology of the past. However, hardly any young men are learning the craft, and there is no school or institute founded in Thrapsano to undertake the difficult task of a double change: in the ceramic technology and in the public's response to new ceramic forms.

In the case of this craft, laden with such a long tradition, total obliteration seems more probable than adaptation to new social conditions.

Notes

1. The term "center of production" is proposed by the author.

2. The term "special artifact" is proposed by the author.

3. The technical terms used in the special ceramic technology are often metaphors of words used in the agricultural household, such as "fireplace" for the place where the turntable is set up, "spindle" for the axle of the turntable, "pie" for the lump of clay from which the base of the jar is made, "milking" for one of the dry operations, or "leaven" for the small piece of clay left in the hand of the Second Master at the end of the kneading process.

References

Casson, S. 1938. The Modern Pottery Trade in the Aegean. *Antiquity* 12: 464–73.

Hampe, R., and A. Winter. 1962. *Bei Töpfern und Töpferinnen in Kreta, Messenien, und Zypern*. Mainz.

Voyatzoglou, M. 1972. *Tὰ Πιθάρια στὸ Θραψανὸ Σῆς Κρήτης*. Thessaloniki.

Voyatzoglou, M. 1973. The Potters of Thrapsano. *Ceramic Review* 24: 13–16.

Voyatzoglou, M. 1974. The Jar Makers of Thrapsano in Crete. *Expedition* 16, no. 2: 18–24.

Xanthoudides, St. 1927. Some Minoan Potter's-wheel Discs. In *Essays in Aegean Archaeology Presented to Sir Arthur Evans*, ed. S. Casson, 111–28. Oxford.

18

Traditional Pottery Production in Kentri, Crete: Workshops, Materials, Techniques and Trade

Harriet Blitzer

Ο᾽ τσικαλάς, ὅπου θέλει, κολλάει τ᾽ἀυτί.
—TRADITIONAL SAYING[1]

The potters' village of Kentri[2] is situated on a small rise (pl. 14E) roughly three kilometers north-northwest of Ierapetra, Crete, close to the dry southern coast of the Lasithi nome (figs. 18–1 and 2). Previous visitors to the village included the pioneers Hampe and Winter who visited the pottery center for one day and briefly described some aspects of production in the ten potters' workshops then functioning (1962:11–13). This present study examines in greater detail the materials and techniques of the Kentri craftsmen, the character and arrangement of their workshops, and the tradition of ceramic production in the village (insofar as it may be reconstructed).[3]

Three potters presently maintain workshops in the Kentri environs, one of whom has little connection with traditional methods of pottery production.[4] Of these three, all stem from local families with a history of involvement in pottery manufacture, and two, who are brothers, continue to produce limited quantities of some of the traditional forms of vessels (figs. 18–5 and 6 and pl. 17D, E, and F, 5c, and d).

History, Local Tradition and Trade

According to the elderly inhabitants of the village, there were at least twenty individuals (ten potters, and as many helpers) working in Kentri, then a village of five to six hundred inhabitants, in the years prior to World War II.[5] As at other pottery production centers in Greece, the Kentri villagers place the origin of their craft quite far back in time.[6] And, while the existence of the village of Kentri is attested by documents as far back as the fourteenth century,[7] it is not clear exactly when the production of pottery began in this location. Four generations of potters are recalled by present-day villagers, taking the history of the craft in Kentri back roughly one hundred years.

Only one other village in the Ierapetra locale is said to have had its own potter. This was Vainia (fig. 18–2) where a Kentrianos, having married into the village, constructed a kiln and began a workshop. With his retirement, however, the craft persisted no longer in Vainia.

Pottery production in Kentri was shared, during its

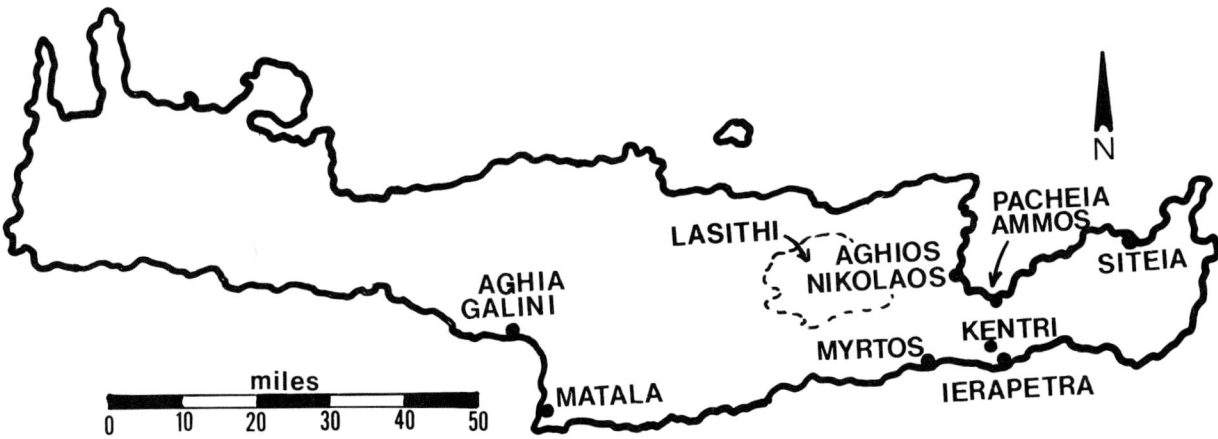

Fig. 18–1. Map of Crete showing locations mentioned in the text.

heyday, between two work forces, consisting of the potters (known locally as τσικαλάδες) and their helpers (προγούς).[8] The potters were responsible for the actual manufacture of the vessels at the wheel and for the loading and firing of the kiln. The helpers mined the clay and transported it to the workshop, prepared the clay body as needed, assisted in loading the kiln, procured fuel for the firings, and generally kept the workshop in order. This arrangement was established in economic terms with the helper and the potter

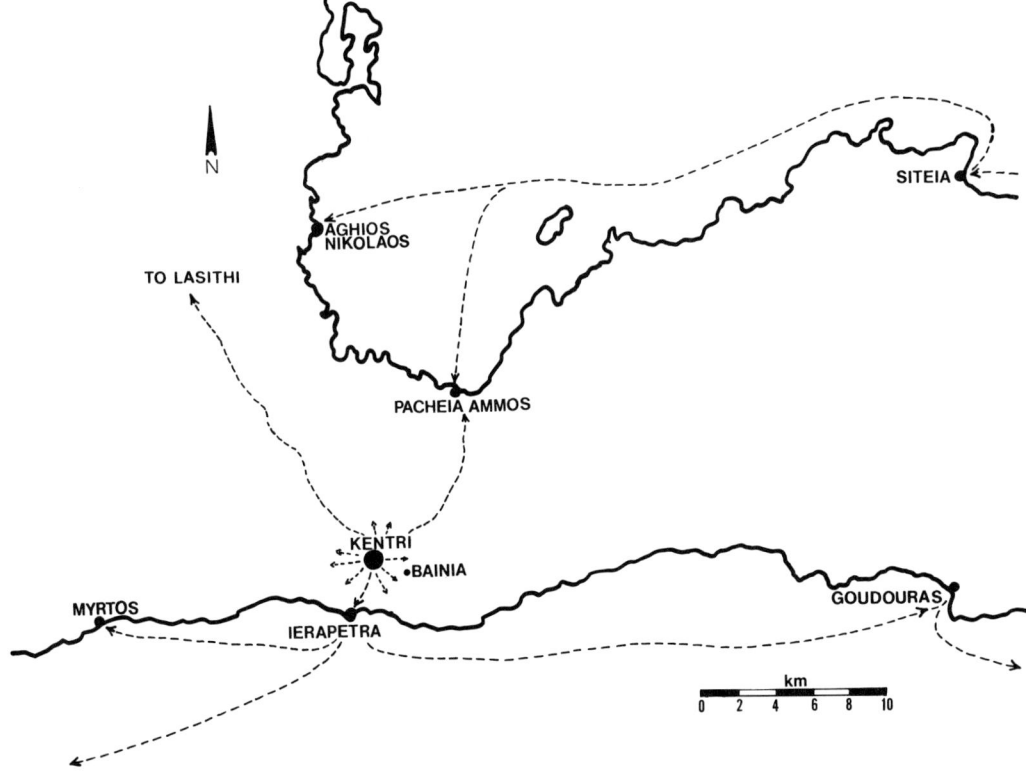

Fig. 18–2. Detail of the Eparchy of Ierapetra, showing Kentri and the land and sea routes by which Kentri pottery was distributed in Crete.

sharing equally in the profits of the workshop. While this particular system is recalled by most inhabitants, there are individuals who remember earlier workshops (for example, those of their grandparents) in which the potter worked alone. In those cases, it appears that the helper had not yet been established as a necessary figure in the production process.

In the history of the village families, it is not uncommon to find that a family member of one generation might serve as a helper in the workshop of an unrelated potter, and in the next generation one of the family might actually learn to be a potter. Early on, the youth of the village were often provided with their own wheels, were taught by their elders, and when they reached a suitable age (about twelve or thirteen) were incorporated into the production process. This, of course, no longer takes place. All of the Kentri inhabitants are aware that the production of traditional vessels will soon cease in their village because no young potters have been trained, and the knowledge of the elders is swiftly being lost.[9]

The working season of the potters in Kentri ran roughly from May through October, that is, during the warm months of the year in which the weather might interrupt production as little as possible. During this season, the potters worked every day except Sunday, from dawn till dusk, with a short midday break for a meal. The colder months of the year were devoted mainly to agricultural labors (such as the olive harvest) although vineyards, requiring attention during the spring and summer, were also important in the local economy.[10] While no other crafts were practiced by the Kentri potters, it may safely be stated that the members of each workshop were dependent on the income from both their ceramic and their agricultural labors.[11]

Women, according to all, were never taught how to make pottery, but often, following the establishment of the helper system, served as helpers in their husbands' workshops.[12] Their workload extended to traveling with a laden pack animal (carrying twenty or thirty vessels) into Ierapetra or to smaller villages in the locale. Such marketing ventures were restricted, for women, to villages within easy reach of Kentri. Very often the potter himself would travel on foot (with a pack animal) to more distant locations.

Villagers estimate that formerly as many as forty or fifty thousand water jugs (σταμνιά) (pl. 17D) would have been produced each year by all of the Kentri potters combined. Indeed, the σταμνί was the vessel for which Kentri became famous in the early twentieth century. Ἱεραπήτρικα σταμνιά were preferred by the villagers of East and Central Crete to similar products from such villages as Thrapsano, a potters' center in the Herakleion nome (see Chap. 17).[13] The sale and trade of the small vessels produced in Kentri included their distribution by means of pack animal (both donkey and mule) to Ierapetra and Pakheia Ammos (fig. 18–2). The pottery was also sent, by boat, from Ierapetra to Siteia and Aghios Nikolaos on the north coast of Crete, and to Goudouras, Myrtos, Matala, and Aghia Galene on the south coast (fig. 18–2).[14] Dealers (ἐμπόροι) stopped their boats at Ierapetra and loaded orders which had been placed during previous visits. Shipments of three to five hundred vessels were not uncommon.

Exchange, or ἀνταλλαγή for pottery did not occur very often, and when it did it was usually on a small scale. On an annual trading venture to the Plain of Lasithi, in the Dictaean Range (fig. 18–2), a Kentri potter might exchange twenty empty σταμνιά (each capable of holding fifteen kilos of liquid) for one hundred ὀκάδες of potatoes (one ὀκά equals roughly 1.25 kilograms).[15] Pulses, grains, and other dry food goods were also procured in exchange on these trips to the interior of Crete.[16]

While pottery was produced in quantity in Kentri in the first half of this century, it is clear that this industry was centered around the production of small portable vessels (figs. 18–5 and 6) in contrast to the production of large storage vessels such as was prevalent at Thrapsano and other centers (see Chap. 17). Preserved examples of the types of vessels made commonly in Kentri include smaller storage jars, a maximum of 0.75 m in height (cf. κουρούπια, below). Only one Kentri potter is said to have tried his hand at πιθάρια of 1.50 m and greater heights, and he did this only rarely. Potters from the village of Thrapsano visited the Kentri locale and produced the large storage jars needed by the locals. These are still visible in household storerooms today (pl. 17E).

One other clay vessel, the τσικάλι (cooking dish) was imported into the village of Kentri from the island of Siphnos. As with πιθάρια, only one potter in Kentri ever attempted to manufacture τσικάλια, but the Siphniote variety was said to have been preferred by local housewives.[17] All other ceramic vessels used in Kentri were produced by the villagers themselves.

The Clays and Their Properties

Three types of local earth are used today by the two Kentri potters who work in the traditional mode. Of these, one type is a recent discovery. The remaining two, when mixed together, form the standard clay body which has "always" been used in Kentri.[18]

Of the two earths used in this Kentri mixture, type one is a bluish white earth called γαλανό or ἀσπρόχωμα mud and the white clay of the Kentri mixture. According to the potters, an enclosed workroom was viable (pl. 15A), only if it had a good source of sunlight (usually a double door left open), was free of windy passages, and (in a preference expressed only by a few) had a door facing south (figs. 18–3 and 4).

The floors of the workshops were usually of beaten earth (pl. 15B), the stone walls might or might not be plastered with clay or mud, and the interior arrangement was simple. It is clear, however, that the term τσικαλαριό in Kentri was not limited, in villagers' perceptions, to the enclosed workroom, but referred, rather, to the entire working area of the potter and helper, most of which was situated out-of-doors (fig. 18–3).

Among the disused potters' workshops in Kentri there appeared to be no standard plan, with the various spaces needed for daily production arranged as each potter saw fit. The potter's kick wheel was, however, always situated against one wall (pl. 15E and figs. 18–3 and 4) with access of light in that location, usually through a door.[21] Immediately within the structure one would find a column of clay (κολόννα) roughly three to four feet high and perhaps 0.50 m wide, situated either in the center of the room or off to one side (fig. 18–3 and pl. 15B). The wheel (τροχός) was set into a pit (λάκκος) dug into the earth floor of the workroom. A stone and mud or wooden set of shelves behind and in front of the wheel provided the potter with a place to sit, a resting place for the tools needed in potting (pl. 15E and F) and a place to set down the newly made pots. Drying racks might be found along the walls of the workshop and trays for drying smaller vessels might take up much of the available floor space. Burlap was often spread out on the floors as well, to receive clay βόλια (balls of clay) which were prepared by hand just prior to their use at the wheel.

The stone-walled workroom, requiring a very small space in the workshop complex, was surrounded outside by well-defined but visually homogeneous areas in which most of the necessary steps for clay preparation and firing were carried out.[22]

The Preparation of the Clay Body

The white clay and the red earth needed for the Kentri mixture were deposited and stored on the ground, in the outdoor part of the workshop (fig. 18–3 and 4). The earths were kept in separate piles, uncovered, until they were prepared for use.

Each earth was beaten separately with a wooden hammer (κόπανο) (pl. 15A and C) into pieces a little larger than one centimeter in size. The κόπανο was made, by the potter, from a tree branch (preferably of a heavy wood such as mulberry) and employed the forking of the branch in the creation of the tool head.[23]

The earths were then sieved (again separately) so as to remove stone pebbles and granules which would interfere later with production. Sieving took place in the same area where the earths had been beaten. The red earth is no longer prepared in this fashion, settling basins having replaced the dry-sieve method of purifying such earth (fig. 18–3).[24]

Following this preparation, five containers of dried red earth and slightly less than six containers[25] of white clay (also dry) were piled up to form a small hill of earth in the center of which was a depression. Six containers of water were poured gradually into this basin, and the water was folded into the clay mixture with a stick. The mixture was then stamped with the bare feet of the potter in a process known as the πάτιμα. Depending on the weather, more or less water might be used in the mixture (a wet or humid day would require less water).

The clay body, now shaped like a large pie, was then cut into pieces and placed in a corner of the workshop, under cover (burlap or canvas were used) until the potter was ready for the next step. The clay might be used immediately in which case it was laid out on the workroom floor, stamped again by the potter with his bare feet, and then made into βόλια or balls of clay of the proper size needed for the vessels to be made that day. The size of these βόλια was determined by the weight of the clay in the hand of the potter or helper.[26]

If the clay was intended for later use it was at some point placed on the workroom floor, stamped again by the potter or helper, and then fashioned into a κολόννα or column which could sit for as much as a year with a constantly moistened burlap or canvas cover (pl. 15B). The amounts of clay body needed for daily production would be measured by hand and extracted from this column. If, on occasion, the clay had dried out, water was again added to it, and flattened lumps of clay were set outside to reach the proper consistency (pl. 15D). A softer and wetter clay was used in Kentri (by all accounts) in the production of σταμνιά as compared with that used for all other vessels. The proper ratio of clay to water was learned by the potter and helper through experience.

The Tool-Kit of the Workshop

In addition to the implements cited above, a standard complement of tools was used on a daily basis. Among these were the σφουγγάρια (sponges), ταβλάκια (potter's ribs), καλάμια (stamps made from reed segments), and κτένια (wooden or metal combs) utilized in the fashioning of the vessels on the wheel (pl. 15F).

The wheel, consisting of the πανοκούτσουρο or iron upper wheel attached to the άξονας (axle) and the κάτωκουτσουρο or wooden kick wheel (pl. 15E) at the base, was made in two separate parts. An ironworker fashioned the upper wheel and axle to order. This frame was then brought to a carpenter who built and attached the kick wheel. The wood used for this lower wheel consisted of planks of the same material used locally in the construction of barrels.[27] This same wood was also employed by the carpenter in the production of the potter's ribs (ταβλάκια), which, according to all informants, were constantly "eaten up" by the heavy wear of daily production.

In order to remove vessels from the wheel, the potter cut the base of each vessel with a wire known as a τέλη. Trays of wood and of clay (πλακάκια) received the freshly made vessels. Pieces of cloth (πανιά) and rags were kept for various uses in the workroom, and during the winter the sieves (δίχτια), beating tools (κόπανα), and stoking tools (διχάλια) were all stored inside as well.

The Vessels Made in Kentri

Thirty types of clay vessels have been produced in Kentri within recent memory. Of these, two types were attempted, without much success, by a single potter of an earlier generation who soon abandoned their manufacture. It is possible that other kinds of vessels were made as well in Kentri, but recollection of the types which have gone out of use is limited.[28]

Examples of some of the vessels no longer produced in Kentri were unavailable in the village itself, and were located in other villages in eastern Crete. In addition, each individual questioned in Kentri recalled a different set of ceramic products. What is presented here is therefore a composite list of all clay vessels remembered by the elders of Kentri and those produced today. Each vessel is described with its Greek name, the English equivalent, the number of sizes in which this shape was produced, and the uses to which the vessel was put.

1. σταμνί (fig. 18–5.1), water jar, two sizes, unglazed, used to contain water only, either at home or in the field.
2. φλυτζάνα (fig. 18–5.2), drinking cup, one size, unglazed, used in drinking all liquids.
3. κουλούρι (fig. 18–5.3), stand, one size, unglazed, used as a base for the σταμνί.
4. λαϊ (fig. 18–5.4), small water jar, one size, unglazed, used to contain water for drinking, in the home, workshop, or in the field.
5. πετρολεκανίδα (fig. 18–5.5), all-purpose basin, three sizes, glazed and unglazed, used for kneading bread, washing clothes, and general food preparation.
6. τσικάλι (fig. 18–5.6), cooking vessel, one size, glazed and unglazed, used for general cooking whether in oven or on coals. This glazed vessel was made by only one potter for a very brief period of time.
7. λεκανάκι (fig. 18–5.7), eating bowl, one size, glazed and unglazed, used in food preparation and serving, and in eating.
8. μαγκάλι (fig. 18–5.8), portable heating vessel, one size, unglazed used to heat small parts of a room (πιρήνες or crushed olive pits, or charcoal was burned in this vessel).
9. γλάστρα (fig. 18–5.9), flowerpot, at least two sizes, unglazed, used for all types of plants, most frequently βασιλικό, or basil.
10. γουβέτσι (fig. 18–5.10), baking vessel, one size, unglazed or glazed, used for baking food in oven.
11. θυμιατό (fig. 18–5.11), incense burner, one size, unglazed, used for burning of incense at home and in church.
12. δοχείο or καθήκη (fig. 18–5.12), chamber pot, one size, unglazed, used as a portable toilet at home.
13. λαδικό (fig. 18–5.13), oil jug, possibly two sizes, unglazed and glazed, used as a pouring vessel and container for oil in the home.
14. κουρούπι (fig. 18–5.14), small storage jar, several sizes, unglazed, used for storage of cheese, oil, olives, dried foods.
15A. βρασχή (fig. 18–5.15), food container, one size, unglazed, used as a feeder for larger animals and as an occasional storage vessel for animal food.
15B. μπουγαδόβρασχη (fig. 18–5.15), washing basin, one size (25 kilos), unglazed, used by housewives for washing clothes.

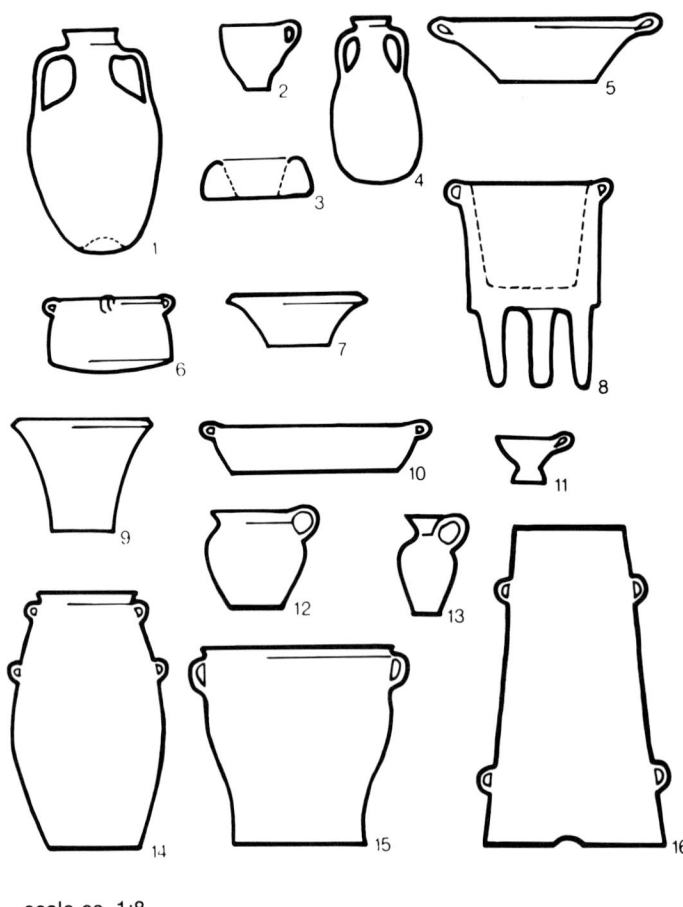

Fig. 18–5. Types of vessels formerly and presently produced in Kentri: 1) σταμνί or water jar; 2) φλυτζάνα or cup; 3) κουλούρι or stand for a σταμνί; 4) λαï or small water jar; 5) πετρολεκανίδα or household all-purpose basin; 6) τσικάλι or cooking vessel; 7) λεκανάκι or eating bowl; 8) μαγκάλι or portable heating vessel; 9) γλάστρα or flowerpot; 10) γουβέτσι or baking vessel; 11) θυμιατό or incense-burner; 12) δοχείο or καθήκη, or chamber pot; 13) λαδικό or oil jug; 14) κουρούπι or small storage jar; 15) βρασχή or feed container for larger animals, otherwise (in a larger size) μπουγαδόβρασχή, or vessel for washing clothes; 16) δυψέλι or beehive.

16. δυψέλι (fig. 18–5.16), beehive, one size, unglazed, used in the raising of bees for honey.
17. νερόγλαστρα (fig. 18–6.17), watering vessel for small animals, one size, unglazed.
18. κουμπαράς (fig. 18–6.18), coin bank, one size, unglazed, could be opened only by breaking it.
19. κυνελλόγλαστρα (fig. 18–6.19), rabbit feeder, one size, unglazed.
20. βάσις (fig. 18–6.20), flowerpot dish, several sizes, unglazed, used with γλάστρες.
21. ποτιστήρι (fig. 18–6.21), watering vessel for animals, one size, unglazed.
22. κουρουπάκι (fig. 18–6.22), storage vessel for small amounts of food, one size, unglazed and glazed, used for storing leftovers and for transporting food to the fields.
23. κουμπαράς (fig. 18–6.23), animal feed container, one size, unglazed used frequently with number 21.
24. πιθαράκι (fig. 18–6.24), minature pithos, several sizes, unglazed, made entirely for the tourist trade.
25. πετροφλασχή (fig. 18–6.25), portable water vessel, at least one size, unglazed, used when traveling or working in fields, also used to hold other liquids, such as wine.
26. γλάστρα (fig. 18–6.26), flowerpot, one size, unglazed, variation on number 9, with a spout.

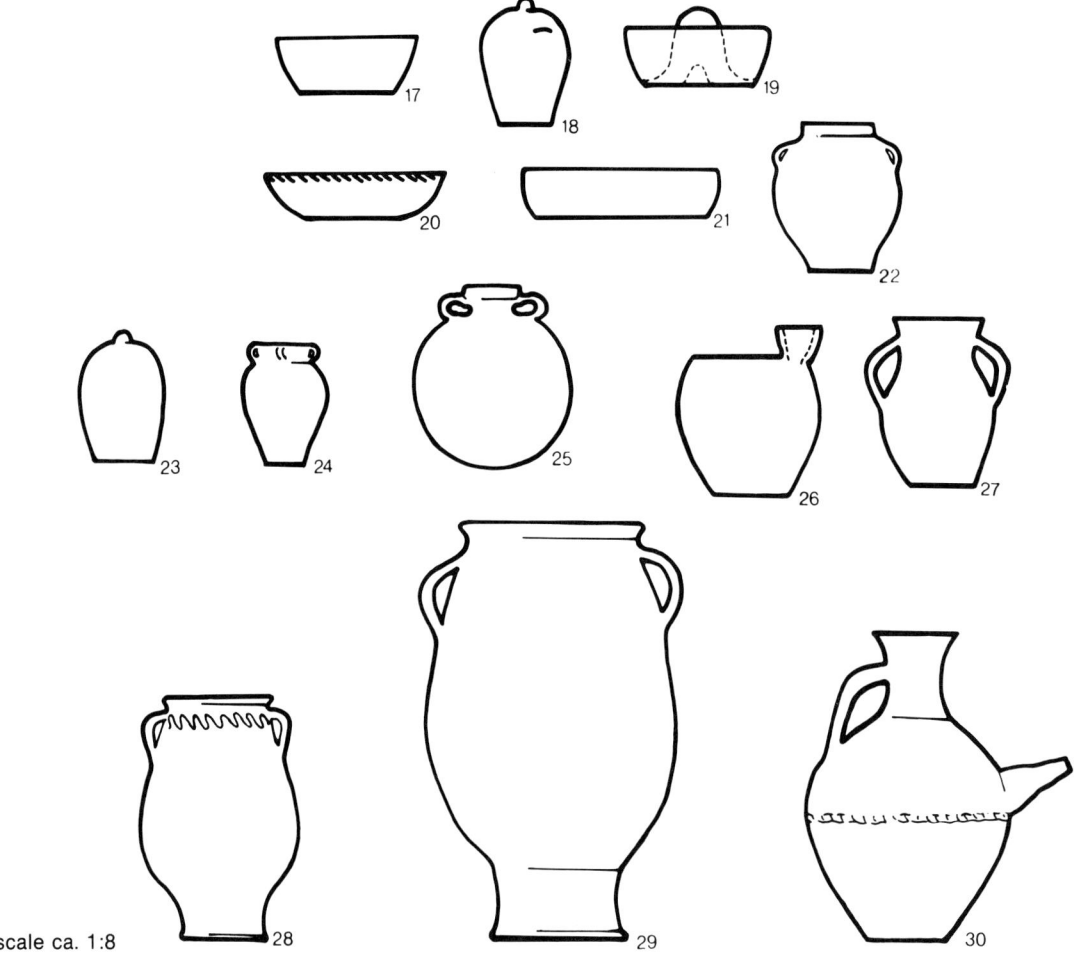

Fig. 18–6. Types of vessels formerly and presently produced in Kentri: (cont) 17) νερόγλασρα or water vessel for small animals; 18) κουμπαράς or coin bank; 19) κυνελλόγλαστρα or rabbit feeder; 20) βάσις or flowerpot dish; 21) ποτιστήρι or water vessel for animals; 22) κουρουπάκι or storage vessel for small amounts of food, sometimes used to transport food to the fields; 23) κουμπαράς or animal feed container to be used with number 21; 24) πιθαράκι or miniature pithos, made for the tourist trade; 25) πετροφλασχή or portable water vessel, used when travelling or when working in the fields; 26) γλάστρα or flowerpot; 27) βάσο or a variation on number 4; 28) κουρούπι or storage jar, variation on number 14; 29) πιθάρι, or large storage jar (attempted by only one potter in memory); 30) μπρίκα or storage vessel for raki. *Of these vessels, types 6 and 29 were made only by one potter (within memory of the villagers) infrequently, within a very short period in the history of Kentri.*

27. βάσο (fig. 18–6.27), water jar (variation on number 4), one size, unglazed, used in the home for water or wine.
28. κουρούπι (fig. 18–6.28), storage jar, (variation on number 14), several sizes, unglazed, used for storage of cheese, oil, olives, dried foods.
29. πιθάρι (fig. 18–6.29), large storage jar, one size, unglazed, used for the storage of grain, oil, olives, wine, other dried goods. Made locally by only one potter for a brief period of time.
30. μπρίκα (fig. 18–6.30), storage vessel for *ρακί*, one size (?), unglazed.

In addition to the vessels described above, there are some shadowy ceramic relatives whose names come up in conversation in the village but whose shapes are difficult to define. (There are no preserved examples in the immediate vicinity.) Among these is the ἐξάρι, or oil measure, which is said to have contained six ὀκάδες of oil, and the φουβού or φουγού, which is said to have been a kind of brazier, with three legs, upon which food could be grilled.

It is clear, however, that the most common products of the Kentri workshops in the first half of this century were σταμνιά, or water jars, and γλάστρες, or flowerpots, both of which were unglazed vessels. Glazing, as a technique, was known to few potters[29] in the village, and was restricted, as illustrated in the above list, to vessels used in the preparation (πετρολεκανίδα), cooking (τσικάλι and γουβέτσι), and serving (λεκανάκι and λαδικό) of food. These same vessels were also used in an unglazed form.

The range of sizes in which each type of vessel was produced was determined, in part, by a convention which had its origins, according to some potters, in an official regulation.[30] Within this established standard a potter could produce several sizes of a particular shape, each of which was described by a number, number *one* being the largest size, number *two* slightly smaller, and so on. With the demise of production in recent years there are few who recall the specific meanings of these numerical designations.

Methods of Production

As all of the vessels produced in Kentri were wheel made, a set variety of techniques was employed on a daily basis. And, while specific vessel types might require additional steps of manufacture at the wheel, the range of techniques employed in Kentri differed very little from those we are familiar with today.[31]

Following the centering of a ball of clay on the upper wheel, the potter made constant use of water (kept in a nearby vessel, usually a broken σταμνί) in the manufacture of each vessel. The potter's ribs (ταβλάκια) were used constantly to shave and shape the vessel walls, and the shavings were simply thrown to the ground near the wheel. This constant deposition resulted in a buildup of clay near the wheel-pit.

Each vessel type required a specific amount of time at the wheel. A πετρολεκανίδα, for example, required a half hour of work in two shifts, interrupted by a drying period. A σταμνί was also made in two shifts (with a drying period in between) and required roughly ten minutes at the wheel. The application of handles to those vessels requiring them was accomplished after the vessels had been set out to dry in the workroom. Handles for a σταμνί took about four minutes to manufacture and apply.

All vessels required some drying indoors before being transferred to the outdoor part of the workshop where further drying under the sun would render them ready for firing. Vessels such as σταμνιά remained in the workroom for one day and dried out-of-doors for six to ten days, depending on the weather. Smaller vessels might require only one to four days inside the workroom. When the yard had filled up with the quantity of dried vessels necessary to load the kiln, the potter and helper prepared for a firing.

The Construction and Use of the Kiln

A wide range of locally available flora was used as fuel for the kilns in Kentri. A helper might be sent to collect wild brush (consisting of dry aromatics or βρομιάδες) from the hills in the Ierapetra locale, or fuel might be purchased from a vendor who made regular trips in search of brush. Aromatic shrubs used in the village firings included θυμάρι (thyme), φασκομηλιά (sage), σκίνος (mastic plant), αλαδάνια (rockrose), and ανωνίδα (restharrow).

The potting season was the ideal time, according to the potters, to collect fuel, which was stockpiled out-of-doors, generally behind the kiln or the workroom (fig. 18–3). Tree roots, especially those of the olive, were also used in the firings, although these κουτσούρες, as they are known locally, were rarely available. The mixed piles of brush which formed the basic fuel were measured in a unit known as an αγκαλιά, or apronful.[32] One firing, of a kiln holding about 300 vessels (of different types), is said to have used forty to fifty αγκαλιές of brush. A larger kiln, holding as many as 600 vessels, might use as much as 120 αγκαλιές of this same fuel.[33] Estimates as to the actual size of one αγκαλιά varied throughout the village. It was generally agreed, however, that the amount of brush which could be gathered up into an apron,[34] used in this part of Greece by both men and women, was the equivalent of one αγκαλιά.

The circular kilns (καμήνια) heated by this fuel were

constructed of stone, clay, and mud. The outer walls of the kiln (fig. 18–3 and 4) were composed of limestone cobbles, boulders, and chunks which were rarely modified into specific shapes. A mortar made of mud or of the standard Kentri clay mixture was often used in the construction of this outer wall, although dry masonry is also present. On the interior face of this limestone frame the potter, or his helper, smeared a clay and earth mixture which formed a layer separating[35] the limestone from the actual heat. This was done to prevent the limestone walls from exploding and burning upon exposure to high temperatures. It was less common, however, to find this same coating on the exterior of the limestone walls (pl. 16A–B).

The floor (πάτος) of the firing chamber (pl. 16C) was made of liquid mud poured onto an arched frame of mud brick and stones which terminated in a mud brick and stone support column (στύλος) in the center of the stoking chamber (pl. 16D). This column, as well as the interior of the stoking chamber, was coated with a mud and clay mixture which eventually hardened into an impermeable surface. The air passages in the floor between the stoking and firing chambers of the kiln (pl. 16C) were created during the construction of the floor by the insertion of wooden shafts into the liquid mud. After the floor had dried, the shafts were removed, leaving behind about forty perforations which were larger in dimension near the walls of the kiln than in the center.

The siting of the kilns in Kentri included their being dug into hillsides (fig. 18–3 and pl. 16A) so that the firing chamber would be accessible from the upper ground level and the stoking chamber entrance would open out to a lower level, usually onto a path or roadway. If it was not possible to utilize a hillside, a rectangular pit was dug into the ground, sloping down to the kiln at one end (pl. 17C and fig. 18–4). In this system the firing chamber entrance was again at ground level but the stoking chamber entrance was situated at the base of the pit.[36]

While most of the kilns in Kentri were constructed by the potters and helpers, some recall the assistance of builders in the preparation of certain kilns. The kilns were fashioned without roofs so that it was necessary, at each firing, to create a temporary covering for the structure (pl. 17A). In recent years, the remains of flattened iron barrels, large broken pottery fragments, and patches of clay have been used to create this temporary roof. No one in the village today recalls the use of any other material in this temporary construction.[37]

There were instances in the history of Kentri when potters maintaining separate workshops shared the use of a kiln. In addition, some workshops might have more than one kiln, as in figure 18–3. According to most potters, it was necessary only that the kiln be near enough to the workshop to permit efficient loading. Where kiln-sharing took place, the workshops were close to one another, if not side-by-side.

The size of a kiln was defined by its σταμνί content. Thus, in Kentri there are kilns which hold up to 300 σταμνιά and others which may contain as many as 600. Generally, however, a mixture of different types of vessels was used to fill the kiln, depending on the kinds of orders which had been placed. All potters agreed that the stacking of the dried vessels in the kiln was the most precarious step in the production process, since one error of placement could reduce the entire contents of the kiln to fragments.[38]

To stack and fill a small kiln required up to two hours, beginning with the arrangement of larger vessels (such as κουρούπια and σταμνιά) in semicircles on the floor of the kiln. All of the vessels which formed the basis of this stacking pattern were placed in the kiln upside down. Following the establishment of this sturdy base of several layers of larger vessels, the remainder of the vases were placed in the kiln (pl. 16E–F) with an eye to the conservation of space and to stability. Many of these upper layers were therefore irregular and included vessels which were right-side-up, sideways, and upside-down. The vessels were stacked to a height of as much as 1.0 m above the termination of the walls of the kiln.[39]

Flattened remnants of barrels were then wrapped around the iron rods set into the kiln walls (pl. 17A), and spaces between these sheets were filled in with broken pottery. The firing chamber door was covered (as in plate 17A, center front) with a mixture of earth and clay which was heavily saturated with water. This clay mixture was also applied to interstices not covered either by iron sheets or broken pottery. And, while this temporary covering might seem to be a precarious form of protection for the pottery, all potters agreed that it was most important to prevent the penetration of wind into the kiln.[40]

Following the sealing of the kiln, the potter and helper moved to the stoking chamber entrance where the first ἀγκαλιά of fuel was placed in the stoking chamber (pl. 17C). The fuel, once ignited, was carefully observed so as to prevent sudden bursts of heat which might disturb the delicate balance of the firing chamber. Fuel was placed in the stoking chamber with a set of stoking tools known as διχάλια, consisting of a wooden pole and a wooden shaft with a forked end.

During the first hour of the firing, very little fuel was used so as to create a uniform slowly rising temperature. During the second hour the potter added a greater quantity of brush to bring the kiln temperature up to the desired point.[41] Finally, during the third hour of the firing, enough fuel was burned to permit the flames to pass through the air passages into the firing chamber and, occasionally, entirely outside of the kiln (through the roof). A firing was generally over in three to four hours.[42]

When all of the fuel had been consumed, it was common to block up the stoking chamber entrance with the same mud and clay mixture used on the temporary roof. The kiln then sat for as much as twelve hours without disturbance and was allowed to cool down. Since firings were frequently scheduled in the late afternoon, the kiln would be opened in the early morning of the following day.[43] The pottery was removed from the kiln with the help of wooden implements (similar to the stoking tools) or by hand. It was then stacked in the outdoor part of the workshop, ready for distribution by whatever means. Vessels which had slipped or cracked during the firing were dashed upon the ground by the side of the kiln, resulting in an accumulation of sherds which were later reused in the stacking and roofing process. At some kilns, however, these sherds were regularly cleaned away from the mouth of the kiln.

The vessels produced in the Kentri workshops were consistently well fired, ranging in color from a pinkish buff to a smokey gray in places. Many of the vessel walls were pitted, and fine but harmless cracks occurred occasionally. And, while the bare remains of a once flourishing industry do not aid the modern observer in a full understanding of the craft, examples of vessels produced in earlier generations exhibit the pride and skill of fine craftsmanship.

Conclusions

The potters' village of Kentri, one of five major ceramic centers on the island of Crete in the first half of this century, filled a need for commonplace vessels used everyday in households in the eastern part of the island. It might almost be suggested that Kentri served as a complementary production center to the village of Thrapsano, where the manufacture of large-scale vessels was a mainstay of the industry.

The distribution of pottery from Kentri, prior to the introduction of mechanized transport in Crete, emphasizes the many possibilities for trade and dispersal of ceramic products by land and by sea. Equally, the diverse origins of pottery found in traditional homes throughout eastern Crete highlight the existence of a more complex network of trade and communication than one might expect in eras prior to our own.

Finally, the character and arrangement of the village of Kentri and the basic knowledge of its craftsmen provides us with a tempting clue to the relationships which are possible between man and his environment. An ability to read a landscape and draw from it needed natural resources, and an understanding of labor and production in an environment of hard and exacting nature—these are the gifts of the Kentri craftsmen, past and present.

Notes

1. "The potter, wherever he wishes, applies the handle." As interpreted by the Kentri villagers, this means that a good potter (τσικαλᾶς) may do whatever he desires with the clay. Ἀυτί (whose literal meaning is "ear") is used in Kentri workshops to describe a handle.

2. The writer wishes to thank the inhabitants of Kentri for their kindness and hospitality during two weeks of research in the village. The three potters still working in the vicinity were especially patient in answering a standardized series of hundreds of questions posed by the writer.

All interviews were conducted in Greek by the writer who is also responsible for the preparation of the plates and figures.

L. V. Watrous kindly read this manuscript, provided enormous support during the research and offered helpful criticism. Sterghios Spanakis of Herakleion, Crete, kindly provided local historical information from his vast store of Cretan history.

Peter Topping of the Center for Byzantine Studies at Dumbarton Oaks graciously provided information on local place names and biographical references.

3. Pottery production in Kentri has suffered the fate of all traditional crafts in Greece. The manufacture of small vessels for consumption by tourists has replaced the production of traditional clay vessels as an income-producing activity.

4. This potter was trained in a workshop at Amaroussi, on the Greek mainland, and uses extremely modern equipment, clay imported from Athens, and a kiln constructed of imported fire brick.

5. The onset of World War II and its accompanying mechanical sophistication changed the char-

acter of traditional industry in rural Greece. In many cases, it encouraged a loss of respect for those who worked on a small scale, and by hand.

6. The writer has encountered belief in the local antiquity of the potter's craft in villages elsewhere on Crete and in the Peloponnese.

7. The map of Coronelli, dated to 1558, shows a village of *Chiedri* located where Kentri now sits, just north of Ierapetra (cf. Spanakis 1971: 472 ff.). A document from the fourteenth century A.D. in Crete attests to the existence of the village of *Chedri* or *Cacoiani* in the *turma* (district) of Ierapetra in 1369 (cf. Santschi 1976: 40–41). It is quite possible that *Chiedri, Chedri,* and *Cacoiani* all refer to what is now called Kentri. The latter reference was kindly provided by Dr. Peter Topping.

Later reference to Kentri occurs in the journal of Robert Pashley (1837: 324) who noted the village of *Kendhri,* containing thirty-five families, in the Ierapetra district. Xanthoudides noted (1927: 118–19) the existence of a reference to "Τσουκολάδες" in the village of Thrapsano in the year 1642. It is possible that potters existed in Kentri at that time as well, although no specific reference to them has been found by the writer.

8. The word for helper in Kentri (προυγός) appears to be derived from the ancient Greek word προῦργου, a contraction of πρὸ ἔργου, meaning useful, or toward a work (cf. Liddell and Scott 1968: 703). Xanthoudides cited the use of the word προγοί at Thrapsano (1927: 128, n.8) and connected it with the term ὑπουργοι. It is common, in Crete, to find ancient Greek words used in conversation to an extent not obvious on the Greek mainland.

9. The general perception of clay vessels as inferior to their plastic equivalents and therefore unworthy of high prices has also contributed to a lack of interest in the craft.

10. This division of the year into six-month periods was not absolute. Clay might be collected in the winter months, as might fuel, and general duties centered around the upkeep of the kiln and the workshop were also carried out.

11. The inhabitants of Kentri suggest that even with an enormous output, a single workshop might not produce enough income to support all those involved.

12. One female helper, in particular, is remembered for her astounding capacity for work and her ability to sell vast quantities of her husband's vessels.

Helpers, in the years prior to the introduction of running water, were obliged to make many trips per day to the single spring which supplied the village. The water was carried in σταμνιά on the helper's shoulders or on a pack animal.

13. The σταμνιά produced in Kentri are repeatedly cited (by villagers in East Crete and in the Mesara) as of better quality than those produced in Thrapsano. The Ἰεραπήτρικα σταμνιά are said to keep water much cooler than water jars produced elsewhere. S. Spanakis of Herakleion, Crete, noted that the Kentri water jars are not as heavy as those from Thrapsano, have thinner walls, and are better made (personal communication, 1981). Thus the following Cretan μαντινάδα: Διάλε τσ'ἀποθαμένους του, τοῦ παλιοθραφανιώτη ποὺ κάνει τὰ σταμνιά βαρειά, καὶ καταλεῖ τη νιότη. "Choose an old-fashioned *stamni*, of an old Thrapsano potter, Who makes his *stamnia* heavy, and wastes away his youth."

14. The distribution of Kentri pottery from these primary destinations is not yet documented. Prior to World War II the potter received 2½ drachmas for each σταμνί. It is not clear what other products were shipped along with the Kentri pottery to coastal sites in Crete. Recollections of such trade are scanty.

15. The measure ὀκά is more frequently used in conversation in Kentri than is the term κιλό.

16. Elders in the Lasithi Plain recall exchanges in which lentils, chick-peas, beans and grain were traded for σταμνιά and λαίνια from Kentri. Other needed vessels in Lasithi such as πιθάρια, κουρούπια, κουρουπάκια, and λεκάνια were also procured from Thrapsano and Panaghia (Pediada) potters. Τσουκάλια came, via Herakleion or Aghios Nikolaos, from the island of Siphnos.

17. It is curious that the local name for potter (τσικαλάς) and potter's workshop (τσικαλαριό), should be derived from the word for cooking dish (τσουκάλι), a vessel produced on Siphnos rather than in Kentri.

The excellent reputation of the Siphniote τσουκάλι, which is based on the special heat-resistant properties of the Siphniote fabric, clearly determined the limited production of such vessels in Kentri (only one potter attempted to make them). Documents from the eighteenth century A.D. in Crete speak of villages described as τσουκαλαριά in the eparchy of Kydonia (Khania) which were known to produce pottery. The local spelling of τσικαλαριό in Kentri is matched by such variations in other parts of Greece as well (cf. Kahane and Kahane 1940: 231–35; Tomadakis 1933: 227–28). Peter Topping notes that the spelling τσικαλαριά is standard in twentieth-century gazetteers while τσουκαλαριά occurs in a document of the eighteenth century (cited in Tomadakis 1933), raising the question of when the spelling τσίκ first appeared in Crete. Kentri villagers today state that their use of these words is not an indication of the Siphniote origin of their craft. Considering the unclear history of pottery production in Kentri, it is tempting to suggest that there may be some relationship between the use of such terms in Kentri and Siphniote influence.

18. "Always" could mean from the beginning of

this craft in Kentri (a date as yet undocumented) or as far back as the villagers can presently remember.

19. This separation of living and working space is in great contrast to the side-by-side placement of home and workshop in the Koroni district of Messenia (cf. Harriet Blitzer, in preparation) and in other Cretan villages.

20. The diffuse light of the potters' workshops in Kentri is especially easy on the eyes, and combined with the slight dampness of the workroom structure creates a rather shadowy and musty atmosphere.

21. There were no windows in any of the structures observed.

22. These outdoor areas, if not defined by actual physical boundaries, are illustrated with dotted lines, as in fig. 18–3 and 4.

23. The red earth (*terra rossa*) separated more quickly into smaller size particles than did the white clay. The κόπανο appears to be manufactured in the same way on Crete and in the Greek mainland.

24. This introduction of settling basins appears to have taken place recently in the Greek mainland as well (cf. Blitzer, in prep.).

25. Each container in the case observed was a τενεκέ capable of holding two kilos of earth.

26. Potters elsewhere in Greece measure "by hand," or μὲ τὸ μάτι (by eye). All traditional potters interviewed by the writer in Crete and the mainland credit their skill and vitality in the craft to πήρα, or experience.

27. The planks, or ντόγες, were made of various types of wood, including πλάτανο (plane tree wood).

28. Differences in recollection are so great that villagers disagree as to which vessels were produced, which were not, and which sizes were commonly manufactured. Vessels were drawn and measured *in situ*. Vessel no. 8 (μαγκάλι) was reconstructed from fragments existing in the village.

29. The standard glaze used was a form of μίνιο, or red lead. Again, the recollection of which vessels were produced in a glazed form is not uniform throughout the village. Presented here is a list of those vessels generally accepted as having been glazed (μολυβοτά).

30. The existence of such a "regulation" could not be documented by the writer. Size variations within this numbering system are visible from one region to another throughout Greece, and within local centers.

31. The actual throwing techniques observed in Kentri and elsewhere throughout Greece are the subject of another study by this writer.

32. The use of this "unit" of measurement (ἀγκαλιά) is similar to the system employed in the Koroni district of Messenia where the standard fuel (grape cuttings) is counted in terms of handfuls, or χούφτες. 'Ἀγκαλιά,' strictly speaking, means armful. In Kentri, however, the ποδιά or apron worn as part of traditional male dress was used in the gathering up of brush.

33. These estimates are based on the use of the wild brush fuel. The use of tree roots, especially those of the olive tree, would change the amount of fuel required.

34. The apron consisted of a wool or cotton piece of cloth, rectangular in shape, and reaching to mid-calf. It is called locally a ποδιά or μπροστομουνά.

35. The earth and clay mixture used in this kiln lining is said by some to have been that of the standard Kentri mixture used for potting, and by others to have been a mixture of different proportions of white clay to red earth.

36. The location of the stoking chamber door at the base of a pit was said to have been preferable since it prevented gusts of air from disturbing the even firing of the kiln. This is a curious observation when one considers the fragility of the roofing on these kilns during a firing.

37. According to all of those questioned, the kilns in Kentri have always been circular in form, made of limestone, and without a permanent roof.

38. The amount of patience needed in this activity was also stressed.

39. Care was taken, in stacking, to keep the mouths of all vessels open and unblocked. Broken pottery fragments were used only to separate pottery from the walls of the kiln. All other stacking involved resting one pot upon or next to another.

40. For this reason the potters stated that a day without any wind at all was preferred for a firing. Some recall windstorms which required the cancellation of a firing.

41. The actual temperature reached in the Kentri kilns is not documented.

42. The brevity of this firing contrasts strongly with traditional methods elsewhere in Greece where ten- and twelve-hour firings are standard. The length of the Kentri firing was the same for both large and small kilns. It is surprising that an even heat could be obtained in such a short period when the potters make little attempt to burn the fuel evenly on both sides of the stoking chamber. In other parts of Greece this alternation of the fuel from one side of the stoking chamber to the other is stressed as a significant part of a successful firing.

43. All of the mud and clay which had been used as a sealant around the roof was thrown to the ground around the kiln. The level of the earth in this area thus rose each year.

References

Blitzer, H. *In preparation*. Storage Jar Production and Trade in Traditional Greece.

Hampe, R. and A. Winter. 1962. *Bei Töpfern und Töpferinnen in Kreta, Messenien, und Zypern*. Mainz.

Kahane, H. and R. 1940. *Italienische Ortsname in Griechenland*. Athens.

Liddell, H. G. and J. Scott. 1968. *An Intermediate Greek-English Lexicon*. Oxford.

Pashley, R. 1837. *Travels in Crete*. London.

Santschi, E. 1976. *Registes des arrêts civils et des mémoriaux (1363–1399) des archives du duc de Crète*. Venice.

Spanakis, S., ed. 1971. Τὸ Ἡράκλειον καὶ ὁ νομὸς τοῦ. Herakleion.

Tomadakis, N. B. 1933. Ειδήσεις καὶ ἔγγραφα τῆς Ἐκκλησίας Κρήτης ἔπι τουρκοκρατίας. Ἐπετηρὶς Ἑταιρείας βυςαντινῶν σπουδῶν 10:227–28.

Xanthoudides, S. 1927. Some Minoan Potter's Wheel Discs. In *Essays in Aegean Archaeology Presented to Sir Arthur Evans*, ed. S. Casson, 111–28. Oxford.

19

Ethnology and the Interpretation of the Archaeological Record

Philip P. Betancourt

The study of traditional Cretan potters offers clues of several types for the interpretation of Minoan pottery. Since the local clay resources have not changed since the Bronze Age, many of the steps between raw clay and fired ware must follow related lines to achieve the same results, no matter what period is involved. In addition, a study of the alternative ways that small-scale potters can meet the needs of a pottery-using community can offer fresh insights into potentially similar operations.

The danger, of course, is in carrying an analogy too far. Even if a similar need can be documented, one should not assume that two different times will respond to a challenge in the same way. Ethnology offers a series of behavioral models; it does not, on its own, suggest that any of these models were ever followed by the residents of another time frame. The theories suggested by ethnoarchaeology must be tested by independent means before they can be incorporated into the interpretation of any ancient culture.

Of the many production centers in twentieth-century Crete (Hampe and Winter 1962), two are discussed here in detail: Thrapsano and Kentri. While they have many points in common, since they both supplied an agricultural society with a necessary commodity, they differ in many basic ways. These differences are as important as the similarities in evolving models for ancient practices.

At Thrapsano the workshops are organized as guilds. The system is patriarchal, with the Master at its head, and each member has precisely defined responsibilities. The system prescribes social behavior as well as professional duties, which operate as an independent social system. Within the system, the work is accomplished through the cooperation of all of the six members. The Thrapsaniot potters specialize in a particular shape, the pithari, using a standardized technology for its production. Because much of the production is established and traditional, innovation and change are discouraged. The craftsmen are farmers as well as potters; their system is tied to the seasonal nature of their agricultural work, and the three summer months must be free for them to pursue a second profession as potters. Since the individual guilds travel away from the home village to set up seasonal work areas, their special society operates essentially away from its members' homes. Yet, as Xanthoudides recorded some decades ago (1927), the Thrapsaniot potters also work a little at their home village during the winter, making jars and other pots as sedentary potters.

At Kentri the workshop system is less rigorously prescribed. Sizes of shops vary, and a wider range of vessels is produced. The group can be a family unit, but it does not constitute a guild of the Thrapsaniot type. Workspaces are more permanent, and the wares travel from there to their places of use or distribution.

The two pottery centers offer interesting alternatives for the manufacture of pottery. One workshop model is stationary; the other travels seasonally, making its pottery from local clays.[1] One is rigorously organized in guilds; the other is not. One specializes in a particular shape; the other makes a greater variety. One uses a potter's wheel; the other employs turntables. The many differences help point up the similarities, for example, in clay preparation and kiln design, that stem from the common ground of modern Cretan ceramics.

The potters from Kentri and Thrapsano prepare their clay in a generally similar way. In the geological setting of eastern Crete, unchanged since the Bronze Age, clays are readily available. Unfortunately for the potter, however, a survey of the region (Chap. 15) suggests that the common white marine clays of this part of the island are unsuited for pottery as found because of their "gummy" nature when mixed with water. To overcome this problem the potters of Kentri and Thrapsano use clay blends. By altering the ingredients or using different proportions, they can adjust their clay bodies to suit the requirements of the moment. The discovery of clay which does not need to be blended is a recent innovation at Kentri. An elaborate levigation operation requiring large settling tanks, common in many parts of the eastern Mediterranean, is not used in eastern Crete (on levigation practices elsewhere see, among others, Hampe and Winter 1962; 1965; Hankey 1974; Lisse and Louis 1956; Noble 1965; Matson 1972; Winter 1978).

Ancient practices must have been similar. Thin sections reveal that the Early Minoan potters tempered their calcareous marine clays with a lateritic soil called terra rossa, adding the coarser and more porous red earth as an essential ingredient (Chap. 6). Additional evidence for blending is provided by differences in the coarseness of cups, lids, and jars, indicating specific clay bodies were differentiated in the mixing process by the addition of a third material, a fine to coarse mixture of stones and mineral particles. The different characteristics which result from varying the coarseness and composition of the temper suggest that the choices were deliberate by the ancient potters, and that they blended specific recipes for particular shapes.

While the stone temper was not added to every vessel, the thin sections show that it was extremely common, particularly for larger shapes (see Chaps. 5 and 6). Stone particles are common in ancient as well as modern pottery, and the advantages they give are well known (for a good recent discussion of the results of tempers see Braun 1982).

Where did the ancient potters obtain this material? The thin sections show a complex composition, with plagioclase, quartz, hornblende, biotite, and several other minerals, some rounded and others with sharp edges indicating a crushing or breaking by the potters. That this material was available in the pottery workshops as a separate mixture (i.e., not as an essential ingredient of one of the clays and never separated) is certain; one of the sherds from Gournia, Penn no. MS 4615–37, has some of the temper adhering to the bottom of the base.[2]

The ethnography suggests that potters try to use readily available materials wherever possible, importing substances only if the local materials are too costly or unsuitable. With this in mind a survey of the region in the immediate vicinity of Gournia was made by the author in July of 1982 in an attempt to locate possible sources for tempering materials. The nearest beaches (toward Pakheia Ammos) do not consist of material like the temper, as they are mainly quartz. Most of the stone near Gournia is not granite, and a suitable candidate which could be ground up by the potters to yield the plagioclase-quartz-hornblende-biotite assemblage was not located. In the ravines and small washes between Gournia and the sea to the north, however, small alluvial deposits of coarse sand to gravel do exist, and these contain small pieces of plagioclase, hornblende, and the other minerals, mostly as slightly waterworn to angular rock fragments with more than one mineral present. If this material were collected (or removed from the earth through levigation) and crushed slightly by the potters, it would yield a proper temper similar to the additive used at Gournia. It is thus likely that the temper in the pottery is local.

Most of the steps in clay preparation—drying, pounding, blending, and wedging—were surely similar in antiquity to what they are today. Evidence from Egypt, like the early Middle Kingdom wall painting in fig. 19–1, suggests related practices were followed elsewhere as well. The painting is from Tomb 2 at Beni Hasan. It shows potters using a low turntable to make pottery and performing other tasks within the ceramic workshop. Many of the vignettes, like the scene of kneading with the men moving the clay with their feet, find good parallels in the modern Cretan potteries.

The kilns also provide good parallels, but the modern structures must be more elaborate than the ancient ones. Replication studies in small built kilns suggest that good results can be achieved with unsophisticated designs (Chap. 16), and the few Middle Bronze Age Cretan kilns which have been excavated are simpler than their modern counterparts (see discussion in Chap. 5). A two-story system with a built floor dividing the firebox from the stacking chamber, as at Kentri and Thrapsano, need not be postulated. Instead, it is more likely the fire was simply at the front of the chamber, with the flames allowed to pass by and come in contact with the pottery. A temporary roof, however, is quite possible. Modern Cretan potters achieve uniform results with roofs built anew each

Fig. 19–1. *A painting from Tomb 2 at Beni Hasan, from the early Middle Kingdom, showing potters at work in a workshop.*

TABLE 19-I
Variables in the sherds from EM III Gournia

Penn Museum Number	Presence of: Siltstone/ Claystone	Cryptocrystalline Quartz	Thickness of Brushes in Centimeters						Motifs (See Chap. 3)	Shape (See Chap. 4)	Careful	Av.	Sloppy
			.6	.5	.4	.3	.2	.1					
MS 4615-6	Siltstone	--		X			X	X	8	6A		X	
MS 4615-7	--	--					X	X	8(?)	6A		X	
MS 4615-8	--	--			X			X	5 mo. 2	6A			X
MS 4615-9	Claystone	--						X	9 no. 6	6A			X
MS 4615-10	--	--							--	2			
MS 4615-11	Siltstone	X		X			X	ck	10	9	X		
MS 4615-12	--	--				X	X		2	2		X	
MS 4615-13	Siltstone	--					X		2	2		X	
MS 4615-15	Siltstone	--					X		12 no. 8	1		X	
MS 4615-16	--	--			X				2	1		X	
MS 4615-17	--	--			X				2	2		X	
MS 4615-18	--	--					X		8	9		X	
MS 4615-20	--	--					X		8	9		X	
MS 4615-21	--	--	X	X					12	9		X	
MS 4615-22	--	--		X				X	9 no. 6	9			X
MS 4615-23	--	--			X		X		5 no. 2	9		X	
MS 4615-24	--	--				X			7	9		X	
MS 4615-25	--	--			X		X		10	9		X	
MS 4615-26	Siltstone	--			X		X		--	9	--	--	--
MS 4615-27	--	X			X		X		14	9		X	
MS 4615-29	--	--	X				X		2	2		X	
MS 4615-31	--	Opalline Chalcedony					X		9 no. 6	6A		X	
MS 4615-32	--	--				X	X		--	10	--	--	--
MS 4615-33	--	--				X			8	9		X	
MS 4615-34	--	--			X				2	13		X	
MS 4615-35	--	--					X		9 no. 6	6A		X	
MS 4615-37	--	--			X				2	2		X	
MS 4615-39	Siltstone	--			X			X	2	13			X
MS 4615-43	--	X					X		6	10	X		
MS 4615-44	--	--	X	X			X		10	9			X
MS 4615-47	--	--					X		--	6A		X	

time a kiln is fired, and there is no reason to exclude the system from consideration for the Minoan kilns as well.

Ethnology also suggests models for the production system in general. Before the 1940s, pottery held an important position in Cretan households, filling many of the needs that are now served by containers made of plastic, metal, and glass. In eastern Crete, this need was supplied from several sources: a large percentage came from Kentri; large jars and a few other vessels were furnished by the traveling workshops based out of Thrapsano in the central part of the island; and a few products, like the *tsikalia* from Siphnos, were brought in from other sources (for the 1930s trade see Casson 1938: 469–73). As Voyatzoglou points out, there were three types of Cretan potteries: isolated workshops; centers of production like Kentri where many shops were located at a single village; and the guild system of Thrapsano. The complex market as a whole allowed for all to coexist, with a specific village filling its needs from several sources, including quite distant ones which might be preferred for special products perceived as superior to the locally made versions.

Did a similar regional system operate for East Cretan White-on-dark Ware? The model can be tested with a combination of shape analysis and ceramic petrology: if true, one would not expect each ancient site to have local peculiarities in the material added as temper, particularly if the differences arise from different methods of preparing the clay bodies, or to have local variations in particular shapes. Studies in both areas (Chaps. 4 and 6) agree in denying the regional model. Most sites studied have their own variations in shapes as well as local characteristics in the temper, suggesting local rather than regional production systems.

Within the local system, it is important to recognize that the pottery was far from standardized. This is an important difference from the products of the modern folk potteries where the output is large and fairly uniform. The degree of variability at Gournia is indicated in Table 19–I, listing rare inclusions in the temper, sizes of brushes used in the painting, choice of motifs and shapes, and skill of the painters. Differences occur at all stages of the production, from clay preparation to choice of tools to technique and skill of decoration.

Gournia is a good site for looking at this aspect of the production because the sherd material is a heterogeneous mixture. The largest group found, from the North Trench (Hall 1904–1905), suggested a cleanup after some destruction or other change in the settlement. The White-on-dark Ware, drawn from 200 basketfuls of pottery (mostly undecorated coarse wares), did not mend into whole or fragmentary vases, suggesting it was randomly mixed before deposition. Sherds from other places on the site came from mixed later contexts and from small patches of early soil below the later buildings. The available material thus comes from many parts of the town; it forms a somewhat haphazard, heterogeneous assortment.

Because of this variability, the model of the village workshop does not really stand up to testing. The speed of manufacture, replicated in Chapter 16, indicates that the needs of a small Early Bronze Age community could be met by a small group of specialized workers, operating seasonally. The high variability within the Gournia material suggests, however, that it is unlikely any substantial amount came from a well organized, specialized workshop with a uniform output. It may be contrasted with the Middle Minoan pottery from the same site where the production is far more uniform. Only occasionally, as with Penn numbers MS 4615–8 and 9, are there sherds from the EM III group which might have been painted by the same hand. The most likely explanation seems to be that a series of small household workshops operated over the course of several years within a common regional tradition. A use of handmade methods has often been taken to imply the same conclusion because the slow, laborious system is more likely to be performed as a household task.

Notes

1. Another variation is found in Cyprus, however, where itinerant potters carried their clay with them (Casson 1938: 467).

2. Pointed out by Frederick Matson. The material was perhaps the result of setting the base on temper before forming or during forming, to prevent sticking to the surface on which it was worked.

References

Braun, D. P. 1982. Radiographic Analysis of Temper in Ceramic Vessels: Goals and Initial Methods. *JFA* 9: 183–92.

Casson, S. 1938. The Modern Pottery Trade in the Aegean. *Antiquity* 12: 464–73.

Hall, E. H. 1904–1905. Early Painted Pottery from Gournia, Crete. *Transactions of the Department of Archaeology, Free Museum of Science and Art* 1: 191–205.

Hall, E. H. 1908. Early Minoan III Ware from the North Trench. In Hawes, H. B. et al., *Gournia*, Appendix E, p. 57.

Hampe, R. and A. Winter. 1962. *Bei Töfern und Töpferinnen in Kreta, Messenien und Zypern*. Mainz.

Hampe, R., and A. Winter 1965. *Bei Töpfern und Zieglern in Suditalien, Sizilien und Griechenland*. Mainz.

Hankey, V. 1974. Pottery Making at Beit Shebab, Lebanon. *The Ceramic Review* 15 (May–June): 4–7.

Lisse, P. and A. Louis. 1956. *Les Potiers de Nabeul, Étude de Sociologie Tunisienne*. Paris.

Matson, F. R. 1972. Ceramic Studies. In *The Minnesota Messenia Expedition*, eds. W. A. McDonald and G. R. Rapp, Jr., 200–24. Minneapolis.

Noble, J. V. 1965. *The Techniques of Painted Attic Pottery*. New York.

Winter, A. 1978. *Die antike Glanztonkeramik, praktische Versuche*. Mainz.

Xanthoudides, S. 1927. Some Minoan Potter's-wheel discs. In *Essays in Aegean Archaeology Presented to Sir Arthur Evans*, ed. S. Casson, 111–28. Oxford.

Part VII

20

Summary, General Conclusions, and Questions for Future Investigation

Philip P. Betancourt

The eastern part of Crete enjoyed its greatest prosperity in the Early Bronze Age. Fine harbors must have played a crucial role in this period for the first time in the island's history, and the eastern settlements were quick to benefit from the new trade and foreign contact. A site like Mokhlos, with its cemetery laden with gold and other precious articles, speaks well for the affluence of the inhabitants.

Toward the end of the Early Bronze Age, the towns and villages began using a new type of pottery, covered with dark underpaint and decorated with pale linear designs. The style flourished from Malia in east central Crete to Palaikastro on the eastern edge, with an especially strong development at the sites that bordered the Gulf of Mirabello on the north coast. At its height the ware was by far the most common fine pottery of the region, filling a need for attractive and well-finished cups and other shapes.

The chronology of East Cretan White-on-dark Ware is now fairly well understood (Chap. 2). It begins in EM IIB with a few experimental vases which have the white painted on top of red, brown, black, or mottled surfaces, either burnished or left plain. These earliest versions of the style have only simple, rectilinear motifs, closely comparable to the designs used in Koumasa Ware and other EM IIA wares that were surely their ancestors. The main phase of the style dates to EM III. In eastern Crete this period is longer than elsewhere, and it persists until after MM IA had begun in other regions. The motifs are now more varied. They include spirals, quirks, wavy lines, and other curvilinear designs as well as rectilinear ones, and the syntax is more complex. The style persists into MM IB, gradually evolving into the provincial Kamares Ware of the middle phases of the Middle Bronze Age. New shapes and motifs enrich its final periods, adding and changing components until the original style can no longer be recognized.

Analyses of the motifs and shapes show the essential unity of the entire style (Betancourt, Chaps. 3–4). The ware develops from earlier Minoan styles on the island itself. The motifs develop very gradually, and the shapes are all variants of shapes used in earlier Minoan periods. The most interesting and complex versions of the style flourish in the eastern part of Crete, with much simpler styles occurring in other parts of the island. While many of the east Cretan sites prefer special shapes or details of ornament, many points link the region as a whole. The ware is primarily used for cups and pouring vessels. Statistical examination of specific contexts is only possible in a few cases due to the nature of the material and the poor publication of most deposits, but in situations where it is possible, it shows that other shapes constitute only a small fraction of the ware. Designed to provide a fine and attractive pottery for serving and consuming liquids, East Cretan White-on-dark Ware flourished for several generations.

Individual aspects of the ware are characterized and measured by a number of different methods. Information on the fabric and its inclusions is provided by smoothly ground cross sections of sherds (Matson in Chap. 5) and by petrographic thin sections (Myer in Chap. 6). This information nicely complements the stylistic determinations because it shows that the eastern ware uses a clay fabric which differs from those used in central Crete, but that individual sites have their own local variations of the regional type. The potters seem to have blended their clays from three ingredients: a white calcareous marine clay; a red lateritic soil called terra rossa; and a stone tempering material. Local differences are most easily traced in the temper, which varies slightly from site to site.

Mössbauer spectroscopy (Gangas and Bakas in Chap. 7) identifies the iron phases which are present in the fabric. It shows that in some sherds a reducing atmosphere was present in the kiln during much of the firing cycle, while in other cases the atmosphere was oxidizing. Since oxidizing atmospheres can only exist in a kiln chamber, this is the first objective and incontrovertible proof for the existence of kiln chambers in the Early Minoan period, although their existence has been conjectured for some time.

The dark slip is examined both with low power microscopy and with the Scanning Electron Microscope by Matson in Chapter 6. He points out its characteristics, suggesting that it was most likely made by grinding up red siltstone. Elemental analyses of the dark slip (Gaisser and Swann in Chap. 11) show that iron is the only coloring agent. The color, which varies from red to brown to black, is caused by the degree of reduction in the kiln.

The white slip is examined by several techniques (Matson in Chap. 5; Betancourt, Gaisser, Matson, Myer, Swann, and White in Chap. 8). It contains several phases, probably including clays and calcium silicates and may have been a naturally occurring marl mixed with lime. It does not include the high magnesium content found in some of the palatial white pigments from the Middle Minoan period.

The firing temperatures are studied by Maniatis (Chap. 9). A maturation in the range from 850–1050° C is indicated for most of the sherds examined, based on observations with the SEM on refired sherds using standards derived from the sherds themselves. Calcareous clays such as those used by the Early Minoans have a stable vitrification stage for about 200° within this range, and produce fired bodies with several advantages (such as resistance to thermal and mechanical shock), suggesting a favorable choice in the type of clays used by the potters.

The porosity is measured by Hartmann (Chap. 10). His studies show that the vessels from Gournia are extremely porous (ranging from just under 25% to over 35% apparent porosity). This characteristic does not seem to have been adjusted by the potters (for example, to make larger shapes more resistant to shock), and the only correlation which is found is between porosity and the degree of vitrification, a function primarily of conditions in the kiln.

Two elemental analyses are documented, by proton induced X-rays (Gaisser and Swann, Chap. 11) and by neutron activation (Rapp and Gifford, Chap. 12). The study by proton microprobe compares the elemental composition of the fabric, dark, and pale slips, and offers comparisons between several groups of samples: EM III Gournia; MM I–III Gournia, Vasilike, Mokhlos, and Knossos. It demonstrates that significant variations exist between the compositions of the fabric and the two slips. Among the differences are a higher Fe and K percentage in the dark slip, with depletion of Ca and Cr. These results indicate it is unlikely the the same material was used for both fabric and dark slip (as has been suggested, for example, for the black glaze of Classical Athens). The analyses of groups show differences between them, but with overlapping of some individual members of the groups. The study demonstrates the essential difference of the Middle Minoan and Early Minoan III fabrics from Gournia, and it suggests that other groups are probably distinct as well.

The study by neutron activation had the objectives of determining if the sherds in the same five groups examined by proton microprobe form distinct groups on the basis of their elemental compositions, as revealed by neutron activation, and if any of the clays collected as potential raw materials could be correlated with the pottery on the basis of this technique. The clays form distinct clusters by their geological groups, confirming the geological framework presented in Chapter 15. While the material from EM III Gournia forms a satisfactory grouping (clusters 4 and 6), and some of the MM Gournian samples form tight groups that are not mixed with samples from other sites, the other sherds do not form unambiguous groupings. The clay samples do not clearly associate with the fired pottery.

Photoacoustic spectroscopy is used to measure the surface layer characteristics of sherds from Gournia (Frost, Chap. 13). The technique detects anomalies which are not visible to the unaided eye, including smoothing to conceal the joins between slabs of clay used in the manufacturing process, and selective burnishing which is not visible beneath surface patination. It helps to confirm the seams detected in Chapter 14.

Xeroradiography is used to study the interior structure of samples (Johnston and Betancourt, Chap. 14). By revealing the shapes and distribution of the temper, it shows the heterogeneous nature of many samples, made from poorly mixed clay bodies. Sizes and shapes of temper can be characterized by this method. Seams, invisible to the unaided eye, are revealed by the alignment of air bubbles trapped during manufacturing, showing that the vessels are built up from slabs.

The clay sources of the Isthmus of Ierapetra are studied in a separate section (Gifford and Myer, Chap. 15). The clays of this region are mostly Miocene in date, deposited as marine sediments between 12 and 6 million years ago. A number of clay formations are available in the area, and they were surveyed and sampled. Analysis by X-ray diffraction shows them to be mostly kaolinite clays with substantial impurities (dolomite, plagioclase, calcite, quartz, zeolites, and other minerals). The region also contains abundant deposits of the red soil called terra rossa. Samples of east Cretan clays were tested for pottery suitability alone and as blends with terra rossa and were fired to ca. 800° C. Blended samples exhibit many of the characteristics of the ancient fabrics. A possible local source for the stone tempering material used at Gournia was also located (Chap. 19).

Comments on the techniques of manufacture are made by Matson (Chap. 5) and by Betancourt, Gosser, and Sapareto (Chap. 16). The technique of hand building with slabs is replicated by Gosser and Sapareto, with the conclusion that a satisfactory cup may be made in 20–30 minutes with completely uniform walls. Test firings suggest that the dark slip can be easily achieved either by levigating or by grinding and levigating a clay to produce a finer slip than was used for the fabric, with the result that it will vitrify at a lower temperature than the body. Firing with wood produces the necessary reducing atmosphere in the kiln to yield uniform, dark slips. Various materials will produce white slips, and when fuel is no longer added at the end of the firing, the oxidizing atmosphere will burn away any surface carbon, yielding a clean product. The replication studies indicate that a considerable margin of error exists for the technique in terms of materials preparation and firing temperatures, which suggests that any potter who was already familiar with the technology could duplicate his or her results under primitive conditions with a variety of raw materials. The forming techniques are fast enough to suggest a household's pottery needs for many months could be satisfied in a short production season lasting only a couple of weeks. It is thus highly unlikely that small communities could support permanent, full time potteries.

Ethnological studies are presented for two centers of pottery production in modern Greece, Thrapsano (Voyatzoglou, Chap. 17) and Kentri (Blitzer, Chap. 18).

They suggest possible models for the interpretation of the archaeological record, and these are discussed in a separate chapter (Betancourt, Chap. 19). The methods of clay preparation and use are particularly instructive, and it is noteworthy that the modern potters use clay blends of white marine clays and red terra rossa, as has been suggested for the Minoan potters. The trade and distribution system for eastern Crete in modern times may also offer some good analogies to help interpret the ancient systems, but an areawide distribution in ancient times does not seem tenable given the apparent local ancient production systems. The sherds from Gournia seem to show too many variables in too many different areas (including size of paint brushes, skill of the potters, choice and preparation of temper, and type of decorative motifs) to support the model of a single specialized workshop for the entire community, and it seems more likely that the pottery was made at the household level, with some intrahousehold and intravillage distribution.

Toward the end of the final phase of White-on-dark Ware, the potter's wheel was introduced into Crete. The Middle Minoan IB and II pottery production is far more uniform in style than White-on-dark Ware, and it is likely that a reorganization of some aspects of the industry accompanied the adoption of the wheel. The motifs of White-on-dark Ware, discussed in detail in Chapter 3, are the best guide to the influence of the ware on the later style. They indicate a considerable amount of continuity, even though the most dynamic developments in MM II occurred in the central parts of the island. Whatever the means of transmission, White-on-dark Ware played an important role in the palatial styles of the Middle Bronze Age.

The present studies have given us a new body of information to build on, but much remains for the future. In many ways the analyses here are only preliminary, and their conclusions need to be checked with further studies, especially from the other sites in eastern Crete with substantial quantities of the same ware: Malia; Sphoungaras; Palaikastro; Pyrgos Myrtou; and others. It remains to be seen if these sites will also have individual peculiarities which will allow their pottery to be objectively identified as local productions.

But especially, the field needs an analysis of a group of many hundred sherds from the same site, from specific contexts in several houses. The chart shown in Table 19–I indicates so many variables for the samples from Gournia that it is not possible to clearly pick out individual household productions with any degree of certainty from a group of only thirty samples. With a large enough body of material, excavated from specific houses and with suitable analyses of tool marks, temper, decoration, and other variables, it should be possible to prove the existence or nonexistence of household productions by comparing the pottery found in different households. Only then can this important aspect of the production be better understood.

As with any complex study, the White-on-dark Ware Project has raised almost as many questions as it has answered. We now know far more about the pottery of the period just before the Minoan palaces than we once did, but much more work remains to be done.

Appendix
Catalogue of Analyzed Sherds and Vases

Philip P. Betancourt

The sherds and vases analyzed by various scientific techniques in this study are arranged by site and shape, as follows:

Gournia, EM III: bowl; conical cup; conical cup or bowl; rounded cup; cup (?); bridge spouted jar; teapot; jar lid

Gournia, MM I-III: bowl; straight sided cup; carinated cup; semiglobular cup; cup or bowl; jug; jug or jar; closed vessel

Knossos, EM III: cup; goblet; teapot; jar

Mokhlos, EM III and EM III–MMI: conical cup; conical cup or bowl; rounded cup; closed vessel; lid

Priniatikos Pyrgos, MM I: rounded cup

Vasilike, EM III: bowl; spouted, conical bowl; conical bowl or jar; conical cup; rounded cup; bridge spouted jar

Eastern Crete, exact site unknown, EM III: bowl

Concordance of Numbers, by Museums

BOSTON, MASS., MUSEUM OF FINE ARTS

1909.66	65	1909.575	61
1909.557	64	1909.575.2	62
1909.573	67	1909.575.3	63
1909.574	66		

OXFORD, ENGLAND, ASHMOLEAN MUSEUM

1909.334	60	AE 752	56
1938.421	57	AE 753.4	59
1938.821	55	AE 1672	58

PHILADELPHIA, PA., UNIVERSITY MUSEUM, UNIVERSITY OF PENNSYLVANIA

MS 4234	72	MS 4615–2	19
MS 4236	74	MS 4615–6	11
MS 4237	69	MS 4615–7	12
MS 4238	70	MS 4615–8	13
MS 4615–9	14	MS 4615–29	7
MS 4615–10	3	MS 4615–31	15
MS 4615–11	20	MS 4615–32	34
MS 4615–12	4	MS 4615–33	31
MS 4615–13	5	MS 4615–34	37
MS 4615–15	1	MS 4615–35	16
MS 4615–16	2	MS 4615–36	8
MS 4615–17	6	MS 4615–37	9
MS 4615–18	21	MS 4615–39	38
MS 4615–19	36	MS 4615–40	18
MS 4615–20	22	MS 4615–41	10
MS 4615–21	23	MS 4615–43	35
MS 4615–22	24	MS 4615–44	32
MS 4615–23	25	MS 4615–45	33
MS 4615–24	26	MS 4615–47	17
MS 4615–25	27	MS 4628–3	41
MS 4615–26	28	MS 4628–6	42
MS 4615–27	29	MS 4628–7	52
MS 4615–28	30	MS 4628–9	46

MS 4628–13	40	
MS 4628–14	51	
MS 4628–15	43	
MS 4628–19	44	
MS 4628–20	47	
MS 4628–21	50	
MS 4628–22	45	

MS 4894	68
MS 4700–1	39
MS 4700–3	48
MS 4700–5	53
MS 4700–9	54
MS 4700–10	49
60–19–14	75

SOUTH HADLEY, MASS., ART MUSEUM
MOUNT HOLYOKE COLLEGE

BAI 14–A	71
BAI 14–B	73

Catalogue

GOURNIA, EM III

1. Penn no. MS 4615–15. EM III. Rim-sherd from a shallow, open bowl. Max. dimension 7.1 cm; d. of rim ca. 23–28 cm. Band on inside and outside of the rim. Fabric breaks roughly; color is even, light red (2.5YR 6/6–8), with a lighter surface; wiped. Paint on rim is reddish brown (2.5YR 4/4) to red (2.5YR 4/6). White decoration: alternating groups of four diagonal lines on interior; alternating groups of three diagonal lines on exterior.
   Bibl.: Luce 1921: 26, no. 78; Silverman 1978: 21, no. 20, fig. 3, no. 5, and pl. ld, no. 15.

2. Penn no. MS 4615–16. EM III. Rim-sherd from a shallow, open bowl. Max. dimension 12.3 cm; d. of rim ca. 35–45 cm. Painted only on rim on interior but overall on exterior. Fabric breaks roughly; color is even, reddish yellow (5YR 6/6) with a lighter surface; surface wiped. Paint is red (10R 4–5/6). White decoration: alternating groups of four diagonal lines on interior; pendant hatched triangles on exterior.
   Bibl.: Hall 1904–1905: pl. 32, no. 3; Luce 1921: 26, no. 78; Zois 1968: pl. 15, no. 98; Silverman 1978: 21–22, no. 21, fig. 3, no. 6, and pl. 2a, no. 8.

3. Penn no. MS 4615–10. EM III. Rim-sherd from a conical cup. Max. dimension 6 cm; d. of rim ca. 6–8 cm. Painted on rim and exterior. Fabric breaks cleanly; color is even, pink (7.5YR 7/4) with a lighter surface; surface wiped. Overall paint is black. White decoration: double band of dots at rim; unknown motifs (not extant) with two bands above and one below.
   Bibl.: Luce 1921: 26, no. 78; Silverman 1978: 20, no. 11 and pl. ld, no. 4.

4. Penn no. MS 4615–12. EM III. Rim-sherd from a conical cup. Max. dimension 4.8 cm. Painted on rim and exterior. Fabric breaks roughly; color varies from dark reddish gray (5YR 4/2) near outer surface to paler tones near interior surface; surface wiped. Overall paint is black. White decoration: pendant hatched triangles.
   Bibl.: Luce 1921: 26, no. 78; Silverman 1978: 21, no. 18 and pl. ld, no. 9.

5. Penn no. MS 4615–13. EM III. Rim-sherd from a conical cup. Max. dimension 8 cm; d. of rim ca. 11–14 cm. Painted on rim and exterior. Fabric breaks cleanly; color is even, pink (7.5YR 7/4) with a lighter surface, wiped. Overall paint is dusky red (10R 3/2–4). White decoration: pendant hatched triangles.
   Bibl.: Luce 1921: 26, no. 78; Silverman 1978: 20, no. 12, fig. 3, no. 7, and pl. ld, no. 14.

6. Penn no. MS 4615–17. EM III. Rim-sherd from a conical cup. Max. dimension 5.2 cm. Painted on rim and exterior. Fabric breaks roughly; color is fairly even, brown (10YR 5/3–4) near exterior and darker near interior, with a lighter surface: surface wiped. Overall paint is black. White decoration: pendant hatched triangles.
   Bibl.: Luce 1921: 26, no. 78; Silverman 1978: 21, no. 17.

7. Penn no. MS 4615–29. EM III. Rim-sherd from a conical cup. Max. dimension 4.9 cm. Painted on interior of rim and on exterior. Fabric breaks cleanly; color is uneven, from reddish yellow (7.5YR 7/6) to slightly grayer, with a lighter surface; surface wiped. Overall paint is red (10R 4/6) on interior and black on exterior. White decoration: pendant hatched triangles.
   Bibl.: Luce 1921: 26, no. 78; Silverman 1978: 21, no. 16, fig. 3, no. 9, and pl. ld, no. 8.

8. Penn no. MS 4615–36. EM III. Rim-sherd from a conical cup. Max. dimension 5.8 cm. Painted on rim and exterior. Fabric breaks cleanly; color is even, reddish yellow (5YR 7/6), with a lighter surface; surface wiped. Overall paint is dark reddish brown (5YR 3/2). White decoration: pendant hatched triangles with double borders, above two bands.
   Bibl.: Luce 1921: 26, no. 78; Silverman 1978: 20, no. 14, fig. 3, no. 8, and pl. ld, no. 7.

9. Penn no. MS 4615–37. EM III. Base-sherd from a conical cup. D. of base ca. 5.6 cm. Painted on rim and exterior. Fabric breaks roughly; color is even, reddish yellow (5YR 6/6–8) with a lighter surface; surface wiped. Overall paint is black. White decoration: probably hatched triangles.

Bibl.: Luce 1921: 26, no. 78; Silverman 1978: 25, no. 42, fig. 3, no. 17, and pl. 2a, no. 14.

10. Penn no. MS 4615–41. EM III (?). Body-sherd from a conical cup or bowl. Max. dimension 5.2 cm. Painted on exterior. Fabric breaks cleanly; color is brown (7.5YR 3–4/2), darker at the core; surface wiped. Overall paint is very dark brown. White decoration: diagonal lines (part of larger design, not preserved).
    Bibl.: Silverman 1978: 26, no. 45 and pl. 2a, no. 16.

11. Penn no. MS 4615–6. EM III. Rim-sherd from a rounded cup. Max. dimension 3.8 cm. Painted on rim and exterior. Fabric breaks cleanly; color is light yellowish brown (10YR 6/4) near surface, darker at core, with a lighter surface; surface wiped. Overall paint in black. White decoration: spirals above two bands.
    Bibl.: Luce 1921: 26, no. 78; Silverman 1978: 19, no. 6 and pl. ld, no. 12.

12. Penn no. MS 4615–7. EM III. Rim-sherd from a rounded cup. Max. dimension 4.8 cm. Painted on rim and exterior. Fabric breaks cleanly: color is even, pink (7.5YR 7/4) with a lighter surface; surface wiped. Overall paint is black. White decoration: portion of multiple connecting lines above three bands.
    Bibl.: Luce 1921: 26, no. 78; Silverman 1978: 19, no. 8, fig. 3, no. 3, and pl. ld, no. 13.

13. Penn no. MS 4615–8. EM III. Rim-sherd from a rounded cup. Max. dimension 4 cm; d. of rim ca. 6–8 cm. Painted on rim and exterior. Fabric breaks roughly; color is even, brown (7.5YR 5/4) with a darker surface; surface wiped. Overall paint is black. White decoration: diagonal band of dots bounded by double lines, with two bands above and one (or two?) bands below
    Bibl.: Luce 1921: 26, no. 78; Silverman 1978: 20, no. 10 and pl. ld, no. 5.

14. Penn no. MS 4615–9. EM III. Rim-sherd from a rounded cup. Max. dimension 4.7 cm; d. of rim ca. 7–9 cm. Painted on rim and exterior. Fabric breaks cleanly; color is even, reddish yellow (5YR 6/6) with a lighter surface; surface wiped. Overall paint is dusky red (10R 3/2–3). White decoration: groups of short lines on rim; rising double arcs of dots within double arcs, with two bands above and one (or more) bands below.
    Bibl.: Luce 1921: 26, no. 78; Silverman 1978: 20, no. 11 and pl. ld, no. 4.

15. Penn no. MS 4615–31. EM III. Rim-sherd from a rounded cup. H. of cup ca. 7–8 cm; d. of rim ca. 8–12 cm. Painted on rim and exterior. Fabric breaks cleanly; color is even, reddish yellow (7.5YR 7/6) with a lighter surface; surface wiped. Overall paint is black. White decoration: double row of dots at rim, above two bands; rising double arcs of dots within one arc, with two bands below.
    Bibl.: Luce 1921: 26, no. 78; Silverman 1978: 19, no. 7, fig. 3, no. 2, and pl. ld, no. 1.

16. Penn no. MS 4615–35. EM III. Rim-sherd from a rounded cup. Max. dimension 5.3 cm. Painted on rim and exterior. Fabric breaks roughly; color is even, very pale brown (10YR 8/3) with a similarly colored surface; surface wiped. Overall paint is black. White decoration: two bands at rim; rising double arcs of dots within one arc, with two bands below.
    Bibl.: Luce 1921: 26, no. 78; Silverman 1978: 25, no. 41 and pl. ld, no. 23.

17. Penn no. MS 4615–47. EM III. Rim-sherd from a rounded cup. Max. dimension 4.8 cm; d. of rim ca. 8–12 cm. Painted on rim, inside and out. Fabric breaks cleanly; color is even, reddish yellow (7.5YR 7/6) with a lighter surface; surface wiped. Paint varies from red (2.5YR 5/8) to nearly black. White decoration: band of dots above two bands on exterior rim.
    Bibl.: Luce 1921: 26, no. 78; Silverman 1978: 19–20, no. 9, fig. 3, no. 4, and pl. ld, no. 6.

18. Penn no. MS 4615–40. EM III. Body-sherd from a cup (?). Max. dimension 4.1 cm. Painted on exterior. Fabric breaks cleanly; color is even, very pale brown (10YR 7/4); surface wiped. Overall paint is black. White decoration: crosshatched triangles.
    Bibl.: Luce 1921: 26, no. 78; Silverman 1978: 26, no. 46 and pl. ld, no. 28.

19. Penn no. MS 4615–2. EM III. Rim-sherd from a bridge spouted jar. Max. dimension 7.1 cm; d. of rim ca. 20–25 cm. Painted on rim and exterior. Fabric breaks roughly; color is even, light brown (7.5YR 6/4); surface wiped. Overall paint is black. White decoration: circles with crosshatched sections and multiple connecting lines, with short lines on the connecting lines.
    Bibl.: Hall 1904–1905: pl. 29, no. 4; Luce 1921: 26, no. 78; Zois 1968: pl. 13, no. 62; Silverman 1978: 24, no. 37 and pl. ld, no. 24.

20. Penn no. MS 4615–11. EM III. Rim-sherd from a bridge spouted jar. Max. dimension 11.7 cm; d. of rim ca. 21–22 cm. Painted on rim and exterior. Fabric breaks roughly; color is even, reddish yellow (5YR 6/6) with a lighter surface; surface wiped. Overall paint is black. White decorations: circles with crosshatched sections and multiple connecting lines.
    Bibl.: Hall 1904–1905: pl. 29, no. 2; Luce 1921: 26, no. 78; Zois 1968: pl. 13, no. 60; Silverman 1978: 23–24, no. 32, fig. 3, no. 14, and pl. ld, no. 26.

21. Penn no. MS 4615–18. EM III. Rim-sherd from a bridge spouted jar. Max. dimension 5.9 cm. Painted on rim and exterior. Fabric breaks roughly; color is even, reddish yellow (5YR 6/6) with a grayer surface; surface wiped. Overall paint is black. White decoration: spirals (probably with multiple connecting lines).
    Bibl.: Luce 1921: 26, no. 78; Silverman 1978: 22, no. 24 and pl. ld, no. 17.
22. Penn no. MS 4615–20. EM III. Rim-sherd from a bridge spouted jar. Max. dimension 6 cm. Painted on rim and exterior. Fabric breaks roughly; color is even, very pale brown (10YR 7/3) with a slightly paler surface; surface wiped. Overall paint is black. White decoration: spirals with multiple connecting lines.
    Bibl.: Luce 1921: 26, no. 78; Silverman 1978: 22, no. 26 and pl. ld, no. 20.
23. Penn no. MS 4615–21. EM III. Rim-sherd from a bridge spouted jar. Max. dimension 5.9 cm. Painted on rim and exterior. Fabric breaks roughly; color is even, dark reddish gray (5YR 4/2) with a grayer surface, surface wiped. Overall paint is black. White decoration: diagonal band of opposed groups of three lines flanked by double lines.
    Bibl.: Luce 1921: 26, no. 78; Silverman 1978: 22–23, no. 27, fig. 3, no. 13, and pl. ld, no. 21.
24. Penn no. MS 4615–22. EM III. Rim-sherd from a bridge spouted jar. Max. dimension 6.1 cm. Painted on rim and exterior. Fabric breaks cleanly; color is even, pink (5YR 7/4 to 6/6) with a lighter surface; surface wiped. Overall paint is weak red (10R 4/4). White decoration: band on rim; rising double arcs of dots bounded by bands.
    Bibl.: Luce 1921: 26, no. 78; Silverman 1978: 23, no. 28 and pl. ld, no. 22.
25. Penn no. MS 4615–32. EM III. Rim-sherd from a bridge spouted jar. Max. dimension 6.4 cm. Painted on rim and exterior. Fabric breaks roughly; color is light brown (7.5YR 6/4) at the core and darker near exterior with a lighter surface; surface wiped. Overall paint is black. White decoration: two bands at rim with groups of short lines above; diagonal double band of dots flanked by triple bands.
    Bibl.: Luce 1921: 26, no. 78; Silverman 1978: 23, no. 29 and pl. ld, no. 23.
26. Penn no. MS 4615–24. EM III. Rim-sherd from a bridge spouted jar. Max. dimension 6.6 cm. Painted on rim and exterior. Fabric breaks roughly; color is even, reddish yellow (5YR 7/6-8) with a lighter surface; surface wiped. Overall paint is uneven dusky red (10R 3-4/2-4). White decoration: diagonal band of quirks flanked by bands.
    Bibl.: Luce 1921: 26, no. 78; Silverman 1978: 23, no. 30 and pl. ld, no. 25.
27. Penn no. MS 4615–25. EM III. Rim-sherd from a bridge spouted jar. Max. dimension 6.2 cm. Painted on rim and exterior. Fabric breaks roughly; color is even, pink (5YR 7/4–7.5YR 7/4) with a grayer surface; surface wiped. Overall paint is black. White decoration: circles with crosshatched sections, with multiple connecting lines.
    Bibl.: Luce 1921: 26, no. 78; Silverman 1978: 23, no. 31 and pl. 2a, no. 7.
28. Penn no. MS 4615–26. EM III. Rim-sherd with handle from a bridge sprouted jar. Max. dimension 10.9 cm; d. of rim ca. 18–22 cm. Painted on rim and exterior. Fabric breaks roughly; color is fairly even, reddish yellow (5YR 6/6), lighter near the exterior, with a lighter surface; surface wiped. Overall paint is dark reddish brown (2.5YR 3/4). White decoration: band on rim; lines on handle; traces of other designs.
    Bibl.: Luce 1921: 26, no. 78; Silverman 1978: 24, no. 36, fig. 3, no. 18 and pl. 2a, no. 9.
29. Penn no. MS 4615–27. EM III. Rim-sherd from a bridge spouted jar. Max. dimension 9.2 cm; d. of rim ca. 15–20 cm. Painted on rim and exterior. Fabric breaks roughly; color is even, yellowish red (5YR 5/8) with a lighter surface; surface wiped. Overall paint is black. White decoration: band on top at rim; crosshatched diagonal area.
    Bibl.: Luce 1921: 26, no. 78; Silverman 1978: 24, no. 34, fig. 3, no. 15, and pl. 2a, no. 2.
30. Penn no. MS 4615–28. EM III. Rim-sherd from a bridge spouted jar. Max. dimension 6.8 cm. Painted on rim and exterior. Fabric breaks roughly; color is even, pink (7.5YR 7/4) with a lighter surface; surface wiped. Overall paint is black. White decoration: circles with crosshatched crescents, with multiple connecting lines.
    Bibl.: Hall 1904–1905: pl. 29, no. 7; Luce 1921: 26, no. 78; Zois 1968: pl. 13, no. 65; Silverman 1978: 24, no. 35 and pl. 2a, no. 3; Andreou 1978: fig. 10, no. 7.
31. Penn no. MS 4615–33. EM III. Rim-sherd from a bridge spouted jar. Max. dimension 6.6 cm; d. of rim ca. 12–15 cm. Painted on rim and exterior. Fabric breaks roughly; color is even, yellowish red (5YR 4–5/6) with a lighter surface; surface wiped. Overall paint is black. White decorations: spirals with multiple connecting lines.
    Bibl.: Luce 1921: 26, no. 78; Silverman 1978: 22, no. 22, fig. 3, no. 10, and pl. ld, no. 19.
32. Penn no. MS 4615–44. EM III. Rim-sherd from

a bridge spouted jar. Max. dimension 7.5 cm; d. of rim ca. 18–24 cm. Painted on rim and exterior. Fabric breaks roughly; color is reddish yellow (5YR 6/6) near interior and darker near exterior with a lighter surface; surface wiped. Overall paint is black. White decoration: two bands at rim; circles with crosshatched sections and multiple connecting lines and zigzags.

Bibl.: Luce 1921: 26, no. 78; Silverman 1978: 25, no. 41 and pl. 2a, no. 5.

33. Penn no. MS 4615–45. EM III. Rim-sherd from a bridge spouted jar. Max. dimension 6.3 cm. Painted on rim and exterior. Fabric breaks roughly; color is even, reddish brown (5YR 5/3) to reddish gray (5YR 5/2) with a lighter surface; surface wiped. Overall paint is black. White decorations: spirals with multiple connecting lines.

Bibl.: Luce 1921: 26, no. 78; Silverman 1978: 22, no. 23, fig. 3 no. 11, and pl. 1d, no. 18.

34. Penn no. MS 4615–32. EM III. Rim-sherd from a teapot. Max. dimension 4.4 cm. Painted on rim and exterior. Fabric breaks roughly; color is uneven, from dark brown (7.5YR 4/4) to black, with a black surface penetrating into the fabric; surface wiped. Overall paint is black. White decoration: dots on top of rim; two bands at rim; part of another design below.

Bibl.: Luce 1921: 26, no. 78; Silverman 1978: 25, no. 40, and pl. 2a, no. 6.

35. Penn no. MS 4615–43. EM III. Rim-sherd from a teapot. Max. dimension 6.6 cm; d. of rim ca. 20–25 cm. Painted on rim and exterior. Fabric breaks roughly; color is even, reddish yellow (5YR 6-7/8) with a lighter surface; surface wiped. Overall paint is black. White decoration: chain above two bands.

Bibl.: Luce 1921: 26, no. 78; Silverman 1978: 25, no. 39, fig. 3, no. 16, and pl. 1d, no. 25.

36. Penn no. MS 4615–19. EM III (?). Rim-sherd from the neck and upper shoulder of a jar. Max. dimension 7.8 cm. Fabric breaks roughly; color is uneven, light red (2.5YR 6/6) with a darker core and a pale surface; surface wiped. Dark brown bands on rim; pendant concentric semicircles on neck; paint on lower neck and body. No white paint preserved.

Bibl.: Silverman 1978: 27, no. 48, fig. 3, no. 20, and pl. 2a, no. 11.

37. Penn no. MS 4615–34. EM III. Complete profile from a lid. H. 4.7 cm; d. of top ca. 22–30 cm. Painted on upper surface and outer edge. Fabric breaks roughly; color is even, light red (2.5YR 6/8) with a grayer surface; surface wiped. Overall paint is black. White decoration: rising hatched triangles on edge; edge of designs on upper surface.

Bibl.: Luce 1921: 26, no. 78; Silverman 1978: 25, no. 43, fig. 3, no. 22, and pl. 2a, no. 13.

38. Penn no. MS 4615–39. EM III. Complete profile from a lid, with the edge of a handle placed at the upper edge of the rim. Max. dimension 6.1 cm; d. ca. 20–30 cm. Painted on both upper and lower surfaces. Fabric breaks roughly; color is even, reddish yellow (5YR 7/6); surface wiped. Overall paint is red (2.5YR 5/8) on underside and darker on upper surface. White decoration: rising hatched triangles on edge; crosshatched triangles on upper surface.

Bibl.: Luce 1921: 26, no. 78; Silverman 1978: 169, no. 418, fig. 3, no. 21, and pl. 2a, no. 12.

GOURNIA, MM I-III

39. Penn no. MS 4700–1. MM IB–LM IA. Rim-sherd from a shallow bowl. Max. dimension 7.5 cm; d. of rim 12 cm. Wheelmade. Painted on top and bottom. Fabric breaks cleanly; color is even, pink (5YR 7–6/4); surface wiped. Overall paint is uneven, reddish brown (5YR 4/3) to black. White decoration: four bands on top and around circumference near edge.

Bibl.: Silverman 1978: 66–67, no. 165.

40. Penn no. MS 4628–13. MM II. Rim-sherd from a bowl. Max. dimension 4.2 cm. Wheelmade. Painted on interior and exterior. Fabric breaks cleanly; color is pink (7.5YR 7–8/4); surface wiped. Overall paint is black. Red decoration: vertical bands on interior. White decoration: quirks between red bands on interior; pendant concentric semicircles on exterior.

Bibl.: Silverman 1978: 35, no. 65 and pl. 26, no. 12.

41. Penn no. MS 4628–3. MM IB–III. Complete profile from a straight sided cup. H. of wall 4.9 cm; d. of rim 7 cm; d. of base 5 cm. Wheelmade. Painted on interior, exterior, and bottom of base. Fabric breaks cleanly; color is reddish brown (5YR 5/4) at surface, dark gray at core; surface wiped. Overall paint is dark brown, almost black. White decoration: band on lower body; diagonal line (crescents?) and small squiggle on body.

Bibl.: Silverman 1978: 34, no. 64 and pl. 2b, no. 3.

42. Penn no. MS 4628–6. MM IB–II. Base-sherd from a straight sided cup. Max. dimension 6.1 cm; d. of base 6.5 cm. Wheelmade. Painted on interior, exterior, and bottom of base. Fabric breaks cleanly; color is even, very pale brown (10YR 7/4); surface wiped. Overall paint is un-

even, dark brown to black. White decoration: bands on lower body.

Bibl.: Silverman 1978: 37, no. 77 and pl. 2b, no. 16.

43. Penn no. MS 4628–15. MM IB–III. Body-sherd from a straight sided cup. Max. dimension 4.4 cm. Wheelmade. Painted on interior and exterior. Fabric breaks cleanly; color is even, pink (7.5YR 7/4) at surface and yellowish red (5YR 5/8) at core; surface wiped. Overall paint is black. White decoration: bands and other designs, only partly preserved.

Bibl.: Silverman 1978: pl. 2b, no. 19.

44. Penn no. MS 4628–19. MM IB–II. Body-sherd from a carinated cup. Max. dimension 6.2 cm. Wheelmade. Painted on interior and exterior. Fabric breaks cleanly; color is even, light gray (2.5Y 7/2); surface wiped. Overall paint is black. White decoration: band and other designs, only partly preserved.

Bibl.: Silverman 1978: 35, no. 69 and pl. 2b, no. 18.

45. Penn no. MS 4628–22. MM IB–II. Body-sherd from a carinated cup. Max. dimension 4.3 cm. Wheelmade. Painted on interior and exterior. Fabric breaks cleanly; color is pink (7.5YR 7/4) at surface, redder toward the center, and gray at the core; surface wiped. Overall paint is black. White decoration: only partly preserved.

Bibl.: Silverman 1978: 36, no. 73 and pl. 2b, no. 17.

46. Penn no. MS 4628–9. MM IB–III. Rim-sherd from a semiglobular cup. D. of rim ca. 4–5 cm. Wheelmade. Painted on interior and exterior. Fabric breaks cleanly; color is even, very pale brown (10YR 7/4); surface wiped. Overall paint is reddish brown (5YR 5/3). White decoration: unk. designs, only partly preserved.

Bibl.: Silverman 1978: 34, no. 63 and pl. 2b, no. 5.

47. Penn no. MS 4628–20. MM II. Rim-sherd with handle from a semiglobular cup. Max. dimension 7.3 cm. Wheelmade. Painted on interior and exterior. Fabric breaks cleanly; color is pale red (2.5YR 6/2) at surface, slightly darker at core; surface wiped. Overall paint is uneven, mostly dark reddish brown. Red decoration: arcs and other motifs, only partly preserved. White decoration: diagonal line and other motifs, only partly preserved.

Bibl.: Silverman 1978: 34, no. 61, fig. 4, no. 4, and pl. 2b, no. 11.

48. Penn no. MS 4700–3. MM IB–III. Base-sherd from a semiglobular cup. Max. dimension 5.7 cm. Wheelmade. Painted on interior, exterior, and bottom of base. Fabric breaks cleanly; color is even, very pale brown (10YR 8/3); surface wiped. Overall paint is black. White decoration: bands on lower body.

Bibl.: Silverman 1978: 67, no. 166.

49. Penn no. MS 4700–10. MM IB–III. Body-sherd from a cup or bowl. Max. dimension 9.3 cm. Wheelmade. Painted on interior and exterior. Fabric breaks roughly; color is even, light gray (2.5Y 7/2); surface wiped. Overall paint is black. White decoration: spirals above two bands.

Unpublished.

50. Penn no. MS 4628–21. MM IB–II. Complete profile from a jug, except for spout. H. (as preserved) 10.9 cm. Wheelmade. Painted on interior of mouth and neck and on exterior. Fabric breaks cleanly; color is reddish yellow (7.5YR 7/6); surface wiped. Overall paint is uneven, dusky red to reddish black. Red decoration: dots on shoulder. White decoration: pendant triangles on shoulder, filled with dots, with one band above and two below; lines on handle. From Deposit A.

Bibl.: Silverman 1974: 14; 1978: 166, no. 406 and pl. 2c.

51. Penn no. MS 4628–14. MM IB–II. Body-sherd from the neck of a jug or jar. Wheelmade. Painted on exterior. Fabric breaks cleanly; color is uneven, light reddish brown (2.5YR 6/4) at surface, gray at core; surface wiped. Overall paint is black. White decoration: zigzags between horizontal bands.

Bibl.: Silverman 1978: 37, no. 76 and pl. 2b, no. 13.

52. Penn no. MS 4628–7. MM IB–LM IA. Body-sherd from a closed vessel. Max. dimension 5.2 cm. Handmade. Painted on exterior. Fabric breaks cleanly; color is even, light brown (7.5YR 6/4); surface wiped. Overall paint is black. White decoration: wide band and thin bands.

Bibl.: Silverman 1978: pl. 2b, no. 7.

53. Penn no. MS 4700–5. MM II. Body-sherd from a closed vessel. Max. dimension 6.3 cm. Handmade. Painted on exterior. Fabric breaks cleanly; color is even, light brown (7.5YR 6–5/4); surface wiped. Overall paint is black. White decoration: dots and foliate ornament.

Bibl.: Silverman 1978: 69, no. 173 and pl. 7c, no. 3.

54. Penn no. MS 4700–9. MM IB–LM IA. Body-sherd from a closed vessel. Max. dimension 10.0 cm. Handmade (?). Painted on exterior. Fabric breaks cleanly; color is very pale brown (10YR 7/3) at surface, redder at core; surface wiped. Overall paint is black. White decoration: running spirals between bands.

Bibl.: Silverman 1978: 66, no. 164 and pl. 7c, no. 4.

KNOSSOS, EM III

55. AM no. 1938.821. MM I. Rim-sherd from a cup with convex profile. Handmade. Max. dimension 6.7 cm. Painted on interior and exterior. Fabric breaks cleanly; color is even, reddish yellow (7.5YR 6/6). Overall paint is dark. White decoration: rectangular box at rim, with three sets of diagonal lines forming vertical herringbone with flanking diagonal lines.
    Unpublished.
56. AM no. AE 752. EM III–MM IA. Rim-sherd from a cup with convex profile. Max. dimension 5.4 cm. Painted on interior and exterior. Fabric breaks cleanly; color is even, pink (7.5YR 7/4) Overall paint is dark. White decoration: three bands at rim and on lower body; diagonal lines across the bands.
    Unpublished.
57. AM no. 1938.421. EM III–MM IA. Complete profile from a goblet. H. 6.0 cm. Painted on exterior. Fabric breaks cleanly; color is even, pink (7.5YR 7/4). Overall paint is red. White decoration: X's formed of double lines, above two bands, at rim.
    Unpublished.
58. AM no. AE 1672. EM III–MM IA. Spout from a teapot. Max. dimension 12.5 cm. Painted on exterior. Fabric breaks cleanly; color is even, reddish yellow (5YR 7/6). Overall paint is red. White decoration: sets of two vertical lines on spout.
    Unpublished.
59. AM no. AE 753.4. EM III–MM IA. Rim-sherd from a jar with an everted rim. Max. dimension 6.3 cm. Painted on rim and exterior. Fabric breaks cleanly; color is even, pink (7.5YR 7/4). Overall paint is black. White decoration: band at rim; pendant triangles composed of three lines.
    Unpublished.

MOKHLOS, EM III AND EM III–MM I

60. AM no. 1909.334. EM III (?). Rim-sherd from a conical cup. Max. dimension 5.4 cm. Painted on rim and exterior. Fabric breaks cleanly; color is even, pink (7.5YR 7/4). Overall paint is red. White decoration: pendant hatched triangles.
    Unpublished.
61. MFA no. 1909.575. EM III–MM I. Complete profile from a conical cup with pronounced base. H. 7.0 cm; d. of rim ca. 8.8 cm; d. of base ca. 5 cm. Painted on inside and outside of rim and on lower part of body. Fabric breaks cleanly; color is reddish yellow (7.5YR 8/6 near surface and 5YR 6/6 at core); surface burnished before applying the ornament. Paint is black. White decoration: pairs of crosshatched ellipses joined by connecting lines and bounded by bands on outside of rim; band on lower body.
    Bibl.: Fairbanks 1928: 14, no. 33.
62. MFA no. 1909.575bis.Ap.2. EM III (?). Rim-sherd from a conical cup or bowl. Max. dimension 6.0 cm; d. of rim ca. 10–20 cm. Painted on inside of rim and on exterior. Fabric breaks cleanly; color is very pale brown (10YR 8/4) near surface, reddish yellow (5YR 7/6) at core; surface wiped. Overall paint is black. White decoration: band of horizontal chevrons with line below at rim, and band of horizontal chevrons bounded by two lines below it.
    Unpublished.
63. MFA no. 1909.575bis.Ap.3. EM III. Rim-sherd from a rounded cup. Max. dimension 5.5 cm. Painted on inside of rim and on exterior. Fabric breaks cleanly; color is even, reddish yellow (5YR 7/6); surface wiped. Overall paint is red on inside of rim, varying from red to black on exterior. White decoration: two diagonal lines; band of quirks flanked by bands on body.
    Unpublished.
64. MFA no. 1909.577. EM III–MM I. Complete profile from a rounded cup (handmade ?). H. 4.4 cm; d. of rim ca. 8 cm. Painted on inside of rim and on exterior. Fabric breaks cleanly; color is pink (7.5YR 7/4) near surface, reddish yellow (5YR 6/6) at core; surface wiped. Overall paint is black. White decoration: triple "connecting lines" forming a zigzag.
    Bibl.: Fairbanks 1928: 14, no. 31.
65. MFA no. 1909.66. EM III–MM I. Rim-sherd from a rounded cup. Max. dimension 5.2 cm; d. of rim ca. 15 cm. Painted on inside of rim and exterior. Fabric breaks cleanly; color is even, reddish yellow (5YR 7/6); surface wiped. Overall paint is red on inside of rim and varies (from dark reddish brown at rim to black on body) on exterior. White decoration: groups of short diagonal lines and tiny dots on rim; pairs of diagonal dot bands flanked by lines, alternating direction.
    Unpublished.
66. MFA no. 1909.574. EM III–MM I. Body-sherd from a closed vessel, probably a teapot. Max. dimension 9.6 cm. Painted on exterior. Fabric breaks roughly; color is even, reddish yellow (7.5YR 6/6–6/4); surface wiped. Overall paint

is black. White decoration: band of triple quirks, between bands.
Bibl.: Fairbanks 1928: 14, no. 33a.

67. MFA no. 1909.573. EM III. Complete profile from a lid. Max. dimension 14.6 cm; d. of top 26 cm; d. of bottom 24–25 cm. Painted on upper surface and sides. Fabric breaks roughly; color is uneven, very pale brown (10YR 7/4) to gray. Marks from burning on surface (from use or a fire?). Overall paint is dark red to black on upper surface and black on sides. White decoration: running spirals on top, around circumference; alternation of spirals and groups of diagonal lines on sides.
Bibl.: Fairbanks 1928: 14, no. 34.

PRINIATIKOS PYRGOS, MM I

68. Penn no. MS 4894. MM I. Rim-sherd with handle from a rounded cup. Preserved h. 5.1 cm; d. of rim 7.5 cm. Painted on interior of rim and overall on exterior. Fabric breaks cleanly; color is pink (7.5YR 7/4) with a paler surface; surface wiped. Paint is reddish brown (5YR 5/4) to dark reddish brown (5YR 2.5/2). White decoration: frieze of isolated motifs consisting of diagonal double rows of dots bounded by double lines, with two bands above and two below; three thin lines on top of handle.
Bibl.: Betancourt 1983: no. 19.

VASILIKE, EM III

69. Penn no. MS 4237. EM III. Conical bowl. H. 5.7 cm; d. of rim ca. 13 cm. Painted on inside of rim and on exterior. Fabric breaks cleanly; color is even, reddish brown (5YR 5/4 to 7.5YR 4/2); surface wiped. Overall paint is reddish black. White decoration: pendant hatched triangles.
Bibl.: Luce 1921: 18, no. 13; Betancourt 1983: no. 240.

70. Penn no. MS 4238. EM III. Spouted, conical bowl. H. 6.6 cm; d. of rim 11 cm. Painted on inside of rim and on exterior. Fabric breaks cleanly; color is even, reddish yellow (5–7.5YR 6–7/6); surface wiped. Overall paint is black. White decoration: pendant hatched triangles.
Bibl.: Luce 1921: 18, no. 13; Betancourt 1983: no. 242.

71. MHC no. BAI 14–A. EM III–MM I. Base-sherd from a conical bowl or jar. Max. dimension 10.5 cm. Painted on exterior. Fabric breaks cleanly; color is even, light brown (7.5YR 6/4); surface wiped. Overall paint is black, White decoration: horizontal chevrons between bands.
Bibl.: Foster 1978: no. 33.

72. Penn no. MS 4234. EM III–MM I. Conical cup with pronounced base. H. 6.1 cm; d. of rim 8.8 cm. Painted on rim, inside and out, and on bottom of wall, with three equally spaced vertical panels. Fabric breaks cleanly; color is even, yellow (10YR 7/4–6); surface is burnished. Background paint is uneven, red to black. White decoration: bands on band at rim; diagonal lines and crosshatching on vertical panels.
Bibl.: Luce 1921: 18, no. 13; Betancourt 1983: no. 239.

73. MHC no. BAI 14–B. EM III. Complete profile from a rounded cup. H. 6.0 cm. Painted on inside of rim and on exterior. Fabric breaks cleanly; color is even, very pale brown (10YR 7/4); surface wiped. Overall paint is red to black. White decoration: band of quirks at rim; three bands on body.
Bibl.: Foster 1978: no. 32.

74. Penn no. MS 4236. EM III. Section of the rim from a bridge spouted jar. Max. dimension 24.5 cm. Painted on inside of rim and on exterior. Fabric breaks roughly; color is yellowish red (5YR 5/6) at exterior surface, shading toward light yellowish brown (10YR 6/4) toward interior surface; surface wiped. Overall paint is red. White decoration: pendant semicircles at rim and rising semicircles at band below shoulder zone, with reserved diamonds between them; spirals and possibly other designs on body.
Bibl.: Luce 1921: 26, no. 77; Betancourt 1983: no. 243.

EASTERN CRETE, EXACT SITE UNK, EM III.

75. Penn no. 60–19–14. EM III. Rim-sherd from a conical bowl. Max. dimension 11.4 cm. Painted on inside of rim and on exterior. Fabric breaks roughly; color is even, light yellowish brown (10YR 6/4); surface wiped. Overall paint is black. White decoration: section of crosshatching flanked by sections with vertical lines on band at inside of rim; pendant triangles hatched at the corners on exterior.
Unpublished.

References

Andreou, S. 1978. Pottery Groups of the Old Palace Period in Crete. Ph.D. Diss., University of Cincinnati.

Betancourt, P. P. 1983. *Minoan Objects Excavated from Vasilike, Pseira, Sphoungaras, Priniatikos Pyrgos and Other Sites. The Cretan Collection in the University Museum, University of Pennsylvania*, vol. I. Philadelphia.

Fairbanks, A. 1928. *Museum of Fine Arts, Boston. Catalogue of Greek and Roman Vases, Preceding Athenian Black-figured Ware*. Cambridge, Mass.

Foster, K. P. 1978. The Mount Holyoke Collection of Minoan Pottery. *Temple University Aegean Symposium* 3: 1–30.

Hall, E. H. 1904–1905. Early Painted Pottery from Gournia, Crete. *Transactions of the Department of Archaeology, Free Museum of Science and Art* 1: 191–205.

Luce, S. B. 1921. *The University Museum. Catalogue of the Mediterranean Section*. Philadelphia.

Silverman, J. S. 1978. The Gournia Collection in the University Museum: A Study in East Cretan Pottery. Ph.D. diss., University of Pennsylvania.

Zois, A. A. 1968. Υπάρχει ΠΜ ΙΙΙ ἐποχὴ; *Πεπράγμενα τοῦ β' Διεθνοῦς Κρητολογικοῦ Συνεδρίου*. Athens.

PLATE 1

White-on-dark Ware from Mokhlos (A–F) and Palaikastro (G). All are from the mature phase of the style, East Cretan EM III.
- A. Anthropomorphic jug in the form of a woman with pierced breasts (HM no. 5499), ht. 18 cm.
- B. Five rounded cups (MFA, clockwise from the back row left, nos 09.556, 09.42, 09.553, 09.554, 09.555), hts. ca. 6 cm.
- C.–E. Jugs (MFA no. 09.33, HM no. 5472, and MFA no. 09.552), hts. ca. 20 cm.
- F. Conical bowl (MFA no. 09.36), ht. 12.3 cm.
- G. Conical bowl with frying pan handle (AM no. AE 742), ht. 10 cm.

PLATE 2

- A. Teapot from Mokhlos (EM III), HM no. 5473, ht. 14.2 cm.
- B. Rounded cup from the Gulf of Mirabello (EM III–MM I), with an open spout and two vertical handles, BM no. A 437, ht. 7.5 cm.
- C.–D. Open bowl from the Gulf of Mirabello (EM III), BM no. A 438, pres. width 24.9 cm.
- E. Cup from the Isthmus of Ierapetra (MM I), BM no. A 441, ht. without handle 5 cm.
- F. Cup from Pseira (MM I), MMA no. 14.89.4, acquired by exchange, 1914, ht. without handle 5 cm.
- G. Carinated cup from Palaikastro (MM I), HM no. 3337, ht. without handle 7 cm.

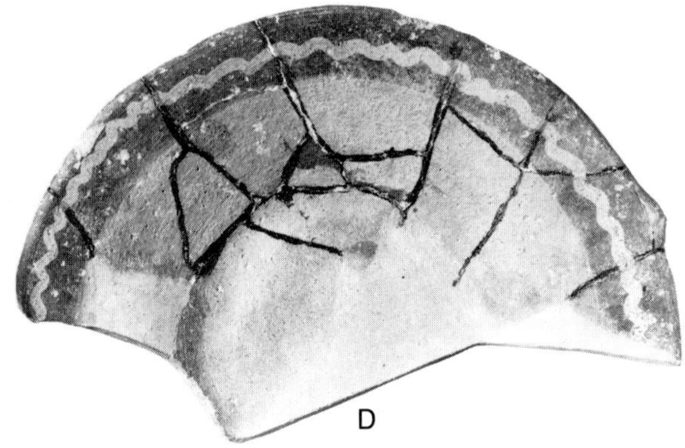

PLATE 3

A. Bridge spouted jug from the Gulf of Mirabello, BM no. A 436, ht. 13 cm.
B. Teapot from Knossos, AM no. AE 749, ht. 13.4 cm.

PLATE 4

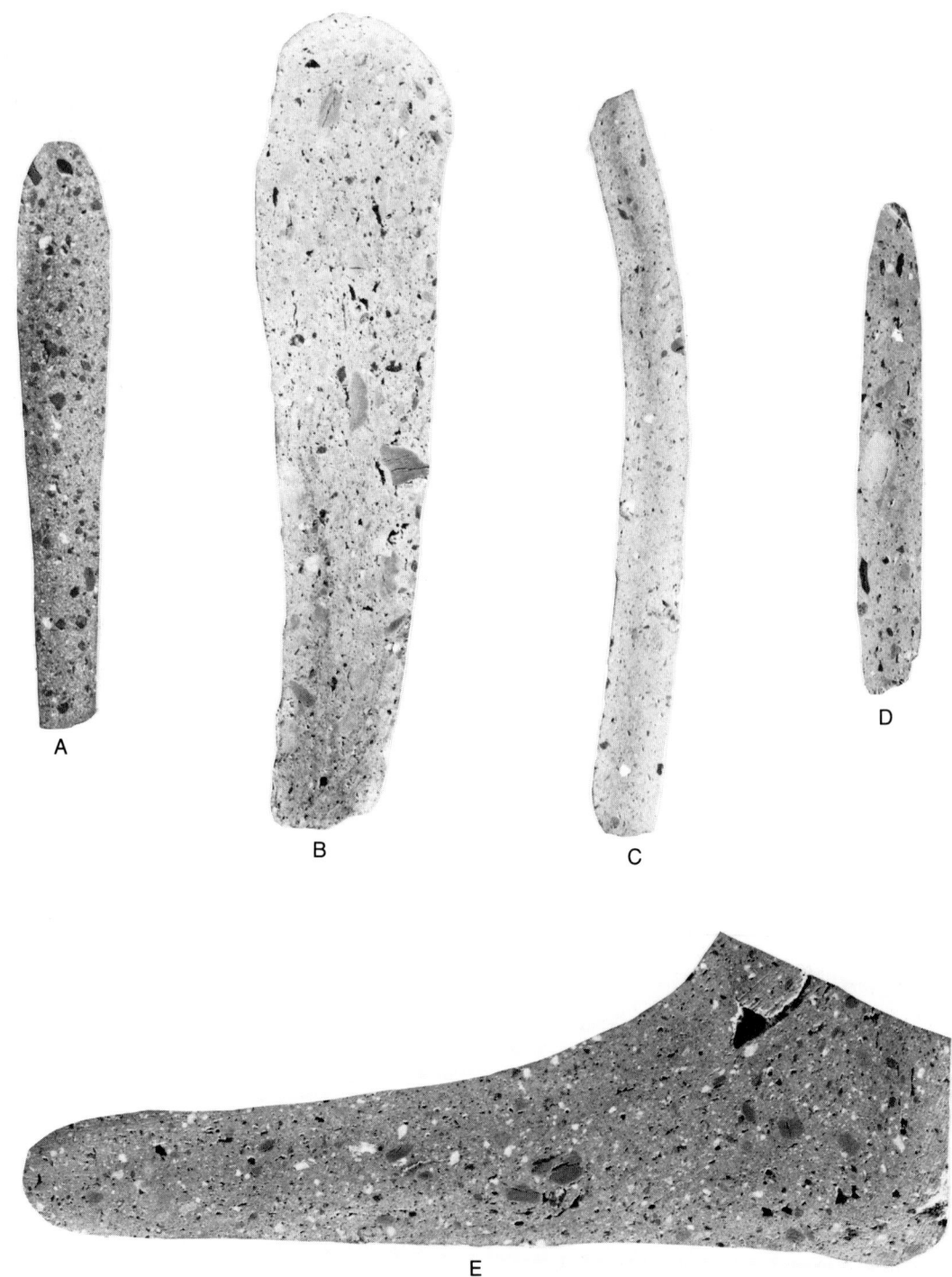

Cross sections through sherds from Gournia showing the variety of the inclusions, three times natural size.
    A. Cup, Penn no. MS 4615-17.
    B. Bridge spouted jar. Penn no. MS 4615-28.
    C. Cup, Penn no. MS 4615-47.
    D. Cup, Penn no. MS 4615-9.
    E. Lid, Penn no. MS 4615-34.

PLATE 5

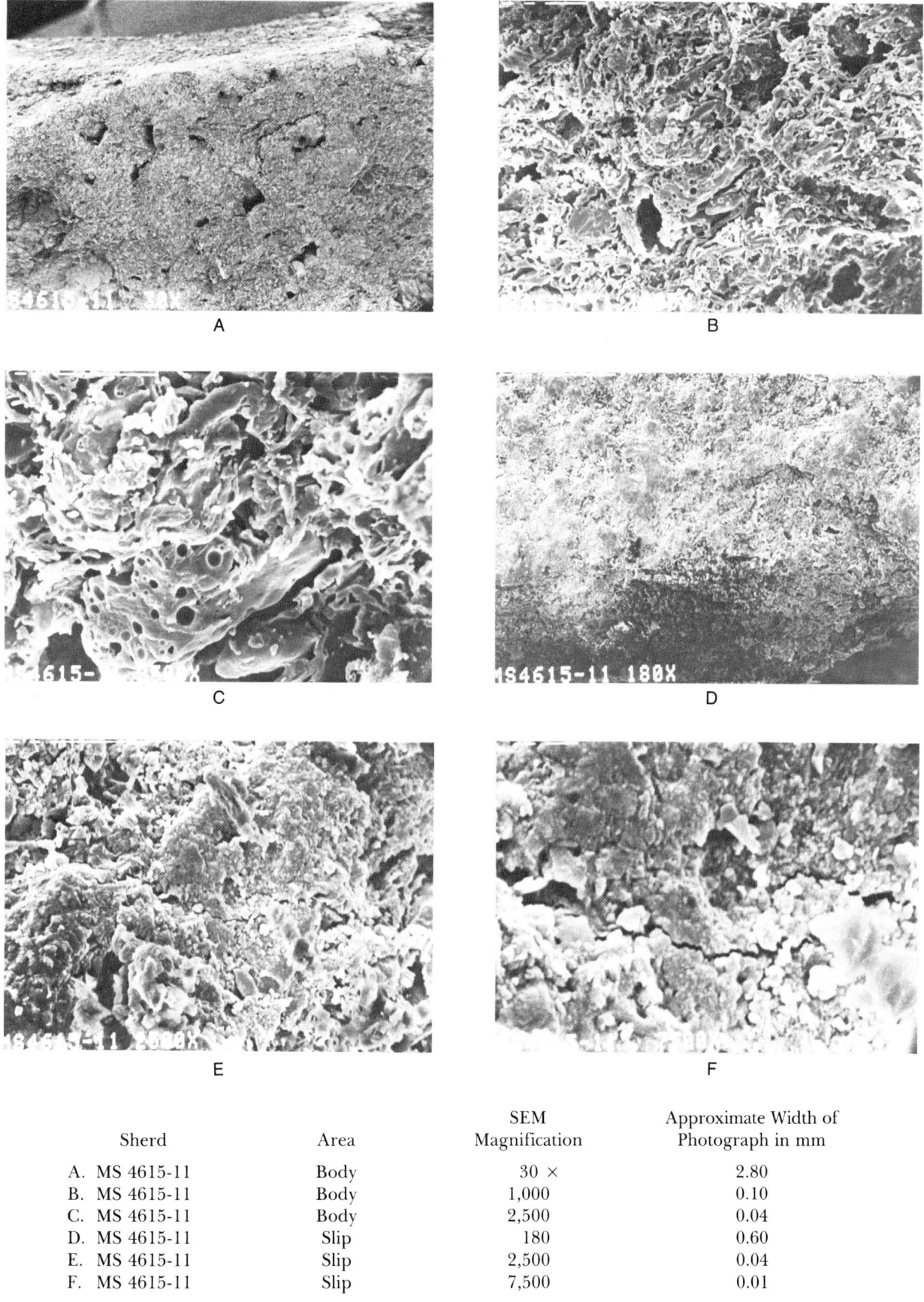

Sherd	Area	SEM Magnification	Approximate Width of Photograph in mm
A. MS 4615-11	Body	30 ×	2.80
B. MS 4615-11	Body	1,000	0.10
C. MS 4615-11	Body	2,500	0.04
D. MS 4615-11	Slip	180	0.60
E. MS 4615-11	Slip	2,500	0.04
F. MS 4615-11	Slip	7,500	0.01

PLATE 6

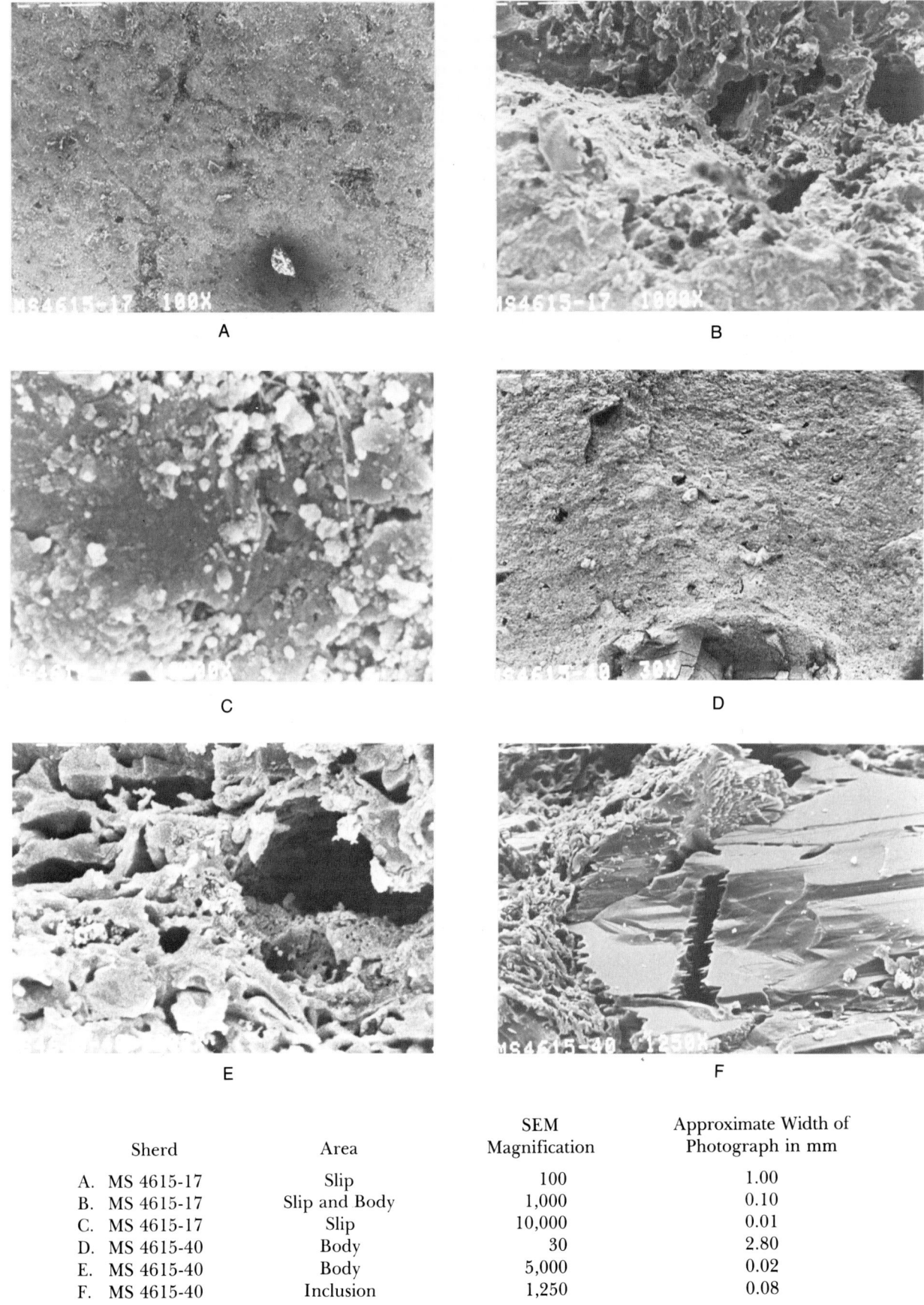

	Sherd	Area	SEM Magnification	Approximate Width of Photograph in mm
A.	MS 4615-17	Slip	100	1.00
B.	MS 4615-17	Slip and Body	1,000	0.10
C.	MS 4615-17	Slip	10,000	0.01
D.	MS 4615-40	Body	30	2.80
E.	MS 4615-40	Body	5,000	0.02
F.	MS 4615-40	Inclusion	1,250	0.08

PLATE 7

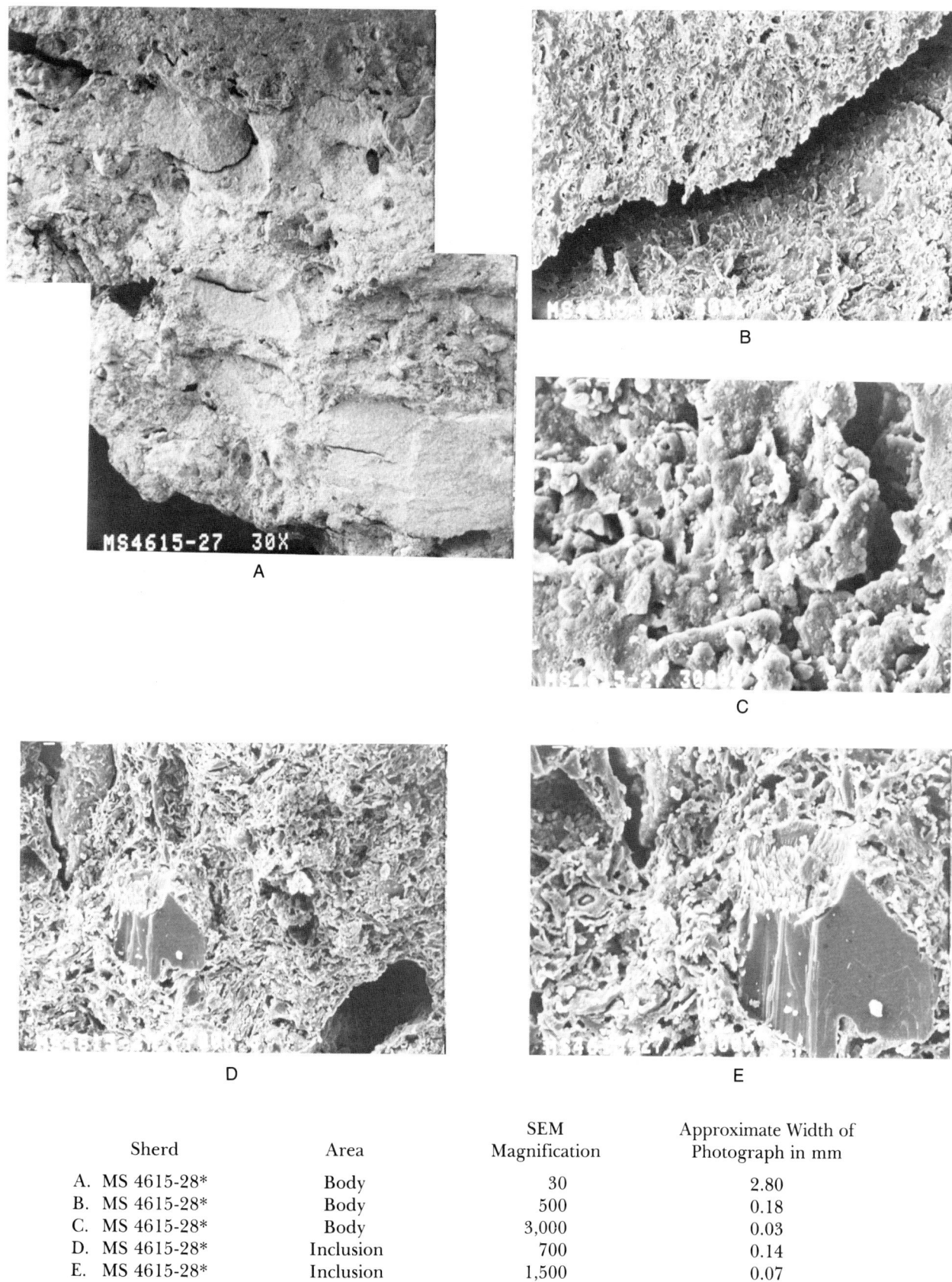

Sherd	Area	SEM Magnification	Approximate Width of Photograph in mm
A. MS 4615-28*	Body	30	2.80
B. MS 4615-28*	Body	500	0.18
C. MS 4615-28*	Body	3,000	0.03
D. MS 4615-28*	Inclusion	700	0.14
E. MS 4615-28*	Inclusion	1,500	0.07

PLATE 8

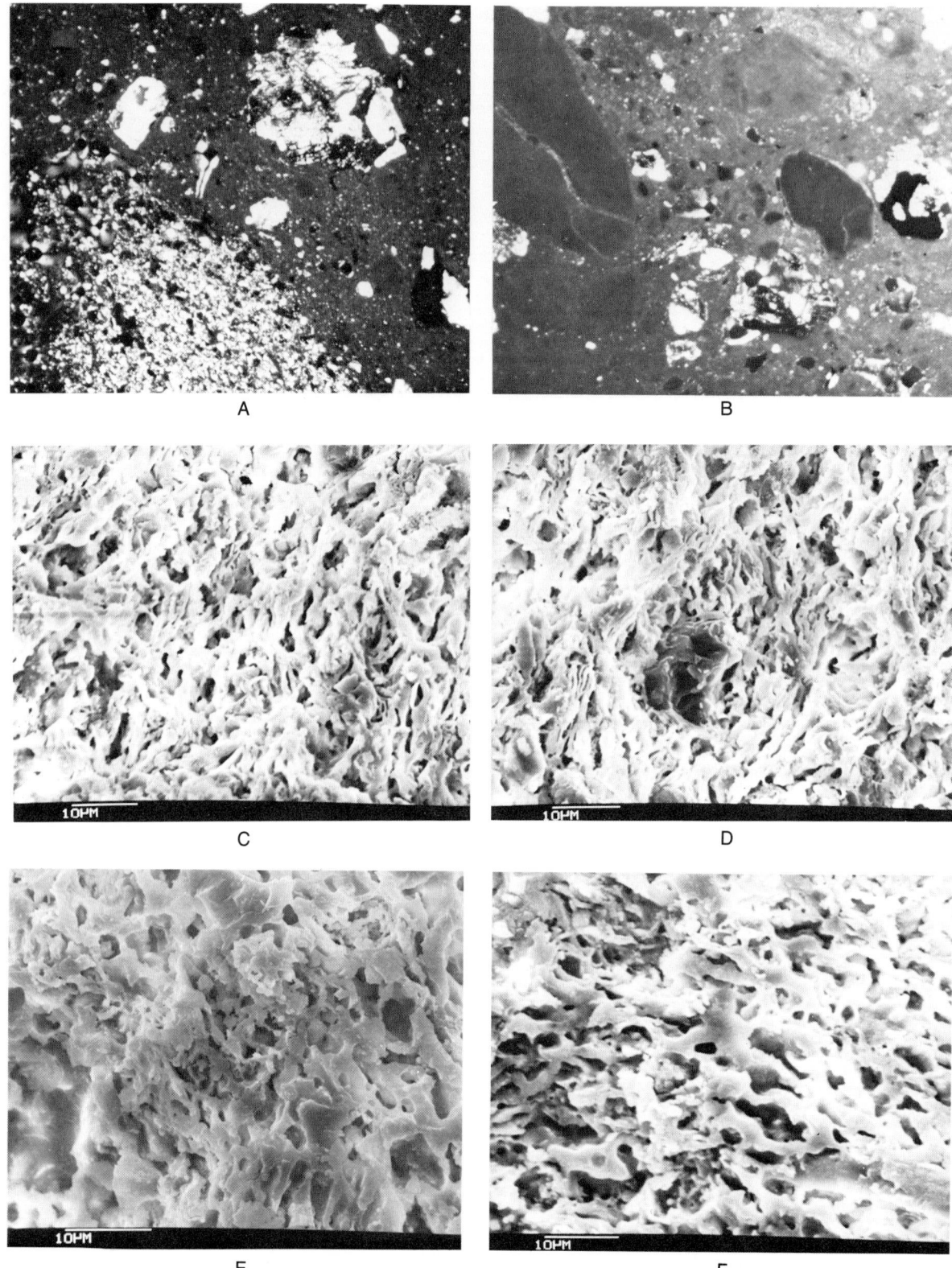

Thin sections (A–B) and SEM photomicrographs (C–F). **A.** Penn no. MS 4615-11 in plane polarized light, showing a fragment of siltstone (large area at lower left) and fragments of plagioclase (white) and hornblende (dark). **B.** Penn no. MS 4615-24 in plane polarized light, showing inclusions of terra rossa (dark gray fragments with rounded contours at left and center), plagioclase (white), and hornblende (dark). **C.** Penn no. MS 4615-26. Characteristic calcareous microstructure (V_c). **D.** Penn no. MS 4615-31. Characteristic calcareous microstructure (V_c). **E.** Penn no. 60-19-14. Advanced calcareous microstructure (V_c+). **F.** Penn no. MS 4615-27. Intermediate/advanced calcareous microstructure.

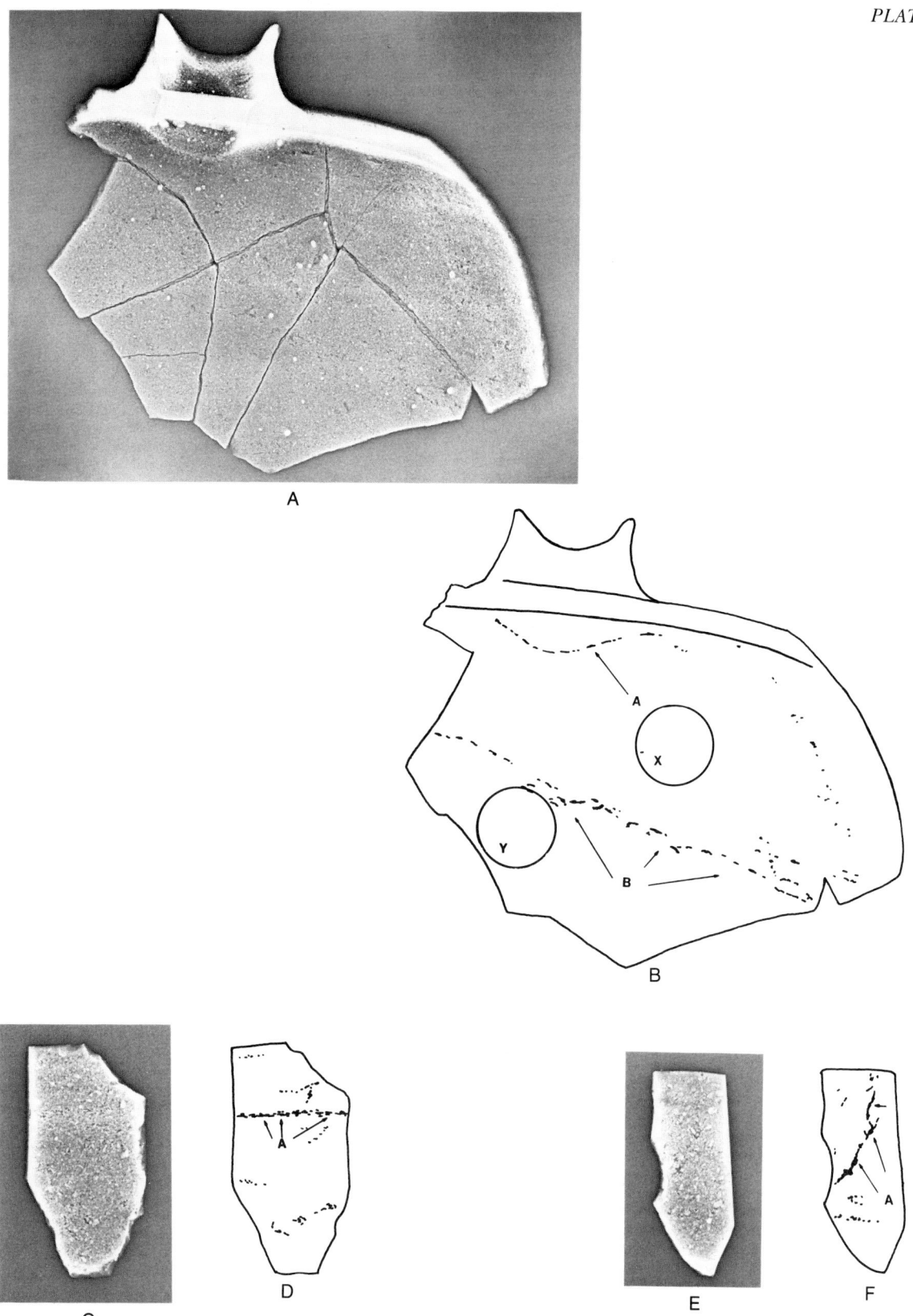

A.–B. Bridge spouted jar from Vasilike (Penn no. MS 4236). Air pockets are dark and inclusions are white. The arrows indicate a seam where the spout was added (A) and a seam between two slabs (B). Compare the density of the inclusions in areas X and Y.
C.–D. Rounded cup from Gournia (Penn no. MS 4615-31). The arrows (marked A) indicate a line of air pockets at seam.
E.–F. Conical cup from Gournia (Penn no. 4615-13). The arrow (marked B) indicates a tiny crack beneath the slip.

PLATE 10

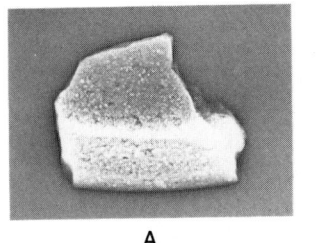 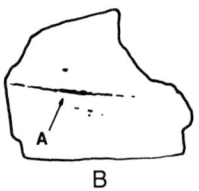

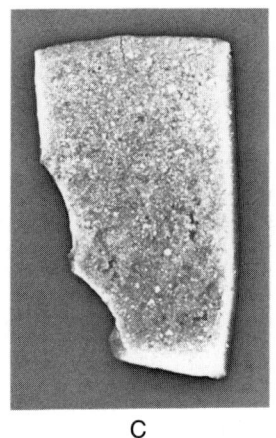 

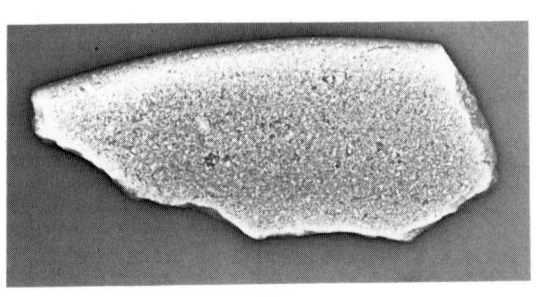

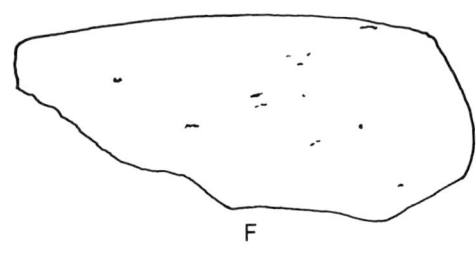

A.–B. Lid from Gournia (Penn no. MS 4615-39). The arrow (marked A) indicates a seam where the edge was joined to the top.
C.–D. Conical cup from Gournia (Penn no. MS 4615-10). The arrow (marked B) indicates a crack.
E.–F. Bowl from Gournia (Penn no. MS 4615-16). No seams are visible.
G. A nearly complete jug, mended from fragments, from Pseira (Penn no. MS 4477). Wheelmade, with no seams, from LM IB. Compare the finer and more uniform consistency of the paste, especially visible on the unbroken part of the upper shoulder, indicating a more carefully prepared and finer clay than was used in EM III.

A. Sample locality 6 in the *Phothia* Formation, approximately 1.3 km NE of Vainia. (The chapel is of Agh. Pandas). View looking NE. Exposed at the head of a gulley, this is a natural outcrop of clay-rich marl that shows recent excavation by local potters from Kentri (arrow). **B.** Sample location 8 in the *Makrilia* formation, approximately 800 m N of the main coastal road at a point 5 km E of Ierapetra. View looking N. Two south-projecting spurs, primarily composed of marls with subordinate sandstone beds, show very rounded and subdued relief due to erosion. A 2 meter high outcrop of clay-rich marl (arrow) is the source of sample 8b; it stands out due to its cohesive resistance to erosion. (The area to the left and in the foreground has just been bulldozed in preparation for olive terracing.) **C.** Sample locality 5 in the *Makrilia* formation, about 500 m WNW of the Vasilike site (arrow). View looking NE down a recently-eroded gulley system. Once the vegetation cover over these unconsolidated marls is breached, erosion procedes very rapidly. Four samples (5a–5d) were collected down the stratigraphic section exposed in the gulley, over a horizontal distance of about 80 m. In the background is the active fault bordering the Pakheia Ammos-Ierapetra depression along its E side; its continued uplift has produced the 'classic' talus breccia slope deposits. **D.** Sample locality 17 in the *Pakheia Ammos* Formation, above a small embayment approximately 500 m NE of the site of Gournia. (This locality is also Fortuin's type section for the formation.) View looking SE, with the Pakheia Ammos-Ierapetra fault scarp in the distance. The sample was collected from near the top of the cliff (arrow), in a meter-thick homogeneous marl stratum.

PLATE 12

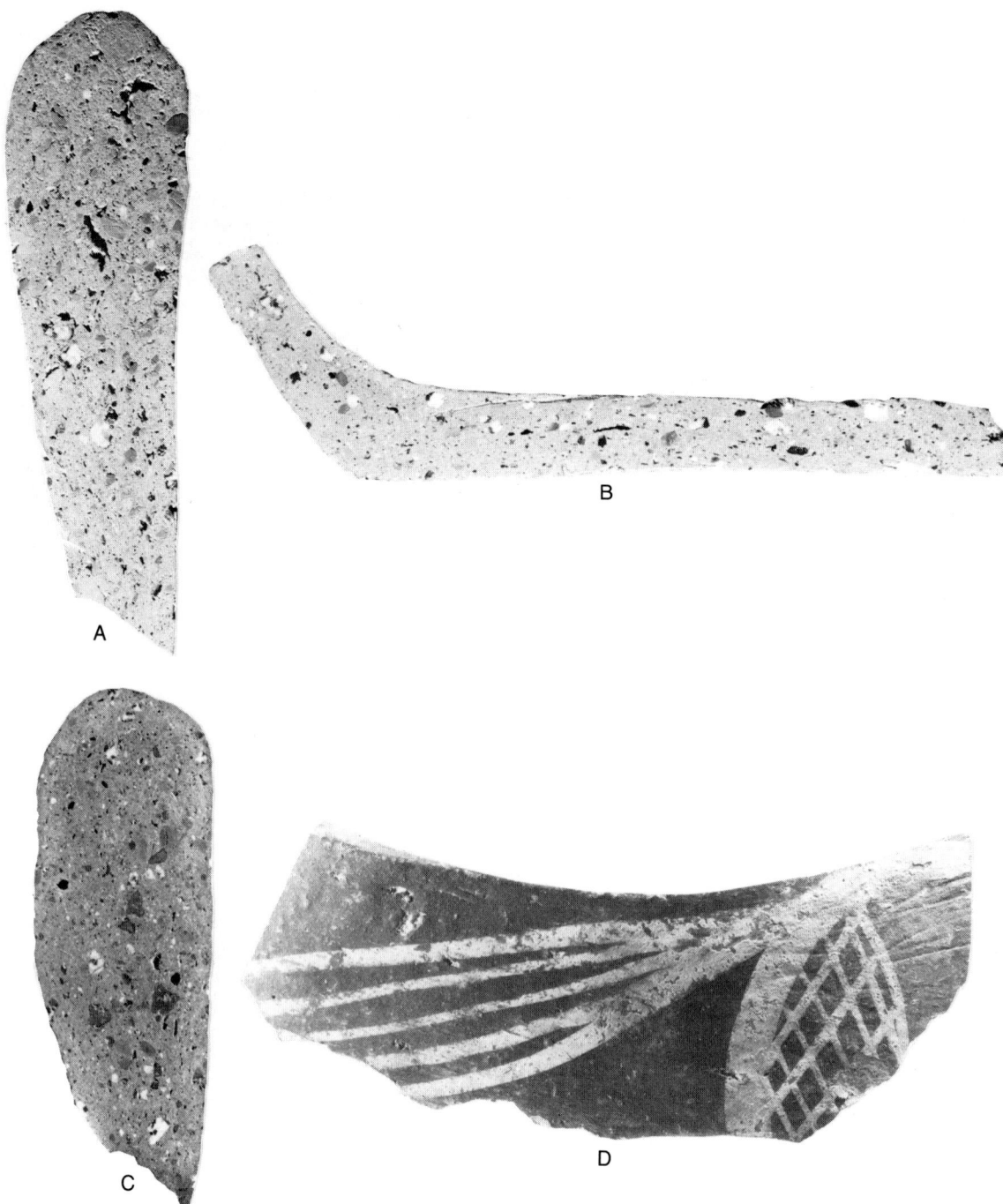

Sherds from Gournia, Crete, from the Middle Phase of White-on-dark Ware (EM III).
  A. Cross section through the wall of a bridge spouted jar, Penn no. MS 4615-23, showing the addition of an extra strip of clay to thicken the rim. The strip may be traced by the difference in coarseness in the clay, finer at the left and coarser at the right of the illustration.
  B. Cross section through the base of a conical cup, Penn no. MS 4615-37, showing different profiles on the exterior and interior. Note the air bubbles elongated parallel to the walls and base, from the smoothing operation.
  C. Cross section through the wall of a bridge spouted jar, Penn no. MS 4615-26, showing irregular voids from air trapped in the forming process.
  D. The exterior of a rim sherd from a bridge spouted jar, Penn no. MS 4615-11, illustrating impressions from something pressed against the wall while the clay was still plastic, best visible at the right of the sherd.

PLATE 13

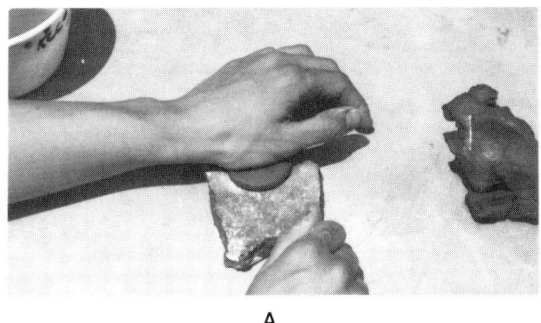
A

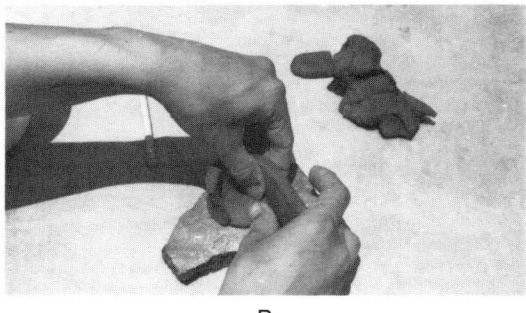
B

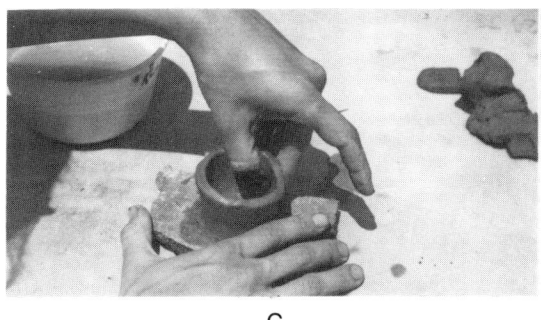
C

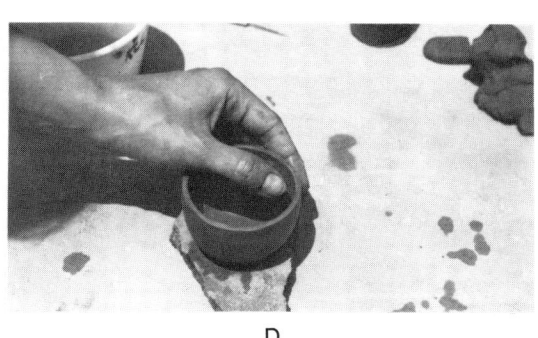
D

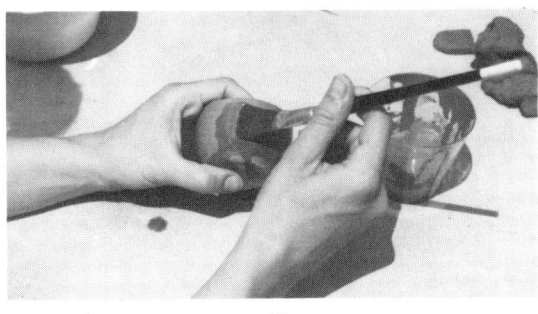
E

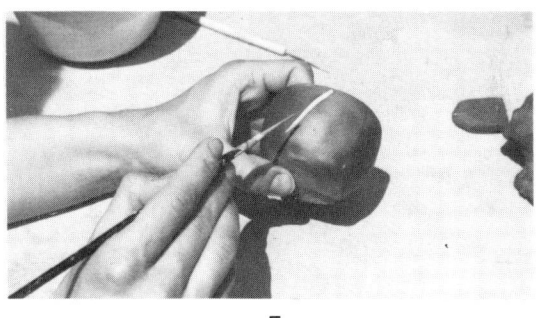
F

Steps in the manufacture of a rounded cup. Potter: Gail Gosser.
    A. Preparing the base.
    B. Attaching a slab to form the wall.
    C. Smoothing the wall with the fingers and thumb with a rotary motion as the vessel is turned.
    D. Finishing the shaping.
    E. Applying the overall coat of slip.
    F. Painting on the white decoration.

PLATE 14

A. A workshop at Thrapsano in 1982, showing the "wheeler-trench" with the Master and Wheeler at work. **B.** The Master performs the "Pulling" operation. **C.** Fixing the coil, performed by the Second Master. **D.** The turntable. A bat is in place on top of the wooden disc. The handles for turning are formed by an iron rod. **E.** The village of Kentri. View from the southeast. **F.** A potter's workshop in the edge of the village. On left, path leading up to the workroom. In center, one of the two kilns used by the potter.

A. The potter's workroom, with limestone walls, a single doorway, and a flat roof made of the white clay also used in potting. Leaning against the building is the κόπανο or wooden branch used to beat the clay, and next to it, a screen. **B.** Interior of the workroom, seen through the doorway. On left, the clay column, covered by burlap. In background, the potter at his wheel. In foreground, newly made vessels set on trays on the beaten earth floor. **C.** Beating the clay into 1–2 cm sized pieces before sieving it. **D.** Clay body mixed with water and allowed to dry on burlap sacks in the workshop courtyard. **E.** The potter's wheel. On left, his seat against the wall. Center, the wheel pit. On right, the stone and mud shelf containing a water supply and the potter's tools. **F.** The potter's tools. From left, moving clockwise: sponges, wooden ribs, perforated and plain, and in center, reed fragments used in decorating pottery.

PLATE 16

A. Two kilns built into a hillside. On lower left, stoking chamber entrance of left kiln. In center foreground are bunches of wild brush (βρομιάδες) ready for use in firing. **B.** Detail of kiln showing firing chamber entrance, iron rods set into kiln walls as part of roof support, and cracked clay lining on the kiln interior. **C.** Detail of floor of kiln showing perforations in the floor allowing passage of hot air from stoking chamber (below) to the firing chamber. Perforations where floor joins kiln walls are larger. **D.** Detail of interior of the stoking chamber, showing thick column (στύλος) which supports the firing chamber floor. Fuel is placed on both sides of the column. **E.** Initial stage in loading the kiln for a firing. The potter enters the kiln and begins to place vessels in a rough size order in layers in half of the kiln. **F.** Kiln almost full. Additional vessels will be added until they exceed the top border of the kiln walls to a height of circa 1.0 m.

A. Kiln ready for firing. Metal sheets (from old barrels) have been wrapped around the stacked pottery within the limits of the metal rods in the kiln walls. Broken pottery is used as extra wrapping, and clay has sealed off the firing chamber door (center foreground). **B.** A firing. During the initial stages smoke pours from the temporary roof. **C.** A stoking chamber during firing. Wooden implements (διχάλια) are used to guide the wild brush (βρομιάδες) into the chamber. **D.** Vessels (ἰεραπήτρικα σταμιά) ready for market. Vessel in center foreground is a λαϊ. **E.** A traditional household storeroom (ἀποθήκη) in the Lasithi nome. From left to right: πιθάρια made by potters from Thrapsano, some with clay and some with wooden lids; on floor below *pitharia,* a λαδικό and a σταμνί, both from Kentri, on right, κουρούπια of various sizes from the Kentri potters. **F.** A λαϊ, or water vessel, hung from a tree in the fields, ready for use during work hours.

PLATE 18

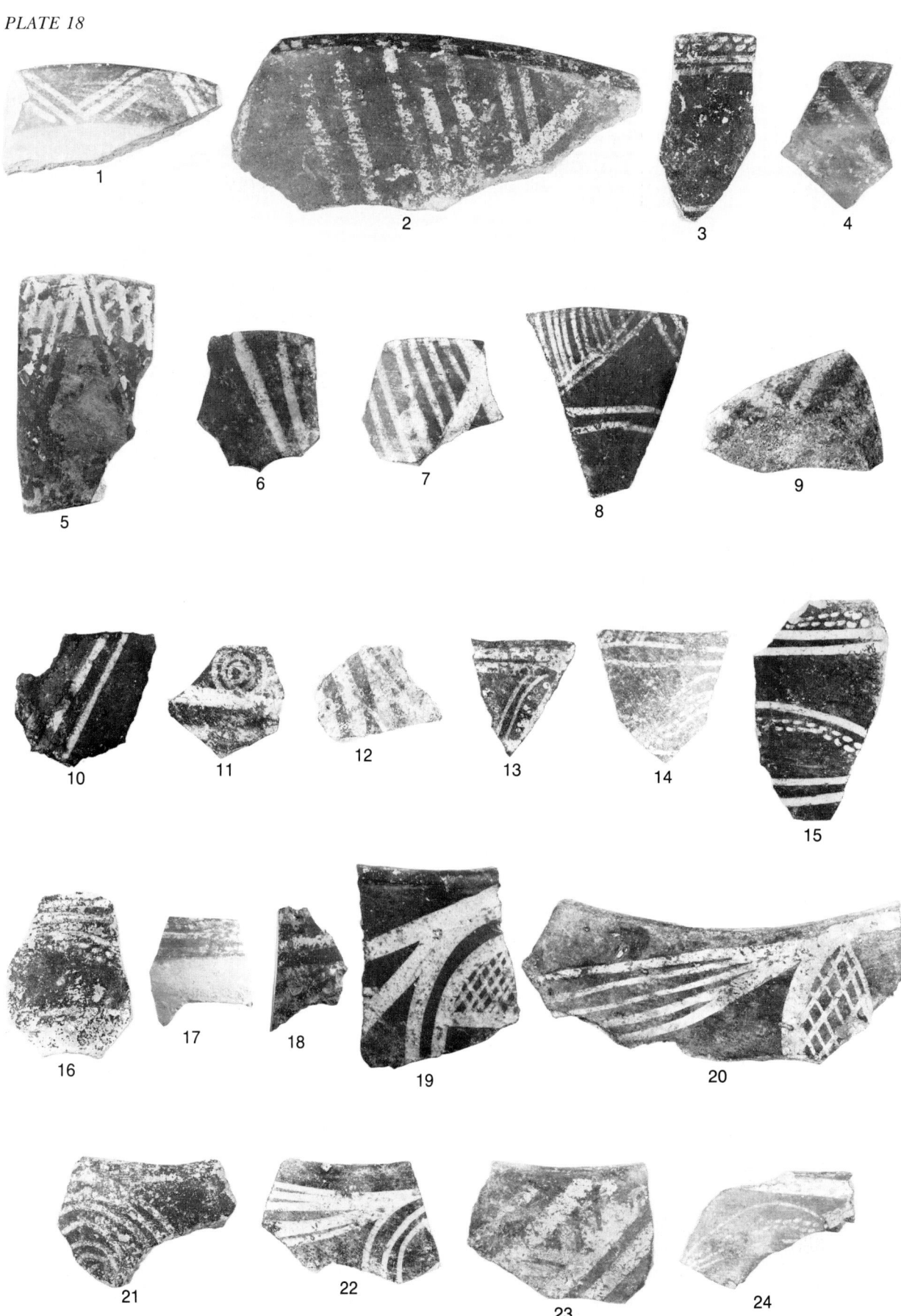

Analyzed sherds listed in the Appendix: Nos. 1–24.

PLATE 19

Analyzed sherds listed in the Appendix: Nos. 25–45.

PLATE 20

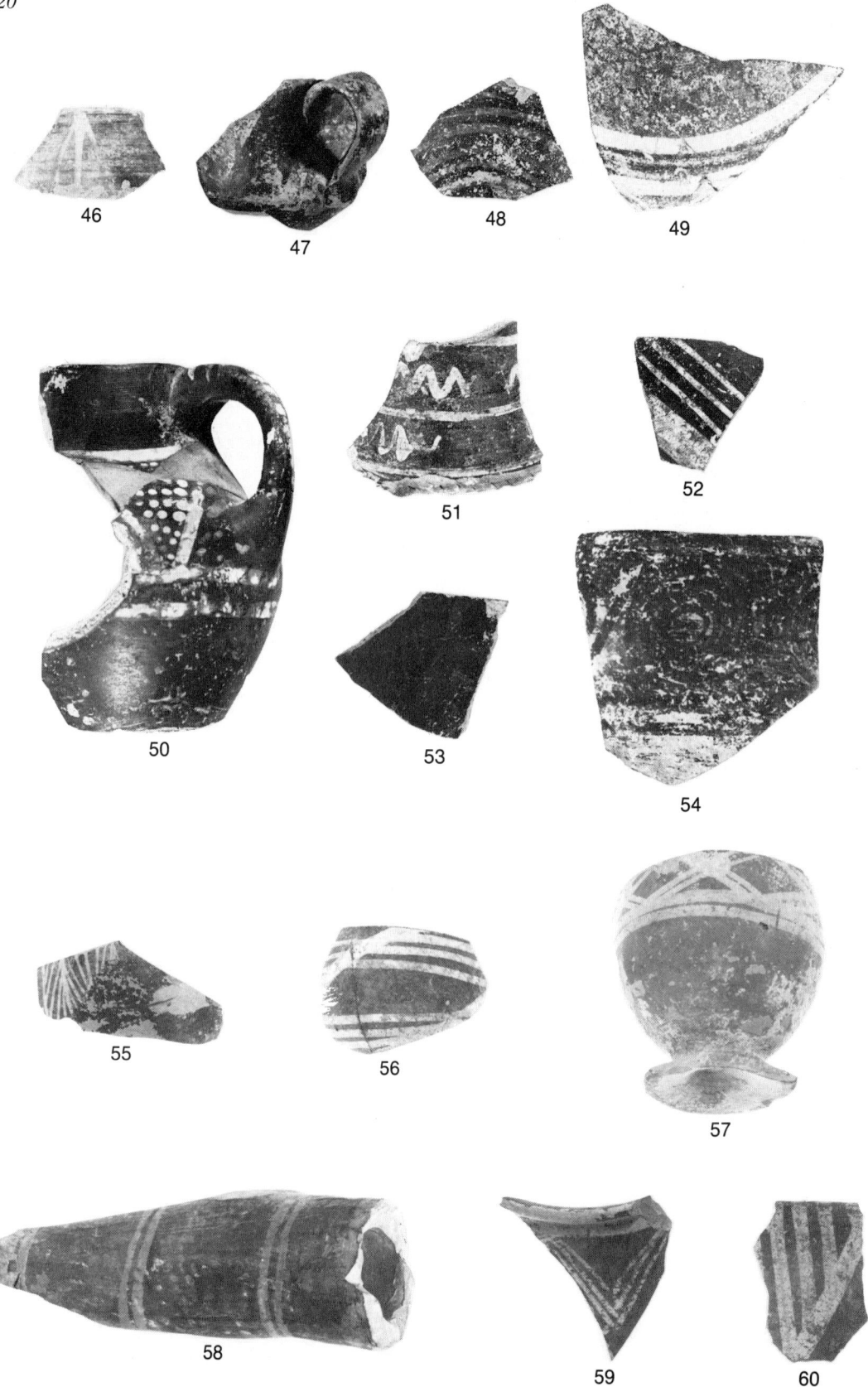

Analyzed sherds and vases listed in the Appendix: Nos. 46–60.

PLATE 21

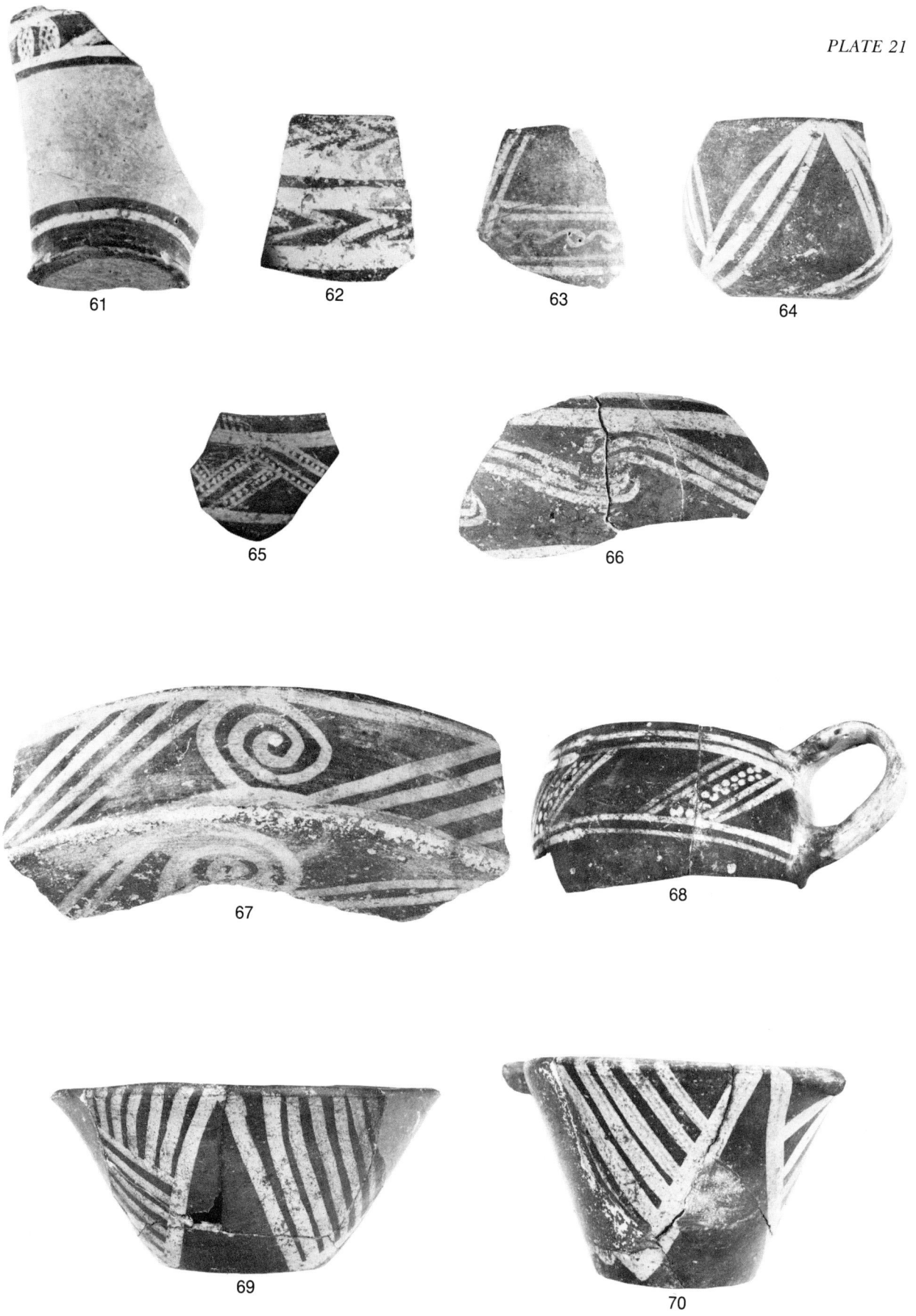

Analyzed sherds and vases listed in the Appendix: Nos. 61–70.

PLATE 22

Analyzed sherds and vases listed in the Appendix: Nos. 71–75.